A CLOUD OF WITNESSES

A CLOUD OF WITNESSES
Opportunities for Ecumenical Commemoration

Proceedings of the International Ecumenical Symposium
Monastery of Bose, 29 October – 2 November 2008

Edited by Tamara Grdzelidze and Guido Dotti

Faith and Order Paper No. 209
WCC Publications
Geneva 2009

Cover Design : Judith Rempel Smucker
Cover photo: The Last Judgement, from an illumination of
the Beato de Liébana Commentary (11th century).
Reprinted with permission from the Monastery of Bose.

Published by WCC Publications
PO Box 2100
CH-1211 Geneva 2
Switzerland
oikoumene.org

ISBN 978-2-8254-1533-7

Printed in France

Table of contents

FOREWORD

The Bose Symposium on *A Cloud of Witnesses: Opportunities for Ecumenical Commemoration* became a testimony to the driving perception in the process towards this event – that witnesses of faith can be commonly shared by all Christians. Despite specific contexts, a witness may bear universal meaning. The means of acquiring the status of witness is also commonly shared: hardship, suffering, endurance, persecution are of a universal nature and move the hearts and minds of all human beings in various parts of the world.

The first person to be mentioned in this volume is Lukas Vischer, former director of Faith and Order and untiring servant of the dialogue among Christians. As soon as Lukas learned about *Il libro dei Testimoni. Un martirologio ecumenico*[1] he connected it with the Bangalore statement[2] which initially inspired the Monastery of Bose to undertake such research, and strove to mobilize ecumenical energy around this theme. It was on his suggestion that the Monastery of Bose and the Faith and Order Secretariat worked jointly on "A Cloud of Witnesses".

Brothers and sisters in the Monastery of Bose come from various Christian churches and this has been for them a stimulus for seeking to retrace their way to the common biblical patrimony, to the teaching and testimony of the undivided church of the first centuries. They are accustomed to celebrate a shared memory in the liturgy of these *sequentiae sancti Evangelii,* these "passages of the holy gospel" that are the witnesses, the martyrs, the saints who have obeyed the commandment "you shall be holy for I our God am Holy" (Lev. 19:2). In this they felt encouraged also by the decree on ecumenism of Vatican Council II, where it says:

> ...Catholics must gladly acknowledge and esteem the truly Christian endowments from our common heritage which are to be found among our separated brethren. It is right and salutary to recognize the riches of Christ and virtuous works in the lives of others who are bearing witness to Christ, sometimes even to the shedding of their blood. For God is always wonderful in His works and worthy of all praise. Nor should we forget that anything wrought by the grace of the Holy Spirit in the hearts of our separated brethren can be a help to our own edification. Whatever is truly Christian is never contrary to what genuinely belongs to the faith; it can always bring a deeper realization of the mystery of Christ and the Church.[2]

Thus, already in the early 1970s, the Community of Bose began to edit a small ecumenical martyrology and to seek ways of commemoration that would conform to the gospel and

1 Comunità di Bose, *Il libro dei testimoni. Martirologio ecumenico,* Cinisello Balsamo, San Paolo, 2002 (French translation: Communauté de Bose, *Témoins de Dieu, Martyrologie universel,* Bayard, Paris, 2005; Polish translation: Klasztor Bose, *Księga świadków. Martyrologium ekumeniczne,* Święty Paweł, Częstochowa, 2004.). Available on line in Italian (http://tinyurl.com/Bose-Martirologio), English (http://tinyurl.com/Bose-Martyrology) and French (http://tinyurl.com/Bose-Martyrologe). on:-http://www.monasterodibose.it/index.php/content/section/34/484/lang,it/

2 *Sharing in One Hope, Commission on Faith and Order, Bangalore 1978,* Faith and Order Paper no. 92, WCC Publications, Geneva, 1978.

respect the deepest convictions of the various churches. The suggestion made at the Faith and Order Commission meeting in Bangalore in 1978 appeared to them to be an ecumenically authoritative confirmation of their path.[3]

When later, in the course of a few months between November 1994 and May 1995, two texts of Pope John Paul II – first the *Tertio millennio adveniente,* then the encyclical *Ut unum sint* – forcefully returned to this hope, Bose found the courage to prepare a volume of common witnesses:

> At the close of the second millennium the Church has again become a Church of martyrs… the witness rendered to Christ to the shedding of blood has become the common patrimony of Catholics, Orthodox, Anglicans, and Protestants… A testimony not to be forgotten… because the ecumenism of saints, of martyrs, is perhaps the most convincing.[4]

In *Ut unum sint,* then, the reflection widened from martyrs in the strict sense to witnesses of the faith.[5]

Two Memoranda

It was in Bose that a project on "Cloud of Witnesses" (later referred to as the "Bose project") initially started. First, in 2004, through the joint efforts of Lukas Vischer and the Community of Bose, representatives of various institutions gathered to discuss the possibility of creating a common martyrology. As a result of conversations over a few days, the initial group (for the constitution of this group see signatures on Memorandum I) was convinced that the common martyrology was one of the outcomes of a much wider and more inclusive project. A Memorandum and a letter signed by the prior of the community and the director of the Faith and Order Secretariat went out to the churches. In 2007, on the basis of the responses from the churches (some of these responses suggested a list of common witnesses) and simultaneous initiatives in different places regarding commemoration of witnesses from different confessions, the Faith and Order Secretariat together with the Community of Bose initiated a new round of communication with the churches and the ecumenical sister organizations. This was Memorandum II which described the process and urged churches to commit themselves to a first step of the Bose Symposium project. Its proceedings are published here.

The Bose Symposium

The style and methodology of papers presented here vary. Speakers at the Symposium were invited *ad personam.* The overarching theme was Christian witness, its biblical, spiritual,

3 *Unitatis redintegratio 4, Enchiridion Vaticanum 1. Documenti del Concilio Vaticano II,* EDB, Bologna, 1981, pp.298-299.
4 *Tertio millenio adventiente 37, in Enchiridion Vaticanum 14. Documenti ufficiali della Santa Sede 1994-1995,* EDB, Bologna, 1997, pp.986-988.
5 *Cf. Ut unum sint 84, in Ibid.,* pp.1668-1671.

historical, confessional, contextual and liturgical expression(s). Most of the speakers took seriously that witness to faith, *martyria*, goes beyond any stereotype about living out one's faith. This spirit which was overwhelmingly present at the Bose Symposium was also reflected in the Message sent to the churches.[6]

The proceedings of the Symposium began with a paper by the primate of the Church of England, Archbishop Rowan Williams. His message affected many participants so that discussion groups between plenary sessions tried to discern this spiritual reflection and some of its themes appeared in the final Message signed by all. The biblical-historical perspective of the theme of witnesses was offered by Enzo Bianchi, the prior of the Monastery of Bose.

The bi-lateral and multilateral treatment of the theme was introduced by Mary Tanner and Tamara Grdzelidze, followed by the traditional understanding of witnesses among the Lutherans (Øysten Bjørdal), Orthodox (Panaghiotis A. Yfantis), Roman Catholics (Marco Gnavi) and Pentecostals (Dale M. Coulter).

The bulk of the papers presented here are on the regional "case studies". In this section organizers used various methodologies for introducing the theme. Along with single presentations from Germany (by Andreas Kurschat), Romania (by Iustin Marchis), South Africa (by Simangasilo R. Kumalo), Melanesia in the South Pacific (Richard A. Carter), there are also paired papers from Russia on witnesses and martyrdom in the Russian church during the 20th century regarding the clergy (by Alexander Mazyrin) and lay women (by Lidia Golovkova). Two other contexts, Korea and Latin America, are presented by the "paper-response" methodology. In the first case Helen Rhee responded to Seong-won Park, in the second case a response was offered by William T. Cavanaugh to the Brazilian (by Karen Bergesch) and Argentinian contexts (Daniel A. Bruno). The analysis of the case studies was shared by Alan D. Falconer.

The final part of this volume covers liturgical reflections on ecumenical commemoration of witnesses. Lutheran (Dagmar Heller), Reformed (Martin Hoegger), Orthodox (Job Getcha) and Roman Catholic (Keith F. Pecklers) share challenges and perspectives according to their own traditions. Liturgical material suggested by these authors as examples to choose from during ecumenical gatherings follow these papers.

The theme of reconciliation through commemoration of witnesses was a special issue at the Symposium: reconciliation between two confessions (Mennonites and Roman Catholics by Helmut Harder), reconciling the memories of the past (Hansulrich Gerber), reconciliation through places of memory (Hans Uytenboogardt, later helped by Guido Dotti), pilgrimage as a way to commemorate anew a saint thus reconciling the past with the present in the church (Knut Kittelsaa).

---

6 See the Message on pp. 299-304.

It is a great pity when the richness of group discussions at symposia similar to the one on “A Cloud of Witnesses” does not reach the reader. However, the Message at the end of the papers highlights some of those riches. This Message has already been sent to the member churches of the World Council of Churches as well as to the other ecumenical organizations with the hope that one day it will bear fruit.

The proceedings end with two Memoranda and a note on bibliography; a bibliography compiled of books suggested in the papers and then extended by some other sources on the theme was too long to be included in this volume. However it can be found on the website of the Monastery of Bose.

A number of persons need to be thanked in connection with this event and the volume. Our gratitude for help in various matters of planning the symposium and final editing of the proceedings goes first to Matthias Wirz. For continual support we thank the sisters and brothers of the Community of Bose whose spirit of love and devotion provided fruitful soil for a successful symposium on witnesses of faith. For their excellent work and dedication we express deep gratitude to the drafters of the final Message, Mary Tanner, Dale Coulter and Job Getcha.

For a grant to Faith and Order to be used for this publication our deep gratitude goes to the Presbyterian Church USA and to Joseph D. Small, the director of Theology, Worship and Education.

The editors
Pentecost 2009

LIST OF CONTRIBUTORS

Karen Bergesch is a pastor of the Evangelical Lutheran Church in Brazil (IECLB), working as a pastor at Cônsul Carlos Renaux School in Brusque, state of Santa Catarina, Brazil. She is also Professor of Philosophy at SENAI University (UNIFEBE), in Brusque, and a member of the Ethical Committee in Research with Human Beings (CEPH) at the University of Blumenau (FURB) in Santa Catarina.

Enzo Bianchi is the founder and prior of the Monastic Community of Bose, author of books on *lectio divina* and spiritual life, and editorialist for several newspapers and journals in Italy and France. Honorary graduate in History of the Church from the Università degli Studi in Turin, he is Professor of Biblical Theology at the Università San Raffaele in Milan.

Øystein Bjørdal is Cathedral dean of Molde, Norway. He was Director of Liturgical Center in Trondheim, Norway, 1997-2000. He undertook musical studies at the Norwegian Conservatory of Music, Oslo. He has published several books and articles on liturgical theology, pilgrimage and spirituality. He is a member of the Lutheran World Federation ecumenical study group on Worship and Culture. Leader of the comission on worship, Church of Norway.

Daniel A. Bruno is professor of history, theology degree at ISEDET (Buenos Aires) and Sacred Theology Master at Drew University (New Jersey). He took part in the National Commission for Disappeared People at Santa Fe province, in Argentina. He was a member of the Ecumenical Movement for Human Rights. He is pastor of the Evangelical Methodist Church in Argentina.

Richard A. Carter is a priest at St. Martin-in-the-Fields, Trafalgar Square, a church which welcomes people from all over the world and has a special ministry to homeless and vulnerable people in London, UK. He was for many years the Chaplain of The Melanesian Brotherhood in the South Pacific and became a Brother himself. He continues to work with refugees and asylum seekers in giving spiritual support to those who have been through situations of loss and conflict.

William T. Cavanaugh is professor of theology at the University of St. Thomas in St. Paul, Minnesota, USA. His degrees are from Notre Dame, Cambridge, and Duke. He is co-editor of the journal *Modern Theology*, and author of four books, most recently *The Myth of Religious Violence* (Oxford University Press, 2009). His books have been published in English, French and Spanish.

Dale M. Coulter is associate professor of historical theology at Regent University, Virginia Beach, Virginia, USA. He is involved in the Roman Catholic - Pentecostal discussion that is part of the annual meeting of the Society for Pentecostal Studies. He is also a member of Evangelicals and Catholics Together, a group sponsored by the Institute for Religion and Public Life, New York.

Guido Dotti has been a monk of the Monastic Community of Bose since 1972. In the monastery he works for the publishing house *Edizioni Qiqajon*. He took part in the Third Ecumenical European Assembly at Sibiu (2007) as co-facilitator for the Forum on Spirituality. He also attended Lambeth Conference 2008 as a personal guest of the Archbishop of Canterbury.

Alan D. Falconer is minister of St. Machar's Cathedral, Aberdeen, Church of Scotland. He is a former director of the Irish School of Ecumenics (1990-1995) and of the Faith and Order Commission at WCC (1995-2004).

Hansulrich Gerber, a Mennonite pastor from Switzerland, is WCC Coordinator for the Decade to Overcome Violence (DOV). Originally a farmer, and trained as teacher and catechist, he studied theology in Elkhart, Indiana, USA. He then worked several years for Mennonite World Conference, first as Executive Secretary of the International Mennonite Peace Committee, and then as Secretary for Program. Prior to joining the WCC, Gerber served ten years as Europe Director for Mennonite Central Committee (MCC).

Job Getcha is a priest of the Ecumenical Patriarchate of Constantinople, he holds a Doctorate of Theology from St. Sergius Orthodox Theological Institute and the Catholic Institute of Paris. Former Dean of St. Sergius Orthodox Theological Institute, he also teaches at the Catholic Institute of Paris. Member of the Central Committee of the WCC, of St. Ireneus Catholic-Orthodox Working Group, of the Committee of Catholic-Orthodox Dialogue in France and of the Society for Oriental Liturgy.

Marco Gnavi is a priest of the Community of Sant'Egidio in Rome, Italy, and Secretary of the Commission for Ecumenism and Dialogue of the Diocese of Rome.

Lidia Golovkova studied music and arts in Moscow, Russia. She started her research on martyrs of repressions in 1989. At present she works at St. Tikhon's Theological University in Moscow.

Tamara Grdzelidze is a programme executive in Faith and Order and serves as an Orthodox theologian since 2001. She belongs to the Orthodox Church of Georgia. She holds a Doctor of Philosophy (in Theology) from the University of Oxford as well as a Doctor of Sciences in Georgian Language and Literature from the University of Tbilisi, Georgia.

Helmut Harder is emeritus professor of theology at Canadian Mennonite University in Winnipeg, Canada. He co-chaired the International Catholic-Mennonite Dialogue (1998-2003), and has published numerous journal articles on ecumenism. He recently translated the major work by Fernando Enns, *The Peace Church and the Ecumenical Community* (Pandora Press and WCC Publications).

Dagmar Heller is an ordained minister of the Protestant Church in Baden (regional church of the Evangelical Church in Germany). 1989 PhD at University in Heidelberg, Germany; 1989-1993 parish service; 1993-2000 executive secretary for Faith and Order in WCC, Geneva; 2001-2007 ecumenical officer of the Evangelical Church in Germany (EKD), Hannover; since April 2007 she is professor for ecumenical theology at the Ecumenical Institute Bossey and executive secretary for Faith and Order in WCC, Geneva.

Martin Hoegger is a pastor of the Evangelical Reformed Church and president of the Council of the Christian Churches in Canton Vaud, Switzerland and General Secretary of the Swiss Bible Society.

Knut Kittelsaa is vicar of Bakklandet parish, Trondheim, Church of Norway.

Simangaliso R. Kumalo is a senior lecturer and director of the Religion and Governance Programme at the School of Religion and Theology, University of KwaZulu-Natal, South Africa. He teaches courses in Practical Theology, Christian Education and Religion and Politics. He is an ordained Methodist minister and a member of the Executive of the KwaZulu Natal Christian Council (KZNCC). He has also participated in a number of commissions of the WCC.

Andreas Kurschat, M.A., 2003-2007 main researcher of the project "Protestant Martyrs of the 20th Century" located at the Research Centre for Contemporary Church History in Munich, Germany; since 2008 research associate of the Institute for Ethics and Related Social Sciences at the University of Münster.

Iustin Marchis studied at the Faculty of Orthodox Theology of Sibiu University, Romania, where he had contacts with Protestant theology students. He became a monk in 1976, entering Cozia Monastery, where he was ordained into the priesthood a year later, in 1977. Superior of Cheia Monastery (from 1982 onward) he has taken part since 1989 in ecumenical meetings in Romania and abroad. He is now the confessor at Stavropoleos Monastery in Bucharest, whose community has always been open to inter-denominational contacts.

Alexander Mazyrin graduated from Moscow engineering-physical institute and St. Tikhon's Theological Institute (now University). Since 2000 he has been teaching at St. Tikhon's Theological University in Moscow, Russia. Since 2004 has been ordained clergy.

Seong-Won Park is a professor of theology at Youngnam Theological University and Seminary in Daegu, Republic of Korea. He is a member of Central Committee of the World Council of Churches. He is also co-moderator of the WCC-WARC-CWM joint programme, "OIKOTREE" movement.

Keith F. Pecklers is professor of liturgy at the Pontifical Gregorian University and professor of liturgical history at the Pontifical Liturgical Institute, Rome. He has been a participant in Durham

University's Project on "Receptive Ecumenism" since its inception and in 2007 was named a member of the Board of Trustees of the American Friends of the Anglican Centre Rome.

Helen Rhee is an assistant professor of history of Christianity at Westmont College in Santa Barbara, California, USA. She specializes in early Christian martyrdom and self-definitions, which resulted in a book, *Early Christian Literature: Christ and Culture in the Second and Third Centuries (*2005). Based on her patristic scholarship and teaching, Rhee has been engaged in ecumenical dialogues in both local and global levels.

Mary Tanner is general secretary of the Council for Christian Unity, Church of England, 1991-1998. She served on the Faith and Order Commission of the World Council of Churches from 1976 and was moderator of the Commission from 1991-1998. She taught Old Testament and Hebrew at Hull and Bristol Universities. In 2008 she became a Dame Commander of the British Empire and is one of the presidents of the World Council of Churches.

Panaghiotis A. Yfantis is a Greek-Orthodox theologian and lecturer in the Department of Theology of the Aristotle University of Thessaloniki, Greece. He has participated in international scholarly conferences and published monographs and articles in Greek and Italian journals.

Hans Uytenbogaardt is pastor-emeritus of the Protestant Church in the Netherlands and former Secretary of the Board for Liturgy of the Dutch Reformed Church, Utrecht, NL.

+ **Rowan Williams** – Archbishop of Canterbury.

INTRODUCTORY SECTION

On Witness and Holiness

+Rowan Williams

In one of the hymns for Vespers on the Sunday of All the Saints in the Orthodox Church the saints are addressed as "Orators of the Spirit". I hope that in this meeting, all participants will feel that the Holy Spirit is truly speaking to them through the company of the saints, and also through the human fellowship of this encounter. For since we are all called to sanctity, then we are all called to speak in and for the Holy Spirit.

Holiness is never an individual matter. For a human person to become holy, so Christians believe, is for them to be taken into the Body of Christ, so that their life is informed, shaped, determined by the eternal life of God the Son as it was and is embodied in Jesus of Nazareth; it is for them to be "immersed" by the gift of the Holy Spirit in the flow of the Son's life towards the Father, the everlasting movement of total adoration and self-giving love. To be holy is to stand with Christ, and to stand with Christ is to be a member of his Body, living in and through the communion of renewed human persons that the Spirit creates.

Hence the naturalness for St Paul of referring to all the baptized as holy – as "saints": in principle, all those who through their baptism are brought into the place where Jesus is, are caught up in this flow of his life towards the Father. But we quite reasonably use the word "saint" more commonly to refer to those in whom we can see that flow evidently at work. The person whom the churches recognize as a saint in the usual sense is going to be one who shows what is true for *all* Christians, one who offers a unique definition of what the baptized life might mean. The holy person will have learned from all those around them how to live in Christ; and they will have learned even from those whose lives may not show the strongest or clearest marks of baptismal faithfulness. And the rest of us, as we receive and reflect on that definition, are called to scrutinize our own lives in its light, asking how our own baptized identities might be deepened and given more integrity. When a saint is recognized and commemorated, the church proposes to its own people and to the wider world a model of life in community with Jesus, and in community with all others who have been called; a saint is someone who is himself or herself *shaped in discipleship* by living in the body of Christ, and also someone whose own life feeds that Body and draws it back to its heart and its calling.

But what about saints in a divided church? Sometimes we may be inclined to think that there is something special about the saints of the "undivided church" – before the schism of East and West, or before the Reformation; or, worse, we may be tempted to use the saints of our particular tradition as proofs that our own confession has been more successful at nourishing holiness than others. This is understandable: if a Roman Catholic looks at a saint of the Eastern Christian world, they may feel that such a saint's witness is somehow weakened or compromised by their separation from or even hostility to the Roman Communion. Anglicans and Protestants cannot fail to be aware that the post-Reformation saints of the Roman Catholic Church belonged to a body that regarded their own Reformed Christian witness as defective and misguided in many ways. Even more problematically, in West and East, there are those who have suffered torment and death at the hands of fellow Christians and who are regarded as martyrs. Roman Catholics, Orthodox, Anglicans and Protestants have all been involved in one way or another in inflicting as well as enduring suffering for what they believed Christ had called them to: but how can we celebrate the memory of someone who died at our own hands?

In Britain, the calendar of the Church of England commemorates those who died as "Protestant heretics" under the persecution of Queen Mary Tudor; it also commemorates those, like John Bunyan and Richard Baxter, who were persecuted by Anglican authority and, in providing a celebration of all the saints and martyrs of the Reformation era, indirectly acknowledges those who died for their loyalty to the Pope at the hands of the British state. Admirable as this is, it needs something of a theology to make it more than just the willingness to acknowledge courage or integrity wherever they occur; it needs exposition in terms of the understanding of the Body of Christ. And it may be that such a theological exposition also gives us better insight into the theology of sanctity overall.

So in relation to this, I want to suggest three perspectives that may help us.

First and most importantly, the Christ whose life we recognize in each other is the Christ who has suffered rejection and humiliation at the hands of human agents like ourselves. To borrow the terminology of the contemporary British theologian who has most eloquently developed this theme, James Alison, Jesus has "the intelligence of the victim". He stands where every victim of every act of human aggression and violent exclusion stands. That is to say, he is not simply a figure with whom we can identify ourselves instantly and straightforwardly, as if he just mirrors back to us who we already are: our identification with him is only fully real if it involves identification also with those whom we as particular agents or our culture or interest group may have made to suffer. To stand where Christ stands is to be exposed to his judgment: it is a place where we must change and grow if we are to live, because to claim the name of Christ is to be committed to a willingness to see ourselves as victimizers as well as victims – as sinners as well as holy people united with the Son of God.

Thus, when we are confronted with the martyr who has suffered at the hands of our own ecclesial body, there is a very particular kind of judgment and gift involved. To the extent that our victim has met his or her death in the conviction that they are being obedient to the law of Christ, they address to us a word from Christ, an invitation to acknowledge our own complicity in violence and the skewed perspectives that both generate and feed violence.

They invite us to cross over to where Christ is: to the place where violence is endured not inflicted. And in this way they draw us deeper into the life of the Body of the crucified.

Secondly: all this is only the most dramatic and clear-cut example of how the holy person manifests to us the reality of a Body constantly broken by betrayal and falsehood, rather than a finished or timeless holiness. Every saint's life, as noted already, arises out of a corporate Christian life in which imperfect (sometimes dramatically imperfect) Christians have played a formative part. Thus if and when we acknowledge signs of Christlikeness – of what I called earlier the "flow" of life and prayer towards God the Father – in someone from another Christian confession, then even when we still feel bound to attend to theological and ecclesiological disagreements at the level of ideas, we are bound to see that this one holy life must entail a presence and activity of the Body of Christ in and through their Christian fellowship. An Orthodox Christian recognizing something of holiness in a Calvinist, a Pentecostal recognizing holiness in a Roman Catholic, would be acknowledging that the actual historical and specific fellowship of this apparently foreign Christian body of believers is a conduit of the life of the Body of Christ, whatever its supposed "deficiencies" in [Catholic] order or in biblical fidelity.

Thirdly: when we celebrate the saints in an ecumenical context, we are celebrating the church that *will be* but is not yet. We celebrate the eschatological Body of Christ in which all those who have truly served Christ and embodied his way and his gospel are equally at home, however they may have been separated from each other in history. And we also acknowledge with gratitude that our own life in Christ's Body is nourished by many invisible sources – indeed, that it is nourished by this eschatological unity. The Spirit of the age to come, the Spirit who is a pledge, an *arrabon* of God's future, works in us through relationships we cannot see or grasp at the moment, acting through the stranger, the victim, the one we cannot now recognize as brother or sister. To celebrate a holy person from the history of another Christian family is at the same time to say, "I do not know today whose life may be used by the Spirit today and tomorrow to bring me to the maturity of faith and witness that God has in mind for me."

The imagery of a "cloud" of witnesses is curiously apt here. Those who by God's grace shape our discipleship are a great multitude whose faces are often hidden from us. It is good that we are able to identify some of those faces – the familiar and obvious ones in our own lives and in the life of our own community, and also the unexpected faces, the strangers who, we begin to see, have been brought into our individual and corporate lives by God for our health and salvation; and in identifying some of these faces, we are reminded of those others whose faces we cannot see, both past and present. And we turn to our Christian brother and sister in another Christian confession with new eyes and new expectations – new penitence as well, since we are faced with the reality of how we consciously and unconsciously ignore, avoid and even violently reject God's gift when it comes in unfamiliar form.

The ecumenical celebration of holiness teaches us two essential things. It alerts us to the various ways in which we may be complicit in Christ's suffering at least as much as sharing it; it teaches us to be very cautious about triumphalistic identification with the cross when, as flawed and fallible disciples, we are always also the crucifiers. It is the same insight that comes at every eucharist, when we acknowledge that we sit at table among those who will betray and abandon their Lord, knowing that we have failed and will fail as they did. And it recalls us to gratitude for the pathless ways of God's grace, given to us constantly in the unexpected person, place or community. In other words, the business of this Conference is not simply one aspect of liturgical life or historical study, but the whole character of the church as a penitent and maturing body, watered by hidden streams and living out of the timeless resource of the Holy Spirit in whom the end, when Christ is all in all, is already real.

May this Conference be blessed by God the Holy Trinity for the enriching of our shared witness and the deepening of our unity.

Witness and Martyrdom in the Bible

Enzo Bianchi

Introduction

> The person who renders testimony (*ho martyrôn*) to the truth, defends it in word and action, can justly be called "witness" (*mártys*). According to the usage of the brethren who have been impressed by the behaviour of those who have fought even to the death for the truth, however, "martyr" (*mártys*) is not used with the full force of this term except for those who in the shedding of blood have given testimony (*martyrésantas*) to the "mystery of piety"[1] (1 Tim. 3:16).

These words by Origen (middle of the 3rd century AD) in his commentary on John[2] fit well to introduce a reflection on the topic of witness (or testimony)/martyrdom in the Bible. It is well-known, in fact, that the Greek terms *martyréo/martyría/mártys,* which originally belonged to the sphere of legal language with the meaning of "witnessing, testifying, making a public declaration", began to be used as technical terms to indicate martyrdom only in the *Passiones* and *Acta Martyrum* of the 2nd century, at the time of the widespread persecution of Christians in the Roman empire. In the Septuagint and in the New Testament, with some rare exceptions, *martyréo* and related words are used rather to signify "testify, give testimony", like the Hebrew root underlying them *'ud* (from which is derived *'ed,* witness).

We likewise know that in the gospels according to Mark (cf. Mark 14:55-56,59,63) and Matthew (cf. Matt: 18, 16:26,65) the language of the *martyría* is always limited to the legal sphere, while in Luke (gospel and Acts) it assumes also a wider significance, that of rendering testimony to Jesus (cf. Luke 4:22; Acts 1:8) and to the resurrection (cf. Luke 24:48; Acts 1:22; 3:15). In the fourth gospel, then, this vocabulary describes the mission of Jesus and consequently that of the apostles: the verb *martyréo,* which recurs a good 33 times, is used to express concisely the testimony that Jesus rendered to the Father (cf. John 5:36) and vice versa (cf. John 8:18), to the truth (cf. John 18:37), to the light (cf. John 1:7-8); it should be noted, however, that Jesus is never designated as *mártys.*

Apart, however, from these lexical considerations, I believe it is more important to reflect on the *reality of martyrdom:* that of a public testimony of faith in God and in Jesus Christ given by men and women, a testimony that does not shrink even before violent death and which from a certain epoch came to be designated by the term "martyrdom", which sums up its meanings. In this sense it is undeniable that sacred Scripture presents models of

---

1 Since the author of this article did not use any official Italian translation of the Bible, but himself translated the quotes he used, the translator of the article translated these quotes into English.

2 Origène, *Commentaire sur Saint Jean II,* 210 (Sources Chrétiennes 120, 350)

"martyrs' *ante litteram,* on whom Christian faithful from the first generations have meditated to strengthen their faith.

I shall try, therefore, to analyze the most significant figures of witnesses/martyrs present in the Bible, exemplary models that attest to the continuity of the tradition of martyrdom for the faithful of the First and of the New Covenant.

Testimony and martyrdom in the Old Testament

a) Martyrdom and prophecy

According to Jewish tradition, as it appears, for instance, in the apocryphal *Lives of the Prophets,* which were composed at the time of the end of the second temple, but transmitted by Christians, the lot of authentic prophets is that of being persecuted. In particular, martyrdom and violent death are the seal *par excellence* on the prophetic mission, the culmination of testimony rendered to God and opposing the dominant idolatry and human disobedience to his will. Conscious of this, the Levites in the expiatory liturgy celebrated upon the return from exile confess that "*[our fathers]* have rebelled against you, o God, have thrown aside the Torah, *have killed your prophets who admonished them to return to you* and have greatly insulted you" (Neh. 9:26). Jesus too in word and deed will place himself in their wake, and Stephen in the long discourse that preceded his being stoned asks his murderers: "Which of the prophets have your fathers not persecuted?" (Acts 7:52).

This long history opens with *Moses,* "the Lord's servant" (Deut. 34:5), whom the children of Israel strongly contested and put to the test in various ways during their wanderings in the desert (cf. Ex. 17:1-7, and others). In a tradition taken up by Hosea there are two verses that, although their interpretation is very uncertain, seem to testify to the sufferings to the point of bloodshed inflicted on the great prophet. I give you a literal translation:

> Through a prophet the Lord made Israel depart from Egypt and through a prophet preserved him. But [Ephraim] provoked him to bitterness: therefore his blood will return to fall on him, and his opprobrium his Lord will render him (Hos. 12:14-15).

The martyrdom of the prophets, however, is attested with certainty already by Elias in the middle of the 9th century BC. When he was fleeing from the persecution of queen Jezebel towards the mountain of God, Horeb-Sinai, the Lord asked him: "What are you doing here, Elias?" He replied: "I am full of zeal for the Lord, the God of the universe, because the sons of Israel have abandoned your covenant, they have demolished your altars, they have killed your prophets with the sword. Only I remain, and they seek to take my life" (1 Kings 19:9-10,13-14). The "guilt" of the prophets is that of opposing idolatrous power, a source of economic and social oppression of the poor: through their defence of justice they testify to the absolute sovereignty of JHWH and confess their faith in him even to the point of giving their life.

Other examples of prophets persecuted to the point of martyrdom could be cited, outstanding examples of which are Uriah (cf. Jer. 26:20-23) and Zachariah, recalled also by Jesus (cf. 2 Chron. 24:17-22; Matt. 23:35; Luke 11:51). I would like, however, to examine more closely only the paradigmatic case of *Jeremias,* who lived at the turn of the 7th and 6th centuries BC. His entire prophetic ministry can be read as one uninterrupted passion, born of the contrast between his announcing the word of God, which "for him is a cause of shame and derision all the day long" (cf. Jer. 20:8), and his persecution by the legitimate religious authorities (cf. Jer. 18:18), so that he comes to feel "like a meek lamb, conducted to the slaughter" (Jer. 11:18). The priest Pascur has him beaten and put in prison (cf. Jer. 20:2), and, on account of his prophecy concerning the temple, Jeremias is arrested and receives the death sentence, commuted at the last moment (cf. Jer. 26).

Just as Zacharias on the point of death had done (cf. 2 Chron. 24:22), so too Jeremias asks God to vindicate him (cf. Jer. 15:15). God, however, does not intervene against his enemies, he lets the prophet descend to the *she'ol* of despair, he confronts him with the false prophets without letting it appear clearly that his testimony is authentic. Jeremias will see burned the roll on which his words were written (cf. Jer. 36:1-26), he will end up in a muddy cistern at the risk of death (cf. Jer. 38:1-12) and will be dragged to Egypt, in solidarity with his people's sin (cf. Jer. 43:1-7). In the tragic moments of this man's existence God appears to abandon him and to refuse him his testimony; Jeremias, however, always gives his testimony to God, remains faithful to him until his death outside the holy land. His death, according to one interpretation of Jewish tradition, is a real and true martyrdom: "Jeremias died at Tafni, in Egypt, stoned by the people."[3]

b) The Servant of the Lord

Within our itinerary a special place belongs to the mysterious figure of the *'eved Adonaj,* the *Servant of the Lord* described by Deutero-Isaias in the middle of the 6th century BC, in the four so-called "Songs of the Servant" (cf. Is. 42:1-9; 49:1-7; 50:4-11; 52:13-53, 12). These are extremely dense and complex texts, which have received through the centuries numerous interpretations. Among these I wish to single out that which sees in him an individual Messiah, an interpretation already present in Judaism and then attested in continuity by Christian tradition, and the collective interpretation that sees in the Servant the people of Israel taken as a corporate personality (cf. Is. 49:3).

In this last view, within a kind of trial before the *gojim,* to the exiled nation among hostile peoples is rendered testimony by the Lord himself. Three times the Lord's oracle resounds with force: *"You are my witnesses"* (*'edaj* [*mártyres* according to the LXX]: Is. 43:10,12; 44:8). The basic testimony rendered by Israel to God is that of perseverance even

3 *Vitae prophetarum* 2. For the Text and Commentary see Anna Marie Schweimer, *Studien zu den Frühjüdischen Propheten-legenden. Vitae Prophetarum,* vol. 2, Tübingen, 1995-1996.

in a situation of extreme suffering. In its apparent passivity the people remain "the servant whom God has chosen" (cf. Is. 43:10) and in this way gives public testimony through its faith, which remains firm even in the midst of persecution.

The songs of the Servant, however, describe also an individual prophet. Filled with the Spirit of God, he is invested with the mission of "manifesting to the people the *mishpat*" (Is. 42:1), "radical judgment in the name of the unique love of God, therefore judgment of salvation for all men."[4] His mission, however, seems to be marked only by a lack of success: a prophet rejected because of the testimony he rendered to God's word, he suffers abuse and persecution; nevertheless, he continues to trust in God and declares himself disposed to testify in tribunal before his enemies (cf. Is. 50:4-9). In the fourth song the mistreatment meted out to the Servant reaches its apex, making of him "a man of sorrows, acquainted with suffering" (Is. 53:3), condemned to suffer an unjust and violent death and a burial among the impious (cf. Is. 53:8-9). Like a lamb without voice the *'eved Adonaj* is led to the slaughter (cf. Is. 53:7), yet his death appears as a true sacrifice of expiation, which permits God's plan to be realized. For the very reason of his ignominious death, in fact, he will see the light, he will be a sign for the multitudes (*rabbim*), he will be a source of justification thanks to his intercession for sinners (cf. Is. 53:11-12).

In the life of this anonymous martyr there is public testimony before worldly authorities, a voluntarily accepted death, the expiatory value of sacrifice and the blessing that follows, which descends on all men, among whom are numbered his killers. These at the sight of him cannot but acknowledge: "He was pierced by our sins, broken for our iniquities… By his wounds we were healed" (Is. 53:5). This is the *absolute uniqueness of the Servant:* by not imputing the sin to the multitudes, but taking upon himself their violence, he puts an end to violence; the killers' guilt falls on the Servant, who assumes the injustice of which he was victim and interposes himself as mediator between God and sinners, in order to ask mercy of God and transmit pardon to the multitudes.

As appears in many passages of the gospel, Jesus must have pondered his deepest vocation in the light of this figure of the Servant, assuming it as the form of his own life, to the point of interpreting by it his own end. Did he not say to his disciples shortly before being arrested: "In me must be fulfilled this word of Scripture: 'He was numbered among the malefactors' (Is. 53:12)" (Luke 22:37)? In consequence, the figure of the Servant will become a stable reference in every Christian reflection on martyrdom.

c) The martyrdom of the Maccabees

If we take a chronological leap to the beginning of the 2nd century BC, the time of the Hellenistic persecution, we come to martyrdom met for the love of God and of his Law on the

4 Alberto Mello, *Isaia. Commento esegetico-spirituale,* Qiqajon, Bose, 1986, p.80.

part of some faithful (*chassidim*) and of some wise men (*maskilim*). Their witness, narrated in the books of the Maccabees and theologically reread by Daniel, will assume the value of an exemplar for Christians oppressed by the Roman Empire. Not by chance *the Maccabee martyrs* were very soon inserted into Christian martyrologies and their tomb in Antioch was taken over by Christians who wanted to honour their memory.

Antiochus IV Epiphanius (175–164 BC), a king of the Seleucid dynasty, began a fierce persecution of the faithful of the Torah who opposed the introduction of pagan customs and of idolatry in Israel. The abolition of the Torah, the substitution of the feast of the Tabernacles by the Bacchanals, finally, the introduction of the cult of Zeus into the temple, an act defined as the "abomination of desolation" (Dan. 9:27; cf. 1 Macc. 1:54), met with strong opposition by the priestly family of the Maccabees. Freed from its nationalistic elements and of its features of "holy war", evident especially in the figure of Judas Maccabeus, this opposition shows paradigmatic characteristics of martyrdom, as is inferred from several passages of the books of the Maccabees. To the enemies who attacked them on a Sabbath day:

> They did not respond or throw stones or obstruct their hiding places, but declared: "We all die in our innocence. Heaven and earth are our witnesses that you unjustly make us die." So they rushed against them in battle, and these died with their wives, their children, and their cattle, to the number of about one thousand persons (1 Macc. 2:36-38).

The scribe *Eleazar* likewise readily met torture, saying under the blows: "The Lord well knows that, although I could escape death, in my body I suffer atrocious torments under the beatings, but in my soul I gladly bear all this out of fear of him" (2 Macc. 6:30–31). The most impressive *testimony,* destined to enjoy enormous fortune, however, is *of the seven brothers and their mother,* ready to die rather than deny the Torah (cf. 2 Macc. 7). While they are tortured one by one, they attest before the king that God will give them consolation, raising them to new and eternal life; that it is good to die on account of men in order to await from God the fulfillment of the hope of being resurrected by him. They sacrifice their own life with *parrhesia* and full faith in the one God, whom they confess as their avenger.

The meaning of the testimony of these faithful is well understood by Daniel who, projecting the historical facts of his times back to the times of the Babylonian kingdom, assimilates the Maccabee martyrs to the three youths thrown into the burning furnace by Nebuchadnezzar (cf. Dan. 3:8-97); in contrast, he judges the armed revolt as an attempt made by human hands, "a little help" (Dan. 11:34), incapable of stopping the persecution because it has little confidence in true help, that of God (cf. Dan. 2:34; 8:25). He recognizes as witnesses of God "those wise persons (*maskilim*) who will teach the multitudes, but will fall by the sword, will be given to the flames, led into slavery and oppressed for many days… Some of them will fall, so that among them there would be those that have been purified, washed, made clean until the time of the end" (Dan. 11:33,35). Their unwavering hope is that of the resurrection: on account of this Daniel can affirm that "they will shine like the splendour of the firmament; those that have led many to justice will shine like stars forever" (Dan. 12:3).

These last elements are already very close to the Christian concept of martyrdom. We could say that only one thing is missing, but that one thing is essential: the event and person of Jesus Christ, the reason of life and of death for his disciples. First, before passing to the second part of my reflections I would like to read a final passage, taken from the book of Wisdom, composed on the threshold of the Christian era. The author, in comparing the lot of the just and of the impious, writes words that constitute an ideal *trait d'union* with what will follow.

> The just who die are in God's hands, no torment can touch them any longer: in the eyes of the foolish they are considered dead, their passing is judged a misfortune, but they are in peace for always. If to men they appeared to be afflicted, yet they have hoped in life without end: after a brief trial they receive a great recompense... On the day of the Lord's visitation they will shine, they will glitter like sparks of fire, they will judge the nations, they will have power over peoples, and the Lord will reign for always over them (Wis. 3:1-5,7-8).

The witness and martyrdom of Jesus of Nazareth

I would like to deal with the topic of witness/martyrdom in the New Testament from a special point of view. It is often said that in the New Testament three episodes of martyrdom are narrated: the beheading of John the Baptist (cf. Mark 6:17-29), the stoning of Stephen (cf. Acts 7:55-60) and the crucifixion of Jesus. Nevertheless, if in the first two cases the character of martyrdom is evident, things are rather different in the death of Jesus. In fact, although it is true that *the death of Jesus* has come to be interpreted in faith and theology as a sacrifice of expiation (cf. Matt. 26:38; 1 Pet. 2:24-25), as the "normative principle for discerning the truth of Christian martyrdom,"[5] it nevertheless remains true that in his historical vicissitude he experienced the death of the cursed through *a shameful end,* through *the anti-sacrifice* par excellence: *death on the cross.* For Scripture this is the death of one cursed by God ("Cursed is he who hangs from the wood": Gal. 3:13; cf. Deut. 21:23), hanging between heaven and earth because rejected by God and by human beings: this is the *mors turpissima crucis*,[6] the extreme torment inflicted on one judged harmful to the *polis* by Roman political authority and enemy of the community of believers by the legitimate religious authority.

What happened in Jerusalem on the eve of the Passover Sabbath, 7 April of the year 30? Jesus, a Galilean who had gathered around himself a community of a few men and

5 Bruno Maggioni, "Il martirio, rivelazione di Dio", *La Rivista del Clero Italiano,* 75/11 (1994), p.738.
6 Origen, *Commentary on Matthew,* xxvii.22, GCS (Die Griechschein Christlichen Schriftsteller) 38, 259.

some women fully drawn into his itinerant life, held as rabbi and prophet by these disciples and by a wider number of sympathizers, was condemned and put to death by crucifixion. This ending in failure at once appeared as a scandal – "the scandal of the cross" (1 Cor. 1:23), Paul will say – an obstacle to faith in him, especially when he began to be confessed as the Messiah of Israel, hence Son of God, sent by God to announce the coming of his kingdom. This is why, still at the beginning of the 2nd century AD the Jewish rabbi Trypho declares in his dialogue with the Christian Justin: "We know that the Messiah must suffer and be led like a sheep (cf. Is. 53:7), but that he should be crucified and die such a shameful and ignominious death, through the death accursed by the Law, this we cannot even begin to conceive."[7] Not by chance, some groups of Christians will end by denying that Christ died on the cross, and it is highly significant that for the Koran Jesus at the last moment was replaced by another man because such a death was impossible for the Messiah.[8]

Yet, for authentic Christian faith it is exactly the one crucified who "has narrated God" (cf. John 1:18); even on the cross, or rather, especially on the cross, Jesus "has rendered testimony to the truth" (cf. John 18:37: verb *martyréo*), transforming an instrument of capital punishment into the place of greatest glory. But how was it possible that a man hanging on a cross become him on whom Christians gaze as Saviour and Lord? That is: can his death be considered a martyrdom? I believe that in order to answer this question it is necessary to ask oneself why Jesus was put to death and how he confronted the prospect of his imminent violent death. Augustine has affirmed: "*Martyres non facit poena sed causa,*"[9] that is, "what makes martyrs is not the torment but the reason for their death". Well then, what was the reason, the cause in the double sense of historical cause and of profound interior principle that animated Jesus' acting as he did?

The gospels take care to tell us clearly that Jesus went towards his death *not by chance or out of necessity, that is, because of a destiny that fell to his lot.* No, Jesus was not arrested by chance: he himself had foreseen his own end, the end that comes to all prophets, the end that fell to the lot of his teacher John the Baptist only a few years before, the end that was the outcome of the growing opposition to him on the part of the religious powers. In this connection his invectives against those who built the tombs of the prophets and in that way showed solidarity with those who had killed them (cf. Matt. 23:29-31; Luke 11:47-48), or his lament over Jerusalem that "kills the prophets and stones those sent to her" (cf. Matt: 23:37; Luke 13:34). Nor was his destiny inevitable: Jesus remained free before the circle that was tightening around him, free to return to Galilee or to terminate in Jerusalem, in the temple, that wandering around and preaching to the people begun in the synagogues and village squares.

7 *Dialogue with Trypho*, 90.1, PG 6, 689.
8 cf. Koran, Sura iv. 157.
9 *Exposition on the Psalms*, 34.ii.13, PL 36, 340.

Neither chance nor necessity: Jesus goes towards his death *in freedom and out of love,* "having loved his own who were in the world, he loved them to the end" (*eis télos:* John 13:1). He had said that his passion "was necessary" (*deî:* Mark 8:31 and parallel), but it was a precise "*necessity*", first of all a *human* one, on which the wise men of Israel had already meditated: "in a world of the unjust, the just man can only meet with hostility, persecution, and, if possible, be put to death", as the first two chapters of the book of Wisdom testify. History confirms this intrahuman necessity: he who is thirsty for justice, who lives and preaches it, finds hostility and rejection, yesterday like today. Jesus could have remained silent or have passed to the part of the unjust: then the hostility towards him would have ceased. By continuing instead to be faithful to the will of God, by continuing to pass among human beings doing good (cf. Acts 10:38), he could only prepare his rejection by the Roman authority, which saw in him a threat to the totalitarian claims of the emperor, and by the Jewish religious authority, which could not stand the face of God narrated by Jesus. Human necessity, thus, becomes also *divine necessity:* not in the sense that God, his Father, wants him on the cross, but in the sense that obedience to the will of God, a will that asks that love be lived to the limit, requires a life of justice and of love even at the cost of a violent death.

Here it is essential to stress that Jesus in assuming this tragic end never separated it from his faith in God who comes to save the just man, who does not abandon his friend forever in the hands of the impious (cf. Ps. 37:28). Yes, the ever clearer revelation of the future that awaited him was lived by Jesus in trusting adherence and in hope placed in the God who intervenes, in the Father who responds: the last word would be God's, who certainly would raise from the dead his beloved Son! In other words, the faith of Jesus in the coming kingdom and his communion with God and with his brethren always remained unshaken and sustained and carried to completion his love: even in the face of death and in death Jesus continued to love his brethren and to accept to be loved by them, continued to believe in God's love.

This Jesus was raised by God in response to the life that he had lived, to his way of living in love to the limit: we could say that it was his love stronger than death that caused the Father's decision to recall him from the dead. Indeed, the resurrection of Jesus is the seal that God placed on his life: by raising him from the dead, God has declared that everything that is essential to know him was testified in the love lived by that man. It is in this that *"the testimony of Jesus"* (*he martyría Iesoû:* Rev. 1:2,9; 12:17; 19:10; 20:4) consists, as the visionary of the Apocalypse defines it; it is this that made him *"the faithful witness"* (*ho mártys ho pistós:* Rev. 1:5; 3:14), the one who from his glorious cross teaches his disciples how to face tribulations and sufferings for the gospel in faithfulness and in love.

Conclusion. The testimony and martyrdom of Christians

Bruno Maggioni has written: "The martyr does not choose death, but a way of living, that of Jesus."[10] This is what distinguishes the Christian martyr, his specific radicality. In the light of this we can go over in summary the testimony given by those who believe in Jesus Christ as it is presented to us in the New Testament:

- Stephen, who before dying in imitation of his Lord asks pardon for his killers (cf. Luke 23:34; Acts 7:60);
- James, put to death by the sword by Herod (cf. Acts 12:2), grandson of the Herod who had persecuted Jesus (cf. Luke 23:7-12);
- Peter, "witness (*mártys*) of Christ's sufferings and participant of the glory that is to become manifest" (1 Pet. 5:1);
- Paul, who in faith exclaims: "Always and everywhere we carry in our body the death of Jesus, so that also the life of Jesus may be made manifest in our body" (2 Cor. 4:10);
- Antipas, who in the Apocalypse is defined by Christ "my faithful witness" (*ho mártys mou ho pistós:* (Rev. 2:13);
- finally, again in the Apocalypse, the multitude of "those who come from the great tribulation and have washed their garments, making them white, in the blood of the Lamb" (Rev. 7:14), "who have overcome the Accuser thanks to the blood of the Lamb and to the word of their testimony (*ho lógos tês martýrias autôn*)" (Acts 12:11).

Where the memory of Christ becomes authentic and efficacious, there the Christian must know that it becomes possible to drink the chalice of a violent death, as Jesus had foretold to James and John (cf. Mark 10:38). Martyrdom is not a project to be plotted, it is not even a project of one's own sanctification, but is pure gift of God in Jesus Christ. *It is always worthwhile to live and to die for Jesus,* and martyrdom is the act *par excellence* by which the Christian lays down his life for Christ, it is the very event by which he testifies that he belongs only to his Lord, that the love of him and for him is worth more than life (cf. Ps. 63:4). Yes, as wrote Ignatius of Antioch on his way towards martyrdom:

> Then I will be truly the Lord's disciple when the world will no longer see my body, because in martyrdom I will begin to be a disciple (cf. *To the Romans,* iv.3; v.3).

10 Bruno Maggioni, p.743.

FAITH AND ORDER ROOTS OF ECUMENICAL COMMEMORATION

From Bangalore 1978 to Bose 2008

Tamara Grdzelidze

The Bose Symposium resulted from a joint effort of the Community of Bose and the Secretariat of the Faith and Order Commission of the World Council of Churches. Without the experience of the Community of Bose to organize large conferences in the field of Christian spirituality, without their skills to find and approach interesting speakers, it would have been difficult to collect so many fascinating presentations. The Faith and Order Secretariat on its part offered its unique capacity of being the largest theological forum of Christian churches today.

Lukas Vischer (1927-2008) stands behind this symposium more than any other person involved in its preparation, including the members of the Steering Group. Certainly, he was fully involved in the work of the Commission as a director of Faith and Order when in Bangalore thirty years ago an initial proposal was made for an "ecumenical list of martyrs".

The Bangalore suggestion for an ecumenical list of martyrs was made in the context of the so called Ecumenical Prayer Cycle – an ecumenical calendar for prayer according to which we pray for churches and peoples of a particular group of countries. Each week churches remember, or as it was said in Bangalore, "visit", two or more countries and pray for those countries and peoples and churches and Christians and for "All God's people".

The first Memorandum, signed by ten persons in Bose in 2004, spoke extensively about the significance of witnesses of faith and drew largely on the image of the Cloud of Witnesses surrounding us, according to Heb.12:1. It also reflected, among other things, on visible boundaries of this cloud that are not established or unchangeable and whose borderlines are known only to God.

It was a strong conviction of the Steering Group at the beginning of the process that remembering together of a cloud of witnesses was one of the paths towards unity between the churches that we seek. Ecumenical commemoration is an act of common Christian witnessing to the world by recognizing the faithful in each other's churches. This is also a path to reconciliation in cases where history made an unfortunate turn by turning heroes of one church into the enemies of the other.

Ecumenical commemoration of witnesses of other churches is a good discipline; in order to acknowledge faith in a challenging context, communities need to re-visit history and take a fresh look at common memory of which we admit to having limited knowledge. Churches, in most cases, tend to be reluctant to take a fresh look at an established historical order, but remembering witnesses of faith in an unusual way, may raise sympathy and elevate the sense that all are surrounded by a cloud of known and unknown martyrs.

Encouragement for ecumenical commemoration resonates differently with the churches. For those with a huge tradition of commemoration of saints and the communion of saints it is a delicate issue. It is one thing to encourage churches that have either lost or rejected the tradition of liturgical commemoration for various reasons, but to ask churches with a strong tradition of commemoration to do so will need clear instruction. What do we wish to evoke? Why do we need to commemorate ecumenically?

The Steering Group started its discussion in 2004 on the basis of the Bose Martyrology, that is, it discussed opportunities to create a similar calendar of witnesses with an extended list of persons nominated by the churches themselves but developing this initiative into a large-scale process. What is this process about and where does the Bose Symposium stand in this process?

The process envisages various activities and the Bose Symposium is one of its significant manifestations. At the end of this symposium, as had been envisaged and hoped for, a Message was produced, directed to the churches and ecumenical institutions and truly to "all God's people". The aim of this process is made clear in the message – *raising awareness about the significance of the ecumenical commemoration for the sake of the unity of the church* – by involving Christian communities at all levels of church life, from the bottom to the top, from the grassroots to the highest authorities. This involvement implies different initiatives on the part of those involved. We are at the beginning but the process has started.

What kind of initiatives do we have in mind to attain the above-mentioned aims? Firstly, the willingness of churches to commemorate witnesses from other traditions at a time they find appropriate, whether at the feast of All Saints or at special ecumenical gatherings. Such commemoration may have a liturgical character and evolve into a service *per se* or simply become a part of meditation. In the papers presented one reads about existing examples of ecumenical commemoration as well as suggestions from different traditions for such a commemoration. Hopefully churches will be convinced by the papers and the message from the Bose Symposium that a path towards unity of the church, towards full recognition of one another by different churches, lies also in reaching reconciliation over the past uncertainties through remembering heroes of faith, martyrs, holy persons, saints, whichever definition will be suitable in each context.

A way to the Bose Symposium was cleared through the above-mentioned first Memorandum - Surrounded by a Great Cloud of Witnesses. It was introduced to the Faith and Order Commission during its Plenary Meeting in Kuala Lumpur in July-August 2004. The Faith and Order Commission accepted a proposal for the Cloud of Witnesses project and gave a positive response to collaboration between the Secretariat and the Bose community. Following this decision, a letter signed by the prior of Bose, Enzo Bianchi, and Tom Best, then director of the Faith and Order Commission, went to the churches together with the Memorandum.

The letter basically attempted to involve churches in a discussion on the significance of awakening the ecumenical memory by remembering witnesses of faith from each other's traditions and requested that the churches answer a few questions (see Memorandum I).

There were several responses from churches for which the Steering Group and Faith and Order Secretariat express gratitude. The second Memorandum from Bose in 2007 (see Memorandum II) again went out to the churches accompanied by a letter from the prior of Bose and the director of Faith and Order. This Memorandum spoke about the interest in the project shown by some churches' replies to the first one; some expressed their interest by organizing dialogues and conferences on the issue.

The Steering Group noted with great satisfaction that the process of encouraging churches to commemorate witnesses of faith ecumenically coincided with a number of publications on the same subject.

Bangalore

Let us see what was at stake in Bangalore and how it fits into or goes beyond what the Bose Symposium has been trying to achieve.

The report from Bangalore – Witness Unto Death – gives a profound examination of martyrdom and interprets it strictly in the eucharistic framework. Christ is "the faithful witness" himself (Rev. 1:5). His earthly life is exemplary, he comes for the sake of sinners and the weak, he heals the sick and frees human beings from death. He brings hope to the hopeless by his voluntary death on the cross. "The Spirit of the Lord is upon me, for he has anointed me to preach good news to the poor. He has sent me to proclaim release to the captives and recovery of sight to the blind, to let the oppressed go free, to proclaim the year of the Lord's favour" (Luke 4:18-19).

For the report from Bangalore, the biblical background of martyrdom is enriched by sayings of martyrs and fathers of the early church: the grace of the eucharist turned impossible into possible. "Already in the 2nd century St Ignatius of Antioch foresees that his martyrdom will 'grind' him into one bread with Christ. Fifty years later the martyr Polycarp will give to his parting prayer the form of an *eucharistia*."[1] The martyrs of Abitanae said in the 4th century: "we cannot do without the Lord's supper".[2] Considering that the Bangalore meeting evolved around the notion of hope, Sharing in One Hope, it is not surprising that the report, Witness Unto Death, emphasized it: "The hope for the future is already prefigured in the fact that the Eucharistic community itself includes pardoned sinners, reconciled adversaries, and the desperate restored to life: all are welcome by the Lord at this table of justice, peace and joy in the Holy Spirit (cf. Rom. 14:17)."[3]

1 *Sharing in One Hope, Commission on Faith and Order, Bangalore 1978*, Faith and Order Paper no.92, WCC Publications, Geneva, 1978, p.198.
2 *Ibid.*, p.197.
3 *Ibid*, p.198.

Martyrs of the church transcend confessional boundaries, they bear witness to Christ, to the coming kingdom, they bring all to the core of the Christian message, to the faith that is the source of hope, the love for God and neighbours. In this respect Christian life may be enriched by accounts of martyrdoms. Thus the Bangalore report says: "It is desirable that an ecumenical anthology of both early and modern accounts of martyrdom should be published... The use of such a book would also strengthen the solidarity of all Christians in prayer and action with those who are in difficult or dangerous situations."[4] (The Community of Bose took this suggestion seriously into account and produced a valuable martyrology.)

At Bangalore a distinction was made between two kinds of martyrdom: the extreme witnessing that ends with death, so characteristic of the early church but also of later periods. Diversity of choices in concrete situations, how to bear witness to Christ, can be a source of tensions yet it can become valuable if it is lived with an effort to transcend divisions and look for things which unite regardless of existing differences.

Bangalore advocated the Ecumenical Prayer Cycle and placed a suggestion for a list of martyrs in this context:

> To intercede for other churches requires that those who pray should know them in their concrete historical actuality, with their problems and their opportunities, their fears and hopes, their particularities of life and worship and witness. This is where the Ecumenical Prayer Cycle will so significantly supplement the existing materials for intercessory prayer, enabling churches to pray for all other churches with at least some knowledge of them. ... To pray for another church requires an energy of will and imagination, a deliberate enterprise, first of thankfulness and then of care and compassion. To pray for another church is to open oneself before God and therefore to open oneself not only to give but also to receive within the fellowship of prayer and service. ... Such a practice of continued intercession for one another will enable the churches to see one another not with the eyes of theological appraisal or historical assessment but as joint petitioners before the throne of him who said, "Behold, I make all things new", who in Jesus Christ our Lord frees and unites us – the God of hope who fills us with all joy and peace in believing so that by the power of the Holy Spirit we may abound in hope (Rom. 15:13).[5]

May I conclude this reflection on Bangalore by evoking one image from the director's report at the Bangalore meeting. Lukas Vischer recalls how once his daughter interpreted the work for church unity after having heard her father's explanation. She found a cartoon of a man watering his plant and increasingly getting tired of his useless work;

4 *Ibid.*, p.200.
5 *Ibid.*, p.262.

however, at the end of the cartoon he was depicted as happy, smiling at a flower which had sprung up before him.

Present Challenges

There are a number of challenges to deal with while introducing ecumenical commemoration of witnesses. One of them is existing differences between traditions on the role attributed to witnesses. For some traditions witnesses are saints and are addressed in a prayer. Some traditions rejected this understanding but developed a different way of remembering witnesses. Through ecumenical commemoration all of them will be treated equally.

The other challenge is to avoid creating an alternative fixed list of witnesses. It is important to keep in mind that the borders of a cloud move and it is beyond human capacity to define its content. Any church may decide to commemorate witnesses at various ecumenical occasions but it will be much more meaningful that local communities or contexts provide concrete material for such a commemoration.

The task of the Bose Symposium is seen as helping to make ecumenical commemoration an active practice at ecumenical prayer services; also, to suggest various ways for such a commemoration in different traditions and at different occasions. This collection of papers together with the Message from the symposium is an open invitation to the churches to express their willingness to undertake a new practice of ecumenical commemoration. Some of the churches may be better prepared than others to face a new challenge in their ecumenical endeavour. The significance of human persons in witnessing to the faith of Christ cannot be diminished or underestimated under any circumstances and when witnessing causes a conflict in relation with other Christians, it is reasonable to seek ways of reconciliation and of re-reading of the past.

The Achievement of Bilateral Dialogues and Some Implications for a Common Martyrology

Mary Tanner

I may be the only person here who was at the Faith and Order Commission Plenary Meeting in Bangalore in 1978 when the commission called for an ecumenical list of saints and martyrs. My search into the bilateral dialogues was defined by the four ideas behind the Bose project[1] aiming at:

- the recognition of each other's witnesses of faith when this is not mutually exclusive;
- the commemoration of witnesses from various traditions at ecumenical meetings;
- developing or recovering a commemoration of witnesses in churches which do not have such a practice;
- and to work towards the production of a common ecumenical martyrology.

What has been done in this direction and what is the potential for future dialogues and how can re-discovery of commemoration and mutual recognition of witnesses enrich dialogues?

Introductory comments

It is an enormous task to ask anyone to do an overview of the bilateral dialogues for since the entry of the Roman Catholic Church into the ecumenical scene after Vatican II everyone, it seems, has been talking to everyone else in a complex network of conversations. The fruits of these conversations are now gathered in four volumes of documents of increasing size: 265 pages, 504 pages, 939 pages, 615 pages, and there are still more texts, important ones, not yet collected together in a single volume.[2] These collections contain not only the results of formal conversations but also Common Declarations made by church leaders, many of which contain significant reflections for our subject.[3]

It is not possible to talk about bilateral statements without taking into consideration the multilateral work of the Faith and Order Commission of the World Council of Churches. Bilateral and multilateral approaches have not been competitive, as was first feared, but mutually enriching and could be even more so in the future, not least of all in the area of the

1 On the Bose project see the Foreword by Guido Dotti and Tamara Grdzelidze.

2 Nils Ehrenstrom & Gunther Gassmann, (eds) *Confessions in Dialogue*, 1975, p 265; Harding Meyer & Lukas Vischer, (eds) *Growth in Agreement* I, WCC, Geneva, 1984, p.504; Jeffrey Gros, Harding Meyer, William Rusch (eds) *Growth in Agreement II*, WCC, Geneva, 2000, p.939; Jeffrey Gros, Thomas Best, Lorelei Fuchs (eds) *Growth in Agreement III*, WCC, Geneva, 2007, p.615. And there are more texts not yet incorporated into volume III – some very important texts like the latest report from the Anglican-Orthodox dialogue, *The Church of the Triune God,* which has been 12 years in the making; the Anglican-Roman Catholic agreed statement, *Growing Together in Mission and Unity*; the Lutheran-Roman Catholic text, *The Apostolicity of the Church*; the Roman Catholic-Reformed agreed statement, *Church as Community of Common Witness to the Kingdom*; etc...

3 It is frustrating for anyone trying to trace a particular theme through these documents that there is no subject index provided in the more recent volumes.

subject of this consultation. Our theme, not surprisingly, is treated more fully in dialogues involving Orthodox (Eastern and Oriental), Roman Catholic and Anglican partners. The subject of the saints and martyrs and "the communion of saints" is most fully treated in the Anglican-Orthodox agreed statements.[4] (In this paper I have worked with the broader, rather than narrower definition of martyrs, in the sense of those who witness unto death to the faith.)

The only bilateral agreed statement on the communion of saints is the *Llandaff Statement 1980* from the Anglican-Orthodox conversation.[5] Conversations between Reformed churches tend to emphasize more a spirituality of common action in the service of justice and peace. This is a generalization and in any case the two aspects can be understood as integrally related within the spirituality of the church. There are exceptions, not least of all in the emphasis the Mennonites bring to their conversation with the Catholics. In spite of the difference of emphases, there are certain commonalities that relate directly to our subject. When you read through this huge corpus with our theme in mind you see things you had not seen before, recognizing both missed opportunities as well as new possibilities for the enrichment of agreements and for forming a more holy vision of the church and its unity in the future.

The way, or pilgrimage, of dialogue and its implications for our subject

First, to enter into theological conversation is to become a part of a transformative experience as we open ourselves to others – to their experience and their traditions. We discover that what we claim theologically, that the personal and relational are prior in the life of communion, is indeed a reality, as deep friendships are forged around the table and what we do in conversation is all of a piece with what we do on our knees. There is a very real spirituality of dialogue, as those of us who have been privileged to be a part of a conversation know. The Lutheran-Catholic conversation was clear early on that theological reflection and spiritual experience had to interact in order to avoid intellectualizing dialogue. Archbishop Rowan's greeting to this meeting recognized this possibility when he wrote – "I hope that in this meeting, all the participants will feel that the Holy Spirit is truly speaking to them thorough the company of the saints, and also through the human fellowship of this encounter." As we share in common prayer, offer to, and receive from, one another, liturgical gifts and, as we celebrate each other's calendars, so we come to recognize the holiness of the other community and thus the holiness of the holy men and women, the saints, they revere.

Secondly, the ecumenical method that lies at the foundation of many of the dialogues contributes to our theme. Since the Faith and Order Conference in Montreal, in

4 The Llandaff Statement 1980, The Communion of Saints and the Dead, in *GinA I*, p.57ff and the more recent *The Church of the Triune God*, The Cyprus Agreed Statement of the International Commission for Anglican-Orthodox Theological Dialogue, ACC, London, 2006.

5 *GinA I*, p.57.

1963, many dialogues have followed the method of going back to Scripture and to the tradition of the undivided church, and then moving through the Scylla and Charybdis of the times of division, in order to restate together, afresh, the common faith for today. That pilgrimage of dialogue, whether undertaken explicitly or implicitly, provides an opportunity to encounter together saints and holy men and women throughout the centuries. First the holy women and men in the Hebrew Scriptures – and here we can all learn from the example of the Orthodox who revere the heroes of the Hebrew Scriptures. We then encounter together the evangelists and apostles of the New Testament and the fathers and martyrs of the early church. As we re-read together the period of division, we meet the heroes of each other's community of faith and in the encounter of dialogue we learn to see them, even those we have demonized in a different way. Methodists and Roman Catholics, for example, early in their dialogue, came to affirm together the treasure of John and Charles Wesley.[6] Without this discovery, there is unlikely to have been the ecumenical celebration of the 300th anniversary of the birth of Charles Wesley in Rome, in December 2007, in which Roman Catholics took part. Similarly, the Lutheran-Catholic and the Anglican-Roman Catholic conversations on justification led to a more balanced understanding of the controversies of the time of the Reformation and with that came a re-assessment of those demonized in the conflicts, even of those who died at our hands for a faith we believed then to be heretical. All of this opened up the possibility of a common re-appropriation of the martyrs on both sides of the Reformation divide.

In this context the Lutheran-Roman Catholic conversations have gone into greatest detail on the problematic practices centred on the saints at the time of the Reformation – the invocation of the saints, the veneration of saintly relics, the offering of the eucharist for the benefit of the dead, the call for heavenly intercession of the saints. Geoffrey Wainwright, in an erudite paper on the saints and the departed, examines a paper from the Lutheran-Catholic bilateral conversation in Germany, *Communion Sanctorum: Die Kirche als Gemeinschaft der Heiligen.*[7] He recognizes the convergences made in understanding the debates of the Reformation and also identifies areas where difficulties still remain. He names purgatory, indulgences and canonization.

In the agreed statement, Salvation and the Church, Anglicans and Catholics came to understand the division over justification by faith through grace, in which both sides stressed particular aspects of the faith and produced caricatures of the beliefs of their opponents. As a result the Commission was led to declare that the matters of dispute in the 16th century no longer justify continuing separation. Although not all Anglicans were happy with the conclusions of Salvation and the Church and called for more work on those areas that

6 *GinA I* p.373.
7 G. Wainwright, "The Saints and the Departed", in *Embracing Purpose: Essays on God, the World and the Church*, Epworth, Peterborough, UK, 2007, pp.222-247.

Geoffrey Wainwright identifies in relation to the Lutheran-Catholic dialogue, nevertheless, the theological convergence of the agreed statements formed the context in which, in the early 1980s, Cardinal Basil Hume and Archbishop Robert Runcie commemorated together the martyrs of the 16th century from both Communions. It also formed the context in which a memorial was placed last year in St Mary the Virgin, Oxford, which sets side by side 23 martyrs, including Church of England bishops, Hugh Ridley and Nicholas Latimer and Archbishop Thomas Cranmer together with Edmund Campion and the Catholic Martyrs. The joint memorial was intended "to create a common memory" and "to provoke contemplation on the sincerity of faith held by both sides".[8] This was to stand in stark contrast to the famous anti-Catholic memorial in Oxford to Protestant martyrs (Ridley, Latimer and Cranmer), close to where they were burnt at the stake on the orders of Queen Mary – a memorial which Dairmaid McCulloch calls "tribal in character", a symbol of religious division.[9] What and who we choose to remember shape us and can keep us apart while our common remembering has the power to draw us together.

A moving example of this way of dialogue is found in the report of the Mennonite-Catholic conversation. Here, a common re-reading of history contributes to "the purification of memories" (para.29). In their common recounting of the Reformation, Catholics and Mennonites had to confront the negative images each harboured of the other. The Catholic partners learnt of the *Martyrs Mirror,* compiled by a Dutch Mennonite of the 17th century which records the stories of many martyrs in which both Protestants and Catholics were the persecutors. Although never suffering at the hands of Mennonites, the fact that Catholics also had an experience of suffering martyrdom led to a recognition that at the Reformation both Catholics and Mennonites shared a common experience. Mennonites, like Catholics, came to hold their martyrs in high regard, singing of their faithful testimony and celebrating their memory by collecting stories in martyrologies, still read aloud in the Mennonite communities today. So, in the memory of both communities, the experience and memory of martyrdom is kept alive. This led the Commission to conclude:

> The common experience of martyrdom and persecution could help both Catholics and Mennonites to reach a renewed understanding of the meaning of martyrdom in the painful division of the Christian church in the early modern period … A common study of the history of 16th century martyrdom and persecution can help Catholics to appreciate and esteem the Mennonite experience of martyrdom and its impact on Mennonite spirituality and identity. Mennonites could benefit from a study of the Catholic Church's minority status in many countries since the

8 Diarmaid MacCulloch, quoted in *The Tablet*, 25 October, 2008, p.16, "When is a martyr a traitor?" by T. Norton.
9 I do not go here into the current controversy over the erection in Oxford of a plaque to the Catholic Martyrs, cf. *The Tablet ibid.*

reformation period and from the knowledge that Catholics have also the experience of being persecuted over the centuries.[10]

So, the actual pilgrimage of dialogue itself provides an opportunity to confront together the painful division of the past, to heal bitter memories and, at the same time, to honour the holy men and women of both communities of faith. This pilgrimage of dialogue thus becomes a way of enlarging our own identity. Those we have seen as traitors, and others have hailed as martyrs, become our common martyrs. Bishop Mark Santer, the co-chairman of the Second Anglican-Roman Catholic International Commission, wrote about this in a moving essay in 1982, just at the time that the theological conversation he was chairing was working at the divisions of the 16th century.[11]

Thirdly, in the 1970s and '80s, excited by the first flush of the results of the ecumenical conversations, the Faith and Order movement was often characterized as interested in theological conversation as an end in itself. But we have come to understand that theological conversations are aimed at bringing about recognition – recognition of our common faith and, through that, recognition of church in one another, as a step on the way to the reception of one another in a single communion of faith and life and witness. The current emphasis on "receptive ecumenism" is one of the promises for the new millennium.[12] Theological convergence and consensus is a crucial step on the way to recognition and ultimately to reception. And this is relevant to our subject again. For what we are to receive is not some finely honed theological document. We are challenged to receive one another, and one another's faithful lives, in a single communion of faith and life. A part of what we receive from the other is the memory of the lives and witness of their holy men and women as our own. As the Anglican-Orthodox, Cyprus Statement, expresses it – "reception is not only a matter of texts but of churches and people. In reacting to texts the churches begin a process of receiving one another as churches." To recognize the saints across historical ecclesiastical boundaries helps in healing of divisions, as we recognize and celebrate the presence and action of the Holy Spirit in communities in which those saints have been raised and nourished.[13]

There are many examples of this happening. In their Patriarchal Letter of 1991, Patriarch Ignatius IV of the Greek Antiochene Church and Patriarch Ignatius Zakka of the Orthodox Church of Antioch, affirm together "the total and mutual respect of the spirituality, heritage and holy fathers of both churches" and agree that "the heritage of the fathers in

10 *GinA III*, pp.219-220.
11 Mark Santer (ed.) *Their Lord and Ours*, SPCK, London, 1980, p.149ff.
12 The Durham Conference in January 2007 captured the imaginations of all who were there who saw it as giving a new impetus to ecumenism in the third millennium.
13 Cf. *The Church of the Triune God*, ACC, London, 2006, p.97ff.

both churches and their traditions as a whole should be integrated into Christian education, curricula and theological studies" of both their communions.[14] The 1993 Communiqué of their theological dialogue, which proposes lifting the anathemas on the basis of the Christological agreement, understands that this would entail acknowledging that the councils and fathers previously anathematized or condemned are orthodox in their teachings. Moreover, "The lifting of condemnations should imply that a catalogue of diptychs of the heads of the churches shall be agreed upon to be used liturgically".[15] There is a similar reference in the Common Declaration of Pope John Paul II and Patriarch Teoctist (of Romania) from October 2002, in which they express joy at being together close to the tombs of the holy apostles, Peter and Paul. Remembering the divisive days of the past they call upon their faithful in Romania to recognize with joy the tradition they have in common, centred on the mystery of the eucharist, to which the saints we have in common in our calendars bear witness. Many witnesses of faith who shared fidelity to Christ in the times of oppression and persecution… are a seed of hope in the present difficulties.[16] One of the most moving examples of the reconciliation of memories of holy men and women is in the Common Declaration of John Paul II and His Holiness Karekin II (Catholicos of the Armenian Apostolic Church), made in 2001 in Holy Etchmiadzin, in which they remember together St Gregory the Illuminator, his collaborators and successors who were an example to the Armenian people. They honour those who were butchered in the genocide of the 20th century who, though not canonized, are among the confessors and martyrs for the name of Christ.[17] There is a rich theme in the conversations of the reconciliation of memories which leads to a common recognition of saints and martyrs, those of the undivided church and those of our separate communities of faith, reclaimed and re-received together as a result of conversation and renewed relationships.

So, the way of dialogue itself, with its seed-bed in friendship, its ecumenical method, and its goal of recognition on the way to the reception of one another as churches, all have implications for our subject. They lead to the recognition of each other's witnesses of faith and to finding occasions of commemorating together. This forms a secure basis for the establishment of a common martyrology.

The subject matter of the dialogues

It is not only the way of dialogue that contributes to our theme but also the subject matter of many of the dialogues. No theme could be more important than the one which echoes through so many dialogues – the theme of communion, *koinonia. Koinonia* refers first to the divine relation of the persons of the Holy Trinity into which, through faith and baptism, Christians

14 *GinA III*, p.3.
15 *Ibid.*, p.5.
16 *GinA III*, p.179.
17 *Ibid.*, p.195.

are drawn, Thus they participate in that divine life and are brought by this into a relationship with one another, a relation of communion.

Union with God therefore involves us in a personal relationship with all who belong to him through the grace of the Holy Spirit who both unites and diversifies: and this personal relationship, which is not broken by death, is precisely the Communion of Saints.[18]

The emphasis on *koinonia* opens up a number of fruitful avenues. First, it enables divided Christians and churches to recognize that they are already, through baptism, bound together in the communion of God's own life and love. So, the Anglican-Roman Catholic Agreed Statement, Church as Communion, affirms that Anglicans and Roman Catholics are already in a "real though imperfect communion"; they can recognize "the profound measure of communion" that exists both within and between them.[19] Similarly, Methodists and Roman Catholics say that they already enjoy a "certain measure of ecclesial communion".[20] Pentecostals and Roman Catholics recognize "a certain, though imperfect communion" that already binds them to one another.[21] No one expresses this already existing degree of communion more beautifully than Pope John Paul II in Ut Unum Sint. This recognition of the communion that already exists is the basis for accepting one another and thus embracing one another's holy men and women.

Many reports recognise *koinonia* not simply as another image of the church but as *the* fundamental reality of the church. They speak of the church as "the communion of saints" – the *communio sanctorum* which is confessed in the Apostles' Creed. In Faith and Order's explication of the Nicene-Constantinopolitan Creed, the church is identified as "the communion of saints in the Holy Spirit". The communion of saints unites all the faithful of every age and of all places in one fellowship of prayer, praise and sharing in suffering and joy.[22] The Anglican-Orthodox dialogue identifies this communion of saints as a reality which transcends the limitations of space and time, a communion in which we remain joined with those who died. "There is no frontier between the two worlds in the Church. God is not God of the dead but of the living, for all live in and of him. This is the meaning of the communion of saints."[23] It is the communion of saints on earth and in heaven and in that communion the saints and martyrs, the holy men and women of all Christian communities and ecclesial bodies, are united in the life and love of the Holy Trinity. "The Church on earth is united in a single movement of worship with the Church in heaven, with the Blessed Virgin Mary, with angels and archangels, and all the company of heaven."[24]

---

18 The Llandaff Statement 1980, The Communion of Saints, in *GinA I*, p.57.
19 *GinA II*, pp.328 and 340.
20 The Word of Life: A Statement on Revelation and Faith, in *GinA II*, p.621.
21 Perspectives on koinonia, in *GinA II*, p.743.
22 *Confessing One Faith,* Faith and Order Paper no.153, WCC Publications, Geneva, 1991, p.231.
23 The Llandaff Statement 1980, The Communion of Saints, in *GinA I*, p.57.
24 *Ibid,* p.57.

In the Mennonite-Catholic report, where each side gives an account to the other of its understanding of the church, it is the Mennonites that emphasize the church as the "communion of saints". The church, the communion of saints, "includes all who believe in Jesus Christ and seek to follow him in holy living... The communion of saints includes the 'cloud of witnesses' (Heb. 12:1) of the past who have endured faithfully to the end. Sainthood is not based on ethical merit, but is accorded those who have endured and persevered to the end, 'looking to Jesus the pioneer and perfecter of our faith'."[25] What is disappointing is the fact that, surprisingly, there is no reference to the church as the communion of saints in *The Nature and Purpose of the Church,* the most recent ecclesiological report of the Faith and Order Commission. It is a missed opportunity. To have spoken of this, referring back to earlier work of the Commission and drawing upon some of the riches of the bilaterals, would have given a depth of spirituality to the statement.

Closely related to the theme of *koinonia* are the themes of baptism and eucharist. The recognition of common baptism leads in the direction of the recognition of those baptized in other communities of faith and of their holy men and women.[26] The bilaterals on baptism make clear that recognition of holy men and women is not just recognizing those a particular church has canonized or formally recognized. It is as much about identifying those who live out their baptismal vocation in holiness of life, living on the knife-edge of death and resurrection because their lives are conformed to the dying and rising of Christ, whose cross is signed on their foreheads.

The eucharist is expressed in many dialogues as the fullest expression of *koinonia* and as the Anglican-Roman Catholic report says: "eucharistic communion on earth is a participation in a larger communion which includes the martyrs and confessors and all who have fallen asleep in Christ throughout the ages."[27] BEM expresses it for all: "In the eucharist united to our Lord and in communion with all the saints and martyrs, we are renewed in the covenant sealed by his blood."[28] In the list of elements to be included in the eucharistic celebration BEM includes an explicit reference to the communion of saints.[29] The eucharist was the place where, in the ancient prayers of the East and West, the saints were commemorated and intercessions made for the departed, as they continue to be in many churches today. As the eucharist is the proper context for receiving each other and for receiving one another's saints, this means that the continuing search for eucharistic communion must remain central to the ecumenical endeavour.

A number of dialogues speak of the Virgin Mary as first in the communion of saints. The Agreed Statement of the Second International Anglican-Roman Catholic

25 Called Together To Be Peacemakers, in *GinA III*, p.231.
26 Eighth Report of the Joint Working Group 1999-2005, in *GinA III*, p.517 and p.573.
27 Church as Communion, in *GinA I*, p.340.
28 *Baptism, Eucharist and Ministry,* Eucharist, 19, Faith and Order Paper 111, WCC, Geneva, 1982.
29 E, 27.

Commission, Mary: Grace and Hope in Christ, is a splendid example of ecumenical method. It begins with an examination of the scriptural witness to Mary, then claims the early tradition of the undivided church, when communion in Christ included a strong sense of the living presence of the saints, the cloud of witnesses, in which the Lord's mother was believed to have a special place. The statement examines medieval extravagances and then traces how the traditions developed in understanding the place and role of Mary in the separated communions after the Reformation. Only then does it seek to re-state together the shared faith about Mary for today. Among the statement's conclusions are the suggestions that both communions re-receive Mary into their life and spirituality, as a model of holiness, obedience and faith for all Christians, a prophetic figure of the church, the Theotokos, that her festivals be observed, and that honour be accorded to her among the saints.[30] The Commission is bold in adding that: "Mary has a continuing ministry which serves the ministry of Christ, our unique mediator, that Mary and the saints pray for the whole church, and that the practice of asking Mary and the saints to pray for us is not communion dividing."[31] "Our hope is," the Commission says, "that, as we share in the Spirit by which Mary was prepared and sanctified for her unique vocation, we may together participate with her and all the saints in the unending praise of God."[32]

Mary in some conversations is first among the saints. The Anglican-Orthodox Statement encourages Anglicans and Orthodox to receive together Mary and the saints, not only saints from the past but from our own century. Today the church is rich, it points out, in examples of Christian holiness that reflect the selfless love of those who have begun to share in the death and resurrection of Christ and so reflect his likeness. They name Mother Maria Skobtsova, who defended Jews in occupied France... and suffered martyrdom in Ravensbruck in 1945; Archbishop Janani Luwum, who witnessed to the gospel in Uganda, at the cost of his life in 1977; and countless ordinary Orthodox believers who suffered in the camps and psychiatric hospitals in the former Soviet Union as well as many Anglican believers who witnessed to the need for racial equality in South Africa.

It would be unfair to end this whistle-stop tour through the documents without at least mentioning the subject of the invocation of saints. As noted, the Anglican-Roman Catholic agreed statement on Mary finds no difficulty in asking Mary to pray for us. Similarly, the Anglican-Orthodox agreed statement insists that in the church, that is the communion of saints on earth and in heaven, there is no frontier between the two worlds and each member intercedes for the whole. It is the continuing union of the saints in the risen Christ that forms the basis

30 Mary: Grace and Hope in Christ, *GinA III*, p.107.
31 *Ibid.*, p.108.
32 *Ibid.*, p.106.

of prayer for the dead and for the invocation of the saints.[33] The text goes on to say that while Anglicans and Orthodox reject the doctrine of purgatory they nevertheless pray for the departed because we still hold them in love and ask their prayers as similar expressions of mutual love.[34]

Conclusion

The results of the bilateral conversations are important for the Bose project on the commemoration of the martyrs, both in what we can learn from the way of dialogue itself and also in the theological and ecclesiological content of some of the reports themselves. Both support the idea of the production of a common martyrology in its broadest sense as an important shared discipline on the way to unity and, ultimately, as an expression of that life in unity which, we believe, is God's gift and our calling.

But while there is much in the bilateral texts to support the Bose project, there are some missed opportunities. It is a little disappointing to see how much more emphasis there might have been on the communion of saints in the documents, particularly in texts on baptism and eucharist. Often texts seem to lead the reader to expect to find something about the communion of saints only to find nothing when a reference would have been appropriate and would have given spiritual depth to the text. There are many missed opportunities where the dialogue partners could have agreed together something profound about the communion of saints on earth and in heaven and its implications for the church, its sacraments of baptism and eucharist, its life of prayer and its unity.

There are a number of suggestions for future conversations. First, partners in conversation might be encouraged to consider the points at which in their work some reference to the communion of saints and an explicit naming of holy men and women of both communions would enrich the agreements, making us aware that we already share together in the different realm of the gifts of the Spirit and thus help the churches to receive one another's saints and martyrs.

Secondly, in the spiritual life of the conversations, members of both communions might pledge themselves to naming in their daily life of shared prayer, the saints of the church, including the holy women and men of both traditions, perhaps including the heroes of the modern ecumenical movement – Abbe Paul Couturier, Bishop George Bell …

Thirdly, as the conversations turn from convergence in faith to convergence in life, partners might be asked to consider what practical implications a shared understanding of the communion of saints has for a closer lived fellowship in faith, life and witness.

---

33 Here we see the truth of what Pope John Paul II believed when he suggested that at the end of the second millennium, the church has once again become a church of the martyrs and that the witness to Christ is borne even to the shedding of blood. This witness is a common inheritance of Catholics, Orthodox, Anglicans and Protestants. Cf. Pope John Paul II, Apostolic Letter, Tertio Millennio Adveniente, p.37 and Pope John Paul II, Encyclical Letter, Ut Unum Sint, 1995, p.48.

34 Mary: Grace and Hope in Christ, *GinA III*, p.58.

Fourthly, it may be time to ask the multilateral conversation in Faith and Order, in line with the call from Bangalore, to produce a short agreed convergence statement on the communion of saints which would gather together some of the rich insights we have seen in the bilateral dialogues, deepen those reflections and, in that context, clarify terminology, and consider some of the neuralgic issues which have been identified in a few of the documents, namely, the invocation of the saints and canonization. A multilateral convergence document on the saints and martyrs would provide an over-arching framework in which to consider the bilaterals on this subject, just as BEM provided a framework for work on sacraments and ministry. It would serve as a theological foundation for the Bose project, in particular for the formulation of a common martyrology. There could be no better starting point for such work than the message of the Archbishop of Canterbury and the papers offered in the Bose Symposium.

TRADITIONAL INSIGHTS AND PRACTICES FOR WITNESSING

The Sanctity of Blood: Martyrdom as Ecclesiastical Witness According to Orthodox Tradition

Panaghiotis A. Yfantis

The manifestation of martyrdom, the spread of the phenomenon, and the veneration of martyrs

Just as the prophets and all of Israel were called upon to give a living and historical witness to Yhwh's uniqueness and superiority,[1] so the holy members of the church are called to bear witness to the incarnate and ultimate truth about Jesus Christ's theandric identity. And just as Christ did not come to abolish the Law but to fulfil it with the commandment of love even towards our enemies, so martyrdom fulfilled the witness of the prophets and of the liturgical witness of the Old Israel. The relationship between the Old Testament witness and Christian martyrdom is equivalent to the relationship between word and deed or, more revealingly, to the relationship between a foretaste and the realization of the Last Things.

The members of the church very soon ceased calling themselves "the holy ones" (i.e. saints). The term was replaced with the term employed to this day, Christianoi.[2] The term saint (*hagios*) and its derivatives continued to be used in ecclesiastical vocabulary, but with a more radically Christocentric semantic shift: it came to be attributed almost exclusively to those members of the church who followed and imitated Christ with such fidelity so as to share the same fate with him by suffering crucifixion.

This dynamic emergence of Christian holiness through martyrdom allowed the Christian community not only to forge its ecclesiastical self-identity, but also to survive and expand geographically and numerically within the confines of an increasingly hostile world. The blood of the martyrs became the seed for the procreation of Christians, according to Tertullian's apophthegmatic formulation: *Sanguinis martyrum, semen christianorum.*[3]

The appropriation and theological elaboration of the concept of the holiness of blood becomes manifest early in the literature of the apostolic period,[4] which is inspired by the raw realism of the martyrdoms, interpreting them in the new eschatological light of the Christian faith. It is this faith that gives meaning to life through the martyrs' lack of fear and through their victory over death. In his first letter, Clement of Rome refers to the *athlesis* "unto

1 Cf. e.g. Is. 43-44.
2 *Ibid.*, 11, 26.
3 Tertullian, *Apol.*, 50,13. *The Early Christian Fathers*, A Selection from the Writings of the Fathers from St Clement of Rome to St Athanasius, edited and translated by Henry Bettenson, OUP, USA, repr. 1969, p.166.
4 P.Vasiliadis, "Νεομάρτυρες" και η σημασιολογική εξέλιξη των όρων 'μάρτυς' και 'μαρτυρία'", Proceedings of Theological Conference on New Martyrs (17-19 November 1987), edited by Ch. Kontakis, Thessaloniki, 1988 (in Greek), p.445.

death" with which the first among the apostles[5] crowned their teaching, whereas Ignatius, in his letter addressed to the Christians of Ephesus, refers explicitly to the "fight with beasts" (*theriomachia*), namely the martyrdom, that would enable him to become Christ's disciple in Rome.[6] The *Martyrdom of Polycarp*, written in the middle of the 2nd century, has the dual meaning of *martyria*, either as confession of faith or martyrdom of blood.[7]

In light of later patristic tradition and theology, it would be a mistake to interpret this imitation, the act of following (*akolouthein*)[8] and, ultimately, the holiness of martyrdom, along the lines of moral criteria, as a kind of external mimetic replication of Christ's example (and in this case Polycarp's example), dictated by sentimental piety. On the contrary, they refer to an ontological state of a "real Christification (*christopoiesis*)",[9] similar to that described by apostle Paul.[10] In the figures of the martyrs, the ancient church and patristic tradition not only recognized the new examples of moral perfection, worthy of imitation, or the symbols of the church's final victory over its persecutors;[11] more than these, martyrdom was a confirmation of Christ's divinity and of the continuation of his presence in the world and in human history.[12] The martyrs' *parrhesia* in the face of death offered compelling proof that Christ was with them and suffered with them during their martyrdom. If, as Father Justin Popović has remarked, "the lives of the saints are nothing else but the life of Christ the Saviour re-enacted in every saint"[13] this phenomenon started then and, as we are about to see, still continues to this day, mostly through the act of martyrdom.

Christian martyrdom was a dynamic, Christocentric, answer to the anthropological model of the hero of pre-Christian antiquity. However, it was a heroism based neither on the hope for fame after death, nor on the virtuous love for an earthly country, but on the thirst for a meeting with the Bridegroom. In tune with eschatological expectations drastically nurtured in a hostile historical environment, the community of the faithful began to honour their martyrs as citizens of the earthly kingdom, because they stayed faithful unto death, which made them worthy of the "crown of life".[14] This eschatological fervour is condensed in the firm response given by the *milites Christi* to their interrogators. To all the questions about their nationality, their descent or their social status they replied: "I am a Christian."[15]

---

5 I Clement 5, 2. PG 1, 217-220.

6 PG 5, 645A. Cf. Io. Galanis "Η έννοια του μαρτυρίου στην αγία Γραφή", *Proceedings*, p.57.

7 *Martyrdom of Polycarp*, PG5, 1044A; 1040A. Vasiliadis, p.445.

8 Cf. Mark 1:17-20; Matt. 8:19-22; 10:37; 19:6-22; Luke 9:61; Eph. 5:1; 1 Pet. 3,13. Cf. 1 Cor. 4:16; 1 Thess. 1:6, 2:14.

9 P. Nellas, Ζώον θεούμενον. *Προοπτικές για μια ορθόδοξη κατανόηση του ανθρώπου*, Athens,[2]1981, p.41.

10 This same conviction permeates the writings of Symeon the New Theologian cf. *Catechesis*, 7,442-459; 6, 342-352; 27, 335-370. Passages in B. Krivocheine, *Μέσα στο φως του Χριστού, Άγιος Συμεών ο Νέος Θεολόγος 949-1002. Βίος Πνευματικότητα-Διδασκαλία*, translated by P. Skouteris, Thessaloniki 1983, pp.312-314.

11 An. I. Fitrakis "Μαρτύριον και Μοναχικός Βίος", *Θεολογία* ΙΘ (1941-1948), p.305.

12 Al. Schmemann, *Η Εκκλησία προσερχομένη. Εισαγωγή στη λειτουργική θεολογία*, translated by D.Tserpos, Athens, 1991, p.217.

13 J. Popovic, *Άνθρωπος και θεάνθρωπος*, translated by A. Gieftic, Athens, 1970, p.99. Cf. G.D. Metallionos, "Ο άγιος και ο μάρτυρας ως μιμητής του πάθους του Κυρίου", *Saint and Martyr in the Life of the Church, Proceedings of the XII Conference of Patristic Theology*, edited by S.G. Papadopoulos, Athens, 1994, pp.58-59.

14 Rev. 2, 10. Cf. G.P. Patronos, *Η θέωση του ανθρώπου υπό το φώς των εσχατολογικών αντιλήψεων της Ορθόδοξης θεολογίας*, Athens, [2]1995, p. 262.

15 See e.g. deacon Sanctus' response in Eusebius of Caesarea's, *Ecclesiastical History* V, 1, 41. Cf. Fitrakis, p.304.

From the outset, martyrdom was considered equal, if not superior, to baptism.[16] *The Apostolic Constitutions* regard martyrdom as more genuine than baptism, since the latter is a symbolic death of the old man whereas the former is a real co-crucifixion of the faithful with Christ.[17] The community of the faithful, right after the death of a martyr, honoured his body as a receptacle of the grace of the Holy Spirit and a tangible proof of Christian faith. The relics of St Polycarp, for example, were kept by the faithful as "more valuable than precious stones and finer than refined gold" [18] and St Ignatius's relics as "priceless treasure".[19]

The author of the *Martyrdom of Polycarp*, highlighting the inception of the holiness of blood, remarked that "the martyrs we love as disciples and imitators of the Lord, as they deserve, on account of their matchless devotion to their King and Teacher".[20] In the same text is found the first written testimony to the institution of a feast for "the birthday of his martyrdom in commemoration of those who have already fought in the contest and also for the training and preparation of those who will do so in the future".[21] This would later extend to all categories and models of sanctity – among others, the venerable blessed, the educated high-ranking priests and the pious potentates.

The holiness of blood did not constitute an individual accomplishment by a member of the church. Martyrdom as an expression of the ecclesiastical identity of the martyr as well as the ultimate expression of his love of God and neighbour, belonged to the repository of the collective memory of the community. For this same reason, the community honoured and continues to honour the memory of the martyrs in the festive joy of the eucharistic gathering. Every local church on the *dies natalis* of the martyr gathered around his or her tomb, heard about his or her feats and in the name of his proven love gave thanks to God by participating in the banquet of the kingdom of heaven. This particular habit illuminates fully the incident when in a group of Christian prisoners the martyr Lucian (+312) celebrated the eucharist on his chest.[22] Similar testimonies about the liturgical and theological presence of the martyrs in the early church is offered by early Eastern and Western Christian authors such as Cyprian of Carthage, who refers to a Divine Liturgy[23] to honour the martyrs, and also Tertullian, who attests that honouring the martyrs was an ancient tradition kept and affirmed by many churches and Christians.[24]

---

16 Origen, *Psalm* 117: Βιβλοθήκη Ἑλλήνων Πατέρων καί Ἐκκλησιαστικών Συγγραφέων (ΒΕΠΕΣ) 16, 98, 16-18.

17 *Apostolic Constitutions* 5, 6: PG 1, 836-7. The author of the same work exhorts to martyrdom even catechumens, assuring them that this is a more genuine baptism "Καν κατηχούμενος η, άλυπος απίτω έσται αυτώ γνησιώτερον βάπτισμα" (ό.π.). Cf. Galanis p.69.

18 *Martyrdom of Polycarp*: PG 5, 1044A.

19 *Martyrdom of Ignatius*: PG 5, 985D.

20 PG 5, 1041C.

21 PG 5, 1044A.

22 Cf. Philostorgius, Quote from Patriarch Photios, PG 65, 476C. Passage in N. Matsoukas, *Δογματική και Συμβολική Θεολογία Β. Έκθεση της ορθόδοξης πίστης σε αντιπαράθεση με τη δυτική Χριστιανοσύνη*, Thessaloniki, [2]1988, p.486.

23 *Epistle* 39, Corpus Scriptorum Ecclesiasticorum Latinorum (CSEL) 3, 2, ed. Hartel, p.538.

24 *De corona* IV, PL 2, 99.

Theological, liturgical and hagiographical consolidation

The cessation of the persecutions and the *pax christiana* that was inaugurated by the Constantinian turn, seemingly consigned martyrdom to the heroic past of the church. However, as the brief interlude of Julian's reign and the iconoclast controversy (715-843) demonstrate, the struggle for safeguarding Christian identity did not cease to energize the agonistic example of the first heroes of the faith. It is true that the predominant – but not the only – model of holiness as the sanctity of blood gradually gave way to that of monastic asceticism, which was to affect spiritually the Middle Ages in both East and West. This asceticism served as counterweight to the moral laxity that set in and beset the church after its institutionalization as it became the official religion of the empire. Nevertheless, the model of the blessedness of holiness derived theological legitimacy from the effort to sustain, under changed terms and ways, the continuation of the holiness of martyrdom. The symbolic martyrdom of conscience became equivalent to that of blood, and might even surpass it, due to its more protracted and inexorable nature. The visible enemy of the anti-Christian authorities of the past was replaced by multiple invisible enemies, in the form of temptations contrived and rendered perceptible by the devil, the infirmity and weakness of human nature, or simply the monk's imagination. In this connection the parallel in martyrologies and in monastic literature between the struggle of the martyrs and confessors with beasts (*theriomachia*) and the struggle of the monk against the lion of the passions that lurks ready to pounce and swallow them is very interesting.[25]

Although from the 4th century onwards the opportunities for martyrdom of blood clearly became more rare, the period until the end of the Middle Ages coincides with a time of systematic growth of the veneration of martyrs. This can be attributed to the freedom of the official church to organize, celebrate the liturgy and preach the gospel, but also to the creative elaborations of patristic thought. During the Middle Ages, the older perceptions and practices about the cult of the martyrs were consolidated and diffused, acquiring a more intellectual form.

In such a context, although the heroic paradigm of the martyrs' civic disobedience seemed outdated, their *parrhesia* and their friendship with God was exploited pastorally in order to strengthen the community of believers spiritually and psychologically against various dangers that threatened it: natural disasters, infidel intruders or heretics who wanted to falsify the true faith. The enthusiasm for the kingdom of heaven may have been sacrificed for a vision of a Christian *oikoumene* on earth but the unshakeable steadfastness of the martyrs in

25 John Climacus, *Κλίμαξ*, PG 88, 708. See the interesting comparison between the figure of the "Egyptian"' against whom Perpetua struggles in her vision (*Martyrdom of Perpetua*, 10) and the snake and dragon who are threatening the monks. For an analysis of the excerpts see Fitrakis p.311.

their faith could inspire and steel the personal faith of the Christian against the passions. A case in point in the East is St John Chrysostom, who added considerable theological depth to, and updated, the notion of the holiness of martyrdom. According to the great Father of the church, on top of the spiritual benefit that Christians derive from imitating the courage and the piety[26] of the martyr by actively participating in the liturgical commemorations in his or her honour,[27] the memory of the martyrdom enhances not only the "kinship" (*oikeioteta*)[28] between those who honour and those who are honoured, but also the reconciliation of the "heavenly things" with the "earthly".[29]

In this perspective, the preoccupation and struggle of every Christian city to acquire a relic or at least a piece of a famous and if possible, miracle-working, martyr is perfectly understandable. The cutting up, the donation and the transfer of a relic as well as the frequent discoveries of a new one offered many opportunities for the enrichment of the liturgical life of the Christians, combined as they were with the creation of a new local feast. During the same period the modes of honouring the martyrs were crystallized. These modes remain the same to this date in Eastern Orthodox Christianity and apply to all those who are included in its *Synaxaria*. The honour that accrues to the commemoration of the martyr involves the composition of *Life*, the composition of hymns, and the right and Christian duty to create an icon and venerate it, and also to build and dedicate a shrine to his or her honour.[30] Every Christian town in the eastern Mediterranean possessed some tomb of a martyr, the so-called *Martyrion,* that was turned into a grandiose church in honour of the martyr. The eastern and western custom of celebrating the eucharist "upon the blood of the martyrs", remembrance and replication of empirical or historical facts such as the crucifixion, highlights the indissoluble link between the holy communion and the memory of the martyrs. For this reason the holy altar of every church is consecrated by putting in its foundations a piece of a holy relic of either a Christian martyr or saint.[31]

---

26 To the Holy Martyr Ignatius the God-bearer, Archbishop of Antioch, Ἐπετηρίς εταιρείας Βυζαντινών σπουδών (ΕΠΕ) 96, p.121. Cf. *To the Martyrs, Oration 2*. ΕΠΕ 62, p.587.

27 To the Holy Martyr Lucianos, ΕΠΕ 96, p. 41. Cf. *Encomion to the Holy Maryr Romanos,* Oration 1, ΕΠΕ 96, p.169.

28 *Encomion to the Holy Martyrs Verniki and Prosdoki the Virgins and their Mother Domnina,* ΕΠΕ 96, p. 217.

29 *To the Martyrs,* Oration 2, ΕΠΕ 62, p.581. For various aspects of Chrysostom's thought on the function and influence of the martyrs on the church's life see Ch. Arambatzis and P.A. Yfantis, 'Η Εφαρμοσμένη Σωτηριολογία στα Πατερικά Εγκώμια. Η περίπτωση του Χρυσοστόμου', *Sfantul Ioan Gura de Aur. Ierah – Teolog – Filantrop (407-2007)*. Simpozion teologic intenational dedicat implinirii a 1600 de ani de la trecerea sa in vesnicie, Ed. Andreiana, Sibiu 2008, pp.131-140; P.A. Yfantis, "Ο θάνατος στα χρυσοστομικά εγκώμια. Στερεότυπα και εξαιρέσεις". Paper delivered at the 10th Inter-Christian Symposium organized jointly by the Department of Theology of Aristotle University of Thessaloniki and the Pontificial Antonianum University in Rome on the topic 'St John Chrysostom: A Bridge between East and West' held in Tenos 15-18.9.2007 (in press).

30 Cf. D.G. Tsamis, *Αγιολογία της Ορθόδοξης Εκκλησίας*, Thessaloniki, ^{2}2004, pp.54-55; P.B. Paschos, *Άγιοι, οι φίλοι του Θεού. Εισαγωγή στην Αγιολογία της Ορθοδόξου Εκκλησίας*, Athens, ^{2}1997, pp.54-64.

31 G.B. Antourakis, "Αρχαία μαρτύρια και χριστιανικοί ναοί. Η επίδραση της τιμής των Μαρτύρων στη λατρευτική ζωή της Εκκλησίας", in *Saint and Martyr in the Life of the Church, Proceedings of the XII Conference of Patristic Theology,* p.288. This custom is still kept in the East even in those churches in which liturgy takes place before their consecration (εγκαίνια) as well as wherever liturgy takes place outside of a church. In the latter case the presence of the martyrs and the saints is ensured by the use of *antimension* (αντί+mensa=τράπεζα: instead of the table, i.e. altar), a liturgical piece of cloth in which are sewn and sealed relics upon which mass can be celebrated.

Often, though, the extent of the honour of an ancient martyr transcended the boundaries of a geographical area, shaping a liturgical tradition that unites East and West. One characteristic example is that of the ancient martyr George, even as his appeal is intertwined with many and diverse and/or dubious accretions of the popular imagination.

By way of digression it is worth noting that although the theology of sanctity in the West does not differ from that of the East, not all of the saints are common to both traditions, even before the division of the church. As is to be expected, this is due primarily to the increasing linguistic gap, and secondarily to cultural or ecclesiastical causes.[32] Among the Western saints recognized by Eastern Christianity in the period before the Schism it is worth mentioning Pope Agapetus I (+536), who opposed significantly to the condemnation of the non-Chalcedonians by deposing the heretical patriarch Menas (10.3.536), Pope Martin (+655), who supported saint Maximus the Confessor during the monothelite controversy, and for this was arrested and tortured and died in Cherson (modern Sebastopol in the Crimea, Ukraine). His holiness was recognized first in the East and his relic was kept in the church of Panagia of Blachernai in Constantinople before it was transferred in Rome. Also worthy of mention are Pope Agathon (+681), who contributed to the consolidation of orthodoxy in the same period by participating in the preparation of the sixth Ecumenical Council (681), and Pope Gregory the Great (+604), who is otherwise known in the eastern monastic environment *ho Dialogos* due to his writing. Furthermore, among the saints of Western origin who are honoured in the East are Pope Theodore (+649), Gregory, bishop of Agrigento (end of 6th-beginning of 7th century), and bishop Leo of Catania (+780). They were recognized as saints in the Roman church in the 16th century. Also, the church of Constantinople honours the Spanish martyr Ermenegildo who, according to tradition, was executed in 585 by his Arian father because of his loyalty to the Catholic faith. These recognitions of saints took place before the Schism. Hitherto the Eastern Orthodox Church does not share the saints who were recognized by the Roman Catholic Church after the Schism.[33] Let us now return to the presence of martyrdom in the contemporary history of Eastern Orthodoxy.

---

32 Cf. Th.E. Detorakis, "Βυζάντιο και Ευρώπη: αγιολογικές σχέσεις (527-1453)", *Βυζάντιο και Ευρώπη. Α΄ Διεθνής Βυζαντινολογική Συνάντηση, Δελφοί, 20-24 Ιουλίου 1985*, Athens, 1987, pp.86-91.

33 The only case of a Western saint whose reputation transcended confessional and geographical boundaries is that of St Francis of Assisi (+1224). Despite the fact that he has not been formally recognized as a saint by the Orthodox Church, philological, archaeological and ecclesiastical sources that date from the time that Crete was under Venetian rule demonstrate the Orthodox Cretans' sympathy and reverence for St Francis. Cf. Detorakis, pp.91-92; K. E. Lassithiotakis, "Ο άγιος Φραγκίσκος και η Κρήτη", in *Πεπραγμένα Δ΄ Κρητολογικού Συνεδρίου Β΄*, Athens, 1981, pp.146-156; P. Ar. Yfantis, 'La ricezione del messaggio francescano in Grecia', in *Nello spirito di Assisi. Giornata di preghiera e di riflessione insieme ai cristiani ortodossi (Sacro Convento: Salone Papale – Sabato 25 ottobre 2008)*, Assisi (in press).

The 20th Century: Towards an ecumenical martyrdom?

Orthodox Christianity suffered persecution during the 20th century, a century characterized by the emergence of totalitarian ideologies that gave rise to horrific political regimes which threw the whole world into turmoil and horror. Inevitably, once more, the ecclesiastical witness was destined to be tinted by the deep red colour of the blood of lay people, monks, priests and hierarchs who were all disciples of Christ, the *protomartyr*, or first among all the martyrs. Many of the Orthodox martyrs of the 20th century remain anonymous because they were martyred under unknown circumstances, as was the case with the thousands of monks who were put to death by the Soviet government in the Monastery of Oranki in 1918.

However, the recent phenomena of Christian martyrdom are so widespread as to alter the spiritual map of the 20th century into a kind of geography of blood which seems to transcend not only particular national, racial and cultural boundaries, but even confessional ones. Notwithstanding the obvious differences, for example, between the case of the Russian Orthodox nun Maria Skobtsova (+31.3.1945)[34] and that of the Polish Roman Catholic priest Maximilian Kolbe (+14.8.1941)[35], or the case of the American Baptist pastor Martin Luther King (+4.4.1968)[36] from that of the Anglican archbishop Janani Luwum (+16.2.1977) from Uganda,[37] there are more substantial common elements that must be identified: the courageous witness of faith to the God of the Bible, the implicit potential and potent prophetic denunciation of various worldly and inhumane messianisms, the unflinching and/or festive welcoming of death, and finally the living communication with the only source of true life.[38] The overlap between the different theological inspirations of modern martyrs is not at all accidental. The German Protestant pastor Dietrich Bonhoeffer (+9.4.1945),[39] before he was hanged by his Nazi compatriots in Flossenburg at the age of 39, assured us that Christ did not call people to espouse a new religion but he called them to life.[40]

The Orthodox priest Alexander Men (+9.9.1990),[41] victim of anti-Christian forces of his time – forces that are not at all far from our own times – observed that "Christianity is not an

34 On the life and thought of the fool-for-Christ nun and martyr Maria Skobtsova see Sergei Hackel, *Μαρία Σκόμπστοβα. Μία "δια Χριστόν σαλή" στους μοντέρνους καιρούς (1891-1945)*, translated by Niki Tsironi, Athens, 1998· Mother Maria Skobtsova, *Essential Writings*, New York, 2003.

35 For a brief outline of Father Kolbe's life see the relevant entry in A. Sicari, *Ritratti di Santi* Milan, 2007, accessible also on http://www.paginecattoliche.it/MassimilianoKolbe.htm

36 On this inspired pastor see the rich collection of materials in http://worldcat.org/identities/lccn-n79-84324

37 Janani Luwum, the Anglican church leader of Uganda, Rwanda, Burundi and Zaire, was murdered by dictator Idi Amin on February 16, 1977. For a brief biography see http://www.jananiluwumtrust.com/

38 An Orthodox thinker notes "whoever suffers for Christ's glory, his suffering becomes a living relationship with the triune God, the source of life", in N. Matsoukas, p.482.

39 Written sources about this inspired Christian thinker abound. See e.g. http://www.crossbot.de/wwwsearch/cobrand/?q=Bonhoeffer&type=www&site=www.ekd.de&PID=4; also the official website of the Evangelical Church of Germany (http://www.ekd.de/) but also the website of the Bonhoeffer International Society that was founded for the commemoration of Bonhoeffer and for the diffusion of his views: http://www.arts.uwaterloo.ca/~diebon06/index.html

40 D. Bonhoeffer, *Letters and Papers from Prison*, Eberhard Bethge (ed.), Touchstone; New York, 1997 (enlarged ed.), p.362.

41 On the figure and the work of the recent martyr of the Russian Orthodox Church Father Alexander Men see the website of the foundation bearing his name (Alexander Men' Foundation) in Moscow: http://www.alexandrmen.ru/fam/pan.html

'ideology', an abstract teaching or defined system of rituals. The Gospel entered our world as a dynamic message that embraces all aspects of life... Christianity is not simply a religion that has just existed for the last 20 centuries but a Way that focuses on the future."[42]

Ultimately, if the sanctity of blood is the genuine testimony of the church, this is not simply due to the fact that the martyrs reinforced the Christians' heroic super-ego and enriched their liturgical memory of the community of the faithful. It is mostly due to the fact that the martyrs evinced two basic characteristics of the life in Christ: first, the depth of a love that verges upon self-sacrifice on the cross both for the sake of the brethren, but also for that of the executioners; second, the radical nature of a freedom that cannot cease to hope in the fervent anticipation and hastening of the resurrection. In this perspective, the memory of the martyrs is not only an affirmation of the common heritage of a chronologically distant indivisible church or a perpetuation of a recent confessional past, but it is at the same time also an ecumenical challenge to self-awareness for the Christianity of both today and tomorrow.

---

42 A. Men', *Kul'tura i dukhovnoe vozrozhdenie*, Moscow, 1992, p.26.

Spiritual Life, Love, Martyrdom in Roman Catholic Tradition

Marco Gnavi

On the topic of the shedding of blood in the 20th and 21st centuries, a preliminary remark is necessary: contemporary martyrs have lived among us. They have been our companions. Among them is Fr Ragheed Ghanni, a thirty year-old Chaldean, who was killed in Mosul. He had studied in Rome and, together with other members of the Community of Sant'Egidio, he had often provided assistance to the Arab-speaking immigrants in Rome; Br Christian de Chergé, who took part in one of the international prayers for peace that stemmed from the Assisi meeting in 1986; Fr Andrea Santoro, Fr Alexander Men... These people, repositories of the gospel, are signs of contradiction to the death. They embody the order of the Easter liturgy in the Latin church when it says before the reading of the gospel: "Death and life have contended in that stupendous combat."[1] Evil perceived their secret and indeed trembled with fear: evangelical justice, love of God and of one's neighbour, have brought upon them the human *necessitas* of death. They defended life and all that it stands for, and death was afraid of them to the point of killing them. But these were men and women who perceived, felt and believed in divine empathy: the resurrection, which does not cancel the absurdity of a violent and sudden death, is the perspective through which their entire life should be seen. Their existence therefore needs to be examined through the connection between spiritual life and charity which runs through the history of the churches of East and West. Their witness is undivided from that of John Chrysostom and Gregory the Great, Sergey of Radonez and Benedict of Nursia, Seraphim of Sarov and Francis of Assisi, Elizaveta Feodorovna and John XXIII. Charity, as Maximus the Confessor wrote, love of God and of human beings is "one and the same and universal: owed to God and attaching human beings one to another."[2] And though it is not easy to speak of charity, for – as John Climacus reminds us – "To speak of charity is to speak of God",[3] these brothers and sisters of ours have made love of God shine in history.

The reflection of the Catholic Church on the witnesses of faith of the 20th century has gained depth and clarity in the Magisterium of Pope John Paul II, whose insight offers fresh elements in this regard. Their unarmed humanity is marked by ordinary choices of charity in contexts of extraordinary danger. In their weakness they represent a living synthesis of the relationship between sanctity and charity in our times. For contemporary men and women they are the most authoritative interpreters of the language of the gospel beatitudes. Theirs is a language "other" than the present culture, which is more fearful of suffering than

1 Víctimæ paschāli laudes, Sequentia for Eastern Sunday, Missale Romanum
2 Andrew Louth, *Maximus the Confessor, Letter 2: On Love*, Routledge, London & New York, 1996, p.90.
3 The quotation is from T. Špidlik, *Manuale fondamentale di spiritualità,* Casale Monferrato, 1993, p.81.

the past, often lacking a centre, and therefore more exposed to "neurosis". Their language is different, and therefore attractive, and it has allowed them to take part, to a certain extent, in God's *macrothymia.*[4] It was uttered during the tempests of our contemporary history: the communist and nazi totalitarianisms, the two world wars, the Shoah, the Armenian genocide, the tragedies associated with decolonization in the 60s, the genocidal drifts in the great lakes region in the 90s, ethnic and regional conflicts, Mexico and Spain in the 20s and 30s, the Christian attempts to penetrate in the huge continent of Asia (suffice it to mention China), decolonization… And new storms are brewing in Iraq, in India… The humble and beautiful Christian identity, when it is lived trustfully, always leads to the front line of the clash with evil, where evil is opposed by the good of faith, hope and love.

What should we do with their legacy? All of us who have not resisted to the point of shedding our blood, are responsible for it. This legacy needs to be revealed and welcomed humbly, listening to their voices, understanding their secret, at times perceiving also their fear, without forcing our views upon them. They are the source of a strong and eloquent Christian humanism, spread through all denominations. The story of the Poor Sisters of Bergamo, who died in 1995 due to the contagion of the Ebola virus in Congo, is a paradigm of many others. Though they were aware of the risk they were running, they remained at the side of their patients in the hospital of Kikwit, showing a love more enduring than death. How did such fortitude mature? Is it within everyone's grasp? What value does it bear for us today?

The proximity of the contemporary witnesses of faith to our lives

In the first Christian generations, (Catholic) hagiography has stressed the heroic offer of one's life in front of the tyrant. The common characteristics of martyrdom in the 20th century – because these martyrs are closer to our age and to the conditions of our life – give these witnesses a certain proximity to our lives. Their choices of love do not differ from the ones we too can make. The roots of their strength are within the reach of our daily experience. They lie in familiarity with the Scripture and in prayer as contemplation and seeing the face of God; they dwell in a vision of the world where, like the women in the gospel, one does not flee from proximity to the cross, out of love for the Lord Jesus. Vatican II (*Lumen Gentium*, n.42) has emphasized the strong ties between sanctity, martyrdom and charity. Love for God and one's neighbour mark the "true discipleship of Christ" and martyrdom is envisioned as an "exceptional gift and as the fullest proof of love". Christians are a sign of hope for the world, an orientation to the dispersed, even in the darkest of night, an indication of hope in a righteous life, even when they die a violent death, because they – and we with them – are

4 The Greek word *macrothymia* (Latin *patientia)* suggests having a large capacity for absorbing the big and little injustices of life without letting them overwhelm you with anger. And it is also God's capacity (Latin *magnanimitas)* to see beyond the person that acts in a wrong way and to discern the hearts and the whole situation. In this sense it is linked with mercy.

called to live the same luminous life, imbued with the gospel. In this sense *martyria* is for everyone.

Pavel Evdokimov in his work on holiness in the tradition of the Orthodox Church writes:

> The salt of the earth and the light of the world, the saints appear as the obvious and hidden leaders of humanity, those who will assume responsibility for history and accomplish it. At the beginning, the "wounded friends of the Bridegroom Christ", the martyrs, are "the sheaves of wheat harvested by the rulers of this age, and gathered by the Lord as the harvest into his barns". The saints take the torch from the martyrs and continue to illumine the world. But the Gospel's call is to every person.[5]

Unity in witness

Pope John Paul II affirmed that the ecumenism of the saints and the martyrs is "perhaps the most convincing" (*Tertio millennio adveniente*, n.37). During the Way of the Cross in 1994 he meaningfully said: "We are united in these martyrs, in Rome, at the 'mountain of the crosses', on the Solovki Islands and in many other extermination camps. We are united against the background of the martyrs: we must be united".

These profound words are shared by other spiritual men. Metropolitan Evlogy, a relevant figure in Russian Orthodoxy in the first half of the 20th century, said in this same regard: "The saints are the citizens of the one and universal Church, they have broken down the dividing wall raised by Christians unfaithful to the new commandment". It was his belief that "persons like St. Francis of Assisi and St. Seraphim of Sarov have already fulfilled the unity of the Church in their lives".[6]

Theirs is not only a vision of history, but an appeal addressed to the life of Christian communities. In this light, the third Sunday of Easter of the year of the great Jubilee assembled together Orthodox representatives, Latin and Oriental Catholics, Anglicans, Lutherans and Protestants in Rome, near the Coliseum, to celebrate together an extraordinary memory, which overcoming denominational divisions, showed the strength of *martyria* in a terrible and fascinating century. The martyr, or the crowd of martyrs, which is often anonymous as occurs in our contemporary age, draws back to the heart of the paschal mystery. In their humbleness – for they are less apt to lend themselves to hagiography and are more similar to us in their limits, fears and contradictions – they reveal an unexpected power and unanticipated beauty, even when their names are unknown to all, except to God alone. In order to read the book

5 Paul Evdokimov, *In the World of the Church, A Paul Evdokimov Reader*, SVS Press, Crestwood, 2001, p.100.

6 The citations from Evlogy were quoted by Enzo Bianchi in the opening speech for the 8th International Ecumenical Congress of Orthodox Spirituality: *Forme della santità russa,* edited by A. Mainardi, Magnano (BI) 2002, p.30.

of the martyrs of the past century in the different languages of the Christian churches and traditions, we therefore need to start afresh from the universal value of the word martyrdom, in its Greek meaning of "witness", and above all from the common witness of faith that is already given in a number of difficult situations. In this reading, the imitation of Christ, rather than persecution, is the heart of the witness of faith.

In this sense Pope John Paul II wished for the Basilica of St. Bartholomew on the Isola Tiberina in Rome, entrusted to the Community of Sant'Egidio, to become the "memorial place of the witnesses of faith of the 20th century". Six chapels in the church are remindful of the most relevant contexts of persecution and welcome also the memories of the contemporary martyrs and witnesses of all denominations. Pope Benedict XVI confirmed the intuition and desire of his predecessor, paying a visit to the church on 7 April 2008 for a solemn prayer and memorial pilgrimage. On this occasion he emphasized:

> In their defeat, in the humiliation of people who suffer for the Gospel, there is a power the world knows not: "When I am weak, then I am strong" – says the Apostle Paul (2 Cor. 12:10). It is the power of love, defenseless and victorious even in seeming defeat. This power challenges and defeats death. Even the 21st century opened under the sign of martyrdom. When Christians are really the leaven, the light and salt of the earth, like Jesus, they also become the object of persecution, like Him, they are a "sign of contradiction"... [7]

He stopped and meditated in front of the icon of the witnesses of faith that shines over the main altar. In its centre is a cathedral surrounded by barbed wire, like a concentration camp. And in the heart of the cathedral the gospel is open at the page of the priestly prayer of Jesus in the gospel according to John: *"ut unum sint"*. Thanks to the martyrs darkness does not prevail forever...

In the last few years a number of solemn liturgies of the Word have been held here. On this occasion, the Romanian Orthodox Patriarch Theoctist offered a scapular that belonged to *staretz* Sophian Bogiu, who spent 13 years in the prisons of Ceaucescu; the solemn memory of Reformed pastor Paul Schneider was celebrated and an autographic letter was offered by his family, that came accompanied by the Reformed Bishop of Rhineland; Orthodox crosses from Albania dating back to the time of Enver Hoxha were offered... And here have prayed the Catholicos of All Armenians, Karekin II and the Catholicos of Cilicia, Aram; in this Basilica the Archbishop of Canterbury, Rowan Williams, delivered the memories that belonged to the Melanesian Brothers – Anglicans who died in 2003 for reconciliation in the Solomon Islands...

7 Homily of his Holiness Pope Benedict XVI, 7 April 2008, http://www.vatican.va/holy_father/benedict_xvi/homilies/2008/documents/hf_ben-xvi_hom_20080407_san-bartolomeo_en.html

Different sensitivities of the same love

The classical theology of martyrdom in the development of Catholic doctrine employs different terms, with its foundations stated by Pope Benedict XVI (who also defined the criteria for canonization and beatification), Thomas Aquinas, and the apologetics following Vatican I. Martyrdom was explained as an act of virtue, of fortitude commanded by charity and accompanied by patience, and as such an act of the highest perfection, since it requires to endure death because of faith or other virtues bestowed by it. But the liturgical recognition of martyrdom does not exhaust its meaning: martyrdom *coram Deo* indeed includes martyrdom *coram ecclesia*, but also transcends it.[8] Even more: martyrdom in our age, and the novel conditions it occurs in, highlights new themes for theological reflection, broadening the sense of martyrdom "*in odium fidei*" in the Catholic Church – though it does retain its original meaning – and comprehending charity and love that are rooted in Christ as crucial elements for its recognition. The paradigm in this sense was the canonization of Maximilian Kolbe, while over the years many other signs in this direction, consistent with Vatican II, have offered an important key to identify the "supreme witness of love" in the shedding of blood and connect it to the holiness that all the baptized are called to: *Lumen Gentium*, particularly paragraphs 42 and 50, offers a clear example in this respect.

A greater understanding of the richness of each "denominational" perspective of the witness borne to the point of shedding one's blood, would generate a mutual impetus to delve deeper into each tradition. In this sense, Unitas Redintegratio states: "To recognize the riches of Christ and virtuous works in the lives of others who are bearing witness to Christ, sometimes even to the shedding of their blood. For God is always wonderful in His works and worthy of all praise" (n.4).

Pope John Paul II strived to communicate this sense of wonder to Christian awareness, this astonishment, first of all by urging Christians to recover their historical memory in its broader sense, not only examining history to offer models for the emulation and spirituality of the churches, but rather to disclose the treasure of Christian life in the 20th century. The research of Andrea Riccardi on the documentary material sent to the New Martyrs Commission, synthesized in the volume *Il secolo del martirio*,[9] is in this line. Its purpose is to identify the "weak strength" that was the *humus* where the exemplary witness of a few was generated, and which defined the belonging of many more to the people of God. It motivated the reconstruction of a geography of suffering and at the same time of the testimony. Many Christian sacred

8 "In a theological perspective, the basic element of martyrdom is the soul, with its inner frame fully known by God; in a juridical perspective, on the contrary, the basic element is what occurs under the control of the senses: actions, words, attitudes that constitute a sure fundament, on which the Church may found its legitimate assumption of entire heroic charity, which in turn ascertains that every martyr coram Ecclesia is also martyr coram Deo". Therefore "One may be a true martyr in the eyes of God for his excellent inner frame, and not be so in the eyes of the Church, due to the lack, sometimes, of sufficient outer signs", Ernesto Piacentini, *Il martirio nelle cause dei santi,* Vatican Press, 1979, p.72.

9 Andrea Riccardi, *Il secolo del martirio*, Arnoldo Mondadori Editore, Milan, 2000.

places were used as detention camps, as if to conquer through violence places of protection and meeting of human beings with God. One of the best known of these sanctuaries is that "kingdom of the sorrowful" – as Olga Jafa, a deportee, defined it – the lager on the Solovki Islands off the shores of the Baltic Sea, in the former Soviet Union. The tragic epilogue of the Russian Orthodox Spaso-Preobrazhenskiy Monastery (of the Transfiguration of Our Saviour) emblematically embodies the agonic and kenotic path of thousands of Christians. These "cathedrals of sorrow" were not only places of tyranny. In the agony and icy wind of winter, fraternity could crack the meaninglessness of forced labour:

> Joining efforts and working together, a Catholic bishop, still in his youth, and an old, emaciated and gaunt elderly man with a white beard, an Orthodox bishop, old in years but strong in the spirit, vigorously pushed the load… Those who among us will have the fate to return to the world will have to bear witness to what we see here and now. And what we see is faith reborn, pure and authentic as that of the first Christians, the union of the churches in the persons of the Catholic and Orthodox bishops who unanimously take part in the endeavour, union in love and in humbleness.[10]

There was ecumenism in the Gulag, an experience of suffering that in Eastern Europe led Christians of different denominations to proclaim the salvation of Christ in places that seemed to be conquered forever by the power of evil. Inside the labour camps or in the prisons one can catch a glimpse of the fabric of Christian fraternity in times of trial, which runs deeper than divisions. The story of the Romanian intellectual Nicu Steinhardt is significant in this respect. Of Jewish origin, he converted to Orthodox Christianity and was baptized in the harsh prisons of Ceaucescu by an Orthodox priest. He wanted two other prisoners to attend the ceremony: two Greek-Catholic priests. Sorrow and persecution were a school of unity among Christians. Fr Roman Braga remembers: "… a Baptist came with a little Bible hidden in the shoulders of his coat… Since at the time we could move from one cell to another, we divided that Bible into the books it contained and every one received a part with the duty to quickly learn it by heart, and then swap it".[11]

By its nature and expression, the nazi regime embodied the totalitarian manifestation of an anti-Christian system. The dehumanizing conditions of imprisonment in the Nazi concentration camps offer many examples of proximity in faith and of steadfast opposition to the perverse aspiration to brutify man and break his ties to God.[12] Relevant in this respect are the memoirs of Fr Roberto Angeli and Fr Jean Kammerer. In his book *La Baraque des prêtres à Dachau*, Fr Jean speaks of an "ecumenical Europe" condensed in barrack 26 of the camp. And Fr Angeli remembers:

10 J.Brodskij, *Solovki,* p.152.
11 R.Braga, *Ogni monaco ha il suo segreto con Dio*, Lipa, Roma 1999, p.76
12 Cf. Riccardi, pp.63-132.

> ...amidst Catholic priests from all countries, with Protestant pastors and Orthodox popes, all priests in the purest sense – powerless and devoid of any frills and privileges – starving and freezing to death, tortured by lice and fear, with no other dignity than the invisible dignity of priesthood, we learnt to discover the essence of life and of faith.[13]

In his memoirs (written in 1964), he records how, in the camp, "the yearning for union was actually keen and profound among the clergy – whether Catholic, Orthodox or Protestant – thrown by Nazi hatred in a single crucible of unprecedented suffering" – and he continues – "Perhaps one of the currents that feeds the yearning for union that now characterizes the Christian churches, and which is one of the major themes of Vatican II Council, lies in the coexistence and suffering of the priests in the frightening Nazi lagers".[14]

The presence of German Lutheran pastors alongside the Catholics was a reason to "listen to each other" and meditate on the power of faith against Hitlerian paganism. Also Protestant pastor Niemöller spoke "with heartfelt words, supporting the need for the reunification of the church of Christ, torn apart centuries before by political and selfish reasons". Fr Giuseppe Girotti, a Dominican, died in Dachau. During the octavary of prayer for Christian Unity, on 21 January 1945, Fr Girotti held a meditation inside the camp which is in line with this awareness: "And we are all aware that the unity of all the churches and communities is highly necessary in our days... The Church was, is, and always will be, the only shelter for a sense of humanity, love and mercy; shelter of truth, of the principles of reason, of civilization and of culture... Now this extraordinary mission of the Church, in this grave moment of history, dear brothers, cannot be carried out to perfection, if the faithful of Christ, united in the soul of the Church... remain divided in the visible body due to schisms and divisions".[15]

Many other stories could be mentioned, like the emblematic account of four Christians of Lübeck executed on 10 November 1943, after having been arrested in the spring by the Gestapo: Evangelical pastor Karl Friederich Stellbrink, Johannes Prassek, a Catholic active in the parish of the Sacred Heart of Jesus, and the leader of the youth groups of the same parish, vicar Hermann Lange. One week later the assistant of the parish, Eduard Miller, was captured. All four were executed by guillotine. While they were walking to the scaffold they recited together: "Eternal Faithfulness to Christ Our King". In this context we should mention also the White Rose movement, which in 1942-1943 wished for the rebirth of a new Germany stemming from a new Christian spirit. Hans and Sophie Scholl, both Pietists, Kurt Huber, a Catholic teacher at the University of Munich, Willi Grad, medical student, and the married student Christian Probst, from Murnau in upper Bavaria. Christian Probst requested to be baptized by a Catholic priest in

---

13 Testimony of Fr Roberto Angeli in *Aspetti religiosi della Resistenza*, Turin, 1972, p.107.
14 Roberto Angeli, *Vangelo nei lager*, Florence, 1964, pp.144-145.
15 Meditation translated into Italian from Latin and quoted in V. Morello, *Morire per i "fratelli maggiori". Una vita nella carità fino al martirio. Padre Giuseppe Girotti o.p. (Alba 1905, Dachau 1945)*, Bologna, 1995, p.154.

the death cell. Together with them was also Alexander Schmorell, a Russian Orthodox. In 1943 they were all beheaded in the prison of Stadelheim in Munich.

These are only some examples among many others of the resolute will to preserve Christianity and humanity in the tempest of Nazi totalitarianism and the "positive Christianity" postulated by Rosenberg, and they accompany the example of all those people, Catholics and Lutherans, who shared and protected the fate of the Jews; their number included also some Orthodox, such as the Russian nun Mat' Marija (Elizaveta Jur'evna Skobtsova) in Paris, who was deported to Ravensbrück, and died at Jugendlager, for having provided shelter to some Parisian Jews.

They are often found one beside the other, bound in a communion of solidarity that stretches beyond denominational divisions. Their stories are intertwined with each other and illuminate each other. The tenaciousness of one supported the other: such is the case of the testimony of a Catholic religious imprisoned in Buchenwald about Reformed pastor Paul Schneider. Pastor Schneider had been deported in 1937 for his opposition to Nazism, which had grown through his faithfulness to two small villages in the Rhineland that were under his pastoral responsibility. Married, with six children, he did not obey the expulsion decree he had been issued with after being arrested three times (upon the request of Hitler himself) and was therefore imprisoned in total isolation. Leonhard Steinwender from Austria expressed his gratitude for Schneider's shouted preaching.

> In front of the single storey building of the bunker the huge roll call square was spread... On days of festivity, in the silence of the roll call, all of a sudden, from the sullen grille of the bunker, echoed the booming voice of pastor Schneider. He held his preaching like a prophet, or better, he tried to start it. On Easter Sunday, for instance, suddenly we heard his powerful words: "Christ says, I am the resurrection and the life!" The long lines of the prisoners stood at attention, profoundly perturbed by the courage and energy of that unwavering will... He was only ever able to say a few sentences. Then we heard the sticks of the guards strike him."[16]

The words of the last homily proclaimed in freedom, before being deported to Dachau, fifty days before Easter, disclose the source of his strength and his open eyes on the Christian *oikumene*:

> Dear community, again today we cross a threshold, the door that leads us to the holy time of the Passion... If we look at Russia we can learn many things. There any kind of official organization of the church is dismembered and dissolved, the pastors have disappeared, the sacred buildings are nearly dismantled. However the Church

16 Margarete Dietrich Schneider, *Il predicatore di Buchenwald. Il martirio del pastore Paul Schneider* (1897-1939), Italian edition edited by T.Franzosi, Claudiana, Turin, 1996, p.199.

> of Jesus Christ there is more living than ever… in the people who here and there gather in the houses, in the priests reduced to laypeople who continue to proclaim the Word, ready to accept the punishments that are waiting for them. And you! Do not be deceived, for you cannot take part in the victory and glory of Jesus if you do not take upon yourself the holy cross, out of love for him, walking with him on the path of faith… this faith is a hidden strength, silent and quiet; but nevertheless not idle and inactive, rather it is activated by intense and passionate prayer.[17]

Prayer and strength, meekness and steadfast faithfulness together, courage and human frailty, are not antinomic terms: they coexist and are intertwined with the stories of the "new martyrs".

Even in more recent circumstances, where Christians live as a religious minority or where many people have died believing in dialogue, like Br Christian de Chergé, prior of the Trappist Monastery of Atlas in Algeria, or Fr Andrea Santoro, killed in Turkey,[18] tribulation has drawn Christians one towards the other. On 11 December 2003, 18 Methodists were killed while praying in the Catholic Church of St Dominic in Bahawalpur, Pakistan. The place of worship served both communities on alternate days.

We fully understand the meaning of the words of Pope John Paul II in Ut Unum Sint, when he affirms that the unity of the saints and of the martyrs is, in a theocentric perspective, already accomplished. This communion "is already perfect in what we all consider the highest point of the life of grace, *martyria* unto death, the truest communion possible with Christ who shed his Blood, and by that sacrifice brings near those who once were far off" (n.84). It is a unique opportunity for the churches and Christian denominations to converge together, mindful of their children who died and lived for the gospel in the most difficult moments of history in the century. With Franz Jägerstätter, an Austrian farmer beheaded in Tagel prison for not wanting to serve the German army of the Third Reich, together we can make the testimony of Christians shine: "Suffering in unity with the mystical body of Christ, one can speak of the 'sorrow of Christ' or 'torment of Christ'. It works to the advantage of the church, which is the mystical body of Christ and which will end only when the church, divided and suffering, will turn into the triumphant church".[19] It is the humble triumph of the gospel that withstands evil with good: by examining the history of the contemporary witnesses of faith, we shall plunge into an ecumenical memory of the martyrs vaster than the criteria and sensitivities of each church, but nonetheless eloquent and significant.

---

17 *Ibid.*, p.112.
18 Augusto D'Angelo, *Don Andrea Santoro, un prete tra Roma e l'Oriente*, Edizioni San Paolo, Cinisello Balsamo (MI), 2006.
19 Cesare G. Zucconi, *Cristo o Hitler, vita del beato Franz Jägerstätter*, Edizioni San Paolo, Cinisello Balsamo (MI), 2008, p.190.

Norwegian Lutheran Tradition for Commemoration

Øystein Bjørdal

I represent the Church of Norway, a Lutheran state church where about 84 percent of the people are baptized members. The theme of the Bose Symposium – A Cloud of Witnesses, Opportunities for Ecumenical Commemoration – is inspiring and its ecumenical implications are important.

There is no calendar of saints in the Norwegian Lutheran tradition. In American Lutheranism there is something like a calendar of saints. Bishop Eivind Berggrav of Norway – a Lutheran church leader and a resistance-personality during World War II – is mentioned in this context. In Swedish Lutheran tradition there is a similar calendar of saints event though the church does not have a formal recognition or canonization of saints.

Who are the saints…? A little boy in a school class visiting Nidaros Cathedral, raises his hand, answering: "A person through whom the light shines…" He had seen the sun shining through the stained glass window in the cathedral.

Dagfinn Hauge, a Lutheran bishop in our church, was called to Akershus fortress to give the sacrament to prisoners of war in the 1940s. "Was dort" says the guard and points his rifle towards the priest with hymnal, the liturgy and the chalice: "Geistliche Waffen" (Spiritual weapons) the bishop answered and went to serve the prisoners. Saints live and die with "Geistliche Waffen": praying, singing, witnessing to the light of the gospel, sharing the sacraments, caring for others, doing good works…

Four Norwegian saints in the Roman Catholic tradition: St Olav, St Sunniva, St Halvard, St Eystein

How do we commemorate these saints in the Norwegian Lutheran tradition today?

* Olsok or St Olav's day/vigil is in our lectionary – July 29th. There are plays, worship services, concerts and pilgrimages in connection with the celebration of St.Olav.

* Musical plays and drama for children and youngsters connected to the life and mission of the four saints.

* Similar plays and worship services on a lesser scale on the island of Selje, commemorating St Sunniva (July 7th).

* Allehelgensmesse – Mass for All Saints Day by Egil Hovland.

* Many plays in our country with a historical and ecclesial perspective, commemorate local heroes and leaders.

We have much inspiration and spiritual formation from the work and the lives of the saints, not so much in the liturgical calendar as from church music and literature (e.g. Sigrid Undset). And we are humbled by the fact that there is so little deliberate and systematic use of the liturgical and spiritual challenge from the saints, except from Olsok or the St Olav vigil.

Lutheran hesitation and rejection of the saints...

What Martin Luther rejected in the sacrifice of the mass was the syncretism of the divine and human when it comes to the salvific acts.

Penitential acts (*meritum/merita*) have no effect (*satisfactio*) on our salvation, says Luther and points to the gospel and the justification by grace alone (*Sola fide; sola gratia*, cf. Paul's Letters to the Romans and Galatians). Luther sees both the saints and the *tax collection/ tesaurus* as a wrong way of balancing our deficit to God. We are in "minus", and it does not help us that the saints are in "plus" and thus contribute with their prayers and good deeds to the ecclesial balance. For Luther the saints disturbed the fundamental theology of Christ's redeeming life and work. There is both an anthropological and Christological perspective to be considered in Luther's rejection of the saints and of the sacrifice of the mass.

The reformers thought that the saints represented a branch of the great church-tree that had no good fruits and needed to be cut off. However, the branches did not disappear or burn up. Church leaders were more concerned with the misuse of saints, rather than the true biblical and spiritual meaning of the cloud of witnesses. And through the years and up to our own post-industrial times, the paths of the saints, the holy days and traditions survived in more poetical forms, in the newspapers and in the arts. More populist trends may show new ways of commemorations and inspirations than from the spiritual leaders that have preceded us (cf. Hebrews 13:7f).

How do we commemorate "the cloud of witnesses" in the Lutheran Church of Norway?

As I see it, this is clearly in the strong hymnody tradition of Lutheranism. And we should remind ourselves that the hymns are a collective memory of the Christian faith and the experience of Christians since the time of the early church. The hymns are poetic and aesthetic expressions in the worship service, but primarily a strong cultic expression of faith, hope and fellowship, commemorating God's creation, Christ and his life and mission and those who followed him through the ages.

In the first Norwegian hymnal of M.B. Landstad the hymns were without names, in accordance with liturgical customs and understanding. Later, however, the composers and writers were "discovered", and names were introduced in hymnals, including fame, royalties etc. But, on the other hand, these dedicated writers and composers are also part of the cloud of witnesses. They have opened a path of praise and praying and have given so much comfort and inspiration for life and service in the church.

Examples:
"Den store, hvite flokk, å se som tusen berge full av sne" (A cloud of witnesses, blessed sight, like mountain peaks with snow so white…). In Norway we see snow and mountains all the time, but not in Denmark where Brorson lived (and never left!) and wrote these lines. He may have seen picture books, but his images are most likely taken from the Bible.

"For all the saints, who from their labours rest
Who Thee by faith before the world confessed
Thy Name, o Jesus, be forever blessed
Alleluja, alleluja"

This Anglican hymn with its famous melody by Ralph Vaughan Williams resounds with the eternal pilgrimage. The same hymn has a central place in the Norwegian All Saints Mass by Egil Hovland. The melody has a different character but the same pilgrimage spirit as the Anglican version.

A Cloud of Witnesses – who are they?

They are priests and bishops, quite naturally, and they are lay leaders, women and men, giving their life to church and mission. And they are fathers and mothers, grandparents and Sunday-school teachers. With them and with the heavenly hosts we unite in one voice in every eucharistic celebration, singing: "Holy, holy, holy". In the Norwegian Lutheran tradition, with altar rails in our churches to kneel for receiving the sacrament, the altar rail is only half of the circle around the alter. The other invisible half is in the communion of the heavenly hosts.

The Working of God's Power: Towards a Pentecostal Understanding of Martyrdom and its Commemoration

Dale M. Coulter

In the *World Christian Encyclopedia*, David Barrett makes a seemingly startling claim that members of Pentecostal/Charismatic movements are "more harassed, persecuted, suffering, martryed than perhaps any other Christian tradition in recent history".[1] The claim seems less surprising when one considers Barrett's estimation of 524 million Pentecostal/Charismatic Christians in the year 2000, which in itself is rather large. Closer inspection of both claims reveals that Barrett includes 176 million Christians who are part of the Charismatic renewal and yet remain firmly committed to their respective communions. Claims such as Barrett's point out the difficulty in clearly identifying those who belong to the global Pentecostal/Charismatic movement. Before asking a question such as, "How do Pentecostals Commemorate?" one must first ask, "To which streams of this global movement do you refer?"

A quick approach to this question is to employ Barrett's classification of the global movement into three groups: 1) Pentecostal renewal, which refers to denominations that arose out of a series of revivals in different parts of the world at the turn of the 20th century; 2) Charismatic renewal, which refers to members of other Christian communions (Roman Catholics, Orthodox, Anglicans etc.) that experienced Pentecostal phenomena while remaining within their communions; 3) Neocharismatic renewal, which refers to a large body of indigenous denominations primarily located in the global south with various connections to the first two groups. While helpful, this classification is not entirely satisfactory because it does not take into consideration the numerous interconnections historically and theologically between Neocharismatics and Pentecostal renewal denominations, as Walter Hollenweger's work has shown.[2]

As an ordained minister of a Pentecostal denomination associated with the first Pentecostal renewal, I will restrict my comments primarily to publications stemming from it while also recognizing that what may be said of this wave could be applied to Neocharismatics.

An examination of the publications associated with the Pentecostal renewal presents a challenge with respect to the present topic. While one can find testimonies about martyrs, these testimonies function as one kind of witness within a broader framework of testimonies, all of which centre upon the power of God at work within human vessels. Consequently, the

---

1 David B. Barrett, George Thomas Kurian, Todd M. Johnson (eds.), *World Christian Encyclopedia: A Comparative Survey of Churches and Religions in the Modern World*, 2nd ed., Oxford University Press, Oxford, 2001, p.283.

2 See Walter Hollenweger, *Pentecostalism:Origins and Developments Worldwide,* Hendrickson Publishers, Peabody, MA, 1997.

approach taken here is to articulate the rough outlines of a theology of martyrdom as a way of indirectly answering the question of how Pentecostals commemorate their martyrs. In short, I wish to suggest that Pentecostals celebrate martyrdom as a witness of the tangible power of God that enables martyrs to overcome hostile forces in their complete identification with Jesus' sufferings and so receive a "martyr's crown". By virtue of their willingness to identify so fully with their Lord, martyrs are described as heroes of the faith. What remains central to this theology is its understanding of martyrdom as *one kind* of witness to the power of God. As such, despite the honour accorded to martyrs, they are viewed as part of a pantheon of witnesses whose testimony speaks of the in-breaking power of God. To support this contention, I will first briefly explore the role of testimony and its relationship to salvation within Pentecostal discourse and then examine how martyrdom is understood as another form of testimony.

Testimony as personal witness of God's power

Within Pentecostalism, testimony is a public act of bearing witness to or sharing with the community as a whole, either in written or oral form, one dimension of the believer's own personal encounter with God. This act draws on the Pentecostal understanding of salvation as the dynamic in-breaking and steady acquisition of God's own life that serves to deliver the individual from sin in all of its permutations.[3] As each Pentecostal believer experiences the liberating effects of God's presence and power, he or she participates in the broader drama of salvation history. The Exodus narrative or the narratives in the Acts of the Apostles become embodied in the personal narrative of the believer as the continuation of God's saving activity. For Pentecostal theologian Steve Land, testifying is about personal stories merging with *the* story (his emphasis).[4] Testimony, then, functions as a kind of corporate liturgy in which the believer offers a personal narrative as part of the ongoing narrative of the local community and the grand narrative of the divine economy.[5]

By construing salvation as deliverance from sin through the acquisition of God's own life, Pentecostalism offers a holistic soteriology in which the individual is progressively freed from hostile forces or powers. These forces include inordinate desires and emotions that stem from psychological disintegration through the internal power of sin, cosmic powers, social and political powers, and cultural systems that ultimately destroy life. Within this framework, the problem of human existence is not simply or even primarily guilt, but a slavery to sin, death and the devil that must be broken. The story is told of an early

3 See Dale M. Coulter, "Delivered by the Power of God: Toward a Pentecostal Understanding of Salvation", *International Journal of Systematic Theology* 10.4 (October 2008) pp.447-467.

4 Steven J. Land, *Pentecostal Spirituality: A Passion for the Kingdom*, JPT sup 1, Sheffield Academic Press, Sheffield, 1993, p.112.

5 See Cheryl Bridges Johns, *Pentecostal Formation: A Pedagogy Among the Oppressed*, JPT sup 2, Sheffield University Press, Sheffield, 1993, pp.126-127.

Pentecostal missionary to the Bahamas who "shocked" a Bahamian woman, Arabella Eneas, by telling her that God could not only forgive her sins, but heal her sickness as well.[6] The salvation of Eneas was construed in terms of bodily healing and forgiveness of sins, and she went on to become an early leader in a Pentecostal denomination in that island nation. Such a perspective on salvation is summarized by the early Pentecostal theologian, J. H. King (1869-1946) as complete "deliverance from death, spiritual, mental and physical, and all decay in the world around us."[7]

Pentecostal discourse about God's overcoming power primarily concerns the concrete way in which the divine life flows into a believer as the means of deliverance. One can see this in the British Pentecostal, Smith Wigglesworth's (1859-1947) declaration, "If you are definite with [Jesus], you will never go away disappointed. The divine life will flow into you and instantaneously you will be delivered. This Jesus is just the same today, and he says to you, 'I will; be thou clean.' He has an overflowing cup for you, a fullness of life."[8] Wigglesworth is describing a conscious, tangible experience of God's power that forms the basis of a soteriological synergism in which the believer embarks on a cooperative journey of ever-deepening awareness of God's presence. Taken primarily from Lukan narratives, the language of power underscores the explosive way in which the divine presence intersects with the human person so that he or she is caught up in the life of the kingdom.

An important dimension of this soteriology is an experience that Pentecostals describe as baptism in the Spirit, a further release of the Spirit's power and presence signaled by speaking in a kind of heavenly tongue. Tongues speech attests to a theological synergism because the Spirit's activity must have its counterpart in human activity. Moreover, for the Pentecostal believer, tongues speech symbolizes a participation in the eschaton that transforms the person into a witness for the kingdom. As Frank Macchia suggests, "Spirit baptism is power for witness, a power that reveals itself in bold witness and extraordinary gifts like inspired speech and bodily healing."[9]

Grounded in the in-breaking of God's life and subsequent deliverance from slavery to sinful forms of existence, these experiences of the Spirit give rise to the "prophethood of all believers". This prophetic ministry of inspired Christian witness occurs in and through the testimony of the believer as the public act of bearing witness to the power of God. Speaking of his activity in Russia in the 1930s, Herbert Schmidt describes a Russian peasant walking numerous miles to a Pentecostal meeting and then returning to his village with a message of

6 James E. Cossey, *R. M. Evans: The First of His Kind*, Missionary Hero Series n.d. Pathway Press, Cleveland, TN, p. 21. The event most likely occurred in 1910.

7 J. H. King, *From Passover to Pentecost*, fourth ed., revised and enlarged Advocate Press, Franklin Springs, GA, 1976, p.103.

8 Smith Wigglesworth, "Himself Took Our Infirmities", in *Ever Increasing Faith*, revised edition, edited by Wayne E. Warner, Gospel Publishing House, Springfield, MO, 1971, p.62.

9 Frank Macchia, *Baptized in the Spirit: A Global Pentecostal Theology*, Zondervan, Grand Rapids, MI, 2006, p.150.

salvation. Schmidt states, "The other villagers have been waiting for him because they know he has gone to find these strange people. Immediately he begins to unfold to them the story. He repeats it again and again until before he realizes it, he has become a preacher."[10] Because of his own experience of the power of God, the Russian peasant has become a witness to others. This witness is not grounded in a close analysis and interpretation of sacred texts, but in the personal embodiment of the story of salvation in the life of the believer. All believers testify, all become witnesses of God's power that they have experienced, and martyrdom functions as an expression of this testimony to which I now turn.

Martyrdom as testimony of God's power

A Pentecostal understanding of martyrdom places this sacrificial act within the broader rubric of the outworking of divine power in the lives of fragile human beings. In this sense, the boldness of a martyr's testimony bears witness to an extraordinary courage he or she receives as a result of concrete experiences of the Spirit. Secondly, martyrs form one contingent in the constellation of witnesses to the way that God's power frees humans to live heroic lives. While martyrs are honoured for their deeds in proclaiming Christ despite the certainty of their death, they are not viewed as saints if the definition of sainthood includes a special class of individuals through whom the miraculous power of God is displayed coupled with a life of holiness. It is these two dimensions of martyrdom that I will explore in the closing section of the paper.

First, early Pentecostal accounts of martyrdom speak repeatedly of the way in which martyrs become witnesses of God's power. Two examples will suffice to make this point. An early Pentecostal missionary, Andrew David Urshan (1884-1967) reported of the martyrdom of a young Russian girl named Sophia in Urumia, a city located in the north of modern Iran. The martyrdom occurred in 1914, just before thousands of Armenian and Assyrian Christians were slaughtered by Turkish forces. Urshan, himself an Assyrian Pentecostal, reported on the event in several Pentecostal publications. Sophia only lived one week after she was shot by a Russian boy on her way to church one night. During this final week Urshan notes that "Although [the village people] did not believe in what God had done for her, they said her face shone like an angel's. The power of God would rest upon her, and many were brought to Jesus through her."[11]

A second example is provided by Herbert McLean in the Yunnan province of western China in 1926. At the time, the Pentecostal Missionary Union was one of several

10 G. Herbert Schmidt, "Lives of Christians Marked by Tragedy and Sorrow", *The Latter Rain Evangel,* 30.4 (February 1939) p.7.

11 Andrew D. Urshan, "The Martyred Six of Persia", *The Latter Rain Evangel,* 8.11 (August, 1916) p.2. Other accounts of the incident by Urshan are "Martyred in Persia," *The Latter Rain Evangel* (August, 1914) pp.13-14; "Persia: A Martyr's End," *Confidence* (September, 1914) pp.175-176. For more information on the historical context see Allan Anderson, *Spreading Fires: The Missionary Nature of Early Pentecostalism,* SCM Press, London, 2007, pp.154-155.

societies operating in the province. McLean relates the story of a young Chinese woman who was beaten to death by her husband after he discovered that she had converted to Christianity. In his description of the young Chinese woman, McLean notes that she had received visions of heaven and that at her baptism in water "a supernatural light shone around them and the power of God rested upon them heavily. Oh, how the Lord anointed this sister."[12]

These two examples illustrate the relationship between power and witness in the lives of early Pentecostal martyrs. Moreover, the writers employ metaphors of light or brightness to convey the physical manifestation of this power in the facial features and expressions of the martyrs. As with Orthodox iconography, early Pentecostals saw the presence of God's own life as permeating the martyrs' lives. This is similar to the way in which Lossky and Ouspensky depict the icon as "an external expression of the transfigured state of man, of his sanctification by the uncreated Divine light".[13] The halo, in particular, surrounding the face of the saint, points to the manifestation of this light. Likewise, early Pentecostals saw the in-breaking of divine life as being expressed in the bodies of Pentecostal martyrs.

Secondly, while Pentecostals constantly refer to the martyrs' crown and describe these individuals as "heroes of the faith", there is a sense in which martyrdom is given less weight as a witness than it might have in other forms of Christianity. This is because martyrs are not the only kinds of Christians through whom God's power is radically at work. Indeed, the democratization of the Spirit means that all believers are prophets and can receive inspired speech, visions and other charisms as part of their own personal narrative, their testimony. As Dario Lopez points out of Peruvian Pentecostal pastors' mentality towards suffering, it is "because of the Pentecostal conviction concerning the activity of the Holy Spirit in the daily life of the believer that gives the power for testimony and the strength to endure moments of suffering."[14] It is this common conviction, grounded in the liberating effects of God's life that forms the basis for all Pentecostal action. For this reason, Pentecostals would not agree with the statement in the *Passion of Perpetua* that by virtue of her status as a confessor Perpetua may ask God for a vision and he will grant it.

Conclusion

In this brief paper, I have attempted to address the question of how Pentecostals commemorate their martyrs by focusing on the outlines of a Pentecostal theology of martyrdom. The primary group of Pentecostals represented are those Barrett associates with the Pentecostal

12 See H. McLean, "The Second Chapter of Acts Repeated: Martyrs for Jesus in Yunnan", *The Latter Rain Evangel,* vol. 19, no. 12, (August 21, 1927) p.3.

13 Leonid Ouspensky and Vladimir Lossky, *The Meaning of the Icons*, trans. G.E.H. Palmer and E. Kadloubovsky, SVS Press, Crestwood, NY, 1999, p.39.

14 Dario Lopez, *Pentecostalismo y transformación social*, Kairos Ediciones, Buenos Aires, 2000, p.17.

renewal. For these Pentecostals, martyrdom is understood as one kind of witness or testimony within a broader soteriological framework for which testimony is an ongoing liturgical act. Pentecostals “testify” to one another of their own personal encounters with God’s energizing life that delivers them from the hostile forces of sin. Martyrs receive a crown because, like the proto-martyr Stephen, they have overcome, which is revealed in the way that the power of God breaks through in the “brightness” of their countenance. Pentecostals daily seek this energizing presence of the Holy Spirit that is found vividly embodied in the witness of Pentecostal martyrdom.

CASE STUDIES ON WITNESSING FROM DIFFERENT REGIONS

A Witness of Courage and Faith in Brazil: Pastor Richard Wangen

Karen Bergesch

"Este é tempo de divisas, tempo de gente cortada…
É tempo de meio silêncio, de boca gelada e murmúrio,
palavra indireta, aviso na esquina."[1]
Carlos Drummond de Andrade

Historical context

Brazil was under military dictatorship from 1964 until 1985. Military dictatorship can be described as a lack of democracy, suppression of constitutional rights, censorship, political persecution and repression of any manifestation against the military government. The social control of the military was made through secret agents at schools and universities, for example.

Before the military government, politics in Brazil was in conflict. The president Jânio Quadros left the government, in 1961, before the end of his mandate. The vice-president, João Goulart (1961-1964), became president in a situation of political conflict. He was very supportive of social organizations. Students, popular organizations and workers were at the centre of political decisions. The army, bankers and conservative managements did not approve his policy. They were afraid that Brazil would become a socialist country. We should not forget that, at the time, the world political context was the cold war. A liberal government in Brazil was a concern for many countries, especially the USA. The conservative classes in Brazil and the USA were afraid of a communist coup.

Two political parties were against the government, the National Democracy Union (UDN) and the Social Democratic Party (UDN). They accused the president of organizing a communist coup and held him responsible for the economic problems, especially the price of food. On March 13, 1964, João Goulart made a speech at a big rally in downtown Rio de Janeiro. In his speech, he defended new agriculture, economic and educational reforms. Six days later, on March 19, conservative groups organized a demonstration against the government's political proposals. It was called "Family with God for Freedom March" and took place in downtown São Paulo.

So, political tension increased gradually. On March 31, 1964, the army from Minas Gerais state and São Paulo state took the city. To avoid a civil war, president Goulart left the country to go to Uruguay. The military took over the government. As soon as the military

1 Carlos Drummond Andrade, "Nosso Tempo" in *A rosa do povo,* Rio de Janeiro Record, 1945, p.29-37.

regime was installed, a new constitutional act was created on April 9: *Ato Institucional Número 1* (AI-1). Through extra-constitutional decrees dubbed "Institutional Acts" the executive was given the ability to change the constitution and remove anyone from office.

During the military regime the presidents were all from the army. General Castello Branco (1964-1967) was the first. He led the transition from democracy to dictatorship government. One of his decisions was to restrict political party organizations. General Costa e Silva (1967-1969) was the second president. He sacked judges, banned political rights and increased military and political control. A large number of Brazilians were unhappy and an urban guerrilla movement began to be organized.

For a short period of time, a group of military was in charge of the Brazilian government (31 August-30 October 1969). This group was called the "Junta Militar". After the "Junta Militar", general Médici became president (1969-1974). The Médici government is considered the hardest and most difficult period of the dictatorship regime. It is called "anos de chumbo" (the years of lead). Repression increased, especially of the urban guerillas and censorship of newspapers, magazines, books, movies, music, etc. Because of that, many professors, artists, musicians, writers and politicians were investigated, put in prison, tortured or exiled from Brazil.

The next president, General Geisel (1974-1979), began a slow process of return to democracy. In this period, economic problems increased which helped the people in exile to return to their homeland. The Brazilian population was unhappy with the economic policy that included high taxes. The last military president was General Figueiredo (1979-1985). He was in charge of the transition from dictatorship to democracy. An amnesty law was promulgated. In 1979 the government approved a law to ensure freedom for public demonstrations and the organization of political parties.

In the last years of the military regime, the country faced inflation and economic recession. At this time the new political parties and labour unions became strong. In 1984, the country wanted the right to vote. A big march with politicians, artist, soccer players and millions of Brazilians was organized. This march was named "Diretas Já Moviment". This movement was in favour of the Dante de Oliveira amendment to have direct elections that year. Unfortunately, it was not approved.

On January 15, 1985, Tancredo Neves was elected through the deputies to become president of Brazil. He was a member of the Union for Democracy. It was the end of the military regime. However Tancredo Neves became sick before he was installed as president and passed away. He was replaced by the vice-president. In 1988, a new constitution was approved to establish democratic principles.

Witnesses of the military regime in Brazil

Unfortunately, it is impossible to name all the people who were imprisoned and tortured in Latin America under the military regimes. There are no documents to clarify the facts concerning the life of each one. Many people just disappeared. Most of them are on the list of missing people. Many were too afraid to keep documents or even to talk about torture.

In spite of that, there are survivors who can tell us what it was like inside the prisons during the military dictatorship. Take the case of **Frei Tito**, for example. In 1963 he was elected to lead the organization of the National Catholic Youth Group in Brazil. Because of that, he moved to Recife.

At the time, it was forbidden by the military regime to organize assemblies or any kind of meetings. Frei Tito was arrested in October 1968 because he took part in a "clandestine" meeting of the National Catholic Youth Group. After that, the military police persecuted him.

On November 4, 1969, he was arrested and tortured for a month. After that he was put in prison and tortured again. At that time, he wrote a document about his condition and the document went around the world and was considered a symbol of the struggle for human rights. In 1971 he was deported to Chile and, to avoid the risk of being arrested again, moved to Rome. There he did not find support because he was considered a terrorist priest. He finally moved to Paris where the Dominicans helped him.

On August 10, 1974, he was found dead by hanging. How it happened was never clarified. His body was brought back to Brazil on March 25, 1983. On this occasion, in São Paulo, there was a memorial mass for the martyrs (Frei Tito and Alexandre Vannucchi). During the celebration, Dom Paulo Evaristo Arns criticized the tragedy of torture. More than 4000 people took part in this mass.

Vladimir Herzog was a journalist and was also arrested, tortured and killed. He had studied philosophy and worked as news director of TV Cultura; he was as well a professor at the University of São Paulo. On October 24, 1975, he was called to the military police department to clarify his relations with the Communist Party. The following day he was found dead, hanging in prison. He was 38 years old.

As he was Jew, the rabbi prepared Vladimir's body for the funeral. In so doing, he realized that Herzog had been tortured. In protest against the military regime, magazine, newspaper, TV and radio station journalists went on strike. On October 31, 1975 an ecumenical celebration took place in the Catedral da Sé, São Paulo, with more than 8000 people. It was a protest against the military regime. In 1978, the judiciary accused the military of torturing and murdering Herzog.

Paulo Stuart Wright was an American citizen born in Joaçaba, State of Santa Catarina. He helped to organize and found the labour union in Joaçaba. He was the first Protestant candidate to the city hall (he missed election by 11 votes). But he was elected deputy to the Santa Catarina State Assembly. In this political position he helped to organized 27 fisherman's cooperatives and helped them to work together as a federation (FECOPESCA).

In 1964 Paulo Stuart Wright was persecuted, and he moved to Mexico. A year later he returned and was elected as the leader of a clandestine popular movement against the military regime that had its roots in the National Catholic Youth Group and the Christian Academic Association. For eight years he led the movement. In 1973 was arrested, tortured and killed. His body has never been found.

Streets in four cities in Brazil are named after him. In São Paulo, all churches were represented at the opening ceremony of a street named for him. The only church that was not there was the Presbyterian Church, the church of which he was member and which had forbidden him to help in the work with the children, and in prayers, as soon as he became involved in politics.

The three examples above are of brothers in faith who were against the military regime and committed to their faith. There were also people who were committed to the gospel and worked against the military regime, but were not arrested.

Richard Harvey Wangen was born in Harvey, North Dakota, USA, on June 18, 1924. He studied theology in Wartburg Seminary, Dubuque, Iowa. He married Dorothy Marie Weiblen in 1953 and they were blessed with three children: Marie Ann, Stewart Richard (he predeceased his father) and Charlotte Amelia.

In 1956 Richard Wangen came with his family to southern Brazil to work as a pastor in a mission project supported by the LWF (Lutheran World Federation), ELCA (Evangelical Lutheran Church in America) and IECLB (Lutheran Church in Brazil). The aim was to work with students at the University of Curitiba, state of Paraná. From 1957 to 1961, Pastor Wangen and his family lived in Curitiba. From 1961 to 1962, he returned to USA where he worked at the University of Minnesota as a student pastor. On his way back to Brazil, he spent a short time in São Paulo city. He then returned to Curitiba from 1963 to 1970.

In Curitiba, he took the initiative to build a house for the students of the university. This house was opened on February 28, 1970. The aim was to provide accommodation for students from the rural areas. *The Students House,* as it was called, has an excellent structure and the capacity to house 88 students, from that time until today.

In 1971, Pastor Wangen was invited to teach at the Theological Seminary in São Leopoldo, Rio Grande do Sul state. Wangen accepted the invitation, but went first to Luther Theological Seminary of St. Paul in Minnesota to take his masters degree. At the theological seminary, professor Wangen was responsible for the Practical Theology area and the Pastoral Clinic class. It was a new area of studies at the time in Brazil. As part of the Pastoral Clinic, the students needed to visit hospitals, hospices and other organizations that helped marginalized people. The new contribution challenged students to be in contact with social problems from a pastoral point of view.

Like at the university in Curitiba, at the Theological Seminary Pastor Wangen regularly organized visits and helped poor communities. Many times it was to help bring people from the countryside to the hospitals and to translate from German to Portuguese during doctor's appointments. Student accommodation was provided for farmers from the countryside and some students went to the rural areas to help, teaching about agriculture, health and food, for example. All this required organization. Besides all this work, Pastor Wangen always had time to talk and to listen to anyone who asked for pastoral care.

Pastor Wangen was and is considered among friends, colleagues and students, a faithful, dedicated and open person. He is described in the book dedicated to him as a loyal disciple of Jesus Christ who was always concerned about contextualizing the gospel. He was dedicated, active, hopeful, creative, audacious, always ready to talk and to listen. In so doing, he demonstrated that to be faithful to the gospel today can sometimes be compromising and hard, but also it may bring happiness and a life fulfilled.

Richard Wangen and his family were already in Brazil when the military coup took place. Courageous but not naïve, Pastor Wangen proclaimed the gospel with caution, keeping a critical eye on the political and social changes. All the leaders should have been like him at that time, because many people were persecuted and arrested by the military regime. Richard Wangen's work was divided between different projects: education for non-violence and the organization of a book of Bible studies in IECLB that was entitled *Proclamar Libertação,* Proclaiming Liberation.[2]

Proclaiming liberation

At the time Pastor Wangen was in Curitiba, he joined a group of colleagues to organize Bible studies. As mentioned above, the historical context did not permit such meetings. The pastors were going against the law and they needed to be courageous and careful. Just the idea of organizing a group was already something daring.

2 Richard Wangen, "Dia da Independência": 1 Pedro 2, 13-17, in Baldur van Kaick (Coord), *Proclamar Libertação,* Auxílios homiléticos, Ed. Sinodal São Leopoldo, vol. I, 1976, p.102-111.

Because of the historical context it was necessary to be cautious in talking about the Bible studies and in inviting colleagues to join the group. Nothing could be said clearly. It was never really clear where and when the meetings would take place. In spite of all these difficulties, the homiletic studies were conceived, organized and printed. Proclaiming the gospel was a need in those difficult times. Pastors were aware of their responsibility to the community, to society and to colleagues.

Proclaiming Liberation is based on the idea of liberation from Egypt in the Old Testament. It was a time to proclaim liberation from the dictatorship. The first volume of the studies was produced by the organizing group and 22 people, among them Richard Wangen, contributed to it. The Bible studies, now in their 33rd edition, continue to be published to this day.

SERPAZ – a seed that germinated

SERPAZ is a non-profit association, in São Leopoldo, state of Rio Grande do Sul. It stems from another group that was set up in 1978 during the military regime. The main point of the first group was to advocate for human rights, justice and democracy. From the beginning important persons in the church and in society who already had a history of fighting for justice and human rights, such as Dom Helder Câmara, Jaime Wright, Dom Evaristo Arns, Walter Altmann, Domingos Bargé and Richard Wangen, were in the group.

Different religions and professionals make up SERPAZ today: musicians, lawyers, theologians, workers, philosophers, professors, teachers, pastors, priests and students. Therefore, SERPAZ keeps its ecumenical character, working mostly with poor people to empower them to build a new society through knowledge, justice and dignity. Pastor Wangen's family is responsible for the organization of SERPAZ, especially through his daughters and son-in-law (Marie and Allan Krahn and Charlotte).

SERPAZ' goals are:

a) Education for peace through two programmes: Alternative Actions to Violence Project (PAV) and Help to Increase Peace Project (AAP);
b) To promote peace through gender, racism and human rights debates;
c) To promote projects or events against the arms industry, including land mines, looking for a disarmed society;
d) To promote a peaceful solution of conflicts;
e) To promote peace awareness;
f) To help countries or groups suffering because of war;
g) To help to bring children out of war;
h) To promote sexual education without discrimination;

i) To fight for Indians' rights and the right for them to study;

j) To support other organizations that educate for peace.

The dream of freedom, peace and justice becomes real when we look for it, fight for it and when we work to keep it alive. The history of the end of the dictatorship and the beginning of democracy in Brazil can be told through many witnesses. These witnesses were empowered through the love, peace and justice proclaimed by the Old Testament and by the gospel.

The 20th Century Martyrdom in Latin America

Daniel A. Bruno

Introduction

Latin America is not the poorest continent of the world but it is the most unequal in distribution of wealth. This unfair and unequal distribution of economic riches in Latin America has been sustained by a triangle of the three powerful columns: trade and financial power, religious power and military power.

In a continent where 95 percent of the population claims to be Christian and where the Catholic Church has been a constitutive active part of this unfair socio-political construction since the beginning, the question that emerges dramatically is: How to be a Christian in this context? This question has never arisen as dramatically as in the 20th century.

It is important for Christians to understand the difference between the church as an institution in contrast to a church as a charismatic event, to grasp the differences emerging, on the one hand, from the church's alliances with power and, on the other, the faithful walking with the people of Christ. Christians began to understand the gap between the *status quo* of a clerical power in contrast to the revolutionary renovation of prophetic voices; the difference between pulpits that preached patient resignation under poverty or the recovery of historical Jesus for the kingdom of God and its justice.

Theological hermeneutical keys

Martyrdom in Latin America cannot be understood properly without taking into account its historical context. The source of Christian martyrdom there has been the dramatic historical clash between Christian faith and scandalous social injustice.

There are a few hermeneutical keys which serve to understand martyrdom in Latin America:

a) Martyrdom in Latin America comes from the prophets' paradigm seeking justice and the power to fight for it. So, most of the time, in the context of structural violence, the historically established faith develops into persecution, "because in the same way they persecuted the prophets who were before you" (Matt. 5:12).

b) Martyrdom in Latin America comes from the faith which claimed preference for the poor. The big cloud of witnesses in Latin America is composed of all those who were urged to live out the Sermon on the Mount:

> Blessed are those who are persecuted because of righteousness, for theirs is the kingdom of heaven. Blessed are you when people insult you, persecute you and falsely say all kinds of evil against you because of me. Rejoice and be glad, because great is your reward in heaven, for in the same way they persecuted the prophets who were before you. (Matthew 5, 10-11)

c) Defending established faith in Latin America means to seek righteousness for the unequal structure which produces poverty, suffering and pain; to be faithful to Christ and to the victims of violent injustice. Martyrs do not look for death, but remain faithful witnesses, despite the risks. As Karl Rahner states: "The authentic acceptance of a forcible death is certainly and fully verified when someone, in the service of the gospel and justice, knowingly and tangibly enters into a situation in which a forcible death must be reckoned on… so martyrdom in Latin America, even where the martyrs were directly involved in the service of a socio-political ideal, flowed from an expressly Christian motivation and inspiration, and therefore may be considered true martyrdoms."[1] Christianity has become a powerful cultural background in Latin America even for the world view of the aboriginal peoples of the continent. So, when we talk about persecution of Christians in Latin America, we must be clear that:

d) In opposition to most cases of martyrdom in history, all executioners of Christians in Latin America claimed to be true Christians. The hierarchy of the church was silent while some of its bishops, priests and nuns were killed. It was common to see crucifixes, rosaries and pictures of the Virgin Mary in rooms where torture took place.

e) Therefore it is clear that the persecution was not against Christian doctrine *(odium fidei)* but against an involved Christian practice *(odium praxis fidei)*. It was a furious persecution against the historical implications of Christian faith in a context of structural injustice.

f) Martyrdom in Latin America is a reversion to the tradition of historical Jesus and the political consequences of his ministry. His death had the unequivocal mark of a political execution so that his death has to be understood and followed consequently. Jesus died because of his search for the kingdom of God and justice. His executioners were the anti-kingdom forces; the brutal power which linked mutual interests of empire with a religious institution. After Jesus, martyrs in Latin America have also given their lives for the kingdom and justice; the hands of those who forced them to martyrdom made the unequivocal mark of the anti-kingdom regardless of their confession.

g) A Cloud of Witnesses contains martyrs from all ages, however, the radical witnessing in Latin America cannot always be compared to the way the early Fathers of the

1 Martin Lange and Reinhold Iblacker, *Witnesses of hope, The Persecution of Christians in Latin America*, Foreword by Karl Rahner, Orbis Books, Maryknoll, 1981.

church understood martyrdom. The early Christian martyrology is a particular genre which has its specific characteristics. There are some similarities between classical martyrdom and the recent martyrdom in Latin America but there are also many important divergences and the major difference lies in the fact of the persecutors being Christians who often referred to Christ.

Historical framework: The final systematic persecution in Latin America

To put it into a historical frame, we may say that the 60s were a special decade for the awakening of Christian historical commitment; in particular the year 1968 is a milestone in the recollection of our contemporary martyrology. That year marked the end of the general assembly of CELAM II (the 2nd General Episcopal Conference of Latin America) held in Medellin, Colombia. The conclusions of that assembly were a turning point, not only for many Catholics, but also for some Protestant denominations. Since that time many bishops, priests, members of religious congregations, nuns, pastors and laypersons, Catholic and Protestant "in growing numbers, have taken the side of the poor, the exploited, the suffering, and the church has become the voice of the voiceless."[2] The reaction to this Christian social awakening was not long in coming.

Within the framework of the so-called "National Security Doctrine", a strategic plan designed by the United States Joint Military Forces, they turned their cold war towards the interior politics of the Latin American continent by training the armed forces of each country to subdue potential signs of rebellion arising in the Latin American masses and submitted them to extremely poor living conditions and limited possibilities of real development.

The USA started to harass the democracies of Latin America: Brazil (1964); Argentina (1966); Uruguay (1970); Chile (1973); Argentina once again (1976) – leaving behind a trickle of absences, pain and impunity. The USA's interest towards the internal security of the Latin American countries was actually the need to create a balanced political situation, in order to guarantee a safe, riskless business environment for North American and multinational investments. Political stability in the midst of extremely unfair social situations might only be achieved with de facto governments independent of the free play and search for democratic consensus. In this way, the coup, by means of the suppression of individual guarantees, the democratic institutions and the control of all which might imply opposition, left the field free for lucrative foreign investments. In this context, a Christian practical faith committed to the poor and marginalized, was of course, an unpleasant nuisance. It had to be repressed. Regarding this, the words of the so-called Rockefeller[3] Report in 1969 were very

---

2 *Ibid.*, p.xvii.

3 Nelson Rockefeller was the president of the commission which, after a tour through Latin America in 1969, reported to Richard Nixon. This report became the basis of President Nixon's policy in Latin America.

meaningful: "The Catholic Church in the region is vulnerable to subversive penetration and, as we know, it is no longer a trustworthy ally for the USA, they can not warrant any more the social stability in the continent".[4]

It was not necessary to say more. These words had a double effect: on the one hand, they were the starting point for the promotion, re-creation and financial support of fundamentalist evangelical groups which, since the 70s, invested and divided the historical churches, especially those committed to a mission with the poor. On the other, it was the permission needed to act severely towards the prophetic church in order to erase that "wrong" example from history.

In fact, the Christian church had to pay a high price for its partnership with the oppressed and those deprived of their rights... from slander to massacres in Christian communities... from abductions followed by torture and death to public executions by shooting.

Facts, names and absences

It is impossible to collate a complete Latin American martyrology, for the simple reason that most of them are anonymous, and this is one more characteristic of Latin American martyrology. But the anonymity of those martyrdoms does not prevent them being part of that holy cloud of witnesses. Certainly, as Karl Rahner asserts:

> Anonymity does not bar them from the ranks of the martyrs. True, in the books of the blood-witnesses of eternal hope there have always been nameless individuals, but the anonymous *campesinos* are a unique admonition to us that in modern mass society the individual dare not be lost sight of, that those vanquished in anonymity and forgetfulness are the true vanquishers.[5]

But close to the nameless, we have also a lot of names. They are the names of those who could not say "No" to Jesus' call, despite the risk, and menaces, and fear.

Adolfo Pérez Esquivel, Catholic layman and Nobel Prize laureate in 1980, due to his outstanding action in defence of life, and founder of another ecumenical body in defence of Human Rights, the Service for Peace and Justice (SERPAJ), thus narrates his participation in the organization of the Plaza de Mayo Mothers:

> At the beginning, everything was despair, then came reflection. And that reflection was fruitful. And those women were strengthened, as they became aware of something very important: that each was not the mother of her own son only, but also of all the

4 Rockefeller Report on Latin America, 1969, chapter V.
5 *Witness of Hope: the Persecution of Christians in Latin America,* edited by M. Lange and R. Iblacker, Foreword by Karl Rahner, Orbis books, Maryknoll, NY, 1981.

> sons and daughters, and that they could only get to do something by gathering and mutually fortifying each other, in order to fight for the lives of their own sons and of all the other sons. We organized meetings, such as the seminar on "The Gospel and Human Dignity", during which sociopolitical, economic and religious analyses of the situation were elaborated. Towards the end of 1979, facing the increase of the repression to which they were submitted, it seemed necessary for us to organize them as an institution, in order to allow them to delve deeply into their action.[6]

The first president of *Madres de Plaza de Mayo* was kidnapped and murdered. During the first years of dictatorship, the action of Methodist parishes was outstanding, opening their churches so that resistance members could meet there, amongst them the relatives of those disappeared who started to organize their claims. The tower of the central Methodist Church was for months a shelter for a young student persecuted by the repressive forces.

In a cellar of another church, the movement *Relatives of Imprisoned-Disappeared* was organized. In the Methodist Church of Lomas de Zamora, a suburb of greater Buenos Aires, the local group of the *Plaza de Mayo Mothers* met. For this reason, the Methodist Church and many of its members were frequently the target of bombs, kidnappings and threats. On 4 October, 1976 the First Methodist Church of the City of Rosario, where the Coordinating Commission of ACNUR (United Nations High Commissioner for Refugees) functioned, was raided. Seventy persons were arrested from that church. The parish priest Ernesto Nielsen some time after those events said in a sermon: "Our participation in the present problems of the country and the continent shall, many times, require us to run these risks, in obedience to serve the vocation our Lord Jesus Christ granted to us."[7]

A bomb also destroyed the front of the Methodist Church in Mendoza, in the mountainous west of the country. This church sheltered Chilean refugees.

On May 4, 1977, Oscar Alajarín, member of the Methodist Church of Remedios de Escalada, active Ecumenical Movement for Human Rights militant and also a workers union militant was kidnapped and disappeared.

On January 1, 1977, Dr Mauricio López, renowned intellectual in the area of sociology and philosophy, Free Brother in origin, but who was then closely working with the Methodist Church of Mendoza, was kidnapped and disappeared. López worked for many years in the World Council of Churches in Geneva, and in 1973 was nominated Rector of the Universidad Nacional de San Luis. Confidential information indicated that he had been murdered in a concentration camp by the Armed Forces in March of the same year.

---

6 A. Pérez Esquivel, *Las Locas de la Plaza de Mayo*, El Cid Editor, Buenos Aires, 1983 (Prologue).
7 *El Estandarte Evangélico* (December 1976).

Alba Garófalo, the 24 year-old daughter of a Methodist pastor, was my partner in working with poor slum children. She belonged to the Methodist youth and also was a Peronist Youth militant. She had a baby boy and was expecting another one when, on December 8th, (Virgin Mary day in Argentina) she was kidnapped together with her husband. Nothing was ever heard of them, nor of her expected baby.

The militant Catholic Church also suffered at various levels. Bishop Angelelli from La Rioja was murdered in a presumed car accident on 4 August 1976. Around 20 priests were murdered during the years 1974 to 1978.

Father Carlos Mujica, one of the leaders of the Third World Priests Movement was shot after celebrating a mass in the slum where he lived and worked, early in 1974 just before the military junta.

The French nuns from the Foreign Missions, Alice Domon and Leónie Duquet, were arrested on December 8 and 10, 1977, and never heard of again. Some testimonies indicate that after being imprisoned in a concentration camp under control of the Navy, they were thrown into the Río de La Plata in the so-called "death flights", an aberrant practice conceived in order to eliminate the evidence of thousands of disappeared.

It is worth mentioning Salvador Barbeito and Emilio Barletti, of the Palatine Community, murdered on 4 July 1976; Marcos Cirio, novice of the Gospel Fraternity, arrested and disappeared on 17 November 1976; Carlos Di Pietro and Raúl Rodríguez, members of the order of the Augustinians of the Assumption, arrested and disappeared on 4 June 1976.

The military in favour of the coup were self-defined fervent Christians who came to defend the Western and Christian way of life against assumed foreign forces which aimed to dissolve it. Some bishops of the Catholic Church also took an active part in the repression and even torture of Christians, some of them by direct action, others by omission.

The brutality and rage with which Christians from different churches repressed the victims made it clear that their proclaimed Christianity was nothing more than an ideological instrument to repress any expression of genuine faith which could emerge from people's daily life.

Latin American Christian martyrdom has been a result of the gospel of Christ put into practice. A gospel that demands a faithful walk with Jesus, and sometimes following Jesus becomes risky. At the same time, paradoxically, Latin American Christian martyrology came to be the most shameful page of the Christian church.

Celebrating the martyrs

In order to make a contribution to the celebration of martyrs included here is a poem by the Spanish-Brazilian bishop and poet Pedro Casaldáliga entitled Open Letter to our Martyrs[8]:

I write to all you men and women
who have given your lives for Life,
throughout the length and breadth of our America,
in streets and in mountains,
in factories and in fields,
in schools and in churches,
at dark of night or in the sunlight.
You above all have made our America
the continent of death with hope.

I write to you in the name of all our Nations and our Churches,
which owe you the courage to live, to defend their identities,
and the stubborn will to go on defending the Kingdom,
against the wind and the tide of the free-market anti-Kingdom
and despite the corruptions of our governments
or our own surrenders.
We believe that while there is martyrdom there is credibility,
while there is martyrdom there is hope.

You, men and women, have washed the garments of your commitment
in the blood of the Lamb.
And your blood in his blood
still washes our dreams, our weaknesses
and our failures.

8 P. Casaldáliga, in "Rethinking Martyrdom", *Concilium* 2003/1, pp. 149-151, translated by Paul Burns.

While there is martyrdom there will be conversion,
while there is martyrdom we shall see results.
the grains of corn only multiply by dying.

I write to you in the face of prohibition
by the dictatorial powers – military, political or economic –
and in the face of the forgetful cowardice of our own Churches.
I write even though powers and Churches would impose
an amnesty that would be amnesia
and a reconciliation that would be surrender.
In vain.
You know how to forgive, but you want to live.
We shall not permit the supreme cry of your love to be stifled,
nor shall we allow your blood to be fruitless.

Nor shall we be superficially or irresponsibly content
with putting up posters of you,
with singing songs to you on pilgrimage,
with dramatizing you in plays.
We shall take on your lives and your deaths,
taking up your Causes,
those specific Causes
for which you gave your life and death.
Those Causes, so human and so divine,
that in actual events and in effective charity
point to the greater Cause of the Kingdom,
for which the first-born from among the dead,
Jesus of Nazareth, crucified and raised for ever,
gave his life and his death, and for which he rose again.

We remember you all, men and women,
and we say none of your great names now
so that we can call to you all in one great shout
of love and commitment:
Our Martyrs! Women,
men, children, old people,
natives, peasants, workers, artists, writers,
pastors, priests, catechists, bishops…
names that are known and already in your matryrology
or names unknown but written in God's roll-call.
We acknowledge ourselves your heirs, a witness Nation, a martyr Church,
deacons walking through the Continent's long Easter night,
so dark still, yet so unconquerably victorious.
We shall not yield, we shall not sell out; we shall not give up
this great paradigm of our lives
that was the paradigm of Jesus himself
and is the dream of the Living God for all his children
throughout all time and in every nation
and in all worlds, towards the single and plural fellowship
of the Kingdom, the Kingdom – his Kingdom!

With St Romero of America and with all you men and women,
and all uniting in one voice and common purpose
with all the sisters and brothers whose solidarity goes with us,
we declare ourselves "happy to run the same risks as Jesus,
[as you men and women were]
to identify ourselves
with the Causes of the dispossessed."
And in this world prostituted by the global market and selfish wealth
We swear to you with humility and resolve:
"Far be it from us to glory

save in the cross of our Lord Jesus Christ"
and in your crosses that mirror his!
With him and with you all
we shall still hymn Liberation.
through him and through you all
we shall jubilantly learn
that we too shall rise "even at the cost of our lives".

Remembering Rightly:
A Response to Karen Bergesch and Daniel A. Bruno

William T. Cavanaugh

I want to begin by thanking Daniel and Karen for their reflections which situate martyrology properly within a particular context. The way that the martyrs' bones and resting places have been revered throughout the centuries reminds us of the particularity of martyrdom, the emphasis on the concrete historical context in which each martyrdom takes place. Daniel and Karen have likewise based their reflections on martyrdom in the concrete context of Latin America during the period of military dictatorships. I have been asked to respond to their papers presumably because I too lived and worked in Latin America, albeit only for a couple of years, among poor people in the same context (General Pinochet's dictatorship in Chile in the 1980s) and I have written theology based in that context. Now, however, my context is quite different; I teach at a private Catholic university in a comfortable part of St. Paul, Minnesota, in the USA. This is an odd place from which to reflect on martyrdom. We need to be aware not only of the historical context in which martyrdom takes place, but also the historical context in which martyrology takes place. Where, how, and for what purpose the martyrs are remembered must be carefully and critically examined, as I hope to do at the end of my remarks.

First, however, I want to make some comments about Daniel's and Karen's papers, and how they read the dynamics of martyrdom in Latin America. Both rely on an expanded view of martyrdom as extending beyond those who are killed simply because they profess Christianity. In traditional terms, the title "martyr" was reserved to those who were killed *in odium fidei*, out of hatred for the Christian faith. Martyrdom was a much tidier affair when Christians were being persecuted by pagans. It is much more difficult, as Daniel points out, when the persecutors also claim to be Christians, indeed claim to be *the true* Christians. Nevertheless, it is clear that the church has come to use the language of martyrdom for those priests, ministers and laypeople who have been killed in their quest for a more just Latin America. Oscar Romero, for example, is widely revered as a martyr by the common people throughout Latin America. Even Pope John Paul II, in an address six days after Romero's assassination, referred approvingly to the martyrology of modern Latin America. He said:

> We cannot forget those who in our day have suffered death for the faith and for the love of Christ, those who in different ways have been jailed, tortured, condemned to death and even mocked, despised, humiliated and marginalized socially. The

> *martyrologium* of the church and Christians of our day cannot be forgotten. This *martyrologium* is written with different characters from the ancient ones. There are other methods of martyrdom and another way of giving testimony; but all springs from the same cross of Christ and completes the same cross of our redemption.[1]

There is more than just this reference. In officially canonizing Maria Goretti as a "martyr of purity" – she was a young Italian girl who died while resisting rape – the Vatican has opened up the definition of martyr well beyond the traditional paradigm.

I think Daniel is right to expand the definition of martyrdom to include persecution for what he calls "an involved Christian practice". The definition of martyrdom can be expanded if we refuse to accept distinctions between the "religious" aspects of Christianity and their "political" consequences. Martyrdom is not and never was a purely "religious" act of dying because of certain beliefs about Jesus. As the early martyrologies emphasized, the martyrdom was an *imitatio Christi*, an imitation of Christ, a participation in the triumph of Christ over the principalities and powers. In Christ's death, says the letter to the Colossians, God "disarmed the rulers and authorities and made a public example of them, triumphing over them in it" (Col. 2:15). The martyrs participate in the same action, which is a political act, as the very language of the "Kingdom" of God makes clear. As Daniel says, Jesus' executioners were "forces of the anti-kingdom" as are those repressive military forces in Latin America who have thwarted Christian attempts to create a more just social order. Those who give their lives in the service of the kingdom deserve to be called martyrs, because they are witnesses not only to the name of Jesus but to the politics of Jesus.

As scholars like Neil Elliott, Richard Horsley and Dieter Georgi have pointed out, awareness of the political significance of witnessing to Jesus is already present in the Pauline corpus. Georgi has noted that many of the key terms used by Paul were already key terms in Greco-Roman political theology. Two examples of many are εὐαγγελίον, a technical term for "news of victory" in the Roman vocabulary of international diplomacy, and πίστις, which was used with its Latin counterpart *fides*, to describe loyalty to Caesar. Georgi believes that Paul deliberately used imperial vocabulary to establish a context of confrontation between loyalty to Caesar and loyalty to Jesus Christ.[2] As N.T. Wright summarizes this line of thinking, Paul's

> missionary work must be conceived not simply in terms of a traveling evangelist offering people a new religious experience, but of an ambassador for a king-in-waiting, establishing cells of people loyal to this new king, and ordering their lives

1 Pope John Paul II, Angelus address, March 30, 1980, quoted in Paul Debesse, *Mártires latinoamericanos de hoy,* Ediciones Paulinas, Santiago, 1991, p.118.

2 Dieter Georgi, "God Turned Upside Down", in Richard A. Horsley, (ed.), *Paul and Empire: Religion and Power in Roman Imperial Society,* Trinity International Press, Harrisburg, PA, 1997, pp.148-157.

> according to his story, his symbols, and his praxis, and their minds according to his truth. This could not but be construed as deeply counterimperial, as subversive to the whole edifice of the Roman Empire.[3]

The plain sense of 1 Corinthians 15:24 then includes opposition to empire: "Then comes the end, when he hands over the kingdom to God the Father, after he has destroyed every ruler and every authority and power."

The early church was aware of the political implications of martyrdom, and for that reason I would want to be more cautious perhaps than Daniel in drawing sharp contrasts between the Fathers' understanding of martyrdom and the modern Latin American understanding. In Daniel's chart, the Fathers seem focused on martyrdom as a "religious" act, one focused on atonement for sin, the afterlife, and beliefs instead of deeds. The distinction between "religious" and "political" may not have been so sharp in the early church, however. Pliny in Asia Minor applied the Emperor Trajan's ban on "political societies" (*hetaeriae*) to the Christians, ordering suspension of their ritual corporate meals and creating martyrs in the process.[4] Forty years later, the account of Polycarp's martyrdom makes clear that Caesar and Christ were seen as rival monarchs. Christians were, after all, largely persecuted because they refused to offer incense to the emperor, an act as political as it is religious.[5] Christians were persecuted because they were a threat to the good order of Roman society. The *Apostolic Tradition* of Hippolytus refuses to allow entry to the catechumenate to those who want to become soldiers, because "they have despised God". That this was a threat to the Roman military order was lost neither on the Romans nor on the Christians. Hippolytus advises the catechumens that, should they be killed before they completed their catechumenate and were baptized, they would be considered baptized in their own blood.[6] Origen too describes martyrdom as a fully public combat between rival powers: "A great multitude is assembled to watch you when you combat and are called to martyrdom. It is as if we said that thousands upon thousands gather to watch a contest in which contestants of outstanding reputation are engaged."[7] The early church and the church Fathers, in sum, were not innocent of the political implications of their actions. They knew that they were being persecuted not for their beliefs alone, but because the church represented a rival social order, an advance of the kingdom of God which would rival the rule of any earthly monarch.

---

3 N.T. Wright, "Paul's Gospel and Caesar's Empire" in Richard A. Horsley, (ed.), *Paul and Politics: Ekklesia, Israel, Imperium, Interpretation,* Trinity Press International, Harrisburg, PA, 2000, pp.161-162.

4 Robert L. Wilken, *The Christians as the Romans Saw Them,* Yale University Press, New Haven, 1984, pp.12-15, 32-35.

5 Not only does *The Martyrdom of Polycarp* make clear that Polycarp refuses to sacrifice to the luck of Caesar, but the editor of the text adds a postscript in which Christ's name is substituted for the emperor's in giving the date of his martyrdom. The editor adds: "the ruling monarch was Jesus Christ, who reigns forever and ever." *The Martyrdom of Polycarp*, in Maxwell Staniforth, (ed.), *Early Christian Writings,* Penguin Books, Harmondsworth, 1968, p.163.

6 Hippolytus, *Apostolic Tradition*, ed. Geoffrey J. Cuming Grove Books, Bramcote, 1976, §17-20.

7 Origen, *Exhortation to Martyrdom*, trans. John J. O'Meara, Newman Press, New York, 1954, p.158.

I think it is important for the same reasons to see the full political import of apocalyptic language for martyrdom in the early church. Older generations of scholars were accustomed to contrast the apocalyptic with the earthly. Some found Gnostic motifs dominant in much of the Pauline corpus, such that the "rulers of this age" were supernatural powers. Apocalyptic language was considered "religious" and not political. Apocalyptic, however, can be read as a theological interpretation of historical political struggles, and this is crucial to how the early church read martyrdom. An apocalyptic reading of the martyrs sees them as providing the key to reading earthly history. The emperor who appears to rule in putting the martyrs to death does not really rule; it is rather those who have been slaughtered who rule. In an apocalyptic reading, the deaths of the martyrs do not signal the postponement of the kingdom of God; their deaths *are* the coming of the kingdom, the inauguration of the reign of self-sacrificial love. The church of the book of Revelation believed that it was participating in the Lamb's rule. The saints sing:

> You are worthy to take the scroll and to open its seals, for you were slaughtered and by your blood you ransomed for God saints from every tribe and language and people and nation; you have made them to be a kingdom and priests serving our God, and they will reign on earth (Rev. 5:9-10).

The church of the book of Revelation did not believe it would assume Caesar's power and rule like Domitian did, nor that the coming of God's reign was deferred until some decisive future coming of Christ, wielding the same kind of power that Caesar wielded. The church's statement about the slaughtered Lamb was a political statement about the way the world is really governed; despite appearances, the world is not really controlled by the kings and emperors of this world, but by the God who is embodied in the Crucified One. The political task of the church is to witness to the way that Christ rules, through servanthood that does not look much like sovereignty in the world's eyes.[8] The church is meant to make visible to the world what the justice of God looks like. The church claims to be nothing less than the visible body of the slaughtered Lamb.

The visibility of the church is an important theme in the veneration of martyrs. Origen's emphasis on the public nature of the contest, and Tertullian's famous remark about the blood of the martyrs as the seed of the church, show that the martyrs are to make Christ's body visible in the world. The military dictatorships of Latin America unfortunately learned this lesson all too well. They knew Tertullian was right, so they often attempted, in contrast to the Romans, to keep their killings out of the public eye. The word "disappearance" captures this strategy of invisibility. Torture and killing was often done in clandestine ways by secret

---

8 See John Howard Yoder, "To Serve Our God and to Rule the World", *The Royal Priesthood: Essays Ecclesiological and Ecumenical,* Eerdmans, Grand Rapids, MI, 1994, pp.130-135.

police. The strategy was meant to produce victims instead of martyrs, and thus to disappear the church as a rival, visible social body. Karen and Daniel point to this strategy very effectively in their papers. The purpose of repression was to eliminate organized social bodies that would rival the state. The state's strategy was to atomize and individualize the body politic. The church's main form of resistance was therefore to provide a space for people to organize. As Karen puts it, "Just the idea to organize a group was already something daring." The military state knew that the martyrs' bodies provide a rallying point, a visible testimony around which to organize. The church is formed around the "dangerous memory" of Christ in the eucharist and of all the other martyrs who have taken up the cross and followed Christ. The elimination of martyrs was part of the strategy of eliminating the church as a rival social body.

Daniel is right to criticize the church hierarchy for often being complicit with repression. This is especially true, with some notable exceptions, of the hierarchy of the Catholic Church in Argentina, about which Daniel writes. I would be cautious, however, about drawing too sharp a distinction "between church as an institution in contrast to a church as a charismatic event". If the strategy of the military state is based upon the elimination of all rival institutions, then it is precisely as institution that the church can resist oppression. In Chile, this was seen most clearly in the Vicaría de la Solidaridad, a branch of the Catholic archdiocese of Santiago, which was able to survive and carry on its work of documenting human rights abuses and organizing groups of the poor only because it was part of the institutional church. The problem is not the institutionality of the church, but what kind of institution it has often become; charism and institution need not be opposed. Likewise, I would be cautious about drawing too sharp a distinction between "the *status quo* of clerical power in contrast to the renovation of the prophetical voice". Again, Daniel is absolutely right to point out that clerics have too often been silent in the face of repression. But clerical power need not be opposed to a prophetic voice. Not only does Latin America provide us with many examples of bishops, ministers and priests speaking out with a prophetic voice, but their prophecy often took on the power it did precisely because they occupied positions of power within the church. Oscar Romero, for example, could only become the voice of the voiceless because his position as archbishop gave him a platform from which the grievances of the voiceless could be publicly expressed. Even more than this, Oscar Romero only became prophetic when he became archbishop. The office itself seems to have awakened him to his own responsibility to represent the unrepresented. Granted, this does not seem to happen often. But my main concern is to see that we cannot too hastily give up on the institutionality of the church, because it is precisely as institution that the church is often able to resist the relentless atomization and individualization of social bodies that is so typical not merely of military regimes, but of modern states and liberal economies in general.

Nevertheless, Daniel's critical comments about the church must be kept in mind if we are to remember the martyrs rightly. As Daniel indicates, martyrology helps the church remember its most faithful following of Jesus. But, as Daniel says: "At the same time, paradoxically, Latin American Christian martyrology came to be the most shameful page of the Christian church." What he means is that those who were doing the killing were mostly members of the church too. In Christian countries, the failure to enact a just and loving social order must be counted as a failure of the church as well. One of the pitfalls of martyrology, in other words, is that we are tempted to remember only the martyrs on our side, and not the victims we produce. This is a constant temptation in the United States, where a martyrology of September 11, 2001 is incessantly reinforced in public discourse as a way of reinforcing US amnesia about the victims of its own policies. Public martyrology in the United States inculcates the idea that we were just minding our own business when we were suddenly attacked, ignoring the long and often unjust and bloody history of US dealings with the Muslim world and the global south more generally. Martyrology helps us remember September 11, 2001 and forget September 11, 1973. In the church as well, martyrology can produce amnesia if we are not careful. We prefer to remember Oscar Romero and forget the bishops who collaborated with military regimes across Latin America. It is, of course, right to remember and honour the martyrs, all those from bishops to the anonymous poor who truly gave their lives in imitation of Christ. But a true martyrology is not triumphalistic and always must include a confession of sin.

Perhaps an even deeper pitfall of martyrology is that it can become an exercise in tourism or nostalgia, an exciting visit to a place or time that is not our own. I am currently teaching a course on martyrdom in Rome to university students and it is very easy for them and me to get caught up in the drama and gory details of martyrdom, in large part because it doesn't match our own context at all. We celebrate their steadfastness, confident that we too would be steadfast in the face of persecution, but only because we think we will never face it. I find it interesting also that we are here now talking about Latin American military regimes that fell two decades ago. The last time I visited Chile, there was almost a kind of nostalgia for the Pinochet regime among some in the progressive church, because under the military regime the church had a visible opponent and a clear role. No one, of course, was nostalgic for the brutal repression and everyone was happy that Pinochet was gone. But then, the kingdom of light was clearly opposed to the kingdom of darkness. Martyrology was a way of keeping that clarity and visibility of the church alive today, when the church was looking for a clear social role.

In some ways the task of the church is more difficult now that military regimes have been replaced by more-or-less democratic governments that usually do not interfere with the hegemony of corporations and the functioning of the so-called "free" market. What does the church do now that martyrs are no longer being produced, but the kingdom of God is no nearer to being a political reality? The visibility of the kingdom of God is imperiled now as the visibility of the church diminishes as well. How does the church make visible the truth about who really rules the world when martyrdom disappears?

I think it is important to continue to tell the stories of martyrs past, both to warn against the dangers of renewed military rule in the future and to show that the church has resources in the Cross of Jesus Christ to resist oppression. But I think that the most urgent task for any martyrology today is not simply to tell the stories of martyrs past but to understand the social dynamics of martyrdom and the remembrance of martyrs. In particular, we need to understand that the underlying strategy of taming social bodies that would interfere with the state and the market is the same now as it was under the military regimes in Latin America. The martyrs teach us that the church – under any type of earthly rule – is meant to be a visible body witnessing to the kingdom of God, in which rule looks more like servanthood and self-sacrifice than what passes for rule in the earthly city. I think that both Daniel's and Karen's papers give us ample resources for undertaking that task.

Commemoration of Martyrs of the Struggle as a Contested Terrain in a Democratic South Africa: The Case of Inkosi Albert Luthuli

Simangaliso R. Kumalo

Introduction

The term "martyr" in Greek means "witness", referring to those who are witnesses of their faith. Therefore, the Christian martyr is not so much someone who has suffered and has died for Christ, as someone who has witnessed Christ in his life until the end. According to Professor Job Getcha, the Orthodox Church has commemorated the martyrs because it is convinced that they were models for others through their witness to the end.[1] This definition is adequate because it covers those who have been put to death for their faith but also people who witnessed their faith to the end whether they were put to death or died without being killed.

An important point of the Bose Symposium is that it suggests commemorations across denominational lines and ecumenical barriers. Martyrs must be embraced and celebrated by all Christians as long as they witnessed for the faith under difficult circumstances up to the end. For instance Catholic saints like St Francis, Lutherans like Martin Luther and Anglicans like Munchie Masemola are already being celebrated across denominational lines. This requires a continuous dialogue from different faith traditions that will lead to mutual recognition, reception and commemoration of those who belong to the cloud of witnesses from the whole universal church.

The emergence of democracy in South Africa in 1994 brought with it a new era and experience of freedom. This was meant to ensure a better future for all people. From its early inception the government sought ways through which it could bring about national healing and reconciliation for a society that had been at war with itself for over four centuries. This came from the realization that in all the African countries independence only came after difficult wars had been fought between the oppressed and their oppressors, leaving a deeply wounded and divided nation to pick up the pieces and re-build itself. Re-building a wounded nation requires more than economic and political development but also healing and reconciliation. This helps to break down the walls of the past, build relationships and enhance commitment to starting afresh as a nation. Without reconciliation and some kind of spiritual healing of the nation it is impossible to attain life in its real sense which in Zulu is referred to as *impilo,* or *bophelo* in Sotho. *Impilo* or *bophelo* is equivalent to Jewish *shalom* which refers to wholeness.

1 Job Getcha, "Celebrating All Saints, the Known and the Unknown: An Orthodox Approach for an Ecumenical Commemoration of Witnesses", see pp. 233-238.

There is a sense in South Africa in which even hardcore politicians have realized that political stability and development also require addressing the spiritual dimensions of the people which was under constant attack during the times of apartheid. Healing the spiritual dimensions of people's lives requires that we move to the spiritual realm of their lives which includes invoking the spirits of those who died for the cause of the struggle and who, from the Christian perspective, form part of the cloud of witnesses.

Having listened to a number of stories about how people were tortured, burned and killed and sometimes not buried properly, the Truth and Reconciliation Commission's (TRC) reparation committee recommended embarking on strategies of commemorating the lives of those who died in the struggle against apartheid.[2] The main aim was to promote healing of the wounds caused by their death, especially those of the members of their families, and to show appreciation for the contribution and total sacrifices they made in the liberation of the country.[3] It was also done to set their spirits at peace, most of whose bodies were scattered all over Africa where they were killed and buried, and to place their legacies at the disposal of the nation so that they could inspire all people to contribute to the building of a free and democratic South Africa. The work to be done included facilitating healing processes, providing financial resources, exhuming and reburial of the bodies of those killed, erecting monuments in their honour, naming public buildings and roads by using their names etc. It also included the building of Freedom Park, a national memorial centre in Pretoria, which tells the story of the pains and triumphs of the South African nation. A key component of the park is the Sikhumbuto Memorial Wall. This wall has the names of all South Africans who died in the wars that involved this country over the centuries. It can take up to 136,000 names and for now it has 76,000 names. All this is done so that it can keep their memories alive and recognize the ultimate sacrifice they paid for the freedom of the country, thus declaring them martyrs of the South African struggle for freedom.

As a result there has been a commemoration function throughout the country, which included the renaming of roads, towns and public buildings after martyrs. This has led to rigorous debates and contestations, sometimes even protest marches from dissatisfied groups. Public funds have been used unsparingly in these endeavours. With a mere glance at these commemorations we find the names of Oliver Tambo, Gert Sibanda, Solomon Mahlangu, Charlotte Maxeke, Nelson Mandela, Walter Sisulu, Govan Mbeki, Albert Luthuli etc. Such commemorations have been marred by vigorous contestations from different sections of society, thus making it difficult to achieve one of the principal aims which is to unite the nation and contribute to its healing and reconciliation. Instead the opposite has been the

---

2 The TRC was established by parliament through the Promotion of National Unity and Reconciliation Act, No.34 of 1995. See also T. Maluleke, "Dealing Lightly with the Wounds of my People", *Missionalia*, Vol. 25/3 (1997), p.325.

3 Desmond Tutu, *No Future without Forgiveness*, Rider, Johannesburg, 1999.

reality. In some cases, instead of bringing about healing, these commemorations have opened up the wounds of the past and promoted further divisions and anger. The church has not been spared from this confusion.[4] Naturally the church which has the greatest number of followers in the population should have been in the forefront of these commemorations but its role has been ambiguous, inconsistent and sometimes non-existent. Being a neutral-religious state,[5] the constitution of South Africa allows observation and religious practices, even in public institutions, without being biased towards any specific religion.[6]

Amongst those who have been commemorated repeatedly is the former president-general of the African National Congress (ANC) Inkosi Albert John Mvumbi Luthuli. On the surface Luthuli's commemorations have been dignified and without any contestations, but when one looks closer, one recognizes deep contestations ranging from the causes of death, purpose of commemoration, ownership of the person's legacy, beliefs underpinning commemorations, political and religious contestations. The aim of this paper is to highlight those underlying contestations by analyzing the commemorations of Inkosi Luthuli, so that through them we can have a window to the issues around the commemoration of martyrs not only in South Africa but on the whole continent of Africa.

The making of Inkosi Albert Luthuli: The first African Nobel Peace Prize winner

Albert John Mvumbi Luthuli was born in 1898 in Mt Solusi Mission near Bulawayo in Zimbabwe to a family with a tradition of both Christian and tribal leadership. His grandfather Ntaba was a chief of his small tribe at Groutville in the Umvoti Mission Reserve near Stanger, Natal. Luthuli's father was a younger son, John Bunyan Luthuli, who became a Seventh Day Adventist missionary and spent most of the last years of his life in missions among the Ndebele people of the then Rhodesia, the present day Zimbabwe. His mother Mutonya (née Gumede) joined her husband in Rhodesia where her third son, Albert John Mvumbi was born. After the death of her husband in 1909 Mrs Luthuli and her sons Alfred and Albert came back to South Africa. They settled at Vryheid and Albert was sent to Groutville to stay with his uncle Martin Luthuli who was by now the chief of Groutville so that he could be educated at the mission school.

Luthuli received his education at the mission starting with Groutville United Congregational Church (UCCSA), moving to John Dube's Ohlange[7] (another UCCSA

4 In the process of building the nation the Christian church has an important role to play because it influences a significant number of the population in the country since over 82 percent of the population claims to be religious and over 72 percent is Christian.

5 This means that in its constitution South Africa recognizes that it is a religious country and does not relegate religion to the individual level but brings it to the centre of society.

6 When the government passed the bill to build the Sikhumbuto Monument, by default the religious community, through pastors, imams, priests and sangomas, was brought in to play an important role by invoking the spirits of the departed and thus turning the victims of the struggle who died as villains into saints and ancestors of the nation.

7 John Langalibalele Dube had constructed the only mission industrial school to be built by an African in South Africa to promote holistic education e.g. education for the head, heart and hands.

institution) in 1914. Then he went to Edendale (Methodist Mission School and College) for his secondary school education, where he also did his teacher training. After completion he taught at a Methodist school at Blaauwbosch, a mission school under the granteeship of Rev. G.G. Mtembu. Luthuli remembers that it was through Rev. Mtembu's influence that he became more committed to the church and was ultimately confirmed and offered himself as a lay preacher. Then he got a bursary to continue with his teacher training at Adams College, also a mission station of the UCCSA. In 1927 Luthuli married Nokukhanya Bhengu. After finishing his studies at Adams the institution offered him a position as a lecturer under the leadership of Z.K. Mathews.[8] In 1936 he was elected by the elders of his tribe in Groutville to be the chief of the Umvoti Mission Reserve, a position he held till 1952 when he was deposed by the government because of his political activities. In 1944 Luthuli joined the African National Congress (ANC). In 1945 he was elected to the Committee of the Natal Provincial Division of ANC and in 1952 to the presidency of the organization nationally. This marked the beginning of suffering which he had to endure at the hands of the police. He was arrested and banned several times, not being allowed to attend meetings and placed under house arrest. He was ordered by the government to leave the presidency of the ANC or lose the chieftaincy. He refused to leave either of the positions arguing that for both of them he had been democratically elected by the people and not by an illegitimate government so he would not abide by their disposition.

His approach to the struggle was non-violent but by direct action. He believed that violence must be avoided at all costs in favour of what he called extra-parliamentary methods of engagement.[9] He travelled throughout the country preaching the gospel of standing up against the apartheid system but doing this without engaging in violence. He had actually committed himself to carrying the cross of Christ as a way of leading his people to freedom. He once wrote in a statement titled The Road to Freedom is via the Cross:

> In this effort I always pursued what liberal-minded people rightly regarded as the path of moderation. Over this great length of time I have, year after year, gladly spent hours of my time with such organizations of the church and its various agencies such as the Christian Council of South Africa, the Joint Council of Europeans and Africans and the now defunct Native Representative Council.
>
> ...As for myself, with a full sense of responsibility and a clear conviction, I decided to remain in the struggle for extending democratic rights and responsibilities to all sections of the South African community. I have embraced the non-violent passive

8 Z.K. Mathews was the leader of the ANC in the Cape, a professor and head of Fort Hare University. He was highly respected and was the brain behind the Congress of the People and drafted the Freedom Charter which became, and still is, the manifesto of the ANC. Luthuli was mentored by Mathews who was himself a committed member of the UCCSA.

9 Documentary on Chief Albert Luthuli, KZN Dept. of Arts and Culture, 2007.

> resistance technique in fighting for freedom because I am convinced it is the only non-revolutionary, legitimate and humane way that could be used by people denied, as we are, of effective constitutional means to further their aspirations... It is inevitable that in working for freedom some individuals and families must take the lead and suffer: The Road to Freedom is via the Cross.[10]

In 1953 Luthuli made contact with the relatively unknown African American leader Martin Luther King and together they co-signed a declaration against racism. Again in 1962 in a joint statement with Dr King, Luthuli called for economic and arms sanctions against South Africa in the light of the Universal Declaration of Human Rights adopted by the UN in 1948. In this statement Luthuli and King declared: "So there exists another alternative and the only solution which represents sanity-transition to a society based upon equality for all without regard to colour."[11] He also went to India to lobby support for the fight against apartheid. By going to India he followed Mahatma Gandhi's trail and was more inspired to follow the path of non-violence. His commitment to non-violence was recognized in 1960 when he was awarded[12] the Nobel Peace Prize, becoming the first African to win that award.

Inkosi Luthuli died on 21 July, 1967, at the age of sixty-nine. He was found dead on a railway line and it was purported by the authorities that he was hit by a freight train. His family has refused to accept the official version of the story of his death and believe he was assassinated. However there has been no evidence to prove those allegations as there is no evidence that he was hit by a train. This leaves the conclusion open as to whether Luthuli is a martyr or not. Two things emerge from the above discussion. First is the fact that Luthuli's commitment to the struggle and the methods he chose of non-violence were underpinned by his Christian faith. Second, does the controversy around the cause of his death, considering that for the state he was *persona non grata,* allow space for him to be declared a martyr?

The commemoration of Inkosi Albert Luthuli

There are a number of ways through which Luthuli has been commemorated in South Africa. These include the proclamation of his home as a national museum because of the role it came to play as a meeting place for domestic and international leaders who consulted with him on issues of justice and the struggle of the South African people. The home has a statue of him at his desk crafted to provide a symbolic presence. Other ways of commemorating him are the naming of a hospital, the International Convention Centre in Durban and the choir festival known as the Albert Luthuli Choral Music Eisteddfod. One of the main roads in Pietermaritzburg has been named after him. His name also appears

10 K. Asmal, *South Africa's Nobel Laureates,* Jonathan Ball Publishers, Johannesburg, 2004, p.4.
11 http://www.anc.org.za/ancdocs/history/lutuli/let6211.html#appeal
12 The prize to Luthuli was reserved in 1960 and distributed on December 1961.

prominently at the Sikhumbuto national monument amongst the 76,000 names of prominent South Africans who died in different struggles for the freedom of South Africa.[13] The University of KwaZulu-Natal has established the Inkosi Albert Luthuli Peace Chair and an annual Memorial Lecture in his honour. Over two dozen commemoration celebrations have been held so far in his honour. In most of these functions there is prayer, Christian song, sometimes a Bible reading and short messages, speeches, freedom songs, political slogans and the singing of the national anthem. The purpose of these commemorations is, according to the Premier of KwaZulu-Natal, to "immortalize his legacy".[14] In one of these commemorations, while paying tribute to Luthuli, former President Nelson Mandela described him as a "colossus" and foot soldier of our people who chose persecution and taught us the non-violent strategies of engaging government.

Contestations in the commemoration of martyrs in South Africa

Commemorating a person of Luthuli's stature, someone who was an African, a Christian, a politician and traditional leader, has raised a number of contestations. This is because a number of diverse and conflicting groups claim ownership of the person including his/her legacy. This is well demonstrated in Luthuli's case where a number of interest groups have claimed him, his story and name. These groups range from the family, political organizations and even the church. These contestations are inevitable in the commemoration of important people but they demean their legacy and pollute their remembrance by making them symbols of division amongst people instead of points of celebration.

Luthuli may have been killed somewhere by the security forces of the apartheid government and dumped next to the railway line or he might have been pushed onto the rails by the same people from the security forces. An inquest was held which included a lawyer who represented the Luthuli family and it found no reason to believe that he had been murdered. However the family and his followers have continued to hold that he was murdered despite the fact that there is no evidence of this, thus making him a martyr. The level of commitment to God that Luthuli demonstrated in a dangerous ministry when opposing the heretic system of apartheid and his desire to be faithful to the end should alone be enough to qualify him to be declared a martyr in spite of the unclear circumstances surrounding his death. If we use loyalty to the end as the main criteria of commemorating martyrs there are a lot of people who deserve to be commemorated, including Luthuli and many others who have not been commemorated for different reasons.

---

13 Freedom Park celebrating peace: http://www.mediaclubsouthafrica.com/index.php?option=com_content&view=article&id=338:freedompark080408&catid=44:developmentnews&Itemid=111.

14 S. Ndebele, Remarks by KwaZulu-Natal Premier Sibusiso Ndebele at the commemoration of 40 years since the death of Inkosi Albert Luthuli. Held at KwaDukuza on Sunday, 4 November 2008, p.2.

Contestation on whether Luthuli changed his mind about a peaceful means for the struggle or not

In 1961 the ANC formed Umkhonto WeSizwe, a military wing. This was within days of Luthuli receiving the Nobel Peace Prize reserved to him the year before[15]. Contemporary leaders of the ANC claim that he knew about the decision to embark on violence even though he did not agree with it. Others argue that Luthuli did not know about the plan to embark on guerrilla and violent means in the struggle. The commemoration of Luthuli is contested because different interest groups would like to emphasize particular opposing points which favour their agenda. Militant groups have manipulated his legacy to support their actions and agendas. For instance, in the early 1990s when the IFP was blamed for violence and discouraged from carrying traditional weapons in public, they used pictures of Luthuli holding a stick and so argued that even Luthuli carried a traditional weapon. Actually a stick is not necessarily carried as a weapon unless one uses it for that purpose. Groups wanting to promote peace and non-violence have also used Luthuli's legacy of being a pacifist.

Another form of contestation on the Luthuli legacy and commemoration is that among the political organizations, some have sought to use his name to enhance their political agendas and use it as a card to draw political support. Commemorating martyrs therefore requires extensive discussions and processes that will involve as many stakeholders as possible to avoid hidden agendas.

Other contestations are the religious ones where you have African Christianity and Western Christianity contesting for space or the role to play in the commemoration service itself or in teaching the reasons and beliefs on the commemoration. African Christianity was a result of African Christians coming up with their own response to the gospel in a new "popular piety"[16] through which they articulated their own theology that emerged from their context and experienced reality. African Christianity can be found both within the mainline churches and also outside amongst the African Independent Churches. What is important to note is that most African Christians adhere to this form of Christianity, so it is the dominant one in the whole country. This type of Christianity has not been explored enough simply because, as Anderson observed, its "methods do not fit neatly into the Western theological categories".[17] Some of the popular rituals of recognizing the dead in African communities are *ukubuyisa* (bringing back to the home the spirit of the deceased), the unveiling of a tombstone, *ukumbulwa kwetje,* etc., or the naming of a child by the name of a deceased

15 See note 12.
16 Hans-Jürgen Becken, "Beware of Ancestor Cult! A Challenge to Missiological Research in South Africa", *Missionalia*, 21/3 (1993), p.333.
17 A. Anderson, *Bazalwane: African Pentecostals in South Africa,* University of South Africa, Pretoria, 1993, p.39.

person. In African traditional society, although there were tombstones, they were not labeled with the names of the deceased obviously because the community was illiterate, but a sharp stone used to be placed on the head of the tomb to mark the direction of the tomb. In African communities ancestors are understood to influence the living and appear to them through dreams, visions and sometimes in the form of snakes. Dreams would be understood as forms of revelation through which the dead communicate with the living.[18] Other sources of revelation used by Africans are diviners – *iSangoma*. These are people who have the ability to mediate between the living and the dead. Recently the lines between diviners and Christian prophets in the African Independent Church (AIC) have been blurred. Most Sangomas also go to church and pray to God to heal people and prophets would also consult ancestors on behalf of the people. Thus Oosthuizen is right in observing that some "AIC prophets are at the same time diviners".[19]

The close collaboration between diviner's *iSangoma,* AIC prophets and pastors in the celebration of the ancestors or saints demonstrates a possibility of bringing the three together in the commemoration of the departed heroes in a more inclusive and all embracing manner and attitude. The Pentecostal Church and mainline churches that still hold onto western forms of Christianity are churches such as the Methodists, Lutherans and Anglicans and more importantly the United Congregational Church of South Africa (UCCSA) which was Luthuli's church in which he spent his whole life as a lay preacher. The UCCSA has not participated in most of the commemorations of Luthuli simply because its theology is ambiguous if not silent on the commemoration of the dead. Most importantly it is not comfortable with the idea of commemorating him along with competition from the political organizations and proponents of African Christianity who dominate these commemorations. I contend that this calls for a dialogue between the dominant religions and political organizations in the country to work together throughout the processes of commemorating our national ancestors and martyrs. It calls for the recognition that the basic human beliefs that are shared by humankind across the different religious orientations and political divides should be brought into dialogue and form the basis of these commemorations. As Hans-Jürgen Becken has observed:

> For it is not enough to scrap apartheid laws from the rule book; the attitudes of people must be changed if we are to know peace in our country. And the first and most important step on this road is to understand, to respect, and to esteem each other's cultural identity.[20]

---

18 B. Sundkler, *Bantu Prophets in South Africa,* Oxford University Press, 1961, pp.265-275.

19 G. Oosthuizen, *The Healer-Prophet in Afro-Christian Churches,* (Studies in Christian Mission 3), E.J. Brill, Leiden, 1992, pp.165-193.

20 Becken, p.339.

During the Sikhumbuto commemorations the organizers invited priests, imams, Sangomas and pastors to give their blessings. It became an opportunity for the religious leaders of the nation, from their different faiths, to participate collaboratively, each one bringing resources from their tradition to contribute to the commemorations. Instead of the commemorations being a place of contestation and division they became a point of sharing and mutual collaboration. In a number of celebrations on Luthuli the Christian pastors have dominated the religious roles simply because he was Christian; however it is the prerogative of the church to encourage the participation of people of other faiths.

Martyrologies and order of service

Another area of contestation in the commemorations has been on the order of service. The church has not had an upper hand on the order of service because these commemorations are normally organized by the government or ruling party. Churches are invited but they do not determine the order of service. Pastors might be asked to pray, read Scripture, give a short message and then close with a word of prayer. This makes it difficult for the pastor to conduct the service following the liturgy of the church for the commemoration of martyrs. Linked to that is that most of the people who are commemorated have had no church background or belonged to churches that did not have liturgies for the commemorations of martyrs, like for instance, in Luthuli's case, the UCCSA which does not have a liturgy for such a service. So a contemporary prayer will be said and a reading of whatever text he might feel comfortable with to preach on, and sometimes it will have no bearing on the purpose of the service. The songs will be divided into three categories. First you hear songs that mourn the death or sometimes celebrate it as victory over the pain of this world. Other songs that dominate such services are political ones that are full of slogans and have nothing to do with the service, such as Jacob Zuma's *Lethu Umshini Wami*. Such songs are not only inappropriate in this kind of service because they are not Christian, but also because they are revolutionary, they do not take into account the current dispensation of a democratic government. Linked to the above is that the Catholic and Anglican churches that have liturgies for this are normally not included in these services, unless the person commemorated belonged to them. Therefore such services require churches to collaborate and negotiate with the organizers and other officials to allow them to include their liturgy. A more inclusive and all-embracing liturgy which cuts across the denominational divide needs to be developed.

Having discussed the difficulties that confront the church with regard to commemorating the cloud of witnesses in South Africa, I propose that the church needs to start discussing services of commemorating their martyrs, at least ecumenically. The church can participate in the commemorations that government or political organizations invite them to, but they must have their own services, choose the names of people they would like to commemorate, set out the criteria, subject the names to rigorous scrutiny and plan liturgies, commemorate their martyrs and write down martyrologies and inspire their members to conduct commemorations in the future. This requires that the church claim these martyrs who, most of the time, were formed and moulded by it. For instance someone like Luthuli owes his being to the work of the church, born at a mission station, educated in mission schools, taught in mission schools, elected to be chief of a Mission Reserve community, inspired by the Christian faith to join the struggle, preaching the gospel at his local church, seeing his involvement in politics as a form of Christian service, inspired by his Christian faith to hold onto non-violent but peaceful means to the struggle until he died. It is fitting for the church to commemorate him independent of the government and the ANC. In this celebration the church can collaborate across denominational lines, even religious ones, but on its own terms. This will be an opportunity for the South African church to celebrate its own martyrs even before they are celebrated by other countries and global bodies. For instance in Westminster Abbey I was embarrassed to come across the statue of Munchie Masemola among those of Oscar Romero, Martin Luther King and Juanani Luwum. I never knew of Munchie Masemola, a saint from Limpopo who was killed by her parents at the age of 15 for her faith. There is a sense in which the contestations around the commemorations of Inkosi Albert Luthuli should be teaching the South African church to be pro-active in commemorating their own martyrs and those who have joined the cloud of witnesses.

At the Luthuli commemoration the text that was used was Exodus 13:19-20 which talks about Moses taking the bones of Joseph with them to the Promised Land. In other services that I have attended of a similar nature I have heard pastors reading the texts that talk about the laying of memorial stones such as 1 Samuel 12:7, where Moses placed a memorial stone and called it Ebenezer, Genesis 28:10-20 and others. People use texts that relate to death, memory and stones. These texts are read literally without any criticism. The tendency is to use what Gerald West calls the "text itself" mode of reading the Bible.[21] However what is important is that the Bible becomes a resource that is used to justify the commemoration of those who have died and are considered to be heroes of the nation. What are also common in services of commemoration are the opportunities given to the family, friends, comrades and others to share testimonies – *ubufakazi* – about the deceased. These exclude the official speakers who are in the programme but just ordinary people who are given opportunities to share from their own unsolicited perspectives of what the person had done. Usually these stories will tell a lot about the person's convictions, the price he/she paid for them, how they were relevant for the Christian faith and why they should be regarded as heroes of the faith. These unsolicited and usually unprepared testimonies that come from the hearts of

21 G. West, *Biblical Hermeneutics of Liberation: Modes of Reading the Bible in the South African Context*, Cluster Publications, Pietermaritzburg, 1995, p.24.

people are taken seriously and contribute to the justification of the commemoration of the person. Ultimately it is the ordinary people through their testimonies and participation who commemorate a person.[22]

Monuments as meeting points for politics and religion

In the South African situation it is noteworthy that it is not the church that came up with the idea of commemorating some of these martyrs but rather it was an act of government. In fact, with regard to some of them, the church did not play even a small role except to be invited by government to participate in the commemoration and to conduct the rituals which only the church can do. For instance, in spite of the fact that Luthuli was a devout Christian and offered his life both in the church and in the struggle, that he even gave testimony that it was his faith as a Christian that motivated him to be involved in the struggle, the church did not take seriously the need to commemorate his life. However, once the government had decided to commemorate it and invited the church, the church joined in and together politicians and religious people collaborated, planned the proceedings, shared roles and played significant though different roles in the service. Songs, prayers, slogans and symbols were both Christian and political. For instance, there were crosses and Bibles carried, but there were also flags – one of the ANC and the national flag. In this commemoration you see politics and religion coming together. Luthuli is not the only one commemorated by politicians; in fact an extreme case is that of Maqhamsela Khanyile, the first Zulu convert, who was killed by Zulu king Dingane for converting to Christianity thus becoming the first Zulu martyr some 130 years ago. He was Lutheran. However it was the provincial government that facilitated Khanyile's commemoration and the church only joined the day of commemoration and participated in the consecration rituals. This brings to our attention that the commemoration of some martyrs can be a point of collaboration for national unity by bringing together religion and politics for mutual benefit. For Albert Luthuli to be celebrated in a meeting that brings politics and religion together is fitting to his character and his form of Christianity because it brought the two together. He wrote that:

> For myself, I am in the Congress (ANC) precisely because I am a Christian. My Christian belief about human society must find expression here and now, and congress is the spearhead of the real struggle… My own urge, because I am a Christian, is to get into the thick of the struggle with other Christians, taking my Christianity with me and praying that it may be used to influence for good the character of the resistance.[23]

---

22 P. Denis, "Prayers and Rituals to the Ancestors as Vehicles of Resilience: Coping with Political Violence in Nxamalala, Pietermaritzburg (1987-1991)", *Journal of Theology for Southern Africa,* 128, July (2007), p.37.

23 A. Luthuli, *Let my people go*, Collins Fount Paperbacks, London, 1962, p.138.

This qualifies Luthuli to have been commemorated as a martyr and a prominent member of the cloud of witnesses for he dedicated his life and put his Christian faith into practice by fighting against racism and ultimately he lost his life in mysterious ways.

Conclusion

With those words of reconciliation and nation building we shall bring this paper to a conclusion. The vigorous attempts by the government and faith communities to commemorate the lives of heroes who lost their lives in the struggle for liberation are remarkable. South Africa was a highly divided country and for decades the nation was at war with itself. As a result there are deep scars and wounds that need healing. The question that might be asked is where the South African people, especially black people, find the strength to forgive and move forward. One answer to that question is that they find it from their heroes like Albert Luthuli who, like Nelson Mandela, did not drink from the cup of bitterness but rather found peace in forgiving their persecutors. The next question that arises is where they found the strength to fight for justice under persecution and also to be able to forgive. A simple answer is in their religion and culture. There is no evidence that the naming of buildings and roads such as those in honour of Inkosi Albert Luthuli has inspired the people of South Africa to be more committed to national reconciliation and unity. But when you have observed and listened to the people in commemoration services, one is aware that their songs, prayers, readings, testimonies and rituals to God and the ancestors have given them strength to go forward and so the monuments will stand as testimony and inspiration for them to move forward in unity as one nation. The South African church has not yet joined the party of commemorating martyrs of the struggle; I suppose that it is still too early for this. Is it not time to reflect and then embark on the vigorous journey of celebrating those who remained faithful to the faith right up to the end? We will then realize that the commemoration of the cloud of witnesses is always a contested terrain, an unfinished business and work-in-progress, for their contribution and witness is much wider and needs human beings to evaluate it with consensus.

Protestant Martyrs under the Nazi Regime

Andreas Kurschat

In German Protestant theology, views about martyrdom have evolved in the 20th century in the context of reflections and debates about different cases of Christians who were subject to persecution by the National Socialist regime. The first case was that of Pastor Paul Schneider. Two other important cases were those of the pastors Karl Friedrich Stellbrink and Dietrich Bonhoeffer. They had all suffered a violent death and were therefore spontaneously commemorated as martyrs by Christians who knew them. But there were significant differences between these three cases and these differences essentially affected their recognition as martyrs.

Paul Schneider, a member of the Confessing Church,[1] was subject to persecution on account of his open criticism of anti-Christian tendencies emerging from National Socialism. He was determined to defend his belief against this new ideology. Hence, he explained his acts of disobedience to the regime by explicitly referring to his understanding of the Bible, particularly of Acts 5:29: "We must obey God rather than men." In 1937, he was imprisoned in the concentration camp at Buchenwald, where he continued his preaching. He was heavily tortured and died there in 1939, presumably poisoned by a doctor. Soon after his death, many Christians considered him a martyr. The term was attributed to him in early biographical publications as well as in official documents of the Confessing Church, and its appropriateness was undisputed, because it was evident that Schneider had been persecuted for the witness he bore in exercise of his ministry as a pastor of the Confessing Church.[2]

Karl Friedrich Stellbrink, in contrast, never joined the Confessing Church. In the early 1930s, he played an active part in a nationalistic theological association called "Bund für deutsche Kirche". However, he did not participate in the movement of the "Deutsche Christen" (German Christians). Animated by a vision in which religious and political ideas converged, he desired to reorganize the church according to a specifically German reception of Christian traditions. He temporarily viewed the National Socialists as allies in this effort and joined their party in 1933, but was excluded in 1937 for having criticized their youth work. During World War II, he took an increasingly critical attitude towards the regime and associated with three like-minded Roman-Catholic priests for a confidential exchange of opinions and information. After Stellbrink had implied in a sermon that the German

1 The Confessing Church is a movement for revival within the German Protestant churches that developed during the 1930s from their resistance to Adolf Hitler's attempt to make the churches an instrument of National Socialist (Nazi) propaganda and politics. The German Protestant tradition of close cooperation between church and state, as well as dislike for the Weimar Republic that governed Germany after World War I, at first caused the churches to take a favourable attitude toward Hitler. (eds.)

2 Cf. Wolf-Dieter Hauschild, "Märtyrergedenken in der evangelischen Kirche", forthcoming in: *Zeitschrift für Kirchengeschichte* 120 (2009).

war policy might be an offence to God, he was arrested, sentenced to death and executed together with his three Catholic fellows in 1943. Instead of supporting him in his conflict, the church administration showed loyalty to the regime by dismissing him even before he was put on trial. Whereas Catholic Christians soon regarded Stellbrink as well as his three fellow sufferers as martyrs, Protestant theologians – especially from the Confessing Church – forcefully rejected this view for a long time, arguing that he had not been persecuted on religious, but on political grounds. It was implicitly denied that Stellbrink had borne witness, even though he had uttered his critical remarks on the war in a sermon. In fact, like Paul Schneider, he definitely became the target of the secret police in exercise of his ministry. The prolonged refusal to recognize Stellbrink as a martyr was obviously due to the fact that he had not been associated with the Confessing Church, but first with a competing Protestant organization, then with the National Socialist party and finally with a group of Catholics. Because of his highly individual attitude, he was considered some kind of heretic, unworthy of commemoration in a confessionally bound Protestant church. Be that as it may, an ecumenical practice of jointly commemorating Stellbrink and his three Catholic colleagues as martyrs has emerged in the congregational context of their respective parishes. This practice has increasingly been supported by the Catholic and Protestant churches' administrations. In recent years, Stellbrink has received special attention in both churches, because the Catholic clergy has initiated the proceedings to beatify his three Catholic fellow sufferers as martyrs. As a result, the differences between the Catholic and the Protestant concepts of holiness will probably become more overt than they have been during the last decades in the practice of commemorating these four martyrs.[3]

Dietrich Bonhoeffer is undoubtedly the most prominent German Protestant who is commemorated as a martyr today. But although, like Paul Schneider, Bonhoeffer had been a member of the Confessing Church, some of his former associates did not regard him as a martyr in any way. They argued that he had been persecuted for his political activities, but not for his religious beliefs. In contrast to Stellbrink, Bonhoeffer was in fact not arrested and finally executed on account of any activities in exercise of his ministry as a pastor. The reason for Bonhoeffer's death was his involvement in a conspiracy against the government, while he was working for a German military intelligence unit. However, his willingness to support the resistance against the National Socialist regime was definitely based on his religious beliefs. Moreover, he constantly considered his options very carefully within the frame of theological ethics, which is palpable in his writings. As early as 1933, he had stated that the church might

3 Cf. Andreas Kurschat, "Martyrien des 20. Jahrhunderts. Voraussetzungen und Prinzipien ihrer Dokumentation", in Harald Schultze and Andreas Kurschat (eds.), "*Ihr Ende schaut an ....*" *Evangelische Märtyrer des 20. Jahrhunderts*, Evangelische Verlagsanstalt, Leipzig, 2006, pp.33-48, esp. p.36; 2nd improved and enlarged edition 2008, pp.35-50, esp. p. 38; Andreas Kurschat, Stellbrink, in: Harald Schultze and Andreas Kurschat (eds.), *Ibid.*., pp.446-448; 2nd improved and enlarged edition 2008, pp.478-480.

be challenged "nicht nur die Opfer unter dem Rad zu verbinden, sondern dem Rad selbst in die Speichen zu fallen" ("not just to bandage the victims under the wheel, but to put a spoke in the wheel itself").[4] Later, he realized that this option included treason and even physical violence. Consequently, he supported the efforts to assassinate Adolf Hitler and remove the regime by force. But such an attitude was incomprehensible to many Germans, and officials from the Confessing Church were reluctant to appreciate it, even after the end of the regime. In 1945, on the first anniversary of the 20 July plot, Bonhoeffer's home church of Berlin-Brandenburg issued an announcement saying that the church could "niemals gutheißen" ("never countenance") the plot, regardless of its objectives.[5] Viewed from abroad, however, the conspirators were judged completely differently. At a memorial service in London on 27 July 1945, George Bell, Bishop of Chichester, who had been closely related to Bonhoeffer for several years, paid tribute to Bonhoeffer and all the others who had died on account of their resistance to the National Socialist regime and he referred to them all as martyrs.[6] One year later, at a memorial service in Berlin on the first anniversary of Bonhoeffer's death, different views were expressed in two addresses. On the one hand, Winfried Maechler, a pastor who had been a friend of Bonhoeffer's, appreciated Bonhoeffer's political resistance and, in substance, acknowledged him as a martyr, namely as "einen von den Zeugen, die Jesus Christus gewürdigt hat, ihn auch durch ihren Tod zu preisen" ("one of the witnesses to whom Jesus Christ has given the honour of praising him even by their death"); on the other hand, Otto Dibelius, the Bishop of Berlin-Brandenburg, emphasized Bonhoeffer's theological gifts, but avoided any reference to Bonhoeffer's conflict with the regime.[7] The view prevailed that Bonhoeffer was a martyr. In 1948, the newly formed Evangelical Church in Germany jointly commemorated him, Paul Schneider and some other members of the Confessing Church as martyrs and, in 1953, a memorial to them was established in the Cathedral of Brandenburg on Havel and opened on the eighth anniversary of Bonhoeffer's death.[8]

For several years, attention to martyrdom among Protestants under the National Socialist regime remained focussed on these few active members of the Confessing Church. Most of them had been pastors and most of them had been persecuted on account of activities related to their respective function in the Confessing Church. The importance of their religious beliefs was obvious. None of them had been directly involved in violent activities to remove the regime. Bonhoeffer was the only one who had explicitly justified the plans to assassinate Hitler. Consequently, the reception of his writings directed the attention of

4 Dietrich Bonhoeffer, "Die Kirche vor der Judenfrage", in *Dietrich Bonhoeffer Werke*, ed. by Eberhard Bethge et al., vol. 12, ed. by Carsten Nicolaisen and Ernst-Albert Scharffenorth, Chr. Kaiser-Gütersloher Verlagshaus, Munich and Gütersloh, 1997, pp.349-358, quotation on p.353.

5 Leaflet quoted in Eberhard Bethge, *Dietrich Bonhoeffer. Theologe, Christ, Zeitgenosse*, Chr. Kaiser Verlag, München, 1967, p.1042; 8th corrected edition, Gütersloh, 2004, p.1042.

6 Text reprinted in: *Bonhoeffer Gedenkheft*, ed. by Eberhard Bethge, Haus und Schule, Berlin, 1947, pp.7-9.

7 Both texts reprinted in: *Bonhoeffer Gedenkheft*, pp.25-30, 34-35, quotation on p.30.

8 Cf. Kurschat, pp.33-48, esp. pp.35-37; 2nd improved and enlarged edition 2008, pp.35-50, esp. pp.37-39.

Protestant theologians also to those conspirators who had tried to put these plans into action. Under this influence, a modified concept of martyrdom evolved, which was more inclusive vis-à-vis Protestant Christians who had been persecuted on account of political activities, regardless of their relation to the Confessing Church.

The acknowledgement of political activities (including armed resistance against the regime) as forms of bearing witness in terms of Christian martyrdom may perhaps be attributed to the insight that martyrdom arises from a moral conflict, which may be specified as a conflict of loyalties. This kind of conflict was made explicit in the trial of Helmuth James Graf von Moltke, the head of the "Kreisauer Kreis", an opposition group of intellectuals, conservatives as well as liberals and social democrats, most of whom were Protestant Christians but not associated with the Confessing Church. At Moltke's trial in early 1945, the judge pointed out a single analogy between Christianity and the National Socialist regime, namely "wir fordern den ganzen Menschen" (we make demands on the whole person); then he added the following rhetorical questions: "Von wem nehmen Sie Ihre Befehle? Vom Jenseits oder von Adolf Hitler!" and "Wem gilt Ihre Treue und Ihr Glaube?" (From whom do you take your orders? From Beyond or from Adolf Hitler! and To whom is your loyalty and your faith?)[9] Even though Moltke had neither supported an assault on Hitler nor been involved in other violent activities, he was sentenced to death and executed on account of his disloyalty to the regime. He was not persecuted for his Christian beliefs as such, but for the political impact of those beliefs, namely his refusal to give obedience to the National Socialist rulers.

Regarding the moral issue of being loyal to God as the sovereign ruler above all human rulers, there is a parallel between the situation of Christians in National Socialist Germany and the situation of Christians in the Roman Empire, in which the tradition of commemorating martyrs emerged. In the Roman Empire, many Christians were executed on account of their refusal to worship the emperor as *dominus et deus*.[10] In National Socialist Germany, Christians were not required to worship the "Führer" but to display political conformity and, ultimately, to render unquestioning obedience to the "Führer", especially if they had taken an oath to Adolf Hitler as civil servants or soldiers. Such "demands on the whole person" may be regarded as compromising one's loyalty to God in no less a degree than acts of pagan worship had in late antiquity. But the vast majority of Christians in Germany dealt with this issue by somehow reconciling their loyalty to God with a large amount of loyalty to the regime. The few who were in conflict with the regime were left

9 Helmuth James Graf von Moltke, *Briefe an Freya 1939-1945*, ed. by Beate Ruhm von Oppen, Beck, Munich, 2007, p.622.

10 Cf. Wolfgang Wischmeyer, "Märtyrer II. Alte Kirche", in Hans Dieter Betz et al. (eds.) *Religion in Geschichte und Gegenwart. Handwörterbuch für Theologie und Religionswissenschaft*, 4th, completely revised edition, vol. 5, Mohr Siebeck, Tübingen, 2002, col. 862-865, esp. col. 863.

with little support. In this regard, there is a significant difference between the ancient Roman and the modern German context. In the Roman Empire, a Christian's refusal to worship the emperor did not harm his or her moral integrity from the point of view of other Christians, but it was appreciated as a pure act of faithfulness in the imitation of Christ. In National Socialist Germany, however, a Christian's refusal to display conformity was disfavoured by many other Christians and it entailed not only social isolation, but moreover, daily fear of denunciation even by other Christians. Active resistance against the totalitarian regime was not a single act, but a sequence of activities that were more or less illegal and often morally questionable, like deceiving in order to protect other people. The legal or moral dubiousness of these activities discredited the persons involved in them. Therefore, one may consider those Christians who lost their lives in such circumstances as a "neuen Typus des Märtyrers" (a new type of martyr): in contrast to the martyrs of the Roman Empire, they are not distinguished by absolute purity, but rather, to some degree they are tainted with guilt.[11] Nevertheless, as Protestant Christians they are at the same time justified by God's grace. Thus, they may be considered as examples – not of a perfect life, but of a life in which justification by God, loyalty to God and good works are closely related. Article 21 of the Augsburg Confession of 1530 says, "daß man der Heiligen gedenken soll, auf daß wir unsern Glauben stärken, so wir sehen, wie ihnen Gnad widerfahren, auch wie ihnen durch Glauben geholfen ist; darzu, daß man Exempel nehme von ihren guten Werken, ein jeder nach seinem Beruf" (that one should commemorate the saints, so that we reinforce our faith by regarding how grace has befallen them and how they were helped by faith; moreover, that one should follow the example of their good works according to one's calling).[12] The reference to the relationship between good works and one's calling is significant in so far as it implies that different professions may be the causes of different kinds of good works. Regarding the issue of martyrdom, one may conclude that it is not appropriate to focus only on the more obvious examples of pastors and other ministers of the church, but that the cases of ordinary church members are equally important examples.

Such an inclusive concept of martyrdom became manifest in a memorial plaque donated by Otto Dibelius, the Bishop of Berlin-Brandenburg, to be installed in the prominent Kaiser-Wilhelm-Gedächtnis-Kirche in Berlin. This memorial plaque was dedicated to "Den evangelischen Märtyrern der Jahre 1933-1945" (To the Protestant martyrs of the years 1933-1945). It was unveiled on the 20th anniversary of the 20 July plot in 1964, and the significance of this date was evident. It indicated not only that the plot, which the church had harshly

11 Eberhard Bethge, "Modernes Märtyrertum als gemeinsames evangelisch-katholisches Problem", in Eberhard Bethge, *Ohnmacht und Mündigkeit. Beiträge zur Zeitgeschichte und Theologie nach Dietrich Bonhoeffer*, Chr. Kaiser, München, 1969, pp.135-151, quotation on p.136.

12 *Die Bekenntnisschriften der evangelisch-lutherischen Kirche. Herausgegeben im Gedenkjahr der Augsburgischen Konfession 1930*, 12th edition, Vandenhoeck & Ruprecht,Göttingen, 1998, p.83b.

condemned 20 years before, was countenanced after all, but moreover that those Protestant Christians who had not survived persecution for being involved in the plot were acknowledged as martyrs. The mention of any names on the memorial plaque was avoided, so that no decision was implied as to who exactly was to be commemorated and who was not.[13]

Many Christians who might implicitly be included in the dedication of this memorial plaque did not receive any attention from the church for a long time however. Even though the plaque refers to them collectively, the persons to be commemorated remained as isolated and anonymous as they were when they died. The National Socialist regime had adjudged them unworthy of belonging to the German people; in many cases, especially of the 20 July plotters, the regime had even tried to erase their memory by preventing the mention of their names on tombstones. The church had largely failed to protest against this policy, but tacitly approved of it. In this regard, commemoration implies a belated statement of disapproval, and mentioning the dead by their names is probably the only possible form of rehabilitating them individually as members of the church, that is, the community of saints. In recent years, the Evangelical Church in Germany has faced this issue by supporting historical research in order to retrace the lives of these formerly overlooked martyrs.[14]

As a concluding remark, it should be noted that the commemoration of martyrs today is more inclusive than it was some decades ago. Based on the anti-hierarchical Protestant concept of holiness, the broadening perspective on martyrdom is not associated with a tendency towards canonization but with enhanced attempts to capture the scope of Christian witnesses.

---

13 Cf. Kurschat, pp.33-48, esp. p.38; 2nd improved and enlarged edition, 2008, pp.35-50, esp. p.40.

14 Cf. Karl-Joseph Hummel and Christoph Strohm (eds.), *Zeugen einer besseren Welt. Christliche Märtyrer des 20. Jahrhunderts*, Evang. Verlagsanstalt & Butzon & Berger, Leipzig and Kevelaer, 4th edition, 2002; also Harald Schultze and Andreas Kurschat 2nd, improved and enlarged edition 2008. The former book contains the biographies of thirteen Protestant and thirteen Roman-Catholic martyrs from different political contexts of the 20th century. The latter book comprises essays on various aspects of martyrdom as well as a biographical dictionary of more than 200 Protestant martyrs under the Nazi regime and almost 300 Protestant martyrs from other political contexts of the 20th century; its scope is ecumenical in so far as Christians from different denominations (e.g., Lutheran, Reformed, Baptist, Mennonite and Adventist) are included.

Martyrs for Christ in Communist Romania

Iustin Marchis

The Communist regime and the thinking behind its anti-Christian persecution

In Romania as elsewhere, the 20th century was the century of the martyrs. From being subsumed into the Soviet bloc on 23 August 1944 until December 1989, communist power held sway over the country – a totalitarian, pseudo-democratic regime driven by a materialistic, atheistic ideology, just like all the other governments installed by Soviet tanks across Eastern Europe. Communist Russia's own regime had been put in place by a revolution, but in these satellite states, including Romania, communism was imposed through an organized, well-planned and tightly controlled campaign. Having been brought to maturity in Russia, communism could now flex its muscles far more effectively in every way in the territories it had annexed – including with respect to repression.

Installed in pseudo-democratic elections on 6 March 1945, the new regime immediately set about identifying and destroying its opponents. Along with the historic parties and personalities of the old regime, the church was a constant object of preoccupation. The new communist state had two main ways of bending the land and its people into the image of its own programme and its own atheistic religion. The first was to wipe out all opponents, indeed, to eliminate the whole cultural, intellectual and spiritual elite. The second was to force through an institutional restructuring of every part of economic and social life. A first wave of mass arrests was carried out straight after 23 August 1944, in which hundreds of Christian leaders were executed for alleged political crimes. The "Congress of Religious Leaders" held on 16-17 October 1945 was supposed to demonstrate, with the help of the whole propaganda machine, that the new regime had brought religious liberty, and it did indeed herald a relaxation of that first wave of repression.

With the abdication of the king and the complete takeover by the communist regime in 1948, repression became systematic and focused on redefining the whole relationship between the church and society at large through a series of "reforms" passed in quick succession: reform of agriculture, monetary policy, property (nationalization), the economy (socialist industrialization), education and, of course, the church. That institution was hammered into a new shape, with a new status and a new form of organization, bereft of all forms of social expression (it was absolutely forbidden from undertaking any educational, charitable or social work). The stated ambition of the new system went beyond mere politics and economics: it was to change the very nature of human beings. To achieve this, it would orchestrate an unprecedented society-wide programme of "re-education" aimed at gaining control of human consciousness and creating the "new (hu)man" of communism. The regime's militant atheism was itself essentially a religion in negative, which found itself in competition with every other religious belief, and especially with Christianity. As its motives were so strongly ideological, this was a priority area of activity for the communist regime. One of the pillars of this "re-education" was political and ideological repression, with its palette of atrocities, from arrest, through torture and unjust sentencing right up to the physical elimination of its targets. Indeed, "re-education" was the name given to the chilling experiments in dehumanization perpetrated at Piteşti prison in the 1950s. The main targets of this repression were church leaders. While the communist state officially and institutionally accepted and tolerated the church, the truth was that Christians were persecuted for as long as communism reigned in Romania.

Outline chronology of persecution

Persecution was constant and systematic, but varied in intensity. Its harshest and most bloody period was in the 1950s, when communist prisons were filled with thousands of priests, monks and ordinary Christians of every confession, arrested for crimes of conscience under the guise of punishment for public order offences – for, officially, there was no such thing as religious persecution in communist Romania. Certain constant factors ran through all the arrests: the victim of arrest (which was usually carried out at night, for greater psychological effect) would be subjected to an interrogation, during which he would be pressured and tortured (physically and psychologically) to confess to anything his inquisitors desired. Generally, Orthodox Christians would be accused of belonging to the Iron Guard, Catholics of spying for the Vatican.

The first wave of repression eased in 1953-4 following the total annihilation of the Makid armed anti-communist resistance movement in the Carpathians. By the end of this period, almost the entirety of the country's cultural and political elite had also been liquidated, including the hierarchy of the Greek Catholic Church, either by actual execution or indirectly, by extermination in the awful regimes of the detention centres (such as Sighet prison). On 29 October 1952 Christian philosopher Marcea Vulcănescu died in prison from tuberculosis caught after spending several winter nights on the cement floor of the prison, with another, also seriously ill, prisoner lying on his chest, thereby saving that man's life. His last words were, "Don't avenge us". Monsignor Vladimir Ghika also died in prison, on 16 May 1954. Arrested on 18 November 1952 at a sick man's bedside, he was sentenced to three years' imprisonment on charges of espionage for the Vatican. After being tortured to confess to trumped-up accusations, the Cardinal perished in the prison's extermination regime. He was 80 years old.

The second wave of repression, unleashed at the end of the 1950s, targeted one of the most significant movements for spiritual revival, the Burning Bush group. The Burning Bush was led by the formidable journalist and polemicist Alexandru Teodorescu, alias Sandu Tudor who, having held leftist views between the two world wars, had entered monastic life under the name of Agaton in 1948 and first been arrested in 1950 and freed in 1952. He made his perpetual profession at Neamț Monastery and lived near Rarău, travelling frequently from there to Bucharest for Burning Bush meetings. The organization was linked to Bucharest's Antim Monastery and centred on Daniel Sandu Tudor and, at the start, a monk called Ioan Kulighin, a refugee from Russia and someone who practised hesychastic prayer. This connection brought together two of the great cultural and spiritual personalities of Romania. The group's main public activity was conferences on spiritual topics – hesychasm, or the prayer of the heart. The meetings were banned in 1948, and almost completely abandoned when their leader, Daniel Sandu Tudor, went to Moldavia, but were revived to a limited degree after 1955, in the home of the Mironescu family. It was here that Sandu Tudor and 15 others were arrested in the night of 13-14 June 1958. In truth, it had simply been a group interested in lectures and discussions on issues relating to the philokalia, but it had drawn attention to itself by promoting a hesychastic spirituality that went against the ritualistic formalism that the church was forced to follow.

There was another aspect to Daniel Sandu Tudor's activities that displeased the communist regime: he ran an educational and training project, bringing young intellectuals to the monastery and preparing them for the intensive work of translating the Church Fathers and the Bible. Although nothing in this group's activity contravened the framework of communist law, its members were nevertheless sentenced to between five and 25 years' imprisonment for its alleged "legionary", anti-working class activities. (This was an ironic sentence to pass against someone like Daniel Sandu Tudor who had consistently opposed the Legionaries in his writings, even when they had been in power.) In one report, the official prosecuting the group wrote the following notes:

> The prayer of the heart represents the most extreme form of Orthodoxy. It is in dangerous opposition to the current regime because, to perform it correctly, practicants of this form of prayer must give it constant internal repetition during waking hours. This leads to a separation from the regime and even from all activity – especially political activity."[1]

The prosecutor's point is vitally important for understanding the utter incompatibility between authentic Christian living and the model of life promoted by the communists. Sandu

1 Quoted by George Enache in *Orthodoxie et pouvoir dans la Roumanie contemporaine*, Nemira, 2005, pp.396-397.

Tudor received the severest possible sentence of 25 years' imprisonment, and died in Aiud prison on 16 November 1962.

The Burning Bush group included, among others, the following figures: the poet and doctor Vasile Voiculescu (born on 13 October 1884, he was given a mandatory sentence of five years' imprisonment in 1958 for "breach of the peace", the evidence presented by the prosecution being "the spiritual poems of Mr V. Voiculescu"; he contracted spinal tuberculosis and died shortly after release. His life was defined by the saying, "Never live a day without a good deed"); as well as students of that time who would survive prison to become spiritual leaders of great standing in later years, such as Roman Braga, Sofian Boghiu, Arsenie Papacioc, Benedict Ghiuş and Father Dumitru Stăniloae. The great theologian Stăniloae was 55 at the time of his arrest. He had moved to Bucharest in 1947, having been forced under pressure from the communist leadership of the day to leave Sibiu and the faculty of theology of which he had been professor and dean. In Bucharest he made contact with Burning Bush members and attended some of the group's meetings. He was arrested on 4 September 1958 for "opposition activities" and breach of the peace on the evidence of articles he had written in the review *Thought* and his participation in Burning Bush meetings, where discussions unfavourable to the people's democratic government had taken place with which he had been "in agreement"[2]. Professor Dumitru Stăniloae was sentenced to five years' forced labour on 15 January 1958. Happily, he survived prison and was released on 15 January 1963, by which time he was 60 years old. Father Dumitru Stăniloae's imprisonment and that of all the Burning Bush members showed that merely reading and making available the writings of the Church Fathers and, indeed, living the spiritual life itself were deemed such a threat that those who did so risked prison and death, and were seen as enemies of the communist regime.

At the institutional level also, spiritual life was penalized by Decree No. 410 of 1959, which all but destroyed monasticism and evicted thousands of monks and nuns from their monasteries and convents.

After 1965, anti-Christian persecution in Romania eased as the communist regime entered a new phase – that of Nicolae Ceauşescu's national communism. Striving for autonomy from Moscow (as clearly shown in the brief glory of his opposition to the invasion of Czechoslovakia in 1968), Ceauşescu sought support from the West. To get this, he had to alleviate – or at least appear to alleviate – the human rights situation at home. Thus the previous policy of harsh repression was jettisoned in favour of close and comprehensive surveillance of the whole of society. Many victims of persecution were released and resumed religious service after the political prisons were closed in 1964. However, the *Securitate*

2 *Ibid.*, pp.442-443.

continued to pursue them, with a greater or lesser degree of discretion; indeed, in some cases, surveillance and prosecution continued right up to 1989. The victims of this treatment included numerous important spiritual directors, preachers and monks. Some were part of the church hierarchy, others became archimandrites, still others exemplary priests; they can be called true saviours of their time. And yet the relative freedom of the 1970s was nevertheless tightly controlled. Churchmen were no longer actually put in prison, but Christian spirituality was still seen as dangerous. There was a ban on even using the term "Christian mysticism": in his writings, Father Dumitru Stăniloae had to resort to synonyms for it in order for his books to be published. In a way, the various restrictions led to the church taking on the aspect of a kind of "nature reserve", with the state preventing any real religious freedom that would have required a visible manifestation of the faith in public life. The removal of religion from schools and the various obstacles placed in the way of catechizing young people ultimately led to the raising of a generation that knew nothing of Christian values.

The problems of unearthing the past

The fall of the communist Ceauşescu regime in December 1989 marked the start of the huge work of recovering and preserving the collective memory, and sparked a broad public discussion on recent church history. Many issues are still being debated, because the context of the time in which they arose leads to inevitable ambiguities. These include the figure of Patriarch Justinian Marina (1946-1977) and the meaning of the "social apostolate" that he espoused, as well as the matter of collaboration by clergy with the former *Securitate*, particularly in the Ceauşescu period.

Since the religious persecution and repression of the 1950s were, in accordance with the regime's consistent strategy of lies, generally carried out under charges of "legionarism", this is the charge contained in the vast majority of churchmen's files from that period – even those of people who never showed any legionarist sympathies. Unfortunately, the memory of these martyrs continues to be tarnished by the judgments of their communist oppressors, and there remains a reticence and hesitation to [re]appraise them. Investigation files were drawn up with an eye to justifying a predetermined verdict; this means that using only the archives of the former *Securitate* (which became possible with the establishment of the National Council for the Study of the *Securitate* Archives) can hardly be said to provide objective information. These files hold only one part of the truth – the part that suited the prosecutors. The other part is to be found elsewhere – in the archives of prisons and tribunals, the administrative papers of cemeteries and, most importantly, the recollections, memories and testimonies of survivors. It requires painstaking effort in each individual case to separate lies from truth: the lies of communism and the devil (for the devil is the father of lies), from the truth of Christ's witnesses. The

20 years that have passed since the fall of the communist regime have seen the emergence of a whole literature recording the memories of the communist prisons, and an Institute for the Study of Totalitarianism has been established.

Since 1989, Romanian historians have focused consistently and closely on drawing up lists of the priests who were arrested. Researchers at the National Institute for the Study of Totalitarianism have compiled data from publications, pamphlets, reports and personal archives and have published journal articles. Studies and whole books on the outcomes of these investigations into the past have gradually begun to appear.

The first work to tell the stories of a large number of Christian servants from all the different confessions was *Testimonies from Behind Bars. Servants of the Church in the communist prisons* by Paul Caravia, Deacon Ştefan Ilioaie and Virgiliu Constantinescu, published as a supplement to the journal *Rebirth* in 1995. It was followed by a "statistical dictionary" entitled *The Imprisoned Church. Romania: 1944-1989* compiled in 1998 by Paul Caravia, Virgiliu Constantinescu and Florin Stănescu (under the aegis of the National Institute for the Study of Totalitarianism), which contained the records of 2,544 people of all confessions, including 2,398 priests (1,725 Orthodox, 226 Greek Catholics, 165 Roman Catholics and 90 Protestants and neo-Protestants). Furthermore, while they are not included in the dictionary articles themselves, the introduction mentions a further 31 members of the Orthodox hierarchy who were deposed (who were imprisoned or exiled, or who met their deaths in strange, suspicious circumstances, such as Ireneu Mihălcescu or Nicolae Popovici), over 1,500 individuals purged from the church and 60 monks whom we know for certain to have supported the national resistance movement. One notable and monumental study is that by Cicerone Ioaniţiu, whose 9-volume dictionary, *The Victims of Communist Terror. Arrested, tortured, imprisoned, killed* reaches only as far as the letter R. Noteworthy, too, are the volumes by Vasile Manea and Cicerone Ioaniţoiu, *Martyrs and Witnesses of the Church of Romania (1948-1989)* – vol. 1, *The Orthodox Church* (Patmos, Cluj-Napoca, [2]1998), vol. 2, *The Romanian Church United with Rome, Greek Catholic. The Roman Catholic Church* (Patmos, Cluj-Napoca, [2]1998).

In 2000, Vasile Manea released a book devoted to the Orthodox priests who had been sent to communist prisons, while, in 2001, Cristina Păiuşan and Radu Ciuceanu released *The Romanian Orthodox Church Under the Communist Regime. Volume I 1945-1958*, which included 181 *Securitate* information reports on the activities of the institutions of the Romanian Orthodox Church, its authorities and its priests during the years in which the communist regime was gaining and asserting its power.

More recent years have seen the emergence of analytical and interpretive works that go beyond simply compiling records, such as George Enache, *Orthodoxy and Political*

Power in Romania Today (Nemira, Bucharest, 2005) and Cristian Vasile, *The Romanian Orthodox Church in the First Decade of Communism* (Vremea, Bucharest, 2005).

Lists, books and studies have also been published recording the Catholic and Protestant churchmen and those of the Greek Catholic confession who were imprisoned in the communist era. In addition, general works on the anti-communist resistance devote many pages to clergy and those who died for the faith.

The establishment of the National Council for the Study of the *Securitate* Archives in 1999, which has enabled systematic study to be carried out for the first time with institutional support. Whereas this investigation once relied largely on oral sources and personal memoirs, now, thanks to this access to the archives, we may begin a period of solid documentation and scientific study.

We must note that there has been a desire to draw up a body of work testifying to the sufferings of Christian witnesses under the communist regime ever since the second world war. In 1943, when the Soviet troops left Bessarabia, the families of clerics and other Christians who had been persecuted were asked to assist in the creation of a "Martyrology of the Bessarabian Church" (that is, the church in ex-Soviet Moldavia) by gathering information on those who had been martyred, tortured or deported by the atheistic regime. It is not known whether the initiative was brought to completion but, in 1942 and 1943, the Bessarabian press did publish lists of the Bessarabian Orthodox priests arrested, deported or killed during the Soviet occupation – lists which have been of use to the authors of this work.

The Church's concern to remember the martyrs of the communist era – an ecumenical martyrology

The history of the Romanian Orthodox Church has also aroused the interest of researchers from outside the church, who have perhaps misunderstood or distorted certain facts and interpretations through ignorance about the church's history and its rather particular structure. It was therefore necessary for the churches' own point of view to be expressed to all who studied the communist era, and it was the job of the church to put that across – to tell and interpret its own history. In 2007, the Romanian Orthodox Church Bible and Mission Institute Press published a book of nearly 800 pages devoted to those Romanians who had died for Christ under the atheistic communist regime. This was the first time that the church had systematically, and on such a scale, attempted to deal with its past, and represented both a work of research to gain knowledge and a moral obligation to those who had confessed Christ during the years of communist persecution. What is particularly remarkable is that this is the first attempt to step beyond confessional boundaries, through a work that may, through an ecumenism of memory, establish an ecumenism of persecution and martyrdom. The book's pages include martyrs from all the historic churches of Romania – Orthodox, Roman Catholic and the Protestant Church of the Augsburg Confession. It was also hoped that the Greek Catholic Church United with Rome would take part but the author claims that the denomination did not manage to submit its contribution in time. The book was released with the blessing of the then-Patriarch of the Romanian Orthodox Church, Teoctist, the Roman Catholic Archbishop and Metropolitan of Bucharest, Monsignor Ioan Robu and the Bishop of the Lutheran Church of the Augsburg Confession of Romania, his Excellency Cristoph Klein. The editorial committee, too, featured priests and members of the hierarchies of the Orthodox, Catholic and Protestant churches. Of the 241 Christian martyrs included in the book, 207 are Orthodox, 30 Catholic and 4 Protestant. Most of them were clergy or monks.

The project was initiated and published by an association of German Catholics in south-eastern Europe, *St Gerhards Werk*, whose members hail from various countries in that part of the world (namely Hungary, the former Yugoslavia and Romania). In 2003, *St Gerhards Werk*, in conjunction with the Roman Catholic diocese of Tottenburg-Stuttgart and with support from the historic churches of Romania, began a comprehensive search of the archives of the various denominations and of the *Securitate* to identify those who confessed the name of Christ, both clergy and lay, who had suffered under the communist regime. From this was born the idea of bringing together all these people's stories in one volume, as martyrology, of the kind that had already been published in countries such as Austria and Germany.

A series of meetings was held to determine the criteria for granting someone the status of martyr for Christ, during which three criteria were agreed, on a foundation of theology and canon law, for deciding and pronouncing that a person was indeed a martyr. These were approved by all the representatives of the Romanian churches who had taken part in the project of the book: a violent death (*martyrium materialiter*), the hatred of the oppressors who opposed the faith (*martyrium formaliter ex parte tyranni*) and conscious acceptance of the will of God (*martyrium formaliter ex parte victimae*). To draw up the information, compile the materials and write the biographies, each church nominated representatives. These in turn selected a team of researchers, who scoured the archives of all the churches, the *Securitate* and the state, family archives, collections of journals both from the inter-war years and since 1989 and personal writings and memoirs, as well as interviewing eyewitnesses from the period. Finally, they drew up hundreds of historically researched and verified life stories. On the one hand, this ecumenical project represented the recovery of the memory of those who had lost their lives for Christ in the years of communism. On the other, it represented religious reconciliation, for each volume contained the stories of Orthodox, Roman Catholic and Lutheran martyrs.

The files include a diverse range of characters and stories. Some priests ended up in prison simply because they were considered members of the elite or because they had supported the anti-communist resistance in the mountains; others because they possessed or published works exposing the true face of inter-war Russian communism. Some priests were imprisoned for working with the legionaries or being members of the National Peasants' Party, or else for having committed liberal propaganda; others for having opposed collectivization or even for borrowing a religious periodical from a neighbour. Monks were seen as hostile elements, difficult to keep in check; their monasteries as hotbeds of mysticism and religious enthusiasm and hard to monitor. For that reason the monks had to be slandered and their monasteries shut down. In those days, being a believer or interested in theology was enough to make one a suspect, to be classed as a legionary and an anti-communist, pursued, interrogated, imprisoned and tortured. And these stories are written down in the pages of the book dedicated to those who were martyred for Christ, and each of them bears witness to a life of sacrifice for the church and for the faith.

Just as for the whole of Romania, 1948 was a watershed moment for the Roman Catholic Church, for it was then that the communist regime began to plan and put in place a series of overtly hostile actions towards the church. The Catholic Church was hard hit by the unilateral abrogation of the Concordat between Romania and the Holy See, by the closure of Catholic seminaries and other traditionally Catholic schools, by the dissolution of all religious communities and the closure of institutions set up under their patronage – schools, hospitals, clinics, charitable organizations and refuges – and by the suppression of the Catholic press and all traditionally Catholic lay associations, as well as by the confiscation of church real estate and other property – buildings, lands, libraries, archives and so on. Archive documents show the brutality of the communist authorities' actions from 1948-1949 onwards with respect to members of the Catholic and Protestant hierarchy, the clergy and the monastic orders. Other individuals, including members of various renowned institutions, major players in the history of our nation, managed to escape the repression of the *Securitate* and left Romania during this time, choosing the path of exile.

The *Romanian Martyrology* published in 2007 provides a real moral redress, for, while it is true that "the martyrs make the church credible to the world", this credibility is also thanks to the fact that works of this kind keep the martyrs alive in our memory. At the Commemoration of the Witnesses to the Faith in the 20th Century (held in 2000 at the Colosseum in Rome), Pope John Paul II said that the martyrs "must not be forgotten; rather they must be remembered and their lives documented", because "the names of many are unknown; the names of some have been denigrated by their persecutors, who tried to add disgrace to martyrdom".[3] That is why we remain duty-bound to remember their martyrdom. It is far from exhaustive, but this book, published by the Romanian Orthodox Patriarchate, is a first step on the road to reconciliation and to uncovering an ecumenical memory of those who, like the Christians of the first centuries, paid with their lives to witness to their faith in the risen Christ.

3 Homily of His Holiness Pope John Paul II, 7 May 2000, http://www.vatican.va/holy_father/john_paul_ii/homilies/2000/documents/hf_jp-ii_hom_20000507_test-fede_en.html

The Importance of the Self-Sacrifice of the New Martyrs and Confessors of Russia[1]

Alexander Mazyrin

Since the 1980s the New Martyrs and Confessors of Russia have been being canonized first by the Russian Orthodox Church Abroad, then in Russia itself; the process of their glorification reached its climax in the early years of the 21st century. By now about two thousand saints have been canonized, yet we should keep in mind that they are only a small percentage of those who were persecuted by the communist authorities.

In just the first 20 years of the Soviet regime more than one hundred bishops of the Russian Orthodox Church, dozens of hundreds of clergy, hundreds of thousands of monks, nuns and lay people were executed.[2] The number of those who died in captivity, in prisons and labour camps, is comparable to those executed. The total number of the persecuted faithful is estimated from 500,000 to 1,000,000 people.[3]

Yet there is a question: can we consider all of them as martyrs who suffered for Christ? The point is – officially in the USSR there were no religious persecutions of the faithful (in contrast to Albania, for example). Having declared "freedom of conscience" in January 1918, the Soviet government kept on declaring that it was fighting not against religion, but counter-revolution. Most of the church-goers persecuted in the 1920s-1930s were convicted of activities "aiming to overthrow, undermine or weaken the state power [...] of the Government of Workers and Peasants" (Article 58 in the Criminal Code of the Russian Soviet Federative Socialist Republic).

How rightful were the accusations of counter-revolutionary activity against the church? Even supposing that the church was not loyal to the Soviet authorities, of what did this disloyalty that caused so many victims among the faithful consist, and did the church battle against the "Soviet Government" and undertake something like actions aiming "to overthrow, undermine or weaken" it?

To answer these questions we should take into account the following facts. In autumn 1919, at the most crucial point for the Bolsheviks of the civil war for the new Russia, while the White Army was triumphantly advancing on Moscow, the Patriarch of the Russian Orthodox Church, Tikhon, urged the bishops and clergy to obey the Soviet

---

1 The investigation was conducted with the support of RGNF, project № 07-01-00180a.

2 *Православная Энциклопедия.* Русская Православная Церковь. Москва, 2000. С. 186. (*Orthodox encyclopedia,* Russian Orthodox Church, Moscow, 2000, p.186).

3 Емельянов Н. Е. Оценка статистики гонений на Русскую Православную Церковь с 1917 по 1952 гг. (по данным на январь 1999 г.) // Богословский сборник. Вып. 3. М., 1999. С. 264. (Emelianov N. E. The estimate of ROC's persecutions statistics from 1917 till 1952 (according to the data of 1999). *Theological anthology,* 3rd edition, Moscow, 1999, p.264).

government's orders unless they violated the faith and piety, and not to give any cause for suspicion.[4] In the summer of 1923, to reject any political accusations, the Patriarch declared his complete and final separation from both a foreign and a home White Guard counter-revolution to the Supreme Court of the RSFSR.[5] And later the Orthodox bishops continued to issue statements about their loyalty to the Soviet authority. Here are some examples: in summer 1926 the Letter of the Patriarchal Locum Tenens Peter (Polianskiy) called on the church to show examples of obedience to the civil authorities everywhere;[6] the draft of the Declaration of summer 1925 by the Deputy to the Locum Tenens Metropolitan Sergey (Stragorodskiy) who, on behalf of all the Orthodox hierarchy and the faithful, expressed a perfect willingness to be law-abiding citizens of the Soviet Union[7]; the so-called "Letter from Solovetsky Island" issued by the imprisoned bishops almost at the same time said: "We can assure the government with all sincerity that the church does not undertake any political propaganda in churches, church institutions and at church meetings."[8] In summer 1927 Metropolitan Sergey went even further and described all previous declarations of loyalty as "half" ones. He proclaimed: "Now, having established a practical and businesslike basis, we assert that no clergyman in his pastoral activity should undertake any steps to undermine the prestige of the Soviet authority".[9] The Declaration issued by Metropolitan Sergey in 1927 embarrassed many faithful in the Russian Orthodox Church. The Declaration said: "We consider every blow directed against the Soviet Union, as a blow directed against us".[10]

All these statements were backed up with a number of other actions, such as the request to make a written undertaking of loyalty towards the Soviet authorities that was demanded from the Russian clergies abroad; the introduction of the compulsory commemoration of the civilian authority in the liturgy; removal of some bishops who were out of favour with the Soviet government to other dioceses. It might seem that the supporters of Metropolitan Sergey would be spared persecution by the authorities: they proved that accusations of counter-revolutionary activities against them were groundless. (The opposition to Metropolitan Sergey did not object to the request of loyalty towards the civil authorities. The most famous statement of the opposition – the appeal of the bishops from the Yaroslavl diocese who were led by the former Patriarchal Locum Tenens Metropolitan Agafangel – ran

4 Акты Святейшего Тихона, Патриарха Московского и всея России, позднейшие документы и переписка о каноническом преемстве высшей церковной власти, 1917–1943 / Сост. М. Е. Губонин. М., 1994. С. 164. (Acts of H.H. Tikhon the Patriarch of Moscow and all Russia, the latest documents and correspondence about a canonical succession of the higher church authorities 1917-1943, p.164.)

5 Правда. 1923. 27 июн.; Известия ВЦИК. 1923. 27 июн. (*Pravda*. 27 June 1923.; *Izvestiya*. 27 June 1923).

6 Акты Святейшего Тихона, С. 420. (Acts, p.420).

7 *Ibid.*, pp.473-474.

8 *Ibid.*, p.505.

9 Беседа с Митрополитом Сергием (Talking with Metropolitan Sergiy) // Известия ЦИК. 1927. 19 авг. (*Izvestiya*. 19 August 1927.).

10 *Ibid.*

as follows: "We always were, are and will be loyal and obedient to the civil authorities; we always were, are and will be true and honest citizens of our home country."[11])

However, persecutions did not stop. On the contrary, they continually increased from year to year. This fact is proved by the statistics of the persecutions collected in St Tikhon's Orthodox University. If we assume the number of the imprisoned according to "ecclesiastical cases" in 1926 as 100 percent, then the index for 1927 is 164 percent, for 1928 – 223 percent, in 1929 – 785 percent, in 1930 – 2175 percent.[12] Even the majority of those hierarchs who signed Metropolitan Sergey's Declaration of July 1927, mentioned above, were executed; only two were spared – future Patriarchs Sergey and Alexei I. Moreover, many of the so-called "church renovators", or "red priests" as they were called among the people, were fiercely persecuted in the 1930s, although they had acted as zealous supporters of the new regime since the beginning of the 1920s. Thus we can conclude that it was not the imaginary disloyalty of the Russian Orthodox Church to the Soviet regime that was the real cause for the persecution of the church. We should look for the reason in the very nature of Bolshevism.

At the beginning of 1922 the first Protohierarch of the Russian Orthodox Church Abroad (this is the part of the Russian Orthodox Church that found themselves abroad after the Bolshevik Revolution and did not acknowledge the Soviet regime) Metropolitan Antoniy (Khrapovitskiy) defined Bolshevism in his address to the nations of the world as "the cult of murder, pillage and blasphemy".[13] It was a sharp remark, but a true one per se. Triumphant Bolshevism was obsessed with atheism. Bolsheviks considered everyone who did not worship this "cult of murder, pillage and blasphemy" as an enemy, whether an honest citizen of the Russian Republic or not. That is why every faithful, as he could not confess an atheistic ideology, was regarded as a counter-revolutionary by the Bolshevik authorities. The new regime demanded not only respect for the law; it was the fight for men's souls. The very fact of the existence of the church in the USSR was a great challenge for the atheistic authorities. In February 1929, in his secret letter to the local committee of the Communist Party, the Secretary of the Central Committee of the Party, Kaganovich, wrote that religious institutions were "the sole legitimate counter-revolutionary organization influencing people".[14] And this at a time when these religious institutions announced their loyalty to the Soviet authorities every day! Bolshevism considered the ministers of the church (the ministers, in the broad sense of this word) as their spiritual enemies above all, who, eventually, should be destined

---

11 Акты Святейшего Тихона, С. 573. (Acts, p.573).

12 Data for calculations: http://pstbi.ru/bin/code.exe/frames/m/ind_oem.html?/ans.

13 Деяния Русского Всезаграничного Церковного Собора, состоявшегося 8–20 ноября 1921 года (21 ноября – 3 декабря) в Сремских Карловцах в Королевстве С., Х. и С. Сремские Карловцы, 1922. С. 155. (The Acts of the Russian All-foreign Church Council of 8-20 November 1921 (from 21 November till 3 December) which took place in Sremskie Karlovtsy, 1922, p.155).

14 ГА РФ. Ф. 5263. Оп. 2. Д. 7. Л. 2. (State Archive of the Russian Federation).

for total destruction. The degree of their expressed loyalty to the Soviet regime influenced only the order of priority: who was to be arrested in the first place – in any case everyone was to be arrested.

At the high point of the persecutions (the years of the so-called "large-scale terror" in 1937-1938) a believer had to renounce the faith and publicly join in militant atheism in order to guarantee his personal safety (if such a guarantee ever existed in the Soviet state at all). For example, in 1938 the "Leningrad Metropolitan" of the Renovated Church, Nikolas Platonov, declared that he would have nothing to do with the church any more and took the position of curator in the museum of atheism.[15]

However, there was another way to survive in those years. As a rule Bolsheviks did not request a direct renunciation of God. More often they requested something else: from bishops – to unmask "counter-revolutionary" clergy; from priests – to unmask "counter-revolutionary" laypeople. The same role of "informants" was also suggested to laypeople. In 1930, escaping from the USSR, priest Michael Polskiy wrote in his book that at first it was offered only to give a written undertaking to be "an honest citizen of the Soviet Republic" and to report "every act of counter-revolution". Then, a bit later, a second written undertaking was requested – an obligation to follow all the instructions from the GPU (the future KGB).[16] And finally, to escape imprisonment, you should send others to prison and do it zealously enough lest the authorities doubt the usefulness of their informant. In this case, it was acceptable not to renounce God publicly. The Soviet regime readily gave the opportunity to serve atheism while wearing cassocks. And there were people who used this possibility. For example, in 1944 "Metropolitan" of the Renovated Church Vasiliy Kozhin cynically explained to officials that "during all the twenty years of her existence the Renovated Church aimed to extract all the counter-revolutionary members of the Church of Patriarch Tikhon".[17]

Nevertheless, the majority of clergy could not accept either this sort of hidden betrayal or the public renunciation of God. They realized that the betrayal of their brothers in Christ was equal to renunciation of Christ himself: "As you did it to one of the least of these my brethren, you did it to me" (Matt. 25:40). And so, sufferings caused by the refusal to report their brethren were equal to the sufferings of Christ himself. Therefore those who were persecuted for refusing to help the Soviet regime in implanting atheism, we can consider to be martyrs for Christ, beyond all doubt. Their sufferings were the result of accepting the gospel in full. They were expected to do what was contrary to their Christian conscience,

---

15 См.: Левитин А., Шавров В. *Очерки по истории русской церковной смуты*. Москва, 1996. С. 630–631. (See: Levitin, A., Shavrov, V., *Studies in Russian Church Sedition's History*, Moscow, 1996, pp.630-631).

16 См.: [Польский] Михаил, свящ. *Положение Церкви в советской России: Очерк бежавшего из России священника*. Иерусалим, 1931. С. 44, 85. (Priest Polskiy Michael. *The Church's Status in Soviet Russia. The Essay of the Priest who left Russia,* Jerusalem, 1931).

17 ГА РФ. Ф. 6991. Оп. 2. Д. 14. Л. 89–89 об. (State Archive of the Russian Federation.)

though it was called "battling ecclesiastical counter-revolution". They preferred to die. This act revealed the grandeur of their sacrifice.

Metropolitan Seraphim (Chichagov) is a model of the suffering for Christ. Like many others he was executed in 1937. He was executed neither because of his anti-soviet activity, nor because he was metropolitan or of noble birth. At the time, being very weak, the 81-year old metropolitan was bedridden. Usually NKVD left such people alone and Metropolitan Seraphim could have died at home in his own bed, but God did not deprive him of the crown of martyrdom. His former cell-attendant and secretary escaped from a labour camp and asked Metropolitan Seraphim for refuge which was granted to him. But soon after, the escapee gave himself up to the NKVD office and gave Metropolitan Seraphim away during the first interrogation. The only cause to execute Metropolitan Seraphim was that he had not betrayed his lost spiritual son.[18] Soldiers had to carry the prisoner out of his house on a stretcher.

The life of Patriarchal Locum Tenens Peter (Polianskiy) gives us another example. The Soviet regime suggested making a bargain with him, but he was adamant. That is why, after only eight months of ruling the Russian Orthodox Church, he was exiled for many years and then imprisoned in solitary confinement. He was promised liberty and safety in exchange for becoming an informant of OGPU, but he vigorously refused. He explained that this kind of activity would be contrary to his rank and incompatible with his character.[19] After 12 years of imprisonment in unbearable conditions Metropolitan Peter was executed in 1937, just like Metropolitan Seraphim.

There are a great number of stories about sufferings for Christ, for the church of Christ or for one's neighbours, the people of God. By the end of the 1930s the Russian Orthodox Church had been almost completely destroyed; there were only four or five celebrating bishops, in comparison with two thousand bishops before the Bolshevik persecutions began, and a few hundred priests in comparison with more than fifty thousand. But the church was not broken spiritually because, as martyred Metropolitan Joseph (Petrovykh) said: "The death for the Church of martyrs is not a defeat but victory over violence."[20] Having faced such spiritual resistance, militant atheism had to retreat.

During the Second World War God's providential dispensation directed the march of history in such a way that the Soviet authorities had to abandon their plans to exterminate religion in the USSR.

---

18 См.: Головкова Л. А. "Последний подвиг священномученика Серафима (Чичагова)" XV Ежегодная Богословская конференция ПСТГУ: В 2 т. М., 2005. Т. 1. С. 298-303. (Golovkova, L.A. "The Last Heroic Deed of Martyr Seraphim (Chichagov)" Annual Theological Conference of the Orthodox St.Tikhon's University, 2005, V.1., pp.298-303).

19 См.: Акты Святейшего Тихона, (*Acts,* p.883).

20 "Я иду только за Христом…": Митрополит Иосиф (Петровых), 1930 год *Богословский сборник.* Вып. 9. М., 2002. С. 405. ("I follow Christ only…" Metropolitan Joseph (Petrovykh), 1930, *Theological Anthology,* 9th edition, Moscow, 2002, p.405.)

What exactly is the most relevant for Christians not only in Russia, but all over the world? Like the Soviet regime, our modern society often considers itself as post-Christian; it does not demand that we renounce Christ directly. In contrast to communist totalitarianism, present-day democracy does not apply undisguised violence. It is not necessary, because non-violent methods have been worked out. The principles contrary to Christian conscience are proclaimed under the guise of defending human rights – such as abortions, euthanasia, so-called gay marriages and so on. And very often, if you refuse to accept these widely advertised sins, you are in danger of becoming a social outcast in our modern society. And this is where we can find the sacrifice of our New Martyrs and Confessors a very encouraging and inspiring one – they were not afraid to live according to the gospel commandments even during the gravest years of Stalin terror, to live as their Christian faith and conscience directed them and they were ready to die for it.

The Russian Myrrh-bearing Women of the 20th Century

Lidia Golovkova

The 20th century saw the most severe and long-lasting persecutions of the Russian Orthodox Church. Unfortunately, some could not withstand them, some joined the Renovated Church, others defrocked themselves. But mostly the faithful met their passion with joy, as many files testify.

To withstand the persecutions, priests' wives were always at their side ready to sacrifice themselves to help them. As witnesses of 1918-1920, when people were often executed publicly, testify, when priests were taken to be executed, priests' wives watching them said to each other: "How happy we are that our husbands are honoured to suffer for Christ!" One of the letters from his wife to an imprisoned priest in the 1930s ran as follows: "We are glad for you that you are worthy of the crown of martyrdom for our Lord. Rejoice, we have experienced persecutions for Christ too!" It was the letter written by the priest's wife and his little children on their way into exile.[1] Many wives of clergy and laymen followed their husbands without fear to the North, Siberia, Kazakhstan or to the Far East.

Many clergy, hierarchy and nobility were imprisoned in the labour camp on the island of Solovky – among them, a hero of World War I, George Osorgin, from an ancient noble family. His wife, princess Golitzina by birth, came a few times to visit her husband. A month after her last visit George Osorgin was killed there.[2] For the wedding ceremony to her exiled fiancé Sergey Fudel, a young girl, Vera Sytina, went to Kazakhstan and stayed there to live with her husband after the wedding.

Being models of self-sacrifice and love, spiritual daughters followed their spiritual fathers, leaving their own families. They went into voluntary exile to help their spiritual fathers to live and survive somewhere far away in the back woods. Only a few of these girls and women have been canonized by the Russian Orthodox Church. Most of their names will be remembered by God alone. St Tikhon's Orthodox University has created a database of New Martyrs and Confessors of Russia. In this database there are more than two thousand names of these girls, women and nuns. They were often very young and not accustomed to hard work, but they shared all the burdens of the clergys' life in exile. Very often Orthodox women remained almost the only supporters of Christian moral standards in a corrupted world.

---

1 Data from PSTGU (www.pstbi.ru) According to the material of *After the Suffered Christ*.
2 Brodskii Yurii, *Solovki. Twenty years of Special Appointment*, Moscow, 2002, pp.362-365.

One of the most prominent figures of the Russian Orthodox Church was the abbot of St Daniel's monastery in Moscow, archbishop Fyodor (Podseevskiy). Nearly all the years of the Soviet regime till his execution in 1937 he spent in prison and in exile. Nun Hermogena (Karetnikova), who was his spiritual daughter, disguised as his relative, followed him everywhere.

In 1928 archimandrite George (Lavrov) was arrested again. He was charged, as his criminal file said, with playing the role of "an elder" in St Daniel's monastery in Moscow and was banished to Kazakhstan. In his exile his two spiritual daughters, Tatiana Melnikova and Helen Checherin, a kinswoman of Checherin – a diplomat and Minister for Foreign Affairs in the Soviet government – followed him. Only in her twenties, Helen Checherin followed Father George to a tiny village in Kazakhstan. She wrote about their life there: "The steppe begins right behind the house. It was so difficult to deal with the snow in winter… Sometimes by morning our house was buried under snow… It was a constant challenge to survive." They ministered the services on all festal days and during Great Lent they did so daily. A chapel was arranged in the sitting room. In her drawings Helen Checherin depicted the place and Father George in his exile.[3]

With the blessing of her parents and the archimandrite of St Daniel monastery in Moscow Simeon (Kholmogorov), young Agrippina Kutomkin followed hieromonk Paul (Troitzkiy). She arrived at the places Father Paul was sent to before him, waited with parcels for him by the closed gates of the prison, ran after the car or the sledge which was deporting Father Paul under guard to the point of destination, she suffered from hunger and cold. All her life she devoted to Fr Paul, she was true to her obedience also during the years of his imprisonment, and when released he lived in seclusion.[4]

A parishioner of St Nicolas church in Kleniki in Moscow, Helen Bychkov was a spiritual daughter of Fr Sergius Mechev. She graduated from Moscow University where she studied history and philology, philosophy and psychology. But instead of an academic career she became a defender of the faith; she visited her spiritual father during the years of his imprisonment. After his execution she supported other exiled priests. But she experienced injustice and captivity too. Later she married a future secret priest Konstantin Apishkin. All her long life she collected materials about outstanding priests and bishops with whom God had brought her in contact. Based on these materials a few books were published, which supplemented the bibliography on the persecutions of the Russian Orthodox Church in the 20th century.[5]

---

3 "With God All Are Alive. Memoirs of the Elder of Danilov Monastery Archimandrite Georgii (Lavrov)", *Danilov Messenger*, Moscow, 1996, p.29; *Holy New Martyrs and Confessors Shone in Kazakhstan,* Moscow, 2008, pp.441-445.

4 *Hieromonk Paul (Troitskii)*, the Life described by Vladimir Vorobev, Moscow, 2003, pp.24-30.

5 www.pstbi.ru

Martyr Tatiana Greembit chose her way of martyrdom when she was 17. Everything she earned and managed to beg in the churches she spent on food and clothes for imprisoned clergy. Five times she was arrested for her help to exiled priests. People said that visiting and helping prisoners was her way to serve Christ. Some bishops whom Tatiana was helping said that for them she was a new St Filaret the Almsgiver. Bishop John (Pashin) in responding to a letter from her wrote: "You have a kind heart, you are happy, give thanks to God for this… Thanks to God you have understood that the superior happiness on Earth is to love your neighbours and to help them…" From his exile Archbishop Averkiy (Kedrov) wrote to her: "I admire your unshakeable devotion to our Creator…" For the last time Tatiana Greembit was arrested on 5 September 1937. During interrogation she did not hide either her faith or her help to the clergy. When asked about the cross she was wearing she answered: "For the cross I am wearing I am ready to give my head, and till I die nobody will take it off me, because I bear the cross for eternity".[6] Tatiana was charged with anti-Soviet propaganda and "causing death to patients in the hospital she worked at". On 23 September 1937 she was executed and buried in a common grave at the firing ground of Butovo. Now Tatiana Greembit is glorified as a saint.[7]

Women devoted to the church not only shared with the clergy their captivity, taking the risk to be persecuted and killed. They also did many other things, as we now know from different archives: they gave refuge to priests and bishops who were hiding from the communist authorities; they delivered letters, which is why in the investigating files they were called "messengers"; they helped priests to celebrate the liturgy secretly.

With the blessing of Metropolitan Seraphim (Chichagov), his daughter Natalia (after taking the veil she was given the name Seraphima) undertook a very difficult and dangerous correspondence between the Metropolitan and the Russian Orthodox Church abroad. To accomplish her task she went abroad to Finland to meet trustworthy people. She also met Metropolitan Seraphim's spiritual children in prisons and labour camps, helped them to escape and to get papers or money. She was arrested a few times and eventually died in exile. Metropolitan Seraphim (Chichagov) was executed by shooting on the firing field in Butovo.

The "Myrrh-bearing Women" of the 20th century are glorified for taking care of the children of executed or widowed priests and bringing them up steadfast in the faith. Unfortunately these cases are almost unknown and forgotten.

The wife of the priest Nazariy (Gribkov) died leaving a baby, Nicholas. Women from the church choir in a Moscow suburb, Daria and Paraskeva, brought him up. When

6 State Archives of the Russian Federation, no. 10035, op. 1 D.P-78536.

7 *Range of Butovo, Remembrance Book of Victims of the Punitive Measures*, Moscow, 1999, vol. III, p.75. *Butovo-Russian Golgotha*, Moscow, 2003, pp.31, 70, 145.

Father Nazariy was arrested and exiled to Kazakhstan the boy stayed with these women. In 1934 Paraskeva travelled with the boy several thousand kilometers to visit Fr Nazariy in Kazakhstan in order to let the priest see his son. In 1936 Father Nazariy returned home and again became a priest in the same church. But in November 1937 he was arrested for the second time and was killed on the firing ground in Butovo.[8] One hundred ten people were killed that day in Butovo, among them 17 clergymen.[9]

When the children of the persecuted priests grew up they were also persecuted. This was the case with Father Nazariy's son. In 1949 he and his wife were arrested, leaving their little boy in the care of the same nurses. These old ladies were now bringing up Nicholas' son – a grandson of Father Nazariy – devoting their long lives to this family. Priest Nazariy was canonized in the Orthodox Church.[10]

At the firing ground in Butovo 20,760 people were killed during a 14-month period in 1937-1938 alone. About 1000 of them were persecuted for their faith. To date, about 315 clergy and lay people among them have been canonized, including many women. The first among the martyrs of Butovo is Metropolitan Seraphim (Chichagov). A church has been built on the very place where the martyrs died, and next to the church the cathedral dedicated to the New Martyrs and Confessors of Russia was erected.

It is pious and quite natural when a faithful Russian woman brings up a priest's orphaned children. But some cases are surprising, for example, when a village woman from a rural place working as a housemaid for a town family, protects and brings up the children of her imprisoned masters as if they were her own. Baptized nurses from rural places, who were brought up in Orthodoxy, adopted their masters' children from Russian, Jewish, Letton and other families of higher rank – people who had very little in common with Orthodoxy or with any other kind of religion. Many such cases were known in the so-called House of Government in Moscow, which is just opposite the Kremlin. There were 507 flats in this gloomy house with a gloomy history. During the persecutions 738 residents of this house were imprisoned, 338 of them were killed. Many children became orphans, were taken to orphanages and later were lost. God safeguarded some of those orphans as their nurses took care of them.[11] This was the case with the families of deputy minister for agriculture S.E. Heister, minister of communications V.E. Polonskiy, a Letton statesman of higher rank, E.T. Smiglti, and others.

The Orthodox nurses influenced the children from atheistic families by bringing them up in the Christian spirit. It is known that sometimes they secretly baptized their foster

8 State Archives of the Russian Federation, no. 10035, op.1, D.P-58379.
9 *Range of Butovo, Remembrance Book of Victims of the Punitive Measures,* Moscow, 2003, vol. VII, p.311.
10 *Butovo-Russian Golgotha,* pp.47, 55, 77, 20, 66, 131.
11 *The House on the Riverside*, Stories collected by O. Trifonova, Moscow, 2005, p.47.

children, to whom they were very much attached. In spite of the risk of being dismissed, they brought the children to the church and taught them how to pray.

Bronstein, better known as Trotzky, was Stalin's main enemy. The dictator annihilated almost all Trotzky's relatives, both immediate and distant. He chased them all over the world. Yet one of the last Bronsteins still lived in Moscow at the end of the 1930s and even held a high post. There was a nurse in the family. They knew that she was recruited by the NKVD. She was obviously made to report who visited the Bronsteins and what they talked about. But she was deeply religious, and steadfast in her faith. In 1937 Bronstein and his wife were imprisoned. Their 11-year-old son was sent to the central orphanage for homeless children and the children of imprisoned parents housed on the territory of the St Daniel monastery. The main principle of upbringing in the Soviet orphanages of that time was to make children forget their relatives. But Valeriy Bronstein forgot neither his parents nor his nurse. When he returned to Moscow after the orphanage, his service in the war and eight years in labour camps in Kolyma, he had no shelter. Then he found his nurse and she gave him refuge in her tiny room. Only a few years later did he find a flat of his own. When his nurse was dying, at her request he invited an Orthodox priest to hear her confession and to give her holy communion. A church funeral service was held. Trotzky's grandnephew, who had miraculously survived, bid farewell to his Orthodox nurse as to a very dear person. So Christian love and devotion overcame class, religious and national hostility, dictated by the communists.

Konstantin Strievskiy was executed by shooting in April 1938 and was buried in the Moscow region on the territory of a former village house or dacha of the minister of the NKVD, Yagoda (this special place called "Commune" became a cemetery for those executed there in 1937-1941). Konstantin Strievskiy's brother Alexander, who was a high-ranking officer, was also executed near Leningrad. Their wives were exiled. Konstantin Strievskiy's son stayed with his kin. A common village girl, Polina, who had worked as a nurse for Konstantin Strievskiy's family, began to work for the boy's new family. Even today the Strievskiys remember her with gratitude. She was illiterate, but her faith in God was so deep that she certainly influenced the child. And the third generation of the family of atheists, twin grandsons of Konstantin Strievskiy, named after their grandfathers Konstantin and Alexander, began to serve God as a priest and a deacon to pray for their atheist grandparents. They are the clergy of St Nicholas Church in Kuznetzy in Moscow and work for St Tikhon's Orthodox University in Moscow. The land of the former special "Commune" firing ground was turned over to the Russian Orthodox Church and the Strievskiy brothers – priest Konstantin and deacon Alexander – go there frequently for the commemorative services for the dead on the place of execution of their grandfather and many other victims. A church dedicated to the new martyrs and confessors of Russia has been built there.

According to God's will the faith survived among the people, due not only to the sacrifice of great archbishops, priests and deacons, but also to common Russian women, even ordinary faithful Orthodox nurses, who brought up the children of those who had lost their faith. As soon as oppression was lifted, they surprisingly easily and quickly found their way back to their origins – to their religious heritage.

Light and Shadow of a Cloud of Witnesses unto Death An Experience of Korean Churches' Martyrdom and its Theological Reflection

Seong-Won Park

It is rare that the encounter between a new value and an old value is made without conflict. This phenomenon is even more inevitable if a new religious value is involved in an encounter with a traditional value of a given society. As is usual in the case of other religions, a serious conflict occurs as the Christian gospel is proclaimed in a given social context. This was true when the Christian gospel was proclaimed in the context of Jewish society and the Roman empire. It also happened when the gospel was introduced to other cultural contexts in the course of mission work. The Korean case was no exception.

Although exact data is not available it is said that about ten thousand Korean Christians, both Catholic and Protestant, were victimized in the process of the Christian mission in the Korean context. In explaining why such a large number of martyrs were produced during a relatively short period of mission history Professor Lee Deok-Ju points to the fact that the period of Christian mission coincided with a period of political and historical difficulty for Korea. It was a time of confusion and oppression, an eschatological situation in theological terms. He also points out the unique nature of Koreans' loyalty to religious values.

Korean martyrdom in the history of the Korean church

The first contact between the Christian gospel and Korea was made in the 16th century through contacts with the Christian presence in China. Actual mission work in Korea, however, started in the 18th century. Roman Catholicism was introduced in the 18th century and Protestantism in the 19th.

The martyrdom of Korean Christians occurred in five different historical contexts. First, it occurred in connection with the Japanese invasion of Korea in the 16th century. The second was in connection with the Korean Roman Catholic community's conflict with the *Chosun* (the 19th century name of Korea) regime whose political ideology was based on Confucianism. The third was in connection with the Japanese colonial power's persecution of the Korean Protestant Church. The fourth was in connection with the conflict between the church and the Communist regime which was established in the northern half of Korea after the liberation of the Korean peninsula. And the fifth was in relation to the Christians' engagement in the struggles for political democracy and social justice from the 1970s to the mid-1990s.

Korean martyrs in Japan

From 1592 to 1598 Japan invaded Korea and about fifty thousand Korean slaves were taken to Japan after the invasion. About seven thousand of the Korean slaves were converts to the Catholic faith and a number of them were among the victims of Shogunate Dokugawa's persecution of the Japanese Catholic Church in the 17th century. According to the official record of the Japanese Catholic Church, two hundred and five Japanese martyrs were canonized by Pope Pius IX in 1867 and among them nine Korean and three Japanese wives were included. Even though they were the first Korean martyrs, they are not regarded as part of Korea's history of martyrdom.

The Gospel in conflict with the state ideology of Korean society

As mentioned earlier, Roman Catholicism was introduced into Korea during the late 18th century. The Korean Catholic Church was established in 1784 when Peter Seung-Hoon Lee returned to Korea after being baptized in Beijing. The newly-established Korean Catholic community held mass in secret because any Catholic practice was forbidden by the authorities. One of the meetings was disclosed by the officials and Mr Kim Bum-Woo, who had offered his house for the meetings, was arrested and exiled in a remote place where he died. He became the first Korean martyr of the Korean Catholic Church.

Later more serious persecutions began. In 1791 two Korean aristocrats were killed because they refused to practice the ancestral rites which were one of the core values of Confucianism. Systematic persecutions followed. In 1801 three hundred Catholics, including a Chinese priest, were killed. In 1839 one hundred and twenty were martyred and about two thousand more Catholics perished between 1866 and 1868. Among those victims one hundred and three were canonized by Pope John Paul II in 1985.

Catholic martyrdom resulted from conflict between the Catholic confession of faith and Neo-Confucian values. The issue centred around ancestral rites. Neo-Confucianism was the state ideology of Korean (then *Chosun*) society (1392-1910). The socio-political system was established and the political order anchored on the basis of Neo-Confucianism. At the heart of Neo-Confucianism were the ancestral rites and these had strong social implications.

The ultimate value in Confucianism is obeying the "Heavenly Mandate". The ways in which human beings obey the Heavenly Mandate are twofold: one is *Choong*, or loyalty to the king and the other is *Hyo*, or filial piety to the ancestors. The king is an earthly ruler whose rule is based on the Heavenly Mandate. Therefore, only the king becomes the priest who appeals to Heaven. The king offers sacrifices to Heaven on behalf of the people. The *Hyo* is an indirect way through which the people participate. Therefore, rejection of ancestral rites meant not only neglect of parents but also total rejection of the social and spiritual system.

Following the near one hundred years of controversy over ancestral rites in China the Roman Catholic Church made it clear through the papal bull "*Ex Quo Singulari*" proclaimed in 1742 that Christians could not practice ancestral rites because they are in contradiction to Christian teaching. In the beginning, the earliest Korean Roman Catholic converts innocently continued to practice ancestral rites. However, when they learned that ancestral rites were in contradiction to Christian teaching they abandoned them.

The abandonment of ancestral rites by the Christians provoked severe persecution from the government. For the Korean government Christian teaching, such as the rejection of ancestral rites and equality among human beings, threatened their social and political system and therefore the Korean government regarded the Christian community as a subversive group and decided to suppress it.

Shinto shrine worship and the Korean church

While the Roman Catholic community in Korea was persecuted by the *Chosun* regime for their rejection of ancestral rites the Protestant Church in Korea struggled against the Japanese colonial power throughout its colonial period (1905-1945).

In 1905, the Japanese military government launched a colonization process of Korea by forcing the Korean government to agree to a Protectorate Treaty, and in 1910 the annexation was completed. Korean people launched resistance movements against the Japanese annexation and Christians were heavily involved. In 1919, a nationwide independence movement swept across Korean society and the Korean church played a major role in organizing the movement together with other religious communities, such as the Buddhists and *Dong-Hak* (East Learning), which was an indigenous religious group. A number of Christians, both clergy and lay people, particularly young people like Ms Yu Kwan-Soon, one of the martyrs, were actively engaged in the movement. The Korean church was one of the centres of the independence movement. Christian engagement in the independence movement provoked a systematic persecution of the Korean church by the Japanese colonial government.

In 1931 the ultra-conservative military wing of Japan fabricated the Manchurian incident. In 1937 the militarists provoked the Sino-Japanese war and in 1941 the Pacific war, propagating the idea that this was a holy war aimed at the co-prosperity of Great Eastern Asia. The militarists used Shinto as a religious ideology and the wars, therefore, were carried out in the name of Shinto mission.

Shinto, or Way of God, is a Japanese indigenous religion which worships the Sun Goddess, *Amaterasu Omikami* and the spirits of the departed emperors. The Japanese military regime reformed the old Shinto as a State Shinto and abused it as a state ideology for imperial wars against the whole of Asia and the United States.

The Japanese government needed to silence the resistance of the Korean church. And therefore they oppressed the Korean churches by imposing Shinto shrine worship in order to subject them to the Japanese "Emperor System". A number of individual Christians suffered because of their resistance and some of them gave their lives for witnessing to God's sovereignty against the sovereignty of the emperor. It was a situation of *status confessionis* for the Korean church. The Japanese colonial government argued that Shinto shrine worship was not a religious ritual but an expression of patriotism and loyalty. However the bulk of evidence showed that it certainly had a religious connotation.

Why did the Korean church resist Shinto shrine worship? There are several theological reasons for refusing Shinto shrine worship. First, the clearest reason for refusal, particularly among Presbyterian Christians, was that it was idolatry and violates the first commandment. As Karl Barth claimed in a lecture given in Denmark around the time when Hitler declared the Third Reich, the first commandment is an axiom of theology. Korean Christians resisted Shinto shrine worship because they could not worship other gods before God, who alone has the sovereignty over the universe.

The second reason was that for Korean Christians the issue of Shinto shrine worship was an issue of confrontation between God's sovereignty and the sovereignty of the emperor. For instance, the Japanese police distributed a questionnaire to Presbyterian pastors in order to test their stance. The questions were:

> Who is higher, Jehovah God or *Amaterasu Omikami*?
>
> Who is greater, Christ or *Tenno* (the Japanese Emperor)?

This makes it clear that the aim of the Japanese government in imposing Shinto shrine worship was to put the Japanese emperor on an equal level to that of God or even higher than God and this was not acceptable to Korean Christians.

The third reason was the issue of the kingship of Christ or the emperor. In the beginning, the Japanese government simply imposed Shinto shrine worship. Later, the authorities intervened in Christian worship itself. A number of restrictions had been put on Christian worship. All congregations were asked to set up a miniature god-shelf (*kamidana*) in their sanctuary. It was forbidden to read some parts of the Bible, like the Exodus story, in the worship services. Christian hymns also had to be modified – particularly all hymns praising Christ's kingship were prohibited from being sung during worship. Japanese authorities ordered the church to delete the two prominent Christian doctrines in the Apostles' Creed; "Maker of heaven and earth" and "from whence he shall come to judge the living and the dead", for the concept of God as the Creator contradicted the Shinto myth which claimed the Sun Goddess was the creator of the universe and the belief in the final judgment by Christ's return would destroy the idea of Japanese imperial rule without end. One of the Christian teachings with which the Japanese colonial power was highly uncomfortable was Christian pacifism because it contradicts the imperialistic war concept the Japanese government was carrying out in the name of holy war.

Korean Christians' resistance to Shinto shrine worship had strong political implications even though it was around the issue of religious worship. In fact, Korean Christians' resistance revealed hidden political intentions packed with religious discourse and the faith response to it had political implications at a different level even though it was a theological response.

Difficult relationship between church and socialist ideology

On 15 August 1945, with the defeat of Japan, Korea was finally liberated from 35 years of colonial rule by Japan. The liberation was a great joy for the Korean people who had long suffered under Japanese colonial rule. However, the military occupation of the North by the Soviet Union and the South by the United States overshadowed their joy and engendered confusion among Koreans as to what political ideology was appropriate for their liberated country. The superpowers' rivalry over Korea resulted in the division of the country with different ideologies. The division of the country created an irreconcilable hostility between the divided Korean people, including Christians, which is still real today.

The Korean church, particularly the church in North Korea, experienced difficulties with regard to its relationship with the socialist regime. The socialist regime expected the church to collaborate with the regime for the socialist revolution and the church wanted to secure freedom of faith in the new context. Both of them had mutual suspicion of each other and the distrust between them resulted in the socialist regime's persecution of the church.

The conflict between the two can be classified into three different stages. During the period from liberation of the country till the outbreak of the Korean War (August 1945-June 1950), there had been a serious conflict between the leftists and rightists in their ideological orientation. Christians were engaged in the anti-communist struggle and this provoked a militant reaction of the leftists. For four months from the outbreak of the Korean War until the retreat of the North Korean troops to North Korea (25 June-30 October 1950), Christians experienced a different type of suffering from socialists. Christians and the church were regarded by the socialists as anti-socialist revolutionaries or reactionists and this provoked severe persecution. With the intervention of the Chinese Red Army in the Korean War, the UN troops and the South Korean army were pushed back to the 38th parallel and the war continued around the parallel until the armistice treaty was signed in July 1953. During this period (November 1950-July 1953), it is assumed that a number of Christians in North Korea were victimized by the socialist regime, because they did not cooperate with the socialists.

The largest number of Korean martyrs was produced during these three periods. Nowadays, however, questions are raised as to whether the victims of this period can be regarded as martyrs. Certainly they suffered and were persecuted, but their suffering and persecution may have something to do with Christians' or the church's uncooperative attitude with the socialist regime. They may not have been forced to lapse in their faith. Deeper theological reflection might be needed. And there is a need to correct their mutual prejudice for reconciliation in the future.

Christian resistance against absolutization of power

From 1961 to the middle of the 1990s, Korean society experienced radical changes. Korean society had been under consecutive military dictatorships for almost 30 years. In 1961 General Park Chung-Hee seized power through a coup d'état, overthrowing the constitutional government. In 1972 President Park declared the so-called "*Yushin* Constitution" which allowed him to be president for life. His regime was extremely authoritarian and oppressive. After his assassination in 1979 he was succeeded by other military generals. They were in power for 10 years. During this time, Korean society suffered from political oppression, social injustice, human rights violations, ideological confrontation between North Korea and South Korea, militarism and economic deprivation.

In this context, the church, together with the student movement, social movements and people's movements had borne the responsibility of prophetic witness by engaging in the struggle for social justice, human rights advocacy, democratization and reunification of the divided country. During this struggle, a number of Christians, both lay and clergy, suffered because of their involvement. Some of them experienced serious threat to life and some students, a few of whom were Christians, sacrificed themselves by self-immolation in protest against the oppressive military regimes and as a means of advocating social justice and peace.

During this period, the struggle of the churches did not produce martyrs whose resistance had something to do with their advocacy of Christian doctrines. However, their engagement in the struggle for social justice, human rights, democratization and reunification had a strong public theological implication of Christian witness.

Theological reflection on martyrdom

As we have seen in the above survey the Korean church has experienced martyrdom in different contexts. Sometimes it was related to confrontation with the socio-cultural context. Sometimes it happened in the political context. Sometimes it was related to the church's struggle for social justice. What sort of theological reflection needs to be made on the experience of Korean Christians' witness unto death?

Martyrdom as a political witness

Martyrdom means to be a witness unto death to what the martyr believes to be the truth. In that sense it is a radical form of personal piety advocating religious truth. However, attention needs to be given to the fact that often political power is engaged in martyrdom. This was the case for the Korean Roman Catholic community's confrontation with the state ideology of Korea around the issue of ancestral rites. The Korean Protestant community's resistance against Shinto shrine worship was also the case. In fact all four cases of Korean martyrdom could be included in this category.

Even though there might be conflict among religious groups on the question of doctrines, political power is engaged in a process of eliminating its opponents, because the majority exercises its political power by suppressing its opponents. Martyrdom, therefore, has political implications embedded in it.

As we put martyrdom in the context of political witness, the sacrifice of the martyrs cannot be understood as merely an act of personal piety. Even though the martyrs gave their lives for a religious cause, their deaths have already a certain implication of political witness in the particular contexts in which they witnessed.

Actualization of martyrdom

In talking about martyrdom, it is often said that martyrdom is a seed of the church, quoting Tertullian.[1] What does that mean practically? How does martyrdom connect with the present generation who confess the same faith? In what way should the courageous witness of the martyrs be inherited by the next generation's witnesses? What would be a theological link between martyrdom and the church today?

There are two problems in connecting the martyrdom of the past with the present generation. The first one is a sort of distance that the present generation feels toward martyrdom. Martyrdom is a radical form of witness. In fact, therefore, common believers feel some sort of distance from such a courageous act of witness. They do not think that they would do the same if they were in the same situation. How can we bridge such a distance between the two generations?

The second issue is that martyrdom is regarded as something that happened in the past. Even though they admire the martyrs people find it difficult to connect themselves with

1 *Apologeticum 50* in *The Early Christian Fathers*, A Selection from the Writings of the Fathers from St Clement of Rome to St Athanasius, edited and translated by Henry Bettenson, OUP, USA, repr. 1969, p.166.

the martyrs' witness. In other words, it does not provide any significant sense to them in their different contexts. What kind of theological connection should be made?

Of course, the situation is different and the context is different. However, they stand on the same line of confessing faith if the present generation takes the same faith stance that the martyr took. Even though Christians of the present generation are in a different context, their confession could have the same connotation with that of the martyrs if they share that same faith stance. A theological articulation of this needs to be made and liturgical ways for celebrating it need to be explored.

Martyrdom and ecumenism

Recently ecumenical efforts are being made to recognize the martyrs beyond confessional boundaries. Some of the martyrs of the Protestant churches are recognized by the Roman Catholic Church. Dietrich Bonhoeffer is one of them, even though the legitimacy of his martyrdom is still under discussion in Protestant circles. Discussions are also underway for finding possibilities to make a common calendar for ecumenical commemoration of the martyrs.

In the case of Korea, an ecumenical approach to martyrdom is not simply a matter of ecumenical sharing of a common heritage of martyrdom. It touches the issue of reconciliation which is one of the fundamental values of the gospel. For instance, common recognition and commemoration of the Korean Protestant martyrs by both Korean and Japanese churches would bring a real sense of reconciliation between the two churches.

A more difficult question would be how to promote common recognition and commemoration of the martyrs who were victimized in the period of ideological confrontation between the North and South in the Christian community of both North and South Korea. Once the divided country and the churches in the North and the South come together by achieving reunification, how would the churches in the North and South settle the issue of martyrdom together? Would it not be necessary to re-evaluate the martyrdom of this period? What kind of theological criteria needs to be applied in the re-evaluation process? This will become a real acid test case for both churches in the North and the South in their ecumenical commitment to reconciliation through the issue of martyrdom.

Recognition and remembrance of martyrs

There is no appropriate body and process for recognizing the martyrs in the Protestant churches in Korea yet. Recently the Korean Methodist Church established a committee to deal with this issue, but that is not the case for other Protestant churches. Major work on martyrs has been and is still being carried out by the Korean Church Martyrs Missionary Association.

The Association has been carrying out the task in cooperation with some Protestant churches ecumenically. But it is not the church. Now the time has come for the official churches to take full responsibility in dealing with the recognition process. It is needed particularly in the recent context in which criteria is unclear.

The other issue the Korean churches need to consider is to find more significant ways for commemorating martyrs. At the moment, there are two mechanisms for commemorating martyrdom: one is to observe a designated Sunday (the first Sunday in June) for commemoration and the other is to promote a tourist type of pilgrimage to historical sites which are related to martyrdom. For meaningful commemoration of martyrdom, more theological and liturgical ways need to be explored.

Concluding remark

Martyrdom is like a treasure that we have forgotten, hidden away for a long time in a wardrobe. As it shines again when we take it out and polish it, martyrdom also sheds light upon our spirituality when it is re-actualized in today's context and meaningfully commemorated. When it is connected with the witness of the present generation, martyrdom continues to work in our witness today.

Experiences and Theology of Christian Martyrdom in Korea: A Response to Seong-Won Park

Helen Rhee

As a part of the regional case studies on this theme, Prof. Seong-Won Park has led us to the experiences and theology of Christian martyrdom in a Korean context. As I am responding to his paper, I want to take up some of his points for further reflection and discussion. I have the following five points:

First, I want to affirm Prof. Park's point of "martyrdom as a political witness". In highlighting the theme of the political significance of martyrdom, I would in fact suggest that in the Korean context, every act of martyrdom has ultimately been a political act in the sense that the martyr's faith inevitably involved (non-violent) resistance to and/or rejection of the political powers that be – whether it was a foreign or national government – based upon what he or she thought the non-negotiable element of the Christian faith was. In the first three contexts mentioned by Prof. Park (Korean martyrs in Japan; conflict with the state ideology of Korean society; conflict with Shinto worship of Japanese imperialism), where there was no separation of religion, society and politics, and in the fourth context (conflict with the communist ideology and regime), where politics effectively replaced religion, the unqualified Christian claim of the supremacy of God as the King, Lord, and Judge, led to inevitable political confrontations, though the concrete manifestations of those conflicts would take various forms, such as rejection of ancestral rites, Shinto worship, or a communist ideology and regime. In the last and most recent context where there was separation of religion and politics, it was the categorical Christian message of liberation and human dignity that propelled the Christian struggle against military dictatorships for democracy, social justice, human rights and reunification. "Martyrdom as a political witness" in Korea took then a form of political self-definition of Korean Christians and is indicative of the fact that the impact of Christianity "has been greatly dependent upon Korea's political situation" to the effect that "an important reason behind Christianity's success in Korea has been its frequent identification with the political movements of Korean nationalism, the independence movements, democracy, and Korean reunification."[1] In this sense, "martyrdom as a political witness" indeed became a seed of the Korean church.

Second, this political aspect of martyrdom has an interesting twist when Christianity is identified with patriotism or nationalism. Alliance between Christianity and nationalism is not unique to Korea; throughout world history examples are replete: America

1 W. J. Kang, *Christ and Caesar in Modern Korea: A History of Christianity and Politics*, SUNY Press, Albany, NY, 1997, p.vii.

(the US) during the time of the American Revolution and the Greeks and Armenians in their struggles against Ottoman rule, just to mention a few. Under Japanese colonial rule, the Korean church recognized in Shinto worship the fundamental imperial ideology of "union of throne and altar". Much like the ancient Roman imperial cult, Shinto worship symbolized the Japanese "national faith and faith in the nation (Japan)" and as such it expressed the Japanese "imperial theology of power" which demanded religious response to power as well as a political act of loyalty.[2] Therefore, while the Japanese government attempted to describe the Shinto worship not as a religious act but as a civil and political one (and thus attempted to separate religion and politics), Korean Christians saw the inseparable nature of the two and refused to participate in the Shinto ceremonies. Hence, rejection of Shinto meant rejection of both Japanese imperial rule and its idolatrous religion; in this way, Christian faith and Korean patriotism went hand-in-hand for Korean Christians. They did not distinguish between religious and political loyalty; rather, they joined their church and nation (Korea) in a common destiny in their particular historical situation. For that matter, the Christians' struggle against communism and the communist regime became another interesting way of identifying Christian faith with patriotism especially during and after the Korean War in South Korea. Since the communist ideology and regime sought to ban and eliminate freedom of religion, particularly Christianity, (South) Korean Christians identified their faith with the anti-communist and anti-North Korean struggle and therefore with (South Korean) anti-communist nationalism, which was incidentally propagated by the South Korean military government.

However, identification of Christianity with patriotism has its own danger if not careful. Dying for one's God (faith) should be distinguished from dying for one's country, and the affirmation of "martyrdom as political witness" means relativization of any earthly political power, including nationalism. This relativization of earthly power and patriotism heightens absolutism of the Christian claim and the first commandment: "You shall have no gods before me," says the Lord of the universe. The Christian struggle against military dictatorship in South Korea from the 1960s to the early 1990s could be an example of relativizing earthly power and patriotism. On the one hand, there were enough Christians who fought for democracy and human rights and paid the price heavily (though not necessarily with death) along with their non-Christian co-citizens. On the other hand, the majority of Christians during that period did not resist the military government per se, based on the principle of separation of religion and politics; they focused rather on "spiritual matters", e.g, evangelism, discipleship and missions. In fact, those decades were the great periods of both church growth and anti-communist nationalism and the number of actual Christian martyrs

2 Cf. H. Rhee, *Early Christian Literature: Christ and Culture in the Second and Third Centuries*, Routledge, London and New York, 2005, p.160.

in a sense of witnesses by death was indeed few. The political witness of Christian faith calls for a prophetic voice and a challenge to any earthly institution or power that demands absolute allegiance over God whether it be a colonial power, communist regime, dictatorship, nationalistic government, or even democracy.

My third point has to do with actualization of martyrdom in the sense of connecting the past and the present. I agree with Prof. Park that there is a challenge and historical distance "in connecting the martyrdom of the past with the present generation" in Korea. If we look back at early Christianity, they had a similar issue with the dawn of the Constantinian era. With the age of martyrs being a historical rather than a contemporary reality, Christians of the 4th century made a conscious effort to remember and commemorate the martyrs by writing down their accounts (martyr acts) and celebrating their deaths in liturgy (cult of martyrs). At the centre of the early martyr acts was the ultimate confession of the martyr made *in public*: "I am a Christian." According to Ekkehart Mühlenberg, "while death is part of the confession, death or manner of dying has no value of its own apart from the confession."[3] If so, the point of connection between the historical martyrs and today's faithful is not necessarily the same experience but the same kind of confession: "I am a Christian." This common confession and living out this confession is what unites the martyrs and the contemporary faithful together as part of the church catholic; but at the same time this confession and living out allows the individual communities to shape, re-enact and enter into the Christian identity in their particular religious, political, historical and socio-cultural contexts as they remember and commemorate the martyrs.

This leads me to highlight the role of specific communities in acts of commemoration. What makes one a martyr? If it is true that a martyr is determined not only by an individual act of confession but also by a social act of its remembrance and commemoration by a community, this entails that defining and appreciating martyrdom and its confession is certainly *an interpretive and contextual act*. The early Christian martyr acts "present martyrdom as the supreme religious value *for the group* and tells the 'collective stories' of dying for God."[4] In this sense, martyrs made "an ultimate statement of commitment *to the group and what the group represented*"[5] in public spectacles of martyrdom. The martyrs' individual acts of confession then always carried collective significance and reflected and shaped a social self-definition of a community they represented. In turn, the community that commemorated the martyrs interpreted and honoured their martyrdom through its community ethos and values. What does this

3 E. Mühlenberg, "The Martyr's Death and Its Literary Presentation," *Studia Patristica* 29 (1997), pp.85-93.
4 Rhee, p.46; italics added.
5 J. Lieu, *Image and Reality: The Jews in the World of the Christians in the Second Century*, T&T Clark, Edinburgh, 1996, p.82; italics added.

mean for ecumenical commemoration of martyrs? On the one hand, it means that specific faith communities' voices and concerns in a larger body of Christ should be heard in remembering the individual martyrs. On the other hand, it also means that ecumenical recognition of martyrs should aim to be trans-ideological, trans-denominational, trans-confessional, trans-national and trans-territorial as Prof. Park calls for "common recognition and commemoration of the Korean Protestant martyrs by both Korean and Japanese churches" and perhaps even the Christian martyrs by both North and South Korean churches. Going even further, could we envision a common recognition and commemoration of Polish Christian martyrs during the Third Reich by both Polish and German Christians? And countless confessional martyrs among the Catholic, Protestant and Orthodox traditions? For this to take place, a fundamental commitment to reconciliation should accompany the common recognition and remembrance.

Fourth, in the conscious commemoration of Korean Christian martyrs, the Christological interpretation or the theme of *imitatio Christi* (imitation of Christ), which was a prominent theme in early Christian martyr acts, seems to be lacking. According to the early Christian martyr acts, the martyrs are the partakers of Christ in his sufferings and the imitators of Christ in his death, who is "the protomartyr or the first martyr of Christianity in his self-giving death on the cross".[6] Following after Christ, who is "the mighty and invincible Athlete" the martyrs are engaged in the contest as the noble athletes for a crown. Their contest is two-fold: the conflict with the pagan opponents such as the Roman officials and the crowd – the Devil's minions; and the supernatural combat against the adversary, the Devil himself, just like that of Christ.[7] In this contest, especially with the Devil, athletic imagery is combined with military imagery; while still called the noble athletes, martyrs are portrayed as God's prized combatants who fight against the angry onslaught and attacks of the enemy (the Devil) and overcome him. In addition to the agonistic motif of imitation of Christ, the sacrificial motif is also significant. Just as Christ's martyrdom provided atoning sacrifice for those who believe in him, the martyrs' death is a sacrifice of praise and worship to God in response to Christ's own salvific sacrifice. In this day and age where an idea of religious "martyrdom" unfortunately involves and evokes violence and killing of innocent people in certain extreme sects and regions, perhaps a military imagery of martyrdom, however spiritualized, might not be so appealing or helpful. Nonetheless, could not this notion of imitating Christ in his suffering and death be applied to and serve as a paradigm for the Korean martyrs? Furthermore, ecumenical significance of the Christological axis of martyrdom could be further explored and reflected on.

6 Rhee, p.92.
7 *Ibid*, pp.92-99.

Finally, as a way of concluding my response, I want to present martyrdom as an eschatological witness: martyrdom highlights one's belief in the supremacy of God as the ultimate judge who will vindicate the righteous and punish the wicked on the last day. Without faith in the hope of future reward and resurrection of the faithful, judgment on the apostates and persecuting powers beyond death,[8] martyrdom loses its poignancy and potency. At the same time, the supremacy of God also manifests in his unfathomable mercy that will overcome and triumph over evil. Without faith in the hope of eternal life and forgiveness, martyrdom loses its significance and redemptive purpose. Furthermore, the supremacy of God will manifest in glorification of his people, the church, in perfect unity and holiness, delivered from her own divisions, brokenness and blemishes; without faith in the hope of reconciliation and transformation of the body of Christ, martyrdom forfeits its unifying vision and identity. Martyrdom in this sense always looks forward to future fulfillment of God's promises and is a supreme witness to the God who will make things right in his way in his time.

8 Cf. W.H.C. *Friend, Martyrdom and Persecution in the Early Church: A Study of Conflict from the Maccabees to Donatus*, Blackwell, Oxford, 1965, pp.44-49.

Called to be Peacemakers (Melanesia)

Richard A. Carter

Goodness is stronger than evil
Light is stronger than darkness
Love is stronger than hate
Life is stronger than death
Victory is ours because of the love of Jesus Christ

Archbishop Desmond Tutu

From 1990-2005 I served as a tutor, chaplain and priest, and later as a brother myself, to an Anglican community in the South Pacific called the Melanesian Brotherhood. There are more than 400 members of the Melanesian Brotherhood, living a very simple life under the traditional vows of poverty, chastity and obedience. Their founder Ini Kopuria, a Solomon Islander from Guadalcanal, believed that the brothers should take and live the gospel in a Melanesian way, not dragging people away from their culture with the material promises of the West but transforming culture by living among the people Christ's gospel of peace and forgiveness… a radical love for God and for neighbour. The Melanesian Brothers differ from other traditional religious communities in that none of the brothers are asked to take life vows. They simply make temporary vows. Ini Kopuria felt that a brother should be free to leave the community after a period of formation and service to return like yeast or salt. Some of the brothers in our community stay 20-30 years; others leave after 5 years. At the moment the community numbers about 400 brothers and 200 novices nearly all of them under the age of 30.

The Solomon Islands have always been called the "Happy Isles". A place of harmony where different island and tribal groups lived together in peace. We never believed that there would be violent conflict in these islands. Different language groups mixed freely, inter-married, played football together and worshipped together in the same church. When I first heard that conflict had broken out on the Weather Coast of the island where I was living I remember thinking like many others that extreme violence could never happen on these islands. I was wrong. The scenario is familiar from all around the world. For many years since the Second World War migrants from the neighbouring island of Malaita had come to live and work on the island of Guadalcanal. In fact they had helped to build and develop the capital city, the airport, the ports; they were the manpower, the labour, for the plantations. At first they had been welcomed with open arms but the more successful they became, the more their numbers grew, the more some of the native Guadalcanal population came to resent them. Stirred up by local politicians it was the migrant workers who were accused of taking over the land, the police force, the government and exploiting the land the Guadalcanal people claimed was not their own. Resentment led to hatred and then to violence. A rebel group began by expelling the migrants from their schools, then they attacked villages and homes, and in a matter of months 30,000 people had had their homes burnt and their villages destroyed. The Malaitans in response broke into the police armoury, took over the police force, ousted the prime minister and in a matter of months there was a full scale ethnic conflict with murder atrocities and death on both sides

This paper will focus on the impact of conflict on the Melanesian Brothers and in particular on the tragic and brutal death of seven members of the community who died while trying to bring peace to the islands; on the tragedy of loss but also on the transformation it has wrought in the lives of the Brotherhood. It is a gospel story of how even the horror of a crucifixion can become a story of love and resurrection.

During the conflict the community became one of the few groups that people could trust. There is not one moment when you decide to become peace-makers – just the growing realization in the confusion and conflict that you cannot do anything else. As a Christian you simply have to try and help those who come to you for protection and help. And as a Christian too, to provide some way back from the horror of violence, some hope of redemption. There are defining moments in all our lives, moments which change things so that after the experience we know things will never be the same. Moments which we return to in our memories and rewind, memories which can hurt like unhealed wounds or which can also become the source of who we are and who we want to become.

In my own memory I return to Easter day 2003 and the three months which followed. It was the day we learnt that one of the brothers from our community, Brother Nathaniel Sado, had been tortured and murdered by one of the militant militia. Over the preceding years our community had been working for peace. On this island of Guadalcanal torn apart by fighting between two ethnic groups it was our order of Melanesian Brothers that had for many become a symbol of hope. These Melanesian Brothers alone had been able to cross the roadblocks and barricades bringing medical supplies, searching for the missing, protecting refugees, ferrying the wounded to hospital and carrying back the dead for grieving relatives. They had even camped between enemy lines, visiting the camps of the militants, trying to awaken a consciousness that a better way was possible. It had seemed they had charmed lives and weaved their way through bullets unscathed. They had embodied the faith of so many that God and goodness would prevail and that prayer was answered in a real and palpable way. And it was to them to whom people had come to renounce the way of violence and hand over their weapons.

On the day we heard of Brother Nathaniel's murder everything changed. These Melanesian Brothers were of course as mortal as everyone else. There was no divine protection, just the reality of a young man bleeding to death in the misery and rain of the Weather Coast and no one there to help him. Six of the Melanesian Brothers went to search for him and they too were taken hostage and did not return. Our community was now being directly targeted, accused of being spies and collaborators themselves. The peace advocates now had no one to advocate on their behalf – similar in some ways to those Buddhist monks in Burma walking hand in hand, bold humility in the face of brutality and violence.

But what happens when everyone looks away and there is no longer anyone to turn to? What happens when God does not provide the easy answers or the divine protection or we cannot see any way out or any way through? I suppose it is then that real faith begins, we enter the unknown, and often it does not feel heroic or holy at all. It is about trying to get through a flood of chaos and trying to keep those you care about from drowning while trying to keep your own head above water. And yet the knowledge too, deeper than we have ever known, that the love and the care we held for one another is the only thing which can possibly redeem the future. And that knowledge night and day becomes our prayer.

After three months of waiting and praying we heard the news we had most feared: that the six brothers who had gone to look for Brother Nathaniel had also been tortured and killed on arrival.

The Seven Witnesses to Peace[1]

Brother Robin Lindsay was the Assistant Head Brother who spent many years in the community. He was four years Assistant Head Brother in the Solomon Islands and four years Regional Head Brother in PNG. I call him "the encourager", because he has time for everyone and helps build on their strengths. He is known and popular wherever he goes in PNG and the Solomon Islands and even in Norfolk in the UK. With his strong handshake and absolute dedication to his work, the community feels in safe and caring hands whenever he is around. There is no brother more committed to the community or to his fellow brothers. My last memory of him is on Maundy Thursday when together we washed the feet of the novices in the community, he washing and I drying.

Brother Francis Tofi from the time he was a novice was so bright and attentive in all his studies. When you met him you knew straight away that here is someone with a deep spiritual life and gentle wisdom. He asked constant questions and understood intuitively what it meant

1 The following biographies are from: Richard Anthony Carter, *In Search of the Lost: The Modern Martyrs of Melanesia,* Canterbury Press, Norwich, 2006, pp.155-159.

to be a brother. First in Malaita and then on the Weather Coast of Guadalcanal at the time of tension and its aftermath he showed incredible courage. Here was a brother who was prepared to speak out, to condemn violence and the use of weapons and protect the lives of others even at great personal danger. There are stories of how he was able to resolve conflicts and rescue those who were being beaten or in danger from the rebels. His courage was very great. He told me he would be frightened if he died doing something that was evil "but I am not frightened to die in God's service doing something which is good". I reminded him that God wants LIVING sacrifices and he had his whole life ahead of him. We laughed, for death never really seems a possibility in one so brave and full of life. I told him I wanted to visit him in Geneva. Today we packed his only possessions in a small grubby black rucksack: a few shirts, a couple of pairs of shorts, his uniform and some books to return to his family. I cannot believe he is dead.

Brother Alfred Hilly. He is a young and humble brother. For two years he has been looking after Chester Resthouse in Honiara. Sometimes the guests find him a bit quiet and vague but he has great kindness, always giving up his bed and mattress to provide extra room for guests. He takes particular care of the kids who love coming to the house. He makes sure they get fed at lunchtime and has been helping young Selwyn, whose parents have deserted him, learn to read. This year he trained in Malaria research and qualified to read blood slides at the local clinic. And now dead. They shot him in the arm and then they beat him to death, this gentle man. How can I write in the past tense about one so young?

Brother Ini Partabatu, free-spirited and outspoken, brave and full of energy. He is a brilliant actor and became a key member of my dramas and joined me on the brothers' mission and tour to New Zealand in 2000. Ini as a brother has been brave to speak out against all injustice. He even confronted the SI police force when he believed their methods were unjust, brutal or failing to respect the rights of the people.

Brother Patteson Gatu. He is full of joy and so motivated as a new brother. He was only admitted last October and always smiles from ear to ear whenever you meet him. The last time I saw him just before Easter he was telling me about when he was fired at while trying to land on the beach, as well as enthusing about a sermon I had just preached. I was never quite sure whether he was not teasing! He had such youth and warmth and confidence of faith. Not some narrow religiosity, but natural and real and strong. "Blessed are the peacemakers, for they shall be called the children of God." (Matt.5:9)

Brother Tony Sirihi, who lost his father when he was young and found in the Brotherhood a real family and home. He developed from a shy, thin and humble novice into a stocky and bold brother. But he never lost his simplicity. So many memories. I remember so clearly the night before he was admitted as a brother how we climbed Pentecost Mountain together and celebrated the eucharist on top with all those about to make their vows. All night Tony had been lighting fires to keep us warm. The brothers loved having him around. He showed his courage throughout the tension and continued to help the disarmament process.

And **Brother Nathaniel Sado**, the lost brother, for whom they had gone in search. As a novice he was in charge of the piggery and cared for those pigs with great dedication. He made a sweet potato garden for them and cooked for them. They often seemed better fed than the rest of the novices. The dogs followed him round too and he was one of the few novices who got on well with our donkey. He loved to welcome guests to the community and made friends with all the visitors. He had little formal education and had a somewhat childlike nature, always on the move, and as a brother was a bit hard to pin down. Stories say that he was beaten to death after being accused by Keke of being a spy for the government. They say he sang hymns as he died, innocent as a child is innocent when caught up in events out of his depth.

Their sacrifice seems too great and hard to believe. The community sat up telling the stories of these brothers through the night and trying to come to terms with the enormity of their loss. And yet beneath the trauma there is a peace too. The knowledge that each of these young men believed in peace and in goodness. They knew that there was a better way. They were prepared to oppose violence and to risk much. At the end of the day they stand against all acts of brutality which are at present disfiguring our world and bravely, boldly, and with love, lived what most of us proclaim only from the safety of a church. Oh how much the worldwide Anglican Church at the moment could learn from their witness. And when such real life issues are so much at stake in our world, is not this what the gospel should be? A gospel of love great enough to set us free?

Cloud of Witnesses over the Melanesian Brotherhood

As I stand back from this story I see it has also become the saving event of my life. It has become gospel. Strangely I believe these deaths have set us free. Free to realise that this is where, if only we had the courage, we want to stand too. Free to realise the choice we have between life and death, death in life and true life. The story we follow is the story of the victory of a peacemaker, the victory of love, even when they thought they had snuffed it out. It is a message which reaches out to you wherever and whoever you are and however overwhelming the odds against you may seem. There is a story I have heard in which a young disciple comes to his teacher and says "There are two wolves within me. One of them is wild and full of violence and hatred, the other is full of gentleness, compassion and love. I am fearful. Tell me which of these wolves will win?" And the teacher answers, "Which wolf are you feeding?"

A month before he was murdered Brother Robin came to me to ask me about a dream that he had had three times. He told me he dreamt he was on a beach and that he looked up and saw the most terrible storm clouds and cyclone approaching and huge waves mounting. He was full of fear and dreamt that the storm engulfed him. He said he drowned and that everything was swept away by the waves. He dreamt that the wave carried him to the top of a mountain and that as the water receded he was in warm sunshine and that he could see for miles, the world flooded with light. He said that he believed that God was saying to him that he must not be afraid and that all, all would be well, all would be made good. I told him he had a lot at the moment and not to worry.

It is only when you stand back from the pain of their loss that you begin to see another story emerging. Who could have imagined the following months – the arrival of the Regional Intervention Force, the unconditional laying down of guns and surrender of militants, the arrest of leading instigators on both sides and, for the first time a public no longer frightened to speak out in support of justice? No, no one could have ever imagined the aftermath of these brothers' deaths, nor that the funeral of these simple, humble men of faith would stop the nation and line the streets with thousands of those longing for peace, nor that churches throughout the world, even in Rome and Canterbury, would hold requiems in thanksgiving and prayer for these unknown, ordinary, men of God. And for our community, stripped of all pride and pretensions, a melting down too and, we pray, a still deeper heart for the gospel.

Resurrection begins in darkness
There is distraction
There is confusion
And uncertainty
In the mind and stomach
The yawn of despair
And I look round
And I cannot find who I am looking for
And there is fear so caustic that I will never find him again
And then Christ comes
Comes so simply
As though to dispel all fear

He comes like joy comes without introduction
Like healing which has dissolved the pain
He comes
Like rain on a dry brittle land
He is simply there
Like light which ends darkness with no struggle
For then it was dark
But now it is light
He comes with his balance and his beauty
And order returns
Like a bird returning home from another land
Spring comes
He comes with no explanation or reason
And there is song
And a hope
And a future
We are surprised by his love
But he is not
For though he kept us waiting and doubting and trusting
He always knew He would never leave us.
Emmanuel, God with us.

The process of healing within the community too – a long time, for the nation even longer, and it is I believe still taking place. We do not forgive and forget; if we forgive it is by painfully remembering and trying to become all that those who you have lost would have wanted to be. Living out of their courage and their goodness. Trying to be the people that they inspire us to become. "Do not be afraid – believe" is what Francis still seems to say to me. This is not a sentimental remembering. These were real people with real flesh and blood humanity, capable of greatness, capable too of all the same human failures. And yet they live on. They have made me believe… believe in resurrection as well as death.

In their work for peace many of our community had witnessed extreme brutality. In the process of healing as we remembered those who had died and the traumatic events that many of the community had witnessed we became aware both of the desolation and damage the violence had caused but also aware of all that led to consolation and hope.

Describing the experiences of trauma brothers identified how they:

- feared violence would happen again;
- how often their thoughts and dreams were often disturbed and full of sorrow or fear;
- how they felt angry and sometimes unable to control that anger;
- how a smell or a taste or a touch or a noise could remind them of all they had been through;
- how events would repeat themselves over and over again in their memories;
- how they felt restless or lethargic or ill or distant from those around them;
- how they could not understand how God had abandoned them;
- how they felt this feeling of guilt and dread.

When the brothers were asked what strategies brought them hope and healing so much of what they shared was in fact what I can only describe as grace. They said:

"I feel so thankful for life."

"Prayer helps, praying for others and being prayed for and the holy eucharist."

"People who love and care for me without condition."

"Creative activities."

"The forgiveness of God."

"The support of the community and knowing we belong."

"Realizing that something good is still possible and can come out of all of this."

Forgiveness is most difficult when the perpetrators of some of the most brutal acts do not even admit they are wrong or accept any responsibility for the pain they have caused. There is no answer to this. But as I meet these brothers who suffered and read again their list of strategies I realize that healing and forgiveness are a mystery and a miracle of grace. It is not the settling of an account or based on a balance of logic; it is freely offered and undeserved. This gift is not always received, but it is a hand held out against all the odds in the hope of final restoration. I think of the father of the Lost Son watching and waiting. There is profound pain in that waiting, which is the result of the sin which has violated the relationship, but there is an even greater love in the waiting, for it is also an inner realization that the love of God is still more powerful than the worst wrong.

If you ask us how this community can forgive those who murdered our brothers I do not know, and yet when I see Christ in my brothers I realize they are holding no hatred or bitterness, but are free in a way the perpetrators are not. Thus, strangely, even hatred can be transformed into compassion and mercy for those who are still prisoners.

Celebrating the martyrdom of the Melanesian Brothers

Years after these seven brothers gave their lives, peace has returned to the Solomon Islands although of course there still remains much to be addressed. We can never wipe away all that has happened but we can learn from it. The seed that falls on the ground and dies can yield a rich harvest. At the Lambeth Conference 2008 when more than 650 bishops from the Anglican Communion came to Canterbury for prayer and reflection and were led in retreat by Archbishop Rowan Williams – I once again recalled this mystery I live with. The Melanesian brothers and Melanesian sisters were invited to the conference as chaplains and indeed as peacemakers for heaven knows how much the church needs peacemaking even within its own community. At the last holy eucharist in Canterbury Cathedral the Archbishop of Canterbury read out the names of the seven Melanesian brothers who died.

We sang the litany of saints echoing through the cathedral, processing up the steps through the sanctuary past the flame which burns for the martyrdom of Thomas à Beckett to the chapel of martyrs and there on the altar seven candles are burning and there is an icon of the seven martyred Melanesian brothers written by a young Brazilian steward at the conference. And in front of this altar many of the bishops from the Anglican Communion from all around the world come to kneel and pray. And I am so overwhelmed by the gospel we proclaim and how it continues to be realized in our lives. For here it seems to me all pride and power is gone and we are on our knees... remembering seven young village men, without power of possession, without riches or status, ordinary humans, vulnerable men who were led by Jesus Christ with his group of village fishermen and misfits, the one who continues to change our lives and change our world. And the amazing thing is we too are like them, capable of falling so short, but capable too of being filled with the same goodness. The Word made flesh.

Like many others I weep
And like many others I too proclaim the greatness of the Lord and my spirit rejoices in God my saviour:
For the Almighty has done great things
He has pulled down the mighty from their thrones
and lifted up the lowly.
He has filled the hungry with good things
and sent the rich away empty
He has come to the aid of his servant.

United in the Fellowship of Christ: Analysis of Theological Criteria Used in the Case Studies[1]

Alan D. Falconer

Introduction

To draw the threads of "case studies", it is appropriate to try to offer an overall framework, so that the tapestry may emerge. There were two major ecclesiological images which were evident in the presentations. Sometimes these threads have been explicit and at other times more implicit. The two images which form the core of the presentations do not contradict each other but are complementary. They are "the communion of saints" and "the body of Christ". At a midday prayer during the Bose Symposium the reading was taken from John Calvin's *Institutes of the Christian Religion* as was appropriate for Reformation Day. While the Psalms of the day expressed well the theme of the body broken, of suffering and brokenness, the reading from Calvin helped us to celebrate participation in the communion of saints:

> When in the Creed we profess to believe the Church, reference is made not only to the visible Church, but also to all the elect of God, including in the number even those who have departed this life... By the unity of the Church we must understand a unity into which we feel persuaded that we are truly engrafted... All the elect of God are so joined together in Christ, that as they depend on one head so they are as it were compacted into one body, being knit together like its different members; made truly one by living together under the same Spirit of God in one faith, hope and charity, called not only to the same inheritance of eternal life, but to participation in one God and Christ...

Calvin goes on in the extract read at worship from the *Institutes* to explore the term "communion of saints" and to emphasize that the grace given to each is given for the sake of the entire community, and that as God is our common father, and Christ is our head:

> they (the saints) cannot but be united in brotherly love, and mutually impart their blessings to each other.[2]

1 Alan Falconer was asked to listen to the presentation of various case studies, and seek to weave the various strands into a coherent framework and help us to move forward in our appreciation and celebration of the saints and martyrs of the church.

2 John Calvin, *Institutes of the Christian Religion* (ed. John McNeill, trans. Ford Lewis Battles) SCM, London, 1961, Book IV, pp.1,2-3.

As John Calvin stresses, the communion of saints of all ages and places is bonded together in baptism. (This is not the occasion to explore this, but he uses the same expressions of bondedness for baptism, the sacrament of the Lord's Supper, and the communion of saints.)

Through the Holy Spirit we are engrafted into Christ and bound together with all who have also been baptized in his name. That baptism is a participation in the dying and rising of our Lord. It is a lifelong journeying in the community of the baptized and a seeking to be faithful in discipleship. Jesus asks whether we can drink the cup which he drinks and be baptized with his baptism (Mark 10:35-40). Baptism is into the body broken of Christ, and into the fellowship of the Easter Saturday experience.[3]

The Body of Christ

Many of the stories which have been shared at the Bose Symposium bear witness to brokenness, suffering, forsakenness and to the courage of those who have, in the words of Archbishop Rowan Williams, been " orators of the Spirit".

Such a testimony is evident in the witness of the Melanesian brothers – an account which was itself an extended prayer of remembering in the context of thanksgiving to God (a prayer of blessing, of berakah). It therefore seems appropriate to explore the theme of the Body of Christ, of the body broken, and of our fellowship in that body of Christ.

Paul offers an extended meditation on the Body of Christ in his first Letter to the Corinthians chapters 10-13. These chapters have the character of an extended meditation.

In 1 Corinthians 10, Paul asserts that we participate in the one bread; in chapter 11 he describes that participation as focused on and centred in the celebration of "This is my body, broken for you". Then in chapter 12 the community is seen to be the Body of Christ with each member having distinctive yet interdependent exercises of ministry exercised for the sake of the whole community, and finally in chapter 13, there is a reflection on how the community can cohere – can live the reality to which she is called – namely by the exercise of love.

In trying to find a coherent framework for understanding or being able to speak about the saints and martyrs of all ages and places, it may be that an understanding of the Body of Christ can provide a useful starting point. The Body of Christ – the embodied life of God – is the body broken. Such is a profoundly sacramental understanding. Rooted in baptism and the sacrament of the Lord's supper, the saints and martyrs are gifts of grace to the community. We remember them when hearing the stories of courageous witness.

---

3 Alan Lewis, *Between Cross and Resurrection: A Theology of Holy Saturday*, Eerdmans, Grand Rapids, 2001.

The term "remember" is central to the Jewish Christian tradition. Throughout the Hebrew Scriptures the community is enjoined to remember. In Psalm 103 people cry out of their pain and their situation of persecution, laying before God their humiliation. It is a phrenetic cry: "Hear my prayer, let my cry come unto you."

The psalmist goes on to remind God of his acts of love and mercy – of *mishpat* and *sedeqah* (terms held together inseparably throughout the Torah) and of *shalom*. The psalmist reminds God of his act of creating and nourishing the people. This is reinforced by Psalm 74 asking God why he has cast off his people forever, and pleading that he remembers his congregation. The psalmist again recalls God's acts of liberation and salvation and calls the people to the ethos of awe and devotion.

Such remembering of God's gracious acts was central to the life and hope of the community. The very format of Jewish and Christian prayer, as Claus Westermann has shown – the berakah – blessing, places the requests, the petitions of the community in the context of the unfolding story of God's gracious accompanying of the people in their pilgrimage through time.[4]

At the major feasts of the community, a central element was always the recounting of God's presence and liberating activity in respect of the community. Such a recounting was evident in the formulae of faith – "a wandering Aramean was my father" (Deuteronomy 26:5-10), and in the hymns of the community. Such remembering was above all expressed at the celebration of the Passover. The community engaged in a concrete re-living of their deliverance, offered a thanksgiving to God and sealed this relationship with God – the covenant – with a meal. The community gives thanks to God for his mercy and for drawing the community into being. They made a sin offering for the sins they had committed as a community, and made a peace offering, committing themselves to seek to live as the people of God. In such festivals and hymnic creations, there is a constant Hebrew poetic holding together of remembrance and remission of sins – which finds expression in the New Testament holding together of anamnesis and aphesis.

The communities were and are thus enabled to re-live mystically and sacramentally the event of deliverance and liberation. The past becomes contemporary as they experience and appropriate this deliverance in their own time.

For the Christian community, that same experience and appropriating through remembering is also central. Its clearest expression is in the sacrament of the Lord's supper, where the whole drama of salvation in Christ is evident. The very movement of the liturgy – re-members, makes present through the action of the Holy Spirit – the calling, the forgiving, healing, teaching, intercessory ministry of Jesus, and his dying and rising, in the light of which he sends us out to be his body in the world, sharing the brokenness of humankind.

---

4 Claus Westermann, *Blessing in the Bible and the Early Church, translated by Keith Crim*, Fortress Press, Philadelphia, 1978.

Re-membering, as Max Thurian[5] and the Pontifical International Theological Commission Memory and Reconciliation[6] in their report *Memory and Reconciliation* have emphasized, is a dynamic process, where the past is contemporary and the now is lived within the horizon of that which is to be "complete". As Paul stresses, we see through a glass darkly, but then we shall see face to face. (1 Corinthians 13:12) We are a pilgrim people, seeking to understand and to be faithful. We are a pilgrim people, who, as Johannes Metz[7] noted, "stand in the event of the dying and rising of Jesus of Nazareth".

As a community we are brought into being by the death and rising of Christ.

It is therefore not surprising that much of our Christian language and experience focuses on suffering and loss, of struggles to understand, of being a community which is a counterwitness to the values of surrounding societies. We live, as Johannes Metz and Jurgen Moltmann[8] so powerfully expressed it, in the subversive memory of Jesus of Nazareth. That is what participation in Christ entails. Our baptism, Mary Tanner noted, is baptism into the pilgrimage of discipleship. The Christian life is living out the baptismal vocation – "Can you drink the cup of which I must drink. Or be baptized with the baptism that I must embrace?"

The church then in its very essence is a community of a body broken, of a body continually broken by betrayal and falsehood, of a body tortured, re-membering that Christ is raised with the marks of victimhood.

The people of the Beatitudes

Such a community is a pilgrim people, a people on a pilgrimage, a people who undertake this journey ecumenically – the people of the Beatitudes. The vespers for All Saints during the Bose Symposium offered a lesson from Ecclesiasticus – the famous hymn: "Let us now praise famous men", a hymn which, having noted the famous, goes on to emphasize the lasting contribution of those who are not known but have also helped to shape persons, communities and the communion of saints by their lives and witness. The gospel of the day is the Beatitudes. Our pilgrimage as the Body of Christ is undertaken as the people of the Beatitudes. As Marco Gnavi noted in his presentation, the saints and martyrs are "the authoritative exegetes of the Beatitudes".

The Beatitudes are by their very nature counter-cultural; they are, as some of the papers have noted, counter-empire. The testimonies from Latin America, Russia and Korea,

5 Max Thurian, *The Eucharistic Memorial* (trans. J.G.Davies) Lutterworth, London, 1961 (2 vols).

6 International Theological Commission, *Memory and Reconciliation: The Church and the Faults of the Past*, Rome, December 1999.

7 See Jurgen Moltmann and Johannes Metz, *Two Meditations on the Passion*, translated by Edmund Colledge, Paulist, New York, 1979.

8 *Ibid.*

among others, have highlighted the way in which to be a Beatitude People involves critiquing society and culture – "the subversive memory of Jesus".

The Beatitudes call us to be peacemakers. As Dietrich Bonhoeffer, himself a martyr, noted in his *The Cost of Discipleship*,[9] Jesus calls us not to enjoy peace, but to make peace. We have seen testimony to this in our presentations. The Melanesian brothers sought to live Christ's reconciling ministry and suffered death because of it. To belong to the Beatitude people is not a specific confessional tradition. The Latin American stories point to those who are not acknowledged by their own church, but have been seen as sacraments of grace by other communities. They have mentored and inspired others. The Beatitude people seek to promote the fullness of life for all and take the risk of affirming the human rights of others. An aspect of this may be naming the victims as in Russia and giving names and faces to the disappeared in all contexts. In his writings, particularly in his New Year's Day peace statements, His Holiness John Paul II reminded Christians of the need to develop a culture of peace rather than promote a culture of violence; to expend as much energy on working for a just peace in situations of conflict throughout the world as had been expended in developing the principles for a just war. Such peacemaking, as the moving testimony of the Melanesian brothers exhibits, requires an intentionality. It is a call to be pro-active for peace, rather than only reactive to specific conflicts.

The pilgrim people, the Body of Christ, the Beatitude people, are thus called to be prophetic in word and life, to seek justice and to offer a witness to the preferential option for the poor. Such a participating in the ministry of Christ can allow of no distinction between church and society, between religion and politics. We are called to be for others, to embody that ministry of self – giving embodied in Christ.

Those who have died because of their faith, their attempt to be faithful disciples, have died to live. One of the first collections of letters and prayers by those who suffered and were killed in the Holocaust was published under the title "Dying We Live".[10] Many of those who perished, like Paul Schneider, had sought to take the place of others – to give themselves for others. The letters so often express a plea for forgiveness and, like Jesus on the cross, a prayer that the perpetrators of the evil will also receive forgiveness. We are called to be embodiments of "costly grace"[11] (Dietrich Bonhoeffer).

In the Body of Christ, those who have suffered and died are our fellow pilgrims. We are bound to them and to those who suffer in our time, in suffering and hope. This is well expressed in a prayer attributed to John Calvin which we regularly pray in my congregation:

---

9 Dietrich Bonhoeffer, *The Cost of Discipleship*, translated by R.H. Fuller, SCM, London, 1959, p.102.
10 Trevor Huddleston, (Foreword) *Dying we Live*, Fontana, London, 1959.
11 Dietrich Bonhoeffer, p.35ff.

Save us O Lord,

from being self centred in our prayers,

and teach us to remember to pray for others.

May we be so caught up in love for those for whom we pray

that we may feel their needs as keenly as our own,

and pray for them with imagination,

sensitivity,

and knowledge.

We ask this in Christ's name.

Through that prayer we are invited to enter, to inhabit the situations of others with whom we are bound in Christ, so that we can stand alongside them in their predicament. We are also invited to remember those who have formed us, and offered us a witness of discipleship. Like the saints and martyrs we are human. They have mediated grace to us. As Marco Gnavi noted, "we are debtors of mutual love". They are sacraments of grace through whom God's invitation and call to us is made plain.

Remembering ecumenically

It is clear that the celebration of, the remembering of, the living testimony of the saints and martyrs transcends denominational barriers. His Holiness John Paul II emphasized this in the very beginning of his encyclical *Ut Unum Sint.*[12] He began his reflection on Christian and church unity with the holiness of the martyrs of the church, whose testimony is received and celebrated by all Christians. To celebrate the saints and martyrs of the church is of its very nature a celebration of the unity of the church, an anticipation of that which we are called to become.

Just as Christians are baptized into Christ and participation in the One, Holy, Catholic and Apostolic Church, such a baptism is celebrated in the context of a specific community. There the baptized are nourished. There they are formed as part of the pilgrimage to be "conformed" to the image of Christ (Romans 8:29). It is clear therefore that the witness of saints and martyrs is specific to the community in which they have been formed, and yet, as in baptism, they are a gift of grace to the whole Body of Christ. Their witness in their own specific context can and does provide inspiration to Christians in other times and contexts, strengthening their resolve and offering encouragement and insight on the pilgrim way. Some

12 Pope John Paul II, *Ut Unum Sint*, Rome, 1995.

may be honoured outside their own situation for the witness they have offered, while not being recognized in their own context.

The suggestion made at the Bangalore Faith and Order Commission in 1978 which the Community of Bose has progressed through the publication of *Il libro dei Testimoni,*[13] offers a valuable resource whereby we are enabled to share in remembering those who have given shape to communities in different times and places. Through our participation in the Body of Christ they belong to us all and may intimate and express the love and grace of God to us.

Such ecumenical remembering may involve a reconciling of memories. At this conference, the reconciling process of the Mennonite-Roman Catholic international dialogue was opened up for us. Perhaps we might also remember the earlier Reformed-Mennonite Dialogue, where painful memories of persecution and death were remembered, forgiveness sought and an act of reconciliation through the visit to the battlefields in which men of faith in the – at that time – opposing communities were killed. Such symbols are important for letting go of the past and drawing a line which takes communities into new relationships of common witness and acceptance. History cannot be changed. However, the memory of the past which may still imprison us from making positive relations with others can be changed.

Similarly, the Reformed-Roman Catholic dialogue, which issued the report: *Towards a common understanding of the Church,*[14] emphasized the reconciliation of memories, attempted to hear the pain of the other, to move towards a pilgrimage of dialogue, in which there is a mutual sharing and commitment to the pilgrim way.

In these instances the churches are called to seek reconciliation, to accept the sacrifice of the other and to initiate a new relationship as a witness to our fragile and broken world.

The churches together also may seek ecumenically to name and note the forgotten ones – as the passage from Ecclesiasticus enjoins. To name those who have disappeared, those who were placed by others into situations of pain, brokenness and death, those with whom we are bound in Christ.

Churches might also ecumenically repent together of situations of complicity in injustice, as they celebrate those who were brave enough to resist, to speak out, to stand alongside those victimized. Such saints and martyrs remind us of our own betrayal of the gospel, and as their lives are celebrated, so churches might commit themselves to work together for justice and peace. Such occasions would remind us of our calling to be a Beatitude people.

---

13 Enzo Bianchi (Introduction) *Il Libro dei Testimoni*: *Martirologio ecumenico*, Edizioni San Paolo, Cinisello Balsamo (MI), 2002.

14 Reformed-Roman Catholic International Commission: *Towards a Common Understanding of the Church*, in Jeffrey Gros et.al. (eds) *Growth in Agreement II*, WCC, Geneva, 2000, pp.780-818.

The witness of the saints and martyrs of the church of all ages and all places seriously entails the recognition of our common baptism into Christ. The celebration of the saints and martyrs is itself a baptismal celebration. It is a participation in and with each other, and should form the root of our ecumenical pilgrimage and our life together. Such a recognition of baptism should also lead to the awareness of our participating together in the body of Christ – the body broken, the body celebrating, "This is my body". It should lead us to the celebration of the sacrament of the Lord's supper. In his Holy Week sermons, John Calvin reminds us of the water and the blood flowing from the side of Christ – and from this he emphasized the centrality of these two sacraments in Christ and their inseparability. As a sign to a broken world, our celebration of the saints and martyrs should lead us towards the feast of remembering, the meal of the whole community of the broken body. It is in this liturgical setting above all, that the saints and martyrs of the church are most appropriately celebrated. In the light of the Faith and Order statement on the Eucharist at Lima in 1982, Max Thurian was asked to produce a liturgy which expressed the elements of the statement. In the Lima liturgy, which emanated from this request, an important space is evident whereby the saints and martyrs of the church are celebrated. They have offered us their living testimony, which thus strengthens our pilgrimage. They have been and continue to be "exegetes of the Beatitudes", "orators of the Spirit". They mediate to us the grace of God, and as such invite our response in love of God and each other. They offer us a testimony to the community we are called to be "united together in brotherly love, and mutually imparting our blessings to each other".

Perhaps reflecting on and celebrating the saints and martyrs of the church in this tapestry of the communion of saints and the Body of Christ will take us forward on our ecumenical pilgrimage of faithful discipleship.

RECONCILIATION THROUGH MEMORIES AND PLACES

Reconciliation between Mennonites and Roman Catholics

Helmut Harder

Jesus, help us live in peace,
From our blindness set us free,
Fill us with your healing love,
Help us live in unity.[1]

Introduction

In 2002 the Monastery of Bose published a volume of yearly calendric readings featuring the lives of 365 faithful witnesses.[2] In years past it would have been typical of a Catholic-oriented institution to choose only Catholics to fill the pages of such a publication. However when those seeking spiritual sustenance for the day open the pages of this publication and turn for instance to January 23, they read of none other than Menno Simons. Why is this surprising? Menno Simons (b.1496) was an important spiritual leader of the Anabaptist-Mennonite movement in the 16th century, during what Protestants call the Reformation and Catholics prefer to refer to as the great schism.[3] Menno had trained as a Catholic priest and was serving in his home parish of Witmarsum in the Netherlands when, on January 23, 1536, he forsook his calling and joined the Anabaptist movement. The radical sign of his transition was his renunciation of infant baptism and submission to (re)baptism as an adult believer. In the next months Menno gave himself to the intense study of the Scriptures, which led him to centre Christian life on discipleship, or *Nachfolge Christi,* and to join ranks with the non-violent peaceful wing of the Anabaptists. In time Menno Simons became a recognized spiritual leader of the people, eventually referred to as *Mennists*, today's Mennonites.

Menno Simons' decision to join the Anabaptist movement was made at great risk to his personal safety. From the moment of his "conversion" he was marked as a heretic by Catholic and Protestant Reformers alike. Every day he faced the prospect of persecution and death as he went about his pastoral duties of serving the sprouting Anabaptist congregations. This was his fate to the end of his life. Menno died of natural causes in 1561. Mennonites and many others would consider Menno Simons a Christian martyr, according to the biblical usage. Under dire circumstances, he served Christ and the church as a faithful witness (Greek: *martys*) to the very end of his earthly life.

1 JD Martin, "Unity", Gill 'n' Goldie Music (ASCAP), 1971, 2003. Used with permission.

2 Comunità di Bose, *Il libro dei testimoni. Martirologio ecumenico*, San Paolo, Cinisello Balsamo (MI), 2002. French translation: Communauté de Bose, *Témoins de Dieu, Martyrologe universel*, Paris, Bayard, 2005. Polish translation: Klasztor Bose, *Księga świadków. Martyrologium ekumeniczne*, Święty Paweł, Częstochowa, 2004. See the pages designated for January 23. For a partial English translation of the calendar see: http://tinyurl.com/Bose-Martyrology.

3 For a full account of the life and thought of Menno Simons, see Cornelius Krahn, "Menno Simons" in *The Mennonite Encyclopedia*, III, ed. by Harold S. Bender and C. Henry Smith, Mennonite Publishing House, Scottdale, PA, 1957, pp.577-584. Menno Simons' writings can be found in: Menno Simons, *The Complete Writings,* Mennonite Publishing House, Scottdale, PA, 1956.

It is indeed remarkable and commendable that today, almost 500 years after the beginning of the 16th century break, Catholics can invite their faithful to appreciate leaders such as Menno Simons, and even to draw spiritual sustenance from this one-time servant of the Catholic Church turned "heretic". How did this change come about? Among the many factors that could be mentioned, the ecumenical dialogues of recent decades have played a major role in setting the stage for reconciliation between the Mennonite Church and its former persecutors, including not only the Catholic Church, but also Reformed and Lutheran churches.[4] Here I recount something of the international Mennonite-Catholic dialogue, particularly as it relates to efforts at reconciliation in the light of a sorry history of persecution and martyrdom.

Roman Catholic-Mennonite Dialogue (1998-2003)

In the fall of 1998 Mennonites and Roman Catholics initiated an unprecedented conversation. This was the first time since the 16th century rupture that the two churches had entered into official church-sanctioned conversation with each other. Gathered around the dialogue table at the Mennonite World Conference offices in Strasbourg, France was a group of fourteen persons, seven of whom represented the Vatican's Pontifical Council for Promoting Christian Unity (PCPCU) and seven appointed by Mennonite World Conference.[5] The dialogue extended over a five year period (1998-2003), with the group meeting six times, for about a week at a time. At the end of that period, in the summer of 2003, an extensive report was issued, entitled *Called Together to be Peacemakers* [abbr.: *CTBP*].[6]

At the beginning, the aim of the dialogue was quite modest: "to learn to know one another better; to promote better understanding of positions on Christian faith held by Catholics and Mennonites, and to contribute to the overcoming of prejudices that have long existed between them." The conversations were held in an atmosphere of good will, and with the hope of effecting some kind of reconciliation, a "healing of memories". Prayer and worship sustained the dialogue each day. In the end, as the title of the *CTBP* Report implies, the dialogue moved some distance beyond the originally stated purpose, from "becoming acquainted" to a common call to peacemaking.

---

4 Over the past three decades, Mennonites have engaged in official international dialogues with the Baptists, the Reformed, the Lutherans and the Roman Catholics. In addition to exchanges on the global level, numerous local and regional exchanges have taken place. For a comprehensive report of ecumenical dialogues between Mennonites and other Christian communions, see: *Heilung der Erinnerungen - befreit zur gemeinsamen Zukunft: Mennoniten im Dialog.* Berichte und Texte ökumenischer Gespräche auf nationaler und internationaler Ebene, ed. by Fernando Enns, Verlag Otto Lembeck, Frankreich am Main, & Bonifatius Verlag, Paderborn, 2008.

5 Mennonite World Conference (MWC) is a global community of Christian churches who trace their beginning to the 16th-century Radical Reformation in Europe. Today, close to 1,500,000 believers belong to this faith family; at least 60 percent are African, Asian or Latin American. MWC represents 97 Mennonite and Brethren in Christ churches in 53 countries on six continents. MWC has offices in Strasbourg (France), Kitchener (Ontario, Canada), and Fresno (California, USA). The presenter of this case study served as Mennonite co-chair of the dialogue along with Bishop Joseph Martino of Philadelphia.

6 *Called Together to be Peacemakers:* Report of the International Dialogue between the Catholic Church and the Mennonite World Conference (1998-2003) [abbr.: *CTBP*], *Information Service,* the Pontifical Council for Promoting Christian Unity, Vatican City: N. 113, 2003/II/III, pp.111-148. The Report is also available via internet at www.bridgefolk.net/called together.htm. For a translation in German, see *Heilung der Erinnerungen – befreit zur gemeinsamen Zukunft: Mennoniten im Dialog,* pp.29-132.

Underlying the conversation was the keen awareness of a history of persecution and martyrdom that marked the 16th century schism and that had coloured relationships ever since. This meant that a Mennonite-Catholic dialogue would be no simple matter. There would need to be honest and open conversation, careful listening, and the possibility of a change of heart (*metanoia*). In the early course of the dialogue, the Catholic representatives around the table reminded their Mennonite counterparts that there could be some understandable reasons why severe persecution was leveled at the Anabaptist-Mennonites. The Anabaptist protests against infant baptism, against the mass, and against intimate church-state relations were seen by the established church of the day as highly provocative acts that ran counter to cherished Catholic beliefs. Also, the historic medieval indictment against those who engaged in re-baptisms was still the rule-of-thumb[7] with the inquisition as the punishing arm against religious "dissidents". Furthermore, the Anabaptist movement was seen as an ecclesial, social, and above all political threat to the already dubious stability of the times.

This inevitably set the stage for a blood-bath. As historian Peter Nissen, member of the Catholic-Mennonite dialogue, stated: "The history of the Catholic – and Protestant – reactions against Anabaptists is not only written in ink, but also in blood."[8] It is estimated that of the ca. 5000 persons who were put to death for their faith in Europe in the 16th century, about half (2500) were Anabaptist-Mennonites, and that of those about 1500 were persecuted unto death in Catholic territories.[9] Looking back to that time, it appears, as the Catholic dialogue partners conceded, that there was no evident theological justification for the persecutions. It was also noted that while followers of the Anabaptist-Mennonite way were martyred by Catholics and Protestants, there appears to have been no retaliation on the part of those threatened and persecuted.

It became clear within the dialogue group that the healing process would require a careful and sensitive joint re-reading of 16th century history. Both sides were willing to revisit their history in a "matter of fact" way. There would have to be a "purification of memory" before there could be a "healing of memory". While, as the report indicates, considerable progress was made over the course of the five years, the group realized that the 16th century situation still begged a deeper analysis of causes and events. For instance, Professor Nissen observed that Catholic theologians and authorities had a quite limited awareness of the Anabaptist movement(s). They tended to borrow their images of the Anabaptists from medieval

7 Cf. *CTBP*, §40 "The practice of rebaptism had already been condemned in the early fifth century as reflected in Augustine's polemics against the Donatists, a separatist movement in North Africa, who rebaptized all recruits from the established Church. For the state, a law of the Roman emperors Honorius and Theodosius of 413 determined severe penalties for the practice of rebaptism. In 529, the emperor Justinian I, in reproducing the Theodosian edict in his revision of Roman law, specified the penalty as capital punishment. On the basis of this ancient imperial law against the Donatists, the Diet of Speyer in 1529 proclaimed the death penalty for all acts of "rebaptism".

8 Peter Nissen, "The Catholic Response to the Anabaptist Movement in the Sixteenth Century," unpublished paper presented at the Catholic-Mennonite dialogue session in Strasbourg, France (October, 1998), p.4. This paper, along with all papers presented at the Catholic-Mennonite dialogue, is available from the library of Canadian Mennonite University, 500 Shaftesbury Blvd., Winnipeg, Manitoba, Canada R3P 2N2.

9 Brad Gregory, *Salvation at Stake: Christian Martyrdom in early Modern Europe,* Harvard University Press, Cambridge, MA and London, UK, 1999, ch.6. James M. Stayer, "Numbers in Anabaptist Research," in C. Arnold Snyder, (ed.), *Commoners and Community: Essays in Honour of Werner O. Packull*, Herald Press, Waterloo, ON, 2002, pp.51-73.

anti-heretical literature. Furthermore, the issue of baptism with its defence of infant baptism dominated their thinking, with the result that they neglected to listen to the contributions of Anabaptist scholars of the day (e.g. Balthasar Hubmaier), such as the Anabaptist longing for a just and peaceful society. Instead they invoked the inquisition on a wide range of subjects.[10] Fortunately, both sides were able to engage in critical self-examination with a minimum of defensiveness. In this, the spirit of the group was guided by the statement in our Lord's Prayer: "Forgive our debts, as we also have forgiven our debtors." (Matt. 6:12).

After considerable discussion, the dialogue group was able to summarize its major insights and conclusions pertaining to persecution and martyrdom in four paragraphs.[11] While, as indicated, this was not considered an end to the discussion, it did serve as a step forward. The main points are as follows:

> The practice of persecution and martyrdom at the time of the Reformation was largely a result of the close relationship between religion and society at that time. This set up a situation where the established Christian confession of a given territory became intolerant towards persons of other Christian confessions. In such a context Anabaptists were dubbed as heretics, and became objects of persecution.[12]
>
> It was acknowledged that Mennonites suffered greatly during this period, both in Protestant and in Catholic states.[13] The numbers of persecuted far exceeded their Protestant and Catholic counterparts. In some states, discrimination against Anabaptist-Mennonites has continued into the 20th century.
>
> It became clear that the motivation for martyrdom among the Mennonites was their commitment to *Nachfolge Christi* (discipleship) with its consequent openness to oppression, persecution and violent death. Indeed, this became a mark of Mennonite identity. The prospect of persecution placed an indelible mark on "all who joined the group – on their priorities, status and self-consciousness."[14]
>
> The dialogue group recognized that while Mennonites suffered persecution at the hands of Catholics, Catholics were never persecuted by Mennonites.[15] Nevertheless, there was

10 Professor Nissen concludes: "As a matter of fact, Catholic theologians in the 16th century mainly discussed questions of a secondary, derived nature, and not the underlying change in the vision of God, man, Church and world. If they had come to know better the Anabaptist concerns, they would perhaps have recognized it as a radicalization of late-medieval piety, as a movement of conversion and penance, of inner rebirth and of the merciful renewal of the creature by the imitation of Christ. Perhaps this is the acquaintance Catholics still have to make in meeting their Mennonite [brothers and sisters]" (Nissen, p.13).

11 Cf. *CTBP*, §45-48.

12 Cf. *CTBP*, §45. While the Catholic delegation took this as a contextual rationale for persecution of Anabaptists, the Mennonite delegates wondered why the official church in the respective territory had not objected, in principle, to the actions of the state on their behalf.

13 Cf. *CTBP*, §46.

14 *CTBP*, §47.

15 Yet questions were raised by Catholics that suggested this claim should be nuanced. Were not the Anabaptists the troublemakers at Münster? Furthermore, perhaps the Mennonites did not kill with the sword, but what about the vitriolic language Menno and others used at times against their adversaries?

> affinity between Mennonites and Catholics in that Catholics were also persecuted in the post-medieval period.[16] This occurred in England and in territories on the Continent where Reformed and Lutheran churches predominated. Like the Mennonites, in these countries Catholics too were often constrained to go into hiding.[17]

These paragraphs indicate the extent to which Mennonites and Catholics were able to reach a common understanding of their complex and difficult 16th century encounters. What progress were they able to achieve in the matter of reconciliation?

Statements of regrets and a mutual challenge

In some ways the timing of the dialogue was fortuitous. The conversations began just before the arrival of the third millennium with its emphasis on new beginnings. On March 12, 2000, the first Sunday of Lent, Pope John Paul II celebrated the "Day of Pardon". On that day the Pope led the Catholic Church in a universal prayer which included a confession of sins committed by members of the church during the past millennium, and a plea to God for forgiveness. The Mennonites were assured by the Catholic dialogue partners that when the Pope confessed "sins which have harmed the unity of the Church" and "sins committed in the service of truth", these expressions of regret were to be heard also by Mennonites to include actions taken against *them*. The dialogue partners assured the Mennonite delegates that "even the consideration of mitigating factors, such as cultural conditioning in previous centuries, which frequently converged to create assumptions which justified intolerance 'does not exonerate the Church from the obligation to express profound regret for the weaknesses of so many of her sons and daughters'."[18] The Catholic representatives expressed their readiness to "apply this spirit of repentance to the conflicts between Catholics and Mennonites in the 16th century and to express a penitential spirit, asking forgiveness for any sins which were committed against Mennonites, asking God's mercy for that, and God's blessing for a new relationship with Mennonites today."[19]

On a visit to Rome in November 2001, the Mennonite delegation met with Walter Cardinal Kasper, President of the PCPCU. On that occasion Cardinal Kasper added his words of regret:

> Is it not the case that we, Catholics and Mennonites, have mutually condemned one another? Each saw the other as deviating from the apostolic faith. Let us forgive and ask forgiveness. The authorities in centuries past often resolved problems in society

16 Cf., for example, Gregory, ch.7.
17 Cf. *CTBP*, §48.
18 *CTBP*, §202. The quote is a reference to *Tertio millennio adventiente*, 1994, §35. The distinction implied here between "the Church" and "her sons and daughters" became a matter for discussion as this distinction is not familiar to a Mennonite ecclesiology.
19 *CTBP*, §202.

> by severe means, punishing with imprisonment or death those who were seen as undermining society. Especially in the 16th century, the Anabaptists were among those who suffered greatly in this regard. I surely regret those instances when this took place in Catholic societies.[20]

This expression of understanding was received with warm appreciation by the Mennonite representatives, although it remains unclear whether this is an expression of regret on behalf of the Catholic Church or only recognition that "in Catholic societies" such persecution took place. The Catholics at the dialogue table identified with Cardinal Kasper's statement as their expression of regret as well.

The Mennonite delegates responded with a statement of their own, a statement that had been formulated some months earlier by the Executive Committee of Mennonite World Conference. The statement, entitled "God Calls Us to Christian Unity," expressed repentance on behalf of the MWC community of churches for poor relations to other Christians, including Catholics. It reads in part:

> As Mennonites and Brethren in Christ, we give thanks to God for brothers and sisters of other traditions around the globe who accept the claims of Scripture and seek to live as followers of our Lord. We confess that we have not done all we could to follow God's call to relate in love and mutual counsel to other brothers and sisters who confess the name of Jesus Christ as Lord and seek to follow him. We have seen peacemaking and reconciliation as callings of all Christian disciples, but confess that we have not done all we could to overcome divisions within our circles and to work toward unity with other brothers and sisters.[21]

The statement continues:

> In regard to the 16th century rupture, we recognize that as the Anabaptists sought to be faithful followers of Jesus Christ, they called into question the established churches and societies. We acknowledge that there were diverse and sometimes divergent currents within the Anabaptist movement. We believe that it was initially difficult for contemporaries to distinguish between the Anabaptists we claim as our spiritual forebears – those committed to Biblical pacifism, ready to suffer martyrdom for the cause of Christ – and those who took the sword, thinking that they were doing God's will in preparing the way for the return of Jesus. We regret Anabaptist words and deeds that contributed to fracturing the body of Christ.[22]

20 *CTBP,* §202.
21 *CTBP*, §203.
22 *CTBP,* §203.

> We confess also that in spite of a commitment to follow Jesus Christ in daily life, we and others in our family of faith have frequently failed to demonstrate love towards Catholics. Too often, from the 16th century to the present, we have thoughtlessly perpetuated hostile images and false stereotypes of Catholics and of the Catholic Church. For this, we express our regret and ask forgiveness.[23]

These respective expressions of failure and regret led the Mennonite and Catholic delegates to formulate and agree upon a common reconciliatory expression as follows:

> Together we, Catholic and Mennonite delegations, recognize and regret that 16th century Christians, including Catholics and Anabaptists, were unable to resolve the problems of the church of that time in such way as to prevent divisions in the body of Christ that have lasted to the present day.[24]
>
> Together we acknowledge and regret that indifference, tension, and hostility between Catholics and Mennonites exist in some places today, and this for a variety of historical or contemporary reasons. Together we reject the use of any physical coercion or verbal abuse in situations of disagreement and we call on all Christians to do likewise. We commit ourselves to self-examination, dialogue, and interaction that manifest Jesus Christ's reconciling love, and we encourage our brothers and sisters everywhere to join us in this commitment.[25]

As 14 Catholic and Mennonite representatives of the two respective global churches, the dialogue group was gratified that progress had been made:

> We celebrated the common recognition of basic convictions we hold in common. We noted significant differences that continue to divide us and require further dialogue.... Nonetheless, and although we are not in full unity with one another, the substantial amount of the Apostolic faith which we realize today that we share, allows us as members of the Catholic and Mennonite delegations to see one another as brothers and sisters in Christ. We hope that others may have similar experiences, and that these may contribute to a healing of memories.[26]

Finally, the group offered a mutual challenge: "Can we not increase our efforts to create new relationships today so that future generations may look back to the 21st century with positive memories of a time in which Mennonites and Catholics began increasingly to serve

23 *CTBP*, §204.
24 *CTBP*, §205.
25 *CTBP*, §206.
26 *CTBP*, §210.

Christ together?" Their hope is expressed in the very title of the report: *Called Together to be Peacemakers.*

Post-2003 initiatives

This brings us to the summer of 2003, which saw both the Vatican's PCPCU and the General Council of MWC accept the Report and endorse the work of the dialogue group. It is evident that the originally stated purpose of the dialogue has been realized. At the least, the participants in the dialogue have learned to know one another better, have grown in mutual understanding of the other's positions on Christian faith, and have made significant progress in overcoming prejudices. Anecdotal evidence reveals that this is also the case throughout much of the Mennonite constituency and in some Catholic parishes. Since the conclusion of the first stage of the dialogue, various initiatives have carried the vision of reconciliation forward. Here are some examples:

1. The Report, *Called Together to be Peacemakers*, has been disseminated broadly and has been used as a basis for study in the two constituencies. Symposia, lecture series and local dialogues, including both Mennonites and Catholics, have been conducted regionally in such contexts as Bethel College (North Newton, KS); Notre Dame University (South Bend, IN), Toronto Mennonite Theological Centre (Toronto, ON); University of Hamburg (Hamburg, Germany); selected congregations/parishes in Winnipeg, MB, Goshen/Elkhart, IN; and at the Thomashof, Germany. These are samples only.

2. Inspired by the dialogue, leaders of the Catholic and Evangelical churches in Austria have initiated dialogue with the Hutterites in Canada. In the 16th century Austria was the context for severe persecution of Anabaptists. Their leader, Jacob Hutter, was burned at the stake in Innsbruck's town square in 1536. Today efforts are being made to heal this wound.

3. In North America the Bridgefolk movement brings together persons who picture themselves as standing "on the bridge" between the Mennonite and Catholic traditions. The movement sponsors an annual retreat, a newsletter and occasional publications.[27] The Benedictine Monastery at Collegeville, through its Abbot John Klassen, has been a primary promoter of this movement. While the beginning of the Bridgefolk movement preceded the Catholic-Mennonite dialogue, the dialogue has given the movement considerable momentum.

27 Bridgefolk produces monographs under the title "Bridgefolk Series". Publications to date, available through Pandora Press (www.pandorapress.com), include: *On Baptism*, ed. by Gerald W. Schlabach, 2004; *Just Policing*, ed. by Ivan Kauffman, 2004: *Called Together to be Peacemakers* (a study book), ed. by Willard Roth and Gerald W. Schlabach, 2005; *Martyrdom in an Ecumenical Perspective*, ed. by Peter C. Erb, 2007. For more information on the work of Bridgefolk, *cf.* www.bridgefolk.net and follow the links.

4. The Report's challenge to Catholics and Mennonites to be peacemakers *together* has already resulted in several joint initiatives. 1) In Columbia, Catholics and Mennonites are currently addressing the perpetuators of violence in that country with one voice. 2) In October 2007, a group of Mennonites and Catholics gathered in Rome to formulate and submit a "Mennonite and Catholic Contribution to the World Council of Churches' *Decade to Overcome Violence*."[28]

It can be surmised that this sample of initiatives is but the beginning of a rich future of ongoing collaboration that will serve to build a culture of peace.[29] In a slow but sure way, these initiatives also contribute to the process of Catholic-Mennonite reconciliation.

Abiding questions

The sentiments contained in the respective Catholic and Mennonite expressions of regret noted above can be characterized as "soft" statements of reconciliation. Confessional statements are carefully balanced. The call to forgive is issued mutually. No specific sins are named which call for recantation. As such, they point the churches in a direction. But for some critics, the effort at reconciliation has not gone far enough. There are still matters that need tending. I conclude by drawing attention to three voices – two Catholic and one Mennonite – that convey a critical, though constructive note.

1. Drew Christiansen, S.J., a Catholic sociologist and theologian, and a member of the Mennonite-Catholic dialogue, judges that not all roadblocks have been removed in the progress towards reconciliation. He surmises that the hope of a new relationship between Mennonites and Catholics is yet contingent on a repudiation of the historic Catholic doctrine of religious coercion. For this to happen, Vatican II's "Declaration on Religious Liberty" (*Dignitatis Humanae*) could be invoked to effect the reversal of this historic doctrine so that repentance for violence done against Anabaptists becomes clear. If this could happen, the ecumenical commemoration of martyrs would be a matter of even greater significance. And the stage would be set for Catholics to implore God's mercy specifically for their persecution of Mennonites.[30]

2. A stronger word of critique comes from Abbot Eoin de Bhaldraithe, O. Cist., of Ireland. Following a Mennonite-Catholic symposium on martyrology held under the auspices of "Bridgefolk" at the Benedictine Monastery in Collegeville, MN, Abbot Eoin, who attended the event as a special guest, wrote as follows:

---

28 For the text, see "A Mennonite and Catholic Contribution to the World Council of Churches' *Decade to Overcome Violence*, in *Information Service*, The Pontifical Council for Promoting Christian Unity, Vatican City, N. 126, 2007/IV, pp.191-195.

29 For an explication of what a "culture of peace" could entail, see, for example, *Seeking Cultures of Peace: A Peace Church Conversation*, ed. by Fernando Enns, Scott Holland, Ann K. Riggs, Cascadia Publishing House, Telford, PA; WCC, Geneva; Herald Press, Scottdale, PA, 2004.

30 Drew Christiansen, S.J., "The Ecumenical Martyrology: Some Catholic Reflections in Partial Response to Helmut Harder on The Bose Ecumenical Martyrology," in *Martyrdom in an Ecumenical Perspective: A Mennonite-Catholic Conversation*, edited by Peter C. Erb, p.158.

> *Called Together to be Peacemakers* is a beautiful title and, thank God, we all accept this as our calling today…. [But] as a Catholic … I found it disconcerting to read its account of the persecutions. About 5000 persons, it is said, died for their faith in the 16th century. About half were Anabaptists, the majority executed in Catholic territories. So between 1000 and 1500 Mennonites "were executed for their religious beliefs" – Catholics apparently are reluctant to call them "martyrs". It seems to me that this is a great flaw in the document. It is self-defensive when it should manifest profound repentance. A Martyrs Conference has been established [under the auspices of *Bridgefolk*] and has already met twice. One hopes this will lead to a better understanding of "dying for the faith" and "killing for the faith"…. The dialogue report says, "We have mutually condemned one another." This is like saying, "Perhaps we should not have condemned you, but remember that you did condemn us too." This attitude just will not work. If we or our church condemned someone wrongly, it is a sin and we must repent before God. The existence of sin in the other party is irrelevant when coming before God. We cannot say, "Since you forgive me I will forgive you." We repent even if there is no repentance on the other side.[31]

Abbot Eoin calls upon the Catholic Church as such to be more forthright in admitting its implication in persecutions against the Anabaptist-Mennonites. These Catholic voices serve notice that while there has been significant progress in the reconciliatory process, there are still abiding issues, issues that place the onus for repentance on the Catholic Church. It is significant that these issues centre not primarily on doctrine nor on sacramental practice, but on violence related to persecution and martyrdom.

3. A third voice comes from Jeremy Bergen, a young Mennonite theologian teaching at Conrad Grebel University College in Waterloo, Ontario. Bergen observes that the current attempt to clinch ecumenical relations by way of a common recognition of martyrs is no simple matter.[32] This is because two trends in Mennonite theology and church life run counter to each other: a renewed interest in "confessional martyrs" as a way of being Christian in the world, and closer ecumenical relations between Mennonites and Catholics.[33] The problem is accentuated by the reality that 16th century Mennonite martyrs "accept[ed] death at the hands of those who hated the faith". Their steadfastness and courage was a stamp of approval on the truth of the confession which they upheld.

---

31 Excerpt taken from "Bridgefolk Mail", *The Bridge:* Newsletter of the Bridgefolk Movement (Summer, 2005), 15, accessible at http://www.bridgefolk.net/newsletter/08/summer.pdf

32 Cf. Jeremy M. Bergen, "Problem or Promise? Confessional Martyrs and Mennonite-Roman Catholic Relations," in *Martyrdom in an Ecumenical Perspective: ibid.*, pp.175-205.

33 Cf. *ibid.*, p.175.

Bergen observes that here we have a clash of confessions, of truth claim against truth claim.

While in the present ecumenical environment Mennonites do not want to characterize Catholics as "false", yet the historic judgment remains as a historic judgment. But Bergen maintains that "any gifts that Anabaptist martyrs have to give the contemporary church … cannot be received apart from facing the difficult reality that they were 'confessional martyrs' who were killed by other Christians."[34] Two crucial aspects of martyrdom, both pneumatalogical, must come together for there to be a resolution: "[1] the Holy Spirit empowers the martyr to be steadfast and thereby confirms the truth of his or her faith and life; [2] the Holy Spirit also builds up the church through the memory of such deaths."[35] Thus martyrdom as such is dependent on *both* dying for the faith *and* recognizing the truth of the faith on behalf of which the persecuted one has been put to death. The first puts the focus and the onus on the persecuted; the second addresses the persecutor. Of course, this issue applies to all Christian groups that have persecuted faithful witnesses to the faith.

Bergen's approach is to say, basically, that the disunity of the church "written on the broken bodies of confessional martyrs" is sinful; that the responsibility for the sin, marked by provocation, accusation, persecution, violence, extermination, etc., must be owned in general by *the entire church*, and in particular by *both sides* of the conflict. What this means for Catholics is for Catholics to discern. As for Mennonites, the challenge is to restore a "painful communion with persecutors."[36] It behooves them to own and confess the violence and unfaithfulness within the Body of Christ as their own sin as well, given their desire to be part of the *church as a whole*. I can only imagine such a move as the work of the Holy Spirit who continues the enduring work of pointing repentant sinners to Christ together.

Conclusion

The story of the five-year Catholic Mennonite dialogue is encased in the larger story which had its concrete beginning when persons of the like of Menno Simons challenged the church to reform. Instead, a separation born of violence ensued. Now, after almost 500 years, the two churches are working to overcome the dividing wall of hostility between them. While not all stumbling blocks have been removed, the dialogue has laid the foundation for a remarkable restoration of ecclesial unity, a unity assured by "the blood of Christ."

34 *Ibid.*, p.176.
35 *Ibid.*
36 *Ibid.*, p.198.

A Scriptural addendum

"For surely I know the plans I have for you, says the Lord, plans for your welfare and not for harm, to give you a future with hope. Then when you call upon me and come and pray to me, I will hear you. When you search for me, you will find me; if you seek me with all your heart" (Jeremiah 29:11-13).

"But now in Christ Jesus you who once were far off have been brought near by *the blood of Christ*. For he is our peace; in his flesh he has made both groups into one and has broken down the dividing wall, that is, the hostility between us.... that he might create in himself one new humanity in place of the two, thus making peace, and might reconcile both groups to God in one body through the cross, thus putting to death that hostility through it.... So then you are no longer strangers and aliens, but you are citizens with the saints and also members of the household of God" (Ephesians 2:13-14,15b-16,19).

Reconciling Memories and Peace

Hansulrich Gerber

Introduction

It is important to pursue the connection between commemoration and peace in the interest of not only the church, but the good news of peace which Jesus Christ came to proclaim. I am passionately convinced that we need to further pursue non-violence and violence prevention, as we reflect together on commemoration in unity. Our world needs peace – no one will dispute that. But our churches also need peace, they who are called to be peacemakers and claim the legacy of Jesus, and are, in spite of all their immense shortcomings, the body of Christ. The gospel of Jesus Christ compels us to work for peace and nonviolence and to do it in a loving, truthful and non-violent way. The challenge is not only an intellectual one, it is one of mind-set, conscience, sensuality, and indeed, life. And it is a challenge for the churches as many communities and as one community in Christ.

Defenseless martyrs

I belong to the Mennonite tradition, which grew out of the Anabaptist movement of the 16th century. Mennonites do not have a formal martyrology but they do have a long history of remembering those who were put to death because of their faith – not only Anabaptists. Early in the printing era, in the mid-17th century, the first collection of martyr's stories was published and it was called *The Bloody Theatre or the Martyr's Mirror of the defenseless Christians who suffered and died for the testimony of Jesus, their Saviour, from the time of Christ to the year A.D. 1660.*[1] The word "defenseless" was apparently crucial to the Anabaptist movement (or more precisely the pacifist wing of it, which by the way is the one of several streams that survived into modernity) that these Christians were not martyrs at any rate, but that they were defenseless martyrs. Their understanding was one of defenselessness in the physical sense of the term. Not that they endured anything passively. They did resist in ways that upset the powers. They did defend themselves through verbal and written disputes, but they did not defend themselves by force or violence, nor did they accept such forceful defense on their behalf. They lived very much with the conviction that Christians should be unarmed, that they should defend themselves with the gospel. They claimed that the struggle of Christ's disciples is not one against flesh and blood but against the powers and principalities as described in Ephesians 6.[2] Nor does *defenselessness* mean they were powerless. They may not always have acknowledged the power they had, but

1 Thieleman J. Van Braght, *The Bloody Theater or Martyrs Mirror*. First published in Dutch in 1660. English at Herald Press, Scottsdale, 1977; Online version: http://www.homecomers.org/mirror/

2 Eph. 6:12: For our wrestling is not against flesh and blood, but against the principalities, against the powers, against the world-rulers of this darkness… (ASV)

their defenselessness was not one of unconditional submission. In fact, they were accused of insubordination and of troublemaking. The Anabaptists were re-claiming the early Christian movement's non-resistant and non-violent stance as central to their faith in Jesus Christ and for the existence and mission of the church. They distinguished between earthly and violent power and divine power. For them divine power is real and tangible here on earth in the testimonies of the disciples of Jesus Christ through the work of the Holy Spirit. *The Martyr's Mirror* was for a long time in Anabaptist and Mennonite circles, and in Amish homes still today, the only book for Christian reference and worship, next to the Bible and the Psalter or Hymnbook.

In the early Anabaptist movement, in Europe until the pietist revival, and in Amish circles to this day, a crucial role is given to remembering as a way of learning and leading a faithful Christian life. For them, this meant essentially to be at peace and not afraid. Both these two things were not easily within reach at the time.[3] My interest in this presentation is in how remembering can contribute to peace and therefore also to peacemaking, or peace building. I do this with the aim to plead for developing a theology of peace in order to have commemorations that serve peace and reconciliation. For not only does Jesus call his disciples to be defenseless, he also calls them to make peace and so does the entire New Testament.

To be sure, I am working from the premise that the core ministry of the church is its ministry of reconciliation. Just as Jesus was sent so are his disciples. Reconciliation is not an accessory or optional task of the church, although often it has been treated as if it were optional, or a special concern. Reconciliation is part of the *raison d'être* of the body of Christ. Part of our work on memory then includes remembering how easily the church has lost sight of that. Keep remembering what the mission of the church is and remember those who have faithfully carried it out. For when that is forgotten, the church gets tangled up in violent conflict, destruction, misery and death. Too many people, especially in our Western world, accuse the church of its complicity in such actions and thus refuse to have anything to do with it.

Commemoration – for peace and reconciliation

Remembering – or commemoration – is to be measured against whether and how it contributes to reconciliation and peace. The term *reconciliation* is used in its broad sense: reconciliation with self, with the other, with the world – the things that surround us – and with God. God's

3 During the presentations on Latin America, I was struck by an interesting difference between the situation in Switzerland and Germany of the 17th century and Latin America of the 1970s: Anabaptists did engage in social work, and they were not persecuted for that, but for not submitting to state/church orders such as baptism or oath or attending worship or bearing the sword. Hanspeter Jecker, has documented in his research (dissertation from the University of Basel) that quite often, when Anabaptists were to be driven out of their village by the authorities, the local population stood up for them claiming that the village would lose their most competent and effective medicine people.

incarnation in Jesus Christ is intended to bring about reconciliation. If commemoration by the church as the body of Christ does not contribute to reconciliation then what is the point? The question for those who remember is this: what do we learn from these stories, from these witnesses? Healing requires remembering, and peace requires healing. Yet not any and all remembering automatically serves that purpose as we know full well.

For reconciling memories, consulting and acknowledging living witnesses in commemoration may be as important as remembering the martyrs who were put to death. Is commemoration or remembering possible in connection with people who are still among us as witnesses of Christ's love and life-giving presence through the Holy Spirit, and embodied in human beings, as flawed and imperfect as they might be? The criterion then is not whether they are martyrs, but whether they are or have been peacemakers, agents of reconciliation. For that is what we and our children and grandchildren need to learn.

In order for us to engage in the reconciliation of memories – our own and those around us – we need to have some understanding of how memories work, how they are being used, and how they contribute to either violence or peace, or both. We cannot do that in-depth here, but recent years have seen considerable work done on these issues.[4]

The challenge is sensitive, complex and not without risk. It is a profoundly anthropological, sociological, psychological and theological challenge and I do wonder sometimes when we will see more deliberate and orchestrated interdisciplinary work on the issue. There may be some, but from my limited perspective I see little interaction between, say, sociologists and theologians on the issue. To be sure, sociology only recently began to study violence – so did theology, and it seems to me we are still working on spelling and grammar. We cannot assume that Christians are on the same page on healing memories – not yet, for they need themselves to come to terms with their sick or distorted memories, not least of each other.

Violence and memory – living witnesses are essential for the healing of memories

Both the martyr and the one dying peacefully as a faithful witness is worthy of our remembering and can teach us and our children about faithful living. There is a difference, but let us not exaggerate that difference at the expense of the crucial role of witnesses for peace, forgiveness and reconciliation. One of the obstacles to peacemaking and to a more prophetic role of the church in our world is that the cloud of witnesses may be seen as a virtual reality, or one of a dusty or perhaps idealized past. And one of the major challenges in overcoming

4 One of the early publications on the subject in the context of Northern Ireland was edited by Alan Falconer on reconciling memories: Alan D. Falconer, (ed.) *Reconciling Memories*; Columba Press, Dublin, 1988.

violence and in peace building is for people to actually see the reality of these tasks being carried out all over the *oikoumene*. People's eyes are blinded and their perceptions obscured with scandal and blood-driven news so that many feel it is all a lost cause.

Remembering the living witnesses of peace is important, for the very fact that they live as human beings generally contributes to preventing that they become a myth. I recently attended a seminar on Martin Luther King and I was surprised at the degree to which Martin Luther King has become a myth for many, most of whom at the same time cannot remember because they do not know the man Dr King, a human being.

A further reason also to look to living witnesses is that we cannot interact with martyrs or saints of the past. I have often thought to myself while listening to a sermon in a Lutheran church what Martin Luther would say about an interpretation of his words. Or I found myself wondering about how our venerated saints would respond to our ways of telling the stories of their lives, especially when in their time they were seen as cases of sheer deviance. Living witnesses have the immense advantage that we can interact with them. Their very being in our midst challenges us because they are not *so* very different from us.[5]

Violence, memory and understanding – recent topics of study

Sociologists tell us that violence is being looked at from the point of view of victims only since the late 19th century (Henri Dunant and the Red Cross in regard to war) and the 20th century (criminal justice and victim-offender work). French sociologist Michel Wieviorka in his book on violence quotes a statement made by Marlene Young in 1988: "Now, finally, crime is understood from a perspective of the victim and no longer from society that needs to keep it at distance".[6] I insist here on the relative novelty of our notion of victimhood, because it changes the way we look at violence, justice and, not least, war. René Girard in his work points out that the Bible is the first instance in human history where the victim is given a voice and in fact where the vantage point of the victim is a consideration at all.[7] Victimhood is about violence and we owe to the Bible the very fact that we consider violence inconceivable not primarily because it disturbs public order but because it hurts people who are made in God's image and who are loved by God.

It is important that we acknowledge the newness of this insight. That churches of various confessions who condemned each other some generations ago today arrive at joint commemorations of their saints; that people of different traditions begin to sing each others songs,[8] that the victim is worth public attention because it is a human being created and

5 The Nobel Peace Prize certainly is a significant contribution to recognizing living peace makers.
6 Michel Wieviorka, quoting Marlene Young in *La Violence*, Hachette, Paris, 2005, p.88.
7 René Girard, *Violence and the Sacred,* Johns Hopkins University Press, Baltimore, 1977.
8 For ex. Pontanima Choir in Sarajevo, founded by Franciscan monk Ivo Markovic in 1995. The choir brings together people of the Abrahamic faith to sing each other's music. It has contributed much to the healing of memories.

beloved by God and thus has dignity; that violence and memory are now topics of research and analysis. All of this is quite new and is good news indeed.

In the Decade to Overcome Violence the question of churches committed to that cause is this: what does it take to overcome the spirit, logic and practice of violence?

We do need to look back at the history of violence and the history of how violence is being portrayed, perceived and interpreted. An African proverb says: "Until lions start writing down their own stories, the hunters will always be the heroes". Today we are learning about how violence works, and we learn it because the victims do have a voice. Unless we understand violence we will not be very effective in overcoming it. Jesus prayed on the cross "Father forgive them for they do not know what they are doing". (Lk 23:34). Could it be that this is not only referring to the unconsciousness of those who killed the Son of God without knowing he is the Son of God, but also because they are ignorant as to their egregious act of violence per se? Is it not generally true that people who commit acts of violence do not really know what they are doing and understand what is going on? Is there not a level of unconsciousness involved in killing? Is it not deliberate that the hangman is blindfolded, and the soldier or torturer drilled into neither thinking nor feeling? Is it not true that people entangled in violent conflict have lost sight of what is really going on, as well as of the actual cause at stake?

Remembering truthfully, therapeutically, and learning from the past

That memories need to be reconciled is clear to us. But how can memories be reconciled? For it is people who need to be reconciled: with themselves, with each other, with God, with their stories, places, their memories and their lives.

Miroslav Volf in his powerful book *The End of Memory*[9] emphasizes that our remembering must be truthful. This is significant for the commemoration of martyrs, because of the human inclination of turning them into more-than-human ideals, which in turn adds to our sense of dispensation: I do not have to do this, I do not need to try to be like him, for I'm no saint…. Truthful remembering includes acknowledging a witness's weaknesses, contradictions and shortcomings. Applying Saint Paul's self-critical assessment in 2 Corinthians 12 is pertinent here: that God's power is at its best in weakness. Truthful remembering includes listening to the variety of experiences and perceptions. It means to be open to reconsider our bias.

Miroslav Volf points out that is is key to remember rightly and he explores what that right or truthful remembering implies.[10]

---

9 Miroslav Volf, *The End of Memory, Remember Rightly in a Violent World*, Eerdmans, Grand Rapids, 2006.
10 Ibid. p.66f.

Given the flawed nature of human memory, it is important that *what* we remember and *the way* we remember it is truthful. That certainly also applies to commemorations. Great people are not remembered because of their presumed flawlessness or their forgotten weaknesses, but because of their contribution to the history of humanity and of faith – or simply to the legacy left with their family or community.

Truth is not entirely relative, as the post-modern mindset tends to hold, but truth is more fully revealed in the hermeneutic community, the community of believers or community of saints. Where that is not observed, the memories drift so far apart as to lead to separation, segregation and war. The way Croatian memories and Serbian memories were out of sync with each other had much to do with the atrocities of the early '90s. Could anyone have healed these memories before they blew up into their very owner's faces? Tito's ways did not, the European Union's ways did not, nor did the churches' ways. Not to mention the effect of the media which impresses as truthful rendering of reality when in fact what they show is complete distortion that contributes to polarization.

There can be little doubt that churches that have recognized and received each other would have both the leverage and credibility to stand up for truth and common sense against sectarian violence. In this way, dialogue and joint commemoration certainly can and will contribute to prevention of potentially violent conflict.

In short, remembering for peace implies the following elements:

- What we remember (listen to the inner voice and to external voices)
- How we remember (listen to the sound, colour and odour of memory)
- How we relate the memories (the way we articulate what we remember)
- How we relate to those with different memories, or those who have done us wrong (listen to the other side and engage in dialogue).[11]

Miroslav Volf adds to the imperative of truthful remembering the need of therapeutical remembering and the importance of learning from the past. All of this needs to be placed into a larger moral framework, Volf says.[12] This goes right to the heart of what we are about here today. There are many memories and once they are cleansed and made fit for healing and learning, they still need a reference, which Volf calls "regulative meta-memories". These are not memories of wrongs suffered, but redemptive events where God's liberating and saving grace breaks through.

---

11 Swiss Foreign Minister Micheline Calmy-Rey once said that to engage in dialogue does not necessitate to agree to the inconceivable. This was in reference to her engaging in dialogue with the government of Tehran.

12 Volf, p.93.

Ecce Homo – Remembering the ultimate victim who was also the ultimate human being

Christians will not only try to remember truthfully and therapeutically while learning from the past. They will also remember that the One who has drawn them into the love of God has suffered injustice and violence. It is through him that our wounds are healed and thus remembering truthfully and therapeutically is to always remember in the light of the cross of Jesus and the risen Christ.

Here is a testimony of 21st century Amish whose forgiveness has gone around the world like lightning, good news on the front pages for a change! To use Volf's term, the regulative memory for Christians is the passion: Jesus on the cross and the resurrected Christ who reigns with God. But I would add, and to me that seems essential, remembering Jesus' teaching, for instance as expressed in the Lord's prayer: forgive us our trespasses as we forgive those who trespass against us. I mentioned the role the *Martyr's Mirror* plays in the life of the Amish. Also, for the Amish the Lord's prayer is in the centre of prayer life and the plea for forgiveness is in the centre of the Lord's prayer. This place and its resonance in the life of the Amish is beautifully described in the book *Amish Grace* which explores the events and dynamics around the tragedy in Nickel Mines, Pennsylvania, on October 3, 2006.[13] *How Forgiveness Transcended Tragedy*, states the subtitle.

In Anabaptist thought the life and teaching of Jesus is not to be left behind his passion. Perhaps such a theological framework is part of why Mennonites have played a crucial role in pioneering peacebuilding and conflict transformation.

Today, because of the profound work on how violence works and how memories work, we have a wealth of stories about reconciling memories and how they contribute to building peace. Peacebuilding is a concept widely used today. Peacebuilding is not all about reconciling memories, but the former cannot be done without the latter. This subject could be explored further.

Conclusion

Reconciliation is an eminently Christian task. The church is the only institution in human history whose *raison d'être* is reconciliation. For that, remembering is indispensable – remembering truthfully and drawing lessons from the past. Reconciled memories and learned lessons furnish the spiritual house of which Christ is the cornerstone.

13 Donald B. Kraybill, Steven M. Nolt, David L. Weaver-Zercher, *Amish Grace, How Forgiveness Transcended Tragedy*, Jossey-Bass, San Francisco, 2007.

The wish and hope is that as we engage together in our common efforts to commemorate, we will find ways to remember rightly and learn lessons from those who remembered rightly, who followed up on their healed memories, who learned from the past and who teach us to do the same.

René Girard in his recent book entitled *Achever Clausewitz* asserts that today we stand before the choice of total destruction or nonviolence. Bose Symposium nurtures my hope that the church is moving towards confessing that nonviolence is the way of Jesus and therefore making the teaching of nonviolence and the non-violent life a real issue of Faith and Order.[14]

14 Examples of projects contributing to reconciling memories and to remember rightly: http://www.peace-counts.org; http://www.emu.edu; http://www.peoplebuildingpeace.org

Places of Memory

Hans Uytenbogaardt and Guido Dotti

The ancient church first began to celebrate the eucharist "on the blood of martyrs", that is, on the place of memory of their martyrdom or on the tomb with their body or on an altar that contained a relic. No city or town was without a church built over a "martyrion", tangible record of a disciple who had followed his Lord to the point of giving his life for him. The eucharist – and, in a wider sense, the liturgy – and the memory of the martyrs, hence, have been intimately connected from the very origins of Christianity. Now this "seed of Christians", after being disseminated for centuries in the farthest mission regions, rendering them fruitful, in the 20th century again was abundantly spilled at the very heart of the church, in countries that we are used to calling Christian or in any case that for centuries had been permeated by the Christian presence. This reappearance of martyrdom in the 20th century, moreover, has been accompanied by an increased awareness that the testimony rendered to Christ by the shedding of blood crosses over confessional boundaries. It is not surprising, hence, that the ancient link between martyrs and liturgy has called forth the creation of specific places in which the common prayer of Christians can be enveloped by the memory of a cloud of those who bore witness to the point of shedding their blood. These are places in which the individual Christian churches have not hesitated to unite witnesses who belonged to different Christian confessions but were united by undergoing a violent death for the sake of Jesus and of his gospel.

Iconographic monuments

We would like to examine here some typologies of these ecumenical "places of memory" and then to look in greater detail at several of them which have acquired a dimension not only of recalling to memory, but of a genuine space of prayer. There are, first of all, images, inscriptions, commemorative monuments that unite the memory of men and women belonging to different Christian confessions, at times even witnesses who suffered at the hands of other Christians. This is the case of the University of Oxford, where a commemorative tablet has been placed with the following inscription: "Remember the martyrs of the Reformation, both Catholic and Protestant, who lived in Oxfordshire, taught at the University of Oxford or were brought here for execution". A list of 23 names follows, with the dates of their death (from 1539 to 1681), and the concluding phrase: "Those whose names are known stand for all who suffered".

Even more solemn is the prominence given to the memory of some 20th century Christian martyrs whose statues in 1998 were placed in ten niches above the west entrance to Westminster Abbey in London. They stand in the space above the entrance doors where, in the tradition of the Western church, Christ sits upon the throne, judging the righteous and the unrighteous. This collocation of the Last Judgment image was meant to remind the faithful as they left the church that they will be judged on the basis of how they carry out what their faith teaches. To the left and right of the doors, as a sort of foundation for these blood-witnesses of Faith, we see the statues of Truth, Justice, Mercy and Peace.

Here are their names, with the brief information given the visitor or the pilgrim: St Maximilian Kolbe (Polish Franciscan, executed in Auschwitz 1941), Manche Masemola (beaten to death for her faith, Sekokaneland 1928), Janani Luwum (Archbishop of Uganda, assassinated 1977), St Elisabeth of Russia (killed by the Bolsheviks 1918), Martin Luther King (Baptist pastor, civil rights campaigner, assassinated 1968), Oscar Romero (archbishop of San Salvador, assassinated 1980), Dietrich Bonhoeffer (Lutheran pastor and theologian, killed by the Nazis 1945), Esther John (evangelist in Pakistan, murdered 1960), Lucian Tapiedi (killed during the Japanese invasion, Papua New Guinea 1942), Wang Zhiming (pastor and evangelist, killed during the cultural revolution, China, 1972).

We may note that the list presents persons who are significant for their witness of faith, hope and charity, whether or not they have been canonized by their respective churches, and their confessional membership is often not specified. This choice made in Westminster Abbey emphasizes that the blood of the martyrs is the seed of the church. Their testimony is an eloquent invitation to all who enter the church to examine themselves as to what truth, justice, mercy and peace mean in their own lives. Furthermore, the collocation of the statues connects these witnesses with the liturgy, as representatives of the communion of saints.

In other churches, which have been recently built or adapted, stained-glass windows or frescoes associate new witnesses, even such as belonged to different Christian confessions. Such is St Anna Church, Heerlen, the Netherlands, where a stained-glass window represents Pope John XXIII as the initiator of Vatican II and as pastor. It is interesting that he is surrounded not only by Christians. The people of God is composed of adults and children, of scholars and workers, black and white, men and women, clergy and laity, baptized and non-baptized, the living and the dead. We see Anne Frank next to Dag Hammarskjöld and Steve Biko. The people of God cross all borders: God's heaven overarches the whole earth and all its inhabitants. The church is the place to witness that recalls the kingdom of God, and the roster of saints is filled by all God's people.

So also in the Catholic cathedral of Ascoli Piceno (Italy), a new ceramic bas-relief commemorates "The martyrs of the 20th century in the vision of the Apocalypse", placing beside the Catholics Massimiliano Kolbe, Oscar Romero and Edith Stein, also the Lutheran Dietrich Bonhoeffer and the Orthodox Pavel Florenskij. A similar choice was made by Metropolitan Serafim of Germany when he had his Romanian Orthodox cathedral in Nürnberg painted: the Lutherans Dietrich Bonhoeffer and Paul Schneider are "received" into the cloud of witnesses belonging to the Orthodox tradition.

In the Saint Gregory of Nyssa Episcopal Church, San Francisco (USA) we find the same idea expressed in the images of the "dancing saints". The same variety of saints as in Heerlen are depicted as dancing around the altar. So not only the building of the church is a symbol of heaven, where all borders are crossed, but the eucharist itself is the place for all God's people. Something similar has been done by the congregation of Saint Gregory in San Francisco.

Spaces for prayer and memory

Some churches, however, did not stop at images, but wished to create spaces clearly set off for prayer dedicated to a shared memory of witnesses of the faith, beyond every confessional barrier.

The Church of St Bartholomew on the Isola Tiberina in Rome

In 1999, anticipating the celebration of the jubilee in 2000, Pope John Paul II created a commission to study the history of the new Christian martyrs of the 20th century. For two years the commission worked at the basilica of St Bartholomew, entrusted to the community of Sant'Egidio; it collected approximately 12,000 dossiers on martyrs and witnesses of faith from dioceses all around the world. Among the fruits of this study was the ecumenical prayer at the Coliseum of the Pope gathered with representatives of various Christian churches during the jubilee celebrations. This event made clear that the multitude of Christian believers killed or persecuted in the last century is like a continent still waiting to be explored, a heritage that all Christian denominations share. After the jubilee, John Paul II wanted the memory of witnesses of the faith of the 20th century to be made visible in the basilica of St Bartholomew. In October 2002 a solemn ecumenical ceremony took place: a large icon dedicated to the martyrs of the 20th century, arranged according to the symbols of the Book of Revelation was placed on the high altar. Objects belonging to some of the martyrs have been placed in the side chapels, each dedicated to a specific historical circumstance. In 2008, on the occasion the 40th anniversary of Sant'Egidio, Pope Benedict XVI visited it. In his sermon he referred to some martyrs of the 20th century: Franz Jägerstätter, a young Austrian husband and father, decapitated in 1943 for his opposition to the Nazis; André Jarian, a Chilean priest killed in a neighbourhood of Santiago where he worked with the poor; and the martyrs of the religious persecutions in Spain during the 1930s. The pope then said: "These brothers and sisters in the faith are a kind of a large image of Christian humanity in the 20th century, an image of the beatitudes lived to the point of shedding their blood," and he quoted Pope John Paul II: "the witness of Christ to the point of shedding blood speaks with a voice that is stronger than the divisions of the past."

The Chapel of Saints and Martyrs of Our Own Time inside Canterbury Cathedral

Not far from the site of the martyrdom of Thomas Becket, the easternmost end of Canterbury Cathedral opens into a semi-circular chapel with high stained-glass windows. Known as the Corona Chapel (since at one time it housed a portion of his skull as a relic), the East Chapel now directs visitors' attention towards the more recently slain. A sign on the wall explains: "Throughout the centuries men and women have given their lives for Christianity. Our own century is no exception. Their deaths are in union with the life-giving death of Our Lord Jesus Christ the Saviour of mankind. In this Chapel we thank God for the sacrifice of martyrdom whereby truth is upheld and God's providence enriched. We pray that we may be worthy of their sacrifice." On the two sides of the entrance to the East Chapel lecterns hold identical small loose-leaf binders. Plastic-sheeted pages inside offer brief biographical sketches of more than a dozen 20th century martyrs, among them Martin Luther King Jr., archbishop Oscar Romero, Charles de Foucauld. Two nuns, Edith Stein and Maria Skobtsova, are included, along with Bonhoeffer and Kolbe, as victims of the Nazi concentration camps. Turning the pages, one can come across perhaps unfamiliar names of priests killed in Russia, Iran and Uganda. Each biographical entry seems meagre at best, the occasional photograph faded. Set beneath a vaulted edifice with glorious ornamentation, the slim binder of names is probably the flimsiest object in the cathedral. Yet located so close to where Thomas Becket was killed, the list seems to illuminate all those who recognize a higher authority than Caesar's. Without fanfare, in stained-glass stillness, the East Chapel transforms the beatitude, "Blessed are those who are persecuted," into lives of flesh and spilled blood.[1]

During the closing eucharist of the Lambeth Conference on 3 August 2008, amid the soaring stone arches of Canterbury Cathedral, seven martyred members of the Anglican Melanesian Brotherhood were honoured during the service. Archbishop Rowan Williams, in gold-coloured vestments, stood at the main altar of the church and read the names, with the presider, Archbishop Ellison Pogo of Melanesia, by his side. Members of the four religious communities of Melanesia, in white and brown robes and grey habits, sang a haunting chant — the Litany of Saints and Martyrs of Melanesia — as they took a document with the names from Archbishop Rowan. In a procession, joined by Archbishop Ellison, they brought the names through a carved archway in the rood screen into the east end of the cathedral. Their song could be heard echoing through the lofty church after the congregation could no longer see them. They knelt in the chapel as the list of names was placed on the altar. When the

1 Cf. David Douglas, *The Growing Company of Martyrs. Reflections from Canterbury Cathedral's East Chapel,* http://www.touchstonemag.com/archives/print.php?id=13-10-016-f.

eucharist was over, bishops and others came to pray in front of the small altar in the chapel, where the icon of the martyrs was placed.

The Chapel of the Witnesses of Faith in the Domkerk of Utrecht

The Domkerk, dedicated in honour of St Martin, was founded in the 7th century by Willibrord, an English missionary, within the walls of the main Roman fortress in this area along the Rhine river, the border of the Roman Empire. Willibrord became the first bishop of Utrecht. Since that time this church has been the centre of Christianity in the Netherlands and Willibrord is now venerated as the "apostle of the Netherlands". Until the Reformation the Domkerk was the cathedral of the Catholic bishop; from that time on it is the main church of the Protestant Church in the Netherlands (PCN), formed from the union of two Reformed churches and one Lutheran church. For about 40 years the church has been inhabited by the Citypastoraat Domkerk (CP), an ecumenical, Protestant-Catholic supra-local parish within the PCN, a sort of "via media" between the Protestant and the Catholic tradition. Weekly eucharist is celebrated, while a daily office takes place at noon.

There were several premises and motivations for the CP to introduce the commemoration of saints as a source of the spirituality of this ecumenical parish:

- Witnesses are guides: they are transparent unto Christ. In the witness's life and work we can discern something of Jesus. Saints have a referring function.
- As Easter is the heart of the liturgical year, so martyrs are the first witnesses of *imitatio Christi.* The life and death of witnesses who have paid with their lives is in a certain way a "memory" of Good Friday. That is to say: their dying is a sign of the mystery of Christ's passion and resurrection. In commemorating them we put ourselves under the sign of Christ's resurrection.
- "We are not the first" (Niek Schuman). In the Creed we confess the "communion of saints". This communion includes the living and the dead (see again Heb. 11:12). There is a "cloud of witnesses", a long procession of pilgrims before and after Christ on their way to the land of God's promises. The Old Testament figures gave witness of the expectation of the Messiah, those of the New were full of his memory, together they look forward to God's kingdom. The first witnesses, thus, are found in the Scriptures. Prophets and apostles are the first witnesses of salvation. Their footsteps have been followed ever since.
- The awareness of this immense procession of pilgrims encourages the church of today to walk along the road of faith and persistence that is taught her by Scripture. At the end of his letter to the Hebrews the author admonishes his

readers: "Remember your leaders, those who spoke the word of God to you; consider the outcome of their way of life, and imitate their faith." (13:7). A biblical motivation is also found in the Revelation of St John, where witnesses and martyrs have such a prominent role (Rev. 6, Rev. 14).

- As a local church, we are part of a greater whole: the worldwide church. Therefore our point of view is ecumenical. Witnesses come from east and west, Rome and Reformation, Anglicans, Lutherans, Evangelicals. Our calendar revision is also based on existing calendars. There is room for our own choices, to do justice to our own local history.
- That brings us to the calendar of witnesses and its specific categories. It is not simple to make choices. Of course, we follow the outline of the traditional calendars, but there are a number of considerations that continually create difficulties in making choices. Our calendar has a broad spectrum of representatives to guarantee recognition by many people. The categories are not meant to be exhaustive. Some names belong to several categories and some names do not fit any category. So we have the following categories:

  Old and New Testament

  The Virgin Mary *

  Martyrs, church fathers, teachers of the faith

  Mission, ecumenical movement / diaconate

  Musicians / artists

  Witnesses from Utrecht **

  Significant people for the Citypastoraat***, the congregation of the Domkerk.

For every category we use the principle of representation. One witness represents others, who remain unmentioned for now. For example: remembering Dietrich Bonhoeffer we also think of others who died under the Nazi regime.

Some remarks to questions we discussed in connection with the ecumenical position of the congregation of the Domkerk:

* In all calendars of saints Mary has a typical position. She is a unique instrument in the coming of God's salvation to our world: "Be it unto me according to thy word". Mary and her feasts serve Christ. It is due to the special position of Mary in the church and in the liturgy

that the *Magnificat* is sung at evening prayer every day. The Dutch scholar Rudolf Boon calls Mary the icon, the image of God's communion. Mary is the image of Israel-beloved-by-God. We have chosen as Marian feasts the Annunciation (Luke ch.1) on 25 March and the Blessed Virgin Mary on 15 August, because the latter is the feast that is celebrated in the most intense way in the worldwide church.

** *Witnesses from Utrecht* belong to the calendar because historically the local church was always abundantly represented in calendars of saints. In this case we followed the list from the "Utrecht Litany" written by Andries Govaart for All Saints' Day of 1 November 2001. In that list all patron saints of Utrecht are mentioned, first of all St Martin of Tours, patron saint of the Domkerk and of the city. We incorporated all the names from this litany in our calendar. In this category we also remember people who were connected with the city of Utrecht during their life: Willibrord, who came from England as a missionary to become "the apostle of the Frisians" and the first archbishop of Utrecht; sister Bertken, a mystic who lived as a recluse in the choir of the Buurkerk for 57 years; bishop Bernulphus, who built the Utrecht "cross of churches" and is buried in the church of St Peter; Liudger, the first native missionary and first bishop of Münster; and Henriette Swellengrebel, a Dutch deaconess.

*** *Significant people for our congregation* were the subject of a great deal of discussion. Commemorating people who are very close to us is a very direct way of commemoration, but the delicate nature of such commemoration is evident. Placing these recent names on the calendar of our Chapel of Commemoration is not possible at this moment. The danger of unhealthy veneration is too great. Especially for this category great care must be taken. We would like to commemorate these persons all together on a special day, for example during an evening prayer on the commemoration of the consecration of our rebuilt church (after a fire in 1253) on the feast of St Mary Magdalene, 22 July (the exact year is unknown).

Already at the presentation of this calendar in 1986 it was said that the calendar would never be completed. History is continuing, the people of God are walking on up to the end of this world. There is a good reason, hence, to revise the calendar from time to time. Every five years we discuss the need of adaptations. After the presentation in 1986 the working group for the Daily Office began a revision in 1998. A strong motivation for working very intensively on this is the great importance of witnesses of the faith for the spiritual development of the congregation. The commemoration of those who preceded us in life and in death makes it clear to us what it means to live with faith as a source of spiritual life. Faith is passed on to us from generation to generation. Without this tradition there is no church. Finally, a calendar of saints is also an instrument of catechetical instruction for both adults and children: vivid examples of the Christian life are given to us by means of this calendar.

We do not work in a formal way. Thinking about a calendar of saints is a creative work; it is always being elaborated. There is also always a subjective element in the calendar. It is important that we are creating the calendar from the perspective of today. Today's people see models in people from the past. The history of the church is a history of people who are bound together throughout history.

The calendar and the chapel of the Witnesses of Faith belong closely together. Three functions come together here:

a) Christ. His image is represented in three symbols:

- the cross was originally made by Karel Kneulman for the chapel in the former concentration camp in Dachau in Germany. There it was refused for some reason and offered to the Domkerk for this chapel.

- the holy sepulchre opposite the cross behind the medieval high altar.

- the Easter candle stands in this chapel except when in use at baptisms, at Eastertide by the altar, and at funerals. The Easter candle is lit every day of the year, so that people can light their candles at the light of Christ.

b) The commemoration of the saints

- A Book of Commemoration with the names of the men and women who, according to a calendar of saints composed by the then minister of the Domkerk, Reverend Hans Kronenburg, are commemorated on the day of their death. Thanks to this calendar, each day, year after year, our "predecessors in the faith" are recalled to memory.

- The names of the witnesses are also brought together in a painting of the names of all the commemorated saints by the German painter Johann Peter Reuter on the wall above the holy sepulcher.

Thus, we imagine the witnesses of faith only by presenting their names, texts, and prayers, without using their traditional images. We are now engaged in discussing how to represent them by means of a visual expression through their symbols – a typically reformed discussion!

c) Personal commemoration of people who want to light a candle for themselves or someone else.

After some discussion, we decided to keep these three functions together in this one chapel, because in our opinion these three ways of commemoration cannot be kept apart from each other. We propose that the cross be the central viewing point. The Book of

Commemoration has to be placed in such a way that it becomes clear that the commemoration of the saints is placed in perspective of the commemoration of Christ. So the cross has to be the central point of attention.

Personal and liturgical commemoration

On the day of a specific commemoration two texts about the saint of that day are presented in the Book of Commemoration:

The first text gives some characteristics about the life and work of the saint from the perspective of Christian life today. For instance, for 7 November, St Willibrord:

- the stranger among us, who eradicated idolatry
- the preacher who caused the water of baptism to well up in this country
- the bishop who planted a church and through the name of Saint Martin linked it with its mother church
- the apostle to whom we owe our faith
- the meek
- the merciful

On the right there is if possible a short text from the saint or, as in this case, a text or hymn about Willibrord.

On the benches lies a small sheet with a short prayer in which some aspects of the life of the saint are connected with the life of person who prays these words. The prayer always ends with the words: "And so receive us in the procession / of those who preceded us / in the Name of Jesus Christ, our Lord."

In the liturgy of the Daily Office on the day of the saint there is always a collect for the commemoration and often an appropriate hymn or anthem by the choir.

"Stronger than the divisions of the past"

Some final questions concern the commemoration of witnesses of the faith with the celebration of the eucharist in a divided church. Is there a main criterion in defining witnesses of the faith in the Body of Christ, the Church universal? The BEM report says: "The Eucharistic communion with Christ who nourishes the life of the Church is at the same time communion within the body of Christ which is the Church. (…) It is in the Eucharist that the community of God's people is fully manifested. (…) The Eucharist embraces all aspects of life. It is a representative act of thanksgiving and offering on behalf of the whole world. The Eucharistic celebration demands reconciliation and sharing among all those regarded as brothers and sisters in the one family of God and is a constant challenge in the search for appropriate relationships in social, economical and political life. All kinds of injustice, racism, separation and lack of freedom are radically challenged when we share in the body and blood of Christ. Through the Eucharist the all-renewing grace of God penetrates and restores human personality and dignity. The Eucharist involves the believer in the central event of the world's history."[2] So the reference to the communion of the saints[3] is one of the *notae ecclesiae* in the celebration of the eucharist.

The question then is whether the church can choose her "saints" outside the circle of those who are "the believers in the Eucharist as the central event of the world's history". It must also be asked whether the eucharist can be celebrated in its full meaning as an act of universal reconciliation without making place in any way for the witnesses of Truth, Justice, Mercy and Peace, as they welcome the visitors in Westminster Abbey. How "openly" do we welcome participants at the eucharist in view of the communion of saints? Whom shall we choose as witnesses of faith in the church when the four qualifications on the Westminster doors are as important as the confession of Christ as our Saviour?

Finally, how hospitable is the church in her litany of all saints to the communion of martyrs who offered their lives for peace universal? And how hospitable is the church at the table of the Lord to all who accept his invitation to share in his death, resurrection and glorification as a sign of the kingdom we look forward to?

---

2 *Baptism, Eucharist and Ministry*, Faith and Order Paper no.111, WCC Publications, Geneva, 1982. Section on Eucharist, pp.19-20.

3 *Ibid.*, p.27.

Celebrating Saint Olav. An Ecumenical, Contemporary Commemoration of a Saint from the Time of the Undivided Church

Knut Kittelsaa

Over the last hundred years, interest in the medieval Saint Olav has been steadily growing in the Lutheran Church of Norway. The general pattern of development is that interest in doing different things comes first, and then in the following years one reflects on the understanding of what is happening. Basically, many of the initiatives are not coming from church authorities, but grow out of a general interest among people. One will now find an ecumenical commemoration of the medieval saint, bringing thousands of people together every year at the end of July, both in Trondheim and at Stiklestad, 100 km north of the city. This commemoration is now well included in the identity of the Lutheran Church of Norway, the majority church in Norway. Also, other denominations active in Norway, such as the Catholic Church, the Methodist Church, the Baptist Church and some Norwegian free churches participate in the commemoration, according to their interest and capacity. In Norway, some 82 percent of the population are members of the Church of Norway. Around 10 percent belong to other churches, almost half of them to the Roman Catholic Church. The rest of the population are Muslims, members of non-religious life stance organizations or not members of any church or life stance organization. Only a very few are Hindus or Buddhists.

Medieval events

Saint Olav was the most known saint of medieval Scandinavia. He was king of Norway from 1015-1030 and introduced church legislation in Norway. He connected Norway to the European Christian culture and promoted Christian faith in Norway. He had to flee the country in 1028, due to political conflict. After two years in refuge in Novgorod, he returned to Norway in the summer of 1030 in an attempt to regain power, but fell at the battle of Stiklestad on 29 July 1030. He was buried in Trondheim, at that time the only city of Norway and the capital of the country.

Shortly after, people started to venerate his grave. Wonders happened there, and a year after his death, on 3 August 1031, he was declared a saint. This led to a breakthrough of Christian faith in Norway. Veneration of the saint and pilgrimages to his shrine grew, and he was regarded as Rex Perpetuus Norwegiae – everlasting king of Norway.

Throughout the medieval centuries, veneration of Saint Olav was an essential element in Norwegian religious life. He was made patron saint of about 360 churches in the Nordic countries, England and northern Germany. A pilgrimage to Nidaros – the medieval name of Trondheim – was vital through all centuries until the Reformation in 1537.

An archbishopric in Nidaros was established in 1153, including all of Norway and the western Nordic settlements, and Nidaros Cathedral was erected over the saint's grave from 1160, completed around 1308. The cathedral – partly turned into a ruin in the post-Reformation times – was reconstructed over the last 150 years, and has now regained its medieval beauty.

Post-Reformation renewal

Reformation brought a sudden end to the veneration of the saint. In the post-Reformation Lutheran Church of Norway there was no official pilgrimage and acknowledgement of Saint Olav until the end of the 19th century, when he became a symbol of the emerging independent Norwegian state. Between the wars there was a growing interest in celebrating Saint Olav in the Church of Norway as well as in the re-established Roman Catholic Church in Norway. In 1930, the 900 year commemoration of the battle at Stiklestad, where he fell, became a most impressive celebration. More than 40,000 people participated in an open-air service at the battlefield. Unfortunately, the Norwegian Nazi party made use of the saint during the German occupation of Norway, 1940-45. This meant a great setback in the emerging veneration. But from the beginning of the 1950s the saint has been celebrated annually at Olsok – the vigil on the night of his death 29 July – both in Nidaros Cathedral and in the city of Trondheim. The celebration has spread to other places in Norway and become a national church event, included in the ecclesiastical calendar of the Church of Norway. The dramatic events at Stiklestad in 1030 and the introduction of Christianity to Norway have also been made a theme for a historic open-air stage play at Stiklestad. The play is staged annually in a natural amphitheatre with 6000 seats, and is seen by more than 20,000 people every summer.

In 1964 the Roman Catholic Church erected a new diocesan church in Trondheim and dedicated it to Saint Olav. Around 1980 the Saint Olav Festival was established as a week-long celebration with lectures, concerts, performances, pilgrimages and services celebrating the saint. The festival was reorganized and widened over the years and is now one of the biggest festivals in Norway. It was an important and touching event when Pope John Paul II visited Nidaros Cathedral in an ecumenical service in 1989 as the first pope ever to visit the site. This is regarded as a big step in the growing relations between Lutherans and Catholics in Norway.

New pilgrimages to Nidaros

Since around 1990, pilgrims are once more presenting themselves at the cathedral gates and a lot of activities have grown around the organizing of pilgrimages. Since the early 1990s a special ministry to the pilgrims has been organized, both assisting in the organizing of pilgrimages and producing services and activities for pilgrims upon arrival at Nidaros Cathedral. More than 2000 km of pilgrim trails are now marked and made walkable through southern Norway. Also in Sweden many paths lead to Nidaros, allowing people from many directions to go on pilgrimage to the old city. Pilgrim activities are not a result of church initiatives. It has been a natural growth, based on an interest for pilgrimages among the people, and the church has found it necessary to respond to this interest.

In 1997 Trondheim celebrated its first millennium, and made the pilgrim the main symbol of the celebrations. In the year 2000 the churches in Europe organized a European Pilgrimage, and Trondheim was one of the five goals for pilgrimages all through Europe, bringing many people from all over Europe to the Saint Olav Festival that year. In June 2003 the Conference of European Churches came together in Trondheim for their General Assembly, the greatest church meeting ever organized in Norway, with broad representation and important focuses. All the main services took place in Nidaros Cathedral and included an ecumenical veneration of Saint Olav. Later the same year the city celebrated the 850 years of the establishment of the Nidaros Archbishopric, with guests from all churches in the old area of the archdiocese: Norway, Iceland, Greenland, Fareyar, Hebrides, Orkneys and Isle of Man.

Another event in this development of the contemporary, ecumenical commemoration of Saint Olav is the establishment of Nidaros Pilgrim Centre close to the cathedral. It was consecrated in May 2008 and is a guesthouse for pilgrims and a centre for the development and celebration of the old heritage around the saint. The ministry for pilgrims is based in the centre.

It may also be of interest to mention in the context of the Saint Olav Heritage that the last months have brought new interest around an old stone at Stiklestad. The saga tells that the saint died leaning on a big stone. This stone was integrated in the altar of the medieval church that was erected on the battlefield of Stiklestad and was an important element in the local medieval commemoration of Saint Olav. After the Reformation the stone was removed from the altar, and for many years was in a garden not far away. In 2007 the stone was brought back into the church and positioned in its original place in the altar. This took place in a service and the stone was brought in by a procession of ministers. In the first months of 2009 discussion focused on how the stone should be regarded. Is it a relic? Or should it be regarded as of minor meaning to the faithful? Both the Catholic and the Lutheran bishops of the area have given their perspectives in newspaper interviews, scientists have studied the phenomenon, and it is obvious that the stone generates a lot of interest among people in general in the area. Some people say they feel calmed and comforted when touching the stone.

Saint Olav Festival

The contemporary commemoration of Saint Olav is celebrated in the annual St Olav Festival, an 8-12 day church and culture festival in Trondheim around 29 July, with Nidaros Cathedral as a natural focus. It includes a variety of services, more than 40 through the period, as well as pilgrimages – both long distance pilgrimages and evening pilgrimages from the outskirts of the city to the cathedral. On the eve of 29 July a vigil with hourly prayers throughout the night takes place. During the festival there are many concerts with a variety of artists from Norway and abroad, folklore activities and a medieval market. The festival is visited by more than 150,000 people, participating in more than 200 different activities. The basis and identity of the festival is closely related to the saint and the commemoration is also an interpretation of the meaning and importance of Saint Olav for contemporary people. Included in the many services throughout the festival period are ecumenical services in the cathedral and a Catholic high mass celebrated in the cathedral. The vigil includes guests from the ecumenical fellowship locally and internationally. There are also almost every year meetings or conferences in connection to the festival, e.g. in 2008 an international meeting on the world's holy places.

Understanding the veneration

The re-establishment of the veneration of Saint Olav and of the pilgrimages to Nidaros is not the result of church planning. Actually, it was in the beginning something like an obstacle for a Lutheran church to recognize these activities. But both through long-term theological reflection and by the acknowledgement of the different elements of contemporary veneration, the Church of Norway has developed an understanding that is well included in the Lutheran identity and the Norwegian history of the church. The essential interpretation of the saint's history is that Saint Olav by his death mirrors Jesus Christ. Like Christ is victorious when dying and rising from the dead, the saint is also victorious through his death. What he could not gain through his lifelong activities – an unthreatened position as the king of Norway – he gained through his death. All the medieval documentation around the saint's history is based upon this understanding, and from this perspective, as well as from all the wonders happening at his grave, his life is interpreted. The basic quotation from Scripture to interpret the saint's life is the word from the gospel of John 12:24: "Very truly, I tell you, unless a grain of wheat falls into the earth and dies, it remains just a single grain; but if it dies, it bears much fruit." This understanding of the importance of the saint is easy to adopt also for the Lutheran Church of Norway and for the ecumenical community. The saint actually witnesses about Christ in a way that might be an example to all Christians, since we are all called to mirror Christ in our lives.

The liturgical focus on the saint in the services at Olsok in the Nidaros Cathedral draws heavily on this tradition. There are no prayers to the saint, but there are prayers expressing gratitude for his life and death. Histories from his life and death from the Nordic sagas and from other medieval sources are quoted, and the services reflect on the saint as an example also for believers of our time. The spiritual power of his history is still present in these services, and we have numerous witnesses from people attending of the importance of this spiritual power.

The spiritual power of the saint's history is also visible in many other ways. Both the city of Trondheim and the two counties of Trøndelag draw on the Saint Olav heritage in their presentation of life, identity and activities in the area, and have made this heritage a focused element in their development planning. Many cultural institutions use elements from the Saint Olav heritage, e.g. when artists put works related to the heritage on stage or in exhibitions. Many schools include excursions to places related to the saint in their programmes on history, geography and religion. Both tourist agencies and local financial institutions are using elements from this heritage in their activities.

Contemporary reflection on the Saint Olav heritage

As stated before, the reflection over the meaning of the saint in our time is secondary to the actual commemoration and to the pilgrimages to his grave church, Nidaros Cathedral. But a lot of reflection has been made over the years, and this has opened many perspectives on the importance of the Saint Olav heritage. Lines might be drawn from the different perspectives of the life and death of the saint to many important perspectives concerning Christian faith in a Nordic setting in our own time. These are the most focused:

The universality of faith. Olav represents the undivided church and the unlimited fellowship of faith. He was baptized in continental Rouen, he brought bishops to Norway from western England, and he sought refuge in eastern Novgorod, before returning to Norway on his last mission.

The local adaptation of faith. Olav was a person of his time and place, as we all are. He went out as a teenager on Viking raids, and he brought soldiers in his missionary activities in Norway. But he was also deeply touched by other values in Christianity and promoted protection for disabled children and for poor people in society.

The diaconal dimension of faith. All kinds of people sought and received help. The outcome of his martyrdom was a new focus on support and assistance to sick and disabled people.

The ecumenical dimension of faith. The Saint Olav tradition has been rooted in a large area and in many denominations now searching for this tradition as a source for spiritual strength and renewal.

Justice and reconciliation as results of faith. The martyrdom of Olav reconciled Norway and established a society based on Christian values. Former conflicts of power as well as religious diversities were overcome.

Growing in faith. Olav was the Viking king who was baptized and became a martyr for Christ, a well known pattern of growth in faith in Christianity.

The integrating dimension of faith. Olav shows how everything in life becomes united in the perspective of faith. Faith gives life meaning, direction and goal.

For those concerned with the challenges facing churches in our time, it will be easy to see that elements from the Saint Olav heritage can be inspirational to contemporary Christians, and may also be helpful in the discerning of solutions and ways to proceed when dealing with the challenges.

Nidaros as the spiritual centre of Norway

The growth of interest for this tradition over the last hundred years has focused Nidaros as the spiritual centre of Norway. Parallel to the reflection around this contemporary commemoration of the medieval saint, there has been a reflection on whether this should have an impact on the way the Church of Norway is organized. Is it not also natural that the church headquarters, or even a new Archbishop for the Church of Norway, should be positioned near Nidaros Cathedral, since this cathedral is the spiritual centre of the church? When one sees the different opinions over this question, one might say that the Saint Olav heritage is still not regarded as the most important source of spiritual identity for the Church of Norway. Maybe it should never be so either. Contemporary Norwegian Christianity should rather draw on a variety of sources and hope that the Saint Olav heritage can be regarded among the important ones, but not claim to be the only one[1].

1 Further information on these questions can be found on the following websites:
For Nidaros Cathedral and the surrounding complex of buildings, and for the cathedral programme: www.nidarosdomen.no
For the Saint Olav Festival: www.olavsfestdagene.no
For information on pilgrimages and pilgrim trails in Norway: www.pilgrim.info
For Nidaros Pilgrim Centre: www.pilegrimsgarden.no

ECUMENICAL OPPORTUNITIES FOR COMMEMORATION. SUGGESTIONS FROM DIFFERENT TRADITIONS

Reflections on the Question of an Ecumenical Commemoration of Witnesses. Challenges, Obstacles, Possibilities and Suggestions from a Lutheran Perspective

Dagmar Heller

Lutheran theological background

The commemoration of saints is not very much present in Lutheran churches. The reason for this has several aspects. The quote from the Augsburg Confession has become one of the most important basic texts for the Lutheran churches. Article 21 speaks about the veneration of saints and says:

> Of the Worship of Saints they (i.e. the Roman Catholics, DH) teach that the memory of saints may be set before us, that we may follow their faith and good works, according to our calling, as the Emperor may follow the example of David in making war to drive away the Turk from his country; for both are kings. But the Scripture teaches not the invocation of saints or to ask help of saints, since it sets before us the one Christ as the Mediator, Propitiation, High Priest, and Intercessor. He is to be prayed to, and has promised that He will hear our prayer; and this worship He approves above all, to wit, that in all afflictions He be called upon, 1 John 2:1: "And if anyone sins, we have an Advocate with the Father."

From this text we can see at least two reasons for Lutheran hesitation vis-à-vis the veneration of saints: It is Luther's emphasis on the Bible as the only source for the faith, and it is his doctrine of justification, which says that salvation comes through Christ alone. And behind this is, of course, a whole history of abuse of the cult of saints, which Martin Luther was criticizing.

Lutheran practice today

The veneration of saints is not very present in Lutheran spirituality, but saints have never totally disappeared. And to a certain extent, there is even a movement – at least within the German Protestant churches – which brings the saints back, and there is a growing interest in literature about saints etc. [1]

This interest involves three different levels: liturgical, popular, official.

1 Cf. Hans Mayr, *Glaubenszeugen der Einen Kirche. 57 Lebensbilder für die Wochen des Kirchenjahres*, J. Stauda, Kassel, 1984.

Liturgical

On the liturgical level we can say that in the Lutheran tradition saints never disappeared totally, especially the apostles, and some other saints have their place in the liturgical calendar, as well as All Saints day on 1 November[2]. In Germany there is even an official name calendar, prepared by the Liturgical Commission of the Evangelical Lutheran Church in Germany (probably this exists also in Lutheran churches in other countries). On the other hand we have also to be realistic: specific days of individual saints are not celebrated in a popular way.

What has been kept though is a certain feeling for what we would call the "cloud of witnesses" through liturgical texts like, especially, the Preface in the eucharistic liturgy, which always ends with a formula like "...and so, let us join the saints by singing: Holy, holy, holy...." There are also a few hymns which refer to the saints and to the cloud of witnesses.

Popular

On the popular level there are certainly traces of saints to be found within Lutheran spirituality. First of all there are some very popular saints, like Saint Francis of Assisi and two or three others. They are not, however, venerated like in the Roman Catholic Church – especially Lutherans would not pray to saints and ask them to pray for them as is the custom in Catholic litanies for All Saints Day for example – but they would be given as examples in catechism or in confirmand classes.

There are also other persons who are taken as examples, and to a certain extent treated somehow like saints in the Lutheran spirituality, although there is no canonization of saints. Martin Luther himself, also Dietrich Bonhoeffer and others are not venerated in a liturgical sense but are admired, seen as examples and their writings are taken as references and authorities. It is, for example, interesting that from the writings of such people, compilations or anthologies for daily reading are made.

Official

Then there is a third level, the so-called official level, involving the churches' leadership. In Germany, for example, it was an official commission that worked on a book on martyrs of the 20th century presented at Bose Symposium by Andreas Kurschat and Harald Schultze.[3] Of course, this is not meant for liturgical use. It is meant for historical purposes and in order to remember these people.

2 See Lutheran Liturgical Resources pp. 246-254.
3 See pages 118-123.

Challenges and obstacles to an ecumenical commemoration of witnesses from a Lutheran perspective

The traditional Lutheran approach to saints or the commemoration of saints is characterized by an opposition to the Roman Catholic way of dealing with saints. There are a lot of aspects which seem strange to Lutherans – on a theological level, but also on a psychological level. Some expressions of sainthood seem strange and grotesque to the Lutherans and may be interpreted from a psychological point of view as sublimations of sexuality. But what is even more difficult for Lutherans is the cult of relics, as if the bones would guarantee the presence of the respective saint. There is also a political aspect to the veneration of saints which is ambiguous, for example cases when saints have been canonized for political reasons. And finally, the close connection of the veneration of saints with the phenomenon of indulgences, which was one of the main reasons for Martin Luther's 95 theses: The merits of saints together with the merit of Christ were seen as the deposit of the church out of which the pope could give indulgences, the forgiveness of sins. And this idea still exists today, for example in the Codex of Canonical law of 1983[4], and *enchiridion indulgentiarum*, Rome 1967[5].

These questions are still relevant nowadays among Lutherans, and therefore, the positive side of saints and the belonging to the cloud of witnesses has still to be re-discovered by Lutherans. It is even more important when talking about a common commemoration of saints which would take some time until being widely accepted.

Possibilities and suggestions

Even so, there are possibilities and entry points for Lutherans to commit themselves to ecumenical commemoration of witnesses. It is important to remember that Martin Luther did not totally deny saints and their value but he somehow developed a new, or attempted to restore the original, concept of saints.

He was interested in the saints on earth, rather than those in heaven, unreachable by living believers. And he was interested in the human side of the saints. A saint is for him not a morally good man or woman with a religious charisma, but a saint who is aware of his deficiencies. Their own holiness is hidden to the saints. It is the sinful human being who is called to be a saint even in suffering and sin, in temptation and failure.

Therefore the exemplarity of saints is not their ethical performance. But our faith is strengthened when we see how saints received grace and how they have been helped by grace.

4 Schatz der Sühneleistungen Christi und der Heiligen, Kanon 992.

5 "Ausserdem gehört zu diesem Schatz auch der wahrhaft unermessliche, unerschöpfliche und stets neue Wert, den vor Gott die Gebete und guten werke der seligen Jungfrau Maria und aller heiligen besitzen." Zit. Nach Chr. Schütz (Hg.), *Praktisches Lexikon der Spiritualität*, Freiburg i. Br, 1988, 2.

There is a threefold attitude towards saints: to give thanks for their lives, to be strengthened in our faith by their examples, and to imitate them in their way of believing.

In a Protestant understanding saints need to liberate people and not put them under psychological or moral pressure. On the other hand, such liberation also includes a radical Christian commitment.

Thus, for an ecumenical conversation or even an ecumenical agreement on the commemoration of saints, it would be important for Lutherans to come to a clear understanding of how this commemoration is to be understood theologically.

On the basis of this background there are some possibilities to meet with other Christians in the commemoration of saints: Protestant Christians need a better awareness that they are part of a wider community which goes beyond their respective parish or congregation. Therefore commemoration of people is a helpful form for establishing and living out this awareness. The connection of the history of the cloud of witnesses with our present time needs to be developed. An open question though remains: what are the criteria for persons we do not know and do not remember but are still within the cloud?

For Protestants, it is not the actions or outward lifestyle of saints that counts but how a saint experiences his/her faith and what the implications of this experience are for his/her life.

Saints are not just ethical examples, because then they would just motivate to another style of life. This can be important, but there is something more: the human being is called to become a member of Christ's body. And this cannot be achieved by just following after St Francis' lifestyle, for example. This can be achieved only by taking seriously into consideration the fact that we are already saints!

Suggestions for a way towards an ecumenical commemoration of saints

According to the above-mentioned three levels, here are a few suggestions which seem appropriate from a Lutheran perspective.

Liturgical level: For Lutherans there is in principle no difficulty to commemorate saints in worship services, as long as these saints are seen as examples of faith and not as moral ideals.

Some Lutherans, like in Germany, have already a calendar of names of people whom they find it important to commemorate. This calendar is in a way already ecumenical, since it contains names from the time of the early, undivided church. But it would certainly be interesting to continue working on such a calendar together with other churches, and then use this calendar for common commemoration.

Popular level: It is important to encourage churches at the local level to commemorate together controversial witnesses and martyrs. For example, on 16 September 1560 the Waldensian, Giovanni Luigi Pascale, was burnt for his faith just across from the Angels Castle in Rome. For the Catholics and Waldensians in Rome it would be an opportunity to commemorate together those martyrs, as such commemoration has already been a practice of a Waldensian parish and a Roman Catholic parish in Rome.

There are, of course a lot of possibilities at the level of parishes in a very practical and concrete way, for example, organization of common pilgrimages.

Official level: At the official level, firstly, there is a need to do some common theological work, discussing still existing obstacles and theological problems regarding common commemoration.

Secondly another sort of obstacle needs to be discussed bilaterally from a historical background, namely the cases of saints which pose specific problems mutually to our churches, for example, Ignatius of Loyola and the Jesuits at the Lutheran-Roman Catholic dialogue. On the grave of Ignatius, at his feet, is the allegorical figure of the right faith who throws heretics down into darkness. One of those has a book under his arm, on which you can read the name of Martin Luther. And there are certainly cases the other way round. Although today even Lutherans and other Protestants read Ignatius' spiritual exercises, healing of memories is still to come.

It is necessary to develop common calendars and biographies at local and international levels. And this could start with a focus on cases where there was a *common* martyrdom. The Orthodox Archbishop Platon and the Protestant pastor Traugott Hahn in Tartu were killed together in 1919; three catholic priests and a Protestant pastor were executed in 1943 in Hamburg-Holstenglacis one after the other, so that literally their blood on the floor was mixed.

But despite all these proposals, we need to consider that the different spiritualities and the history remain in the background. A few things should be done ecumenically, through the World Council of Churches. It is necessary:

to be aware of different understandings of sainthood and their different practical implications;

to motivate different churches locally to look into the histories of their witnesses and remember together their stories;

to look at saints who are problematic for other churches;

to look at saints whom we can accept in common as examples of witnessing the faith[6].

Propose 1 November or another day of common commemoration of the cloud of witnesses.

Use existing sources, like the ecumenical calendar of saints which can be found on the internet (www.heiligenlexikon.de) and which was – interestingly – prepared by a Protestant pastor!

Finally encourage the WCC to consider including names of saints from different churches in the Ecumenical Prayer Cycle. This does not have to wait until a new edition is prepared, but can be done on the internet where the calendar already exists.

6 Maybe we should not ask churches to name saints whom they would wish to see in a common martyrology, but take the existing martyrologies and send them to other churches with a question: Who are the problematic saints for you?

Ecumenical Experiences in Commemoration of the Cloud of Witnesses from a Reformed Perspective

Martin Hoegger

The Reformed Church, to which I belong, was one of those most opposed to the idea of including the "holy witnesses" in its worship or even of commemorating them in any way. This is due to John Calvin's total focus on Christ alone, thus excluding any reference to the saints in the liturgy.[1] This convergence on Christ remains a characteristic of Reformed churches up to this day.

The Second Helvetic Confession gives a good definition of a saint, which a Protestant may confess:

> We acknowledge them to be living members of Christ and friends of God who have gloriously overcome the flesh and the world. Hence we love them as brothers, and also honor them; yet not with any kind of worship but by an honorable opinion of them and just praises of them. We also imitate them. For with ardent longings and supplications we earnestly desire to be imitators of their faith and virtues, to share eternal salvation with them, to dwell eternally with them in the presence of God, and to rejoice with them in Christ.[2]

Saints and martyrs, even if their faith is exemplary, are not given any place in the worship of the Reformed Church. However, the liturgical and ecumenical movements have led some of the Reformed churches to review this exclusion and to have a more inclusive attitude.[3]

Although I have made another study on the influence of the liturgical movement on the Reformed churches,[4] this contribution is to share some experiences of ecumenical commemorations (especially from the French-speaking part of Switzerland), which may lead the Reformed Church to re-examine its perception of the cloud of witnesses.

---

1 For Calvin there is no place for the witnesses to the faith in worship (*Institutes of Christian Religion* III,20,22); his liturgy of the Last Supper makes no mention of the deceased and the witnesses (cf. B. Burki, "La Sainte Cène selon l'ordre de Jean Calvin 1542", in *Coena Domini. Die Abendsmahlsliturgie der Reformationskirchen.* Hg. V. Imagard Pahl, Freiburg, 1983 pp.347-367).

2 Chapter V.

3 It was only in 1874 that the *memento* reappeared in the *Liturgie à l'usage des Eglises réformées* of the French pastor Eugène Bersier. In the French-speaking part of Switzerland, the movement "*Eglise et Liturgie*" introduced in 1931 in its *Liturgies de communion* the remembrance of the deceased and the triumphant church, plus a complete liturgical year. In 1939 it proposed a commemoration of All Saints day (*Rapport théologique sur la commemoration de la Toussaint et des trépassés.* Eglise et Liturgie, 1939), which provoked a "disputatio" with the theological faculty of Lausanne.

4 Cf. Martin Hoegger: "La nuée des témoins dans les liturgies réformées francophones". (To be published).

Ecumenical pilgrimages

Each year I walk with my wife on some stages of the *Via Francigena*. In September 2008 we did the stage of Saint Maurice and, without knowing it, we arrived on the eve of the feast of Maurice and his companions, martyrs at the end of the 3rd century. This was the first sign of my being a "typical Protestant": my ignorance of the Catholic calendar!

So I took part in the commemorative mass for the martyrs. The abbot of Einsiedeln, Martin Werlen, gave the sermon. Quoting from the rules of St Benedict, he touched on the subject of faith, which is a narrow path at the beginning, but widens as one goes forward, and notwithstanding the difficulties, "our heart expands".[5] It just so happens that the eucharistic preface of the feast of St Maurice mentions that the Theban martyrs "expanded their hearts" thanks to their faith in Christ.

According to Werlen, "to expand our heart" is the aim of commemorating a martyr. Our life is a pilgrimage where, through Christ's death and resurrection, we march on in our "exodus" to God. In this way the Holy Spirit expands our heart, as it did for those witnesses who preceded us.

The Conference of European Churches underlined the ecumenical importance of the pilgrims' roads, which link the various parts of Europe and the diverse churches, in time and history. They give roots and historical reference points. They are a sign of a *"Catholicity in time"* – these roads have been used for more than a 1000 years, they remind us of the faith of our forefathers and also of a sign of *"Catholicity in space"* – the Via Francigena linking Canterbury (Anglican) and Rome (Catholic) through Lausanne (Protestant reformed).[6]

Walking together on a pilgrimage has a great ecumenical significance. On the way, one can pray at the site of a martyr who gave his life, one discovers the spirituality of other churches, one can have exchanges and try to better understand things which surprise us, to cultivate a fraternal communion. In the Canton of Vaud, the Council of Christian Churches, in which I participate, regularly organizes ecumenical pilgrimages. Two years ago we visited the Holy Land; this year we visited the churches of Romania. Our group had Reformed, Catholics, Orthodox and members of Evangelical-Pentecostal churches. We started with the great feast of St Paraskeva in Iasi and we ended it with the feast of St Dimitri in Bucarest.

---

5 *Rule of Benedict,* Prologue, 48s: "But if a certain strictness results from the dictates of equity for the amendment of vices or the preservation of charity, do not be at once dismayed and fly from the way of salvation, whose entrance cannot but be narrow (Matt. 7:14). For as we advance in the religious life and in faith, our hearts expand and we run the way of God's commandments with unspeakable sweetness of love."

6 The CEC chose the city of Trondheim in Norway for its annual meeting in 2003. Its cathedral was a centre of pilgrimage for more than a thousand years, and 20 years ago, the pilgrimage to the cathedral of Nidaros was rediscovered. Several speakers at that meeting went into greater depth on the subject (*Trondheim Report, CEC,* Geneva, 2004). The same for the Ecumenical meeting in Sibiu in 2007 which had the theme of pilgrimage, as well as the last World Conference of Faith and Order in Santiago de Compostela in 1993.

It was a spiritual shock for several Protestants to discover the practice of veneration of relics in the Orthodox Church. Nevertheless every day we spent an hour of *lectio divina,* during which there was an important moment of silence to welcome and to listen to Christ's Word in each of us. With Christ's spiritual presence among us we progressed with a better understanding of each other.

Prayer vigil in memory of martyrs

I have participated on three occasions in the "Prayer vigil in memory of all those who gave up their lives for the Gospel". It is organized by the Saint Egidio Community of Lausanne during Holy Week. Although this community was created in the Roman Catholic Church, it has the particularity of being ecumenical. This ceremony is directly related to the *Ecumenical Commemoration of the witnesses to the faith in the 20th century*, as proposed by Pope John Paul II to mark the Jubilee Year of 2000 in the Coliseum of Rome.[7]

After a meditation on the gospel, it is a long celebration in memory of recent martyrs on various continents. The list of witnesses from different churches is quite impressive. It illustrates what John Paul II wrote on the ecumenical significance of martyrdom:

> In a theocentric vision, we Christians already have a common Martyrology. This also includes the martyrs of our own century, more numerous than one might think, and it shows how, at a profound level, God preserves communion among the baptized in the supreme demand of faith, manifested in the sacrifice of life itself.[8]

This ceremony is held as "a communion with Christians of all churches who have given their lives for the Lord". It brings together Christians in prayer so that they can confess the joy of being disciples of the gospel. As the continents are named one after another, a candle is lit with the following words spoken by those present: "we welcome the cross which has been placed (in that continent) and we pray that it be illuminated by the resurrection."

This approach is based on the detailed research of Andrea Riccardi, the founder of the Community, on the persecution of Christians in the 20th century which are listed and updated each year with the names of new martyrs.[9] The ceremony ends with this prayer underlining the exemplary character of the martyr: "Oh Lord, who gives strength to the weak and perseverance to those who trust you, please ensure that, guided by the example of those who did not hesitate to die for you, we become true disciples and witnesses of the Gospel. Give us a communion of faith and love with your Son, crucified and risen from the dead..."[10]

---

7 Cf. www.vatican.va/holy_father/john_paul_ii/homilies/documents/hf_jp-ii_hom_20000507_test-fede_en.html

8 *Ut Unum Sint, On commitment to Ecumenism*, 1995, § 84.

9 Andrea Riccardi, *Ils sont morts pour leur foi. La persécution des Chrétiens au 20e siècle*, Plon/Mame, Paris, 2002.

10 Cf. www.ceccv.ch

Ecumenical celebration with organizations in favour of the persecuted churches

In January 2007 there was a ceremony in Lausanne Cathedral bringing together four organizations in favour of the persecuted churches: Aid to the Church in Need, Aide aux Eglises en détresse (Hilfe für Mensch und Kirche), Christian Solidarity International and Open Doors.[11] These organizations from the Catholic, Protestant and Evangelical-Pentecostal churches had prepared together a service of prayer for persecuted Christians.

In a time when the churches seek to have a dialogue with all, the word "persecution" may seem obsolete. One can honour the memory of yesterday's martyrs, but to speak of Christians being persecuted today could raise objections. Nevertheless those who have seriously studied the subject are quite clear about it: the list of persecutions inflicted on the church in the 20th century and which continue in the world is long.[12]

During the ceremony an impressive panorama was drawn up of persecuted Christians throughout the world: the situation of the faithful in intolerant regimes, the poignant account of a Syrian-Orthodox deacon who had just received the news that his bishop was martyred in Iraq. The commemoration of martyrs was linked with the prayer for persecuted Christians. In the spirit of the letter to the Hebrews one did not separate the injunction to remember the great cloud of witnesses from the calling to pray for the members of the body of Christ who are in prison or persecuted (Heb. 12:1;13:3,7).

By bringing us together to listen to the word of God and the cries of our brothers and sisters who are suffering – "If one member suffers, all suffer together with it" (1 Cor. 12:26) – we have experienced what is, in my opinion, one of the most authentic forms of ecumenism: to pray together for our friends in Christ who suffer for his name. They remind us that we are also called to be witnesses of Christ's love wherever we are with our personal challenges.

The ceremony included gospels and spirituals sung by the oldest Gospel group of Switzerland, the "Companions of Jordan" created more than 50 years ago. Their founder and director, Olivier Nusslé, told me that he had rarely seen such an intense moment, because the words from the songs, written in a time of oppression, were well suited to the contents of the ceremony.

---

11 www.aide-eglise-en-detresse.ch; www.hmk-aem.ch; www.portesouvertes.ch; http://sb.od.org ; www.csi-suisse.ch

12 Besides A. Riccardi's book indicated above, one can mention Didier Rance, *Un siècle de témoins. Les martyrs du 20è siècle*, Fayard, Paris, 2001; Sergiu Grossu, *L'Eglise persecutée. Entre Goulag et Société opulente*, L'Age d'homme, Lausanne, 2002; Anneke Companjen, *Hidden Sorrow, Lasting Joy: The Forgotton Women of the Persecuted Church*, Hodder & Stoughton, London, 2000.

Let us here open an excursus. In 1927, the delegates to the first world conference on Faith and Order, which took place in Lausanne, were aware that the Christians in Russia were subjected to persecution by the Soviet authorities. The Russian Orthodox Church was prevented from participating in this conference. After specifying the purpose of the pilgrimage begun in Lausanne – the full communion around the Lord's table – the conference's final Declaration stated: "To hasten the union which we all yearn for, there is nothing better than intercession. Either as an individual, or as a Church, let each one of us remember this in our daily worship".[13] For Charles Henry Brent, who organized and presided many sessions of the Faith and Order conference in Lausanne, prayer underlies the search for unity. Without it this search, and even a Christian way of life, would be meaningless. We must also pray for each other, especially for the Christians persecuted for their faith and deprived of their freedom. Thus the last words of Brent and the last lines of the conference's final Declaration are an appeal to intercede for those brothers and sisters who are persecuted: "our prayers rally round them and we reach forth our arms to them with affection".[14] This part of the final declaration, which was written by Brent himself, reminds us of one of his prayers which has become part of our heritage. One can find it in the calendar of the Episcopalian Church on the anniversary of his death:

> Lord Jesus Christ, who didst stretch out thine arms of love upon the hard wood of the Cross, that all men everywhere might come within the reach of thy saving embrace: So clothe us with thy Spirit that we, reaching forth our hands in love, may bring those who do not know thee to the knowledge and love of thee; for the honor of thy Name.[15]

Christians martyred and persecuted remind us of Jesus on the cross when he opened his arms to welcome the world. Today his work of reconciliation is accomplished through our praying hands of compassion.[16]

The cloud of witnesses at the celebrations of the World Council of Churches

In the last assemblies, the WCC introduced some periods of commemoration of the cloud of witnesses. For example, at the 7th assembly in Canberra (1991) they had an All Saints service. One was asked to "remember all those witnesses who can transmit a living faith, even though they have been dead a long time". Photos or pictures of witnesses, either alive or deceased, renowned or unknown were exhibited. During a

13 Actes officiels de la Conférence mondiale de Lausanne, 1927, p.543.

14 *Ibid.*, p.511, 543.

15 *Charles Henry Brent.* Episcopal Calendar. http://satucket.com/lectionary/Charles_Brent.htm

16 On Brent, cf. Martin Hoegger, *Pratique de l'unité chez Charles Henry Brent. A l'Aube d'une spiritualité œcuménique,* Ecumenical Institute of Bossey, 2004.

moment of silence the participants wrote their names on a long paper banner. The service ended with a litany of saints.[17]

At the 8th assembly in Harare (1998) a ceremony, accompanied by prayers of the Oriental Orthodox churches (Coptic, Ethiopian and Syrian), was also held in remembrance of witnesses of faith based on the words of Jesus about "the grain of wheat falling into the earth" (John 12:24). The participants were asked to remember all those, alive or dead, who gave their lives for Jesus: those who served him, those who bore fruit, the blessed who bore witness. At the end the participants could write on a cloth the names of a witness or a martyr. There were also grains on the cloth, where each person could pick one up by giving a name out loud: "This grain will bear fruit, when later on the day and during the whole time of this Assembly, it will remind you of this person's history".[18] During the closing service, we were asked to remember that one is not alone as we are surrounded by a great cloud of ecumenical witnesses ever since the first WCC Assembly in Amsterdam.

Discovering how the other churches commemorate their martyrs

In ecumenical meetings the remembrance of witnesses was carried out in two ways, either by ecumenical prayers, or by joining up in prayer with another church, particularly the Orthodox and Oriental churches. We have a similar experience in Lausanne: since 2004 the Protestant cathedral has welcomed religious services of other churches. For example the Roman Catholic mass and the Orthodox liturgy have been celebrated there. On the first Sunday of each month a different church is given the possibility to prepare a ceremony to which other churches are invited. It is an excellent ecumenical occasion to discover the prayers and the spirituality of various churches. From time to time there are also ecumenical celebrations. In this way we have discovered how certain churches commemorate their witnesses. For instance, thanks to the Roman Catholic mass, we Protestants rediscovered some biblical feasts which had been discontinued by the Reformation, like the Annunciation and the Presentation at the Temple.[19]

Integrating the past in a cathedral

Let us stay awhile in the cathedral of Lausanne. In the course of the 75th anniversary celebration of the first Conference on Faith and Order (August 2002) there was a commemoration of its major events and important personalities.[20] The opportunity to "speak" was given to the

17 *Sinfonia Oecumenica*, Basel, 1998, pp.933ff.

18 *Turn to God - Rejoice in Hope: Orthodox Reflections on the Way to Harare,* edited by Th.E. Fitzgerald, WCC Publications, Geneva, 1998, pp.78ff. http://www.wcc-coe.org/wcc/assembly/morn-e.html

19 The feast of the Annunciation was nevertheless celebrated in the cathedral of Lausanne until 1863 (E. Dupraz *La Cathédrale de Lausanne*, Publ. Notre Dame, Lausanne, 1958, pp.252-257). Bruno Burki made a plea for the Reformed churches to rediscover the feast of Annunciation (25 March), which is one of the oldest Marian commemorations in both the East and West. As it is close to Easter, it reminds us of the Annunciation of Christ's birth in the very midst of the Pascal Mystery (Marie et les anges: "Pertinence liturgique d'un memento dans la liturgie des Eglises réformées" in A. Barnard, P. Post, E. Rose (eds): *A Cloud of Witnesses. The Cult of Saints in past and present*. Peeters, Leuven, 2005, pp.362f).

20 See www.wcc-coe.org/wcc/what/faith/lausanne-service-e.pdf

cathedral so that it could tell us something about its moments of glory. We began with Mary, the mother of our Lord to whom the cathedral was originally consecrated in the 8th century. At an entrance of the cathedral one can see her receiving the crown of martyrs from the hands of Christ. Mary is a model of the church, a faithful witness of Christ, her son.[21]

Then we mentioned the consecration in the 13th century by Pope Gregory X; the end of the Western Schism in the 15th century when the anti-pope Felix V deposited his tiara in this cathedral; the memory of Jean Calvin and Pierre Viret in the Reformation period. Then we passed on to the 18th century with the figure of Antoine Court, the founder of the French seminary which trained the Huguenot pastors, many of whom were martyred. Finally we recalled the personality of Charles Brent, the first president of Faith and Order, and the call for unity at the conference of Lausanne in 1927. We concluded by recalling the recent ecumenical ceremonies, bringing together all the churches of the Canton of Vaud, and which led to the decision to open the Cathedral of Lausanne to the religious services of other churches.

This commemoration showed that it is possible to consider figures of the past. It may seem at first that such diverse elements would mutually exclude themselves in a comparative logic of our liturgical practices. How is it possible to link these very diverse spiritual approaches at the very heart of the belief in the mystery of Christ's resurrection? In the 16th century the radical response of the Reformation was to clear out from the cathedral in one fell swoop everything which was not central to this. The same goes for the calendar, the common and personal prayers of the Reformed churches, which excluded any references to the cloud of witnesses. This reaction was without doubt too extreme to be just and acceptable. Following the second Vatican Council, the Catholic Church's revised liturgy included a simplified calendar which gave priority to the mystery of Christ and to the importance of Sunday worship besides any other occasional course of action. But how can one today confess only the *name* of Christ?

We may find a reply to this question in the way this ceremony was conducted. Although it was strictly centred on Christ, it did mention figures of the past as part of the mystical body of Christ. The meaning of this ceremony was not to reject the past, but to perceive it in a new manner. It led us to a more inclusive approach in our Christian faith; we seek to define ourselves with others instead of opposing them, we incorporate their contributions instead of rejecting them, we underline the value of unity in diversity.

Portraits of gospel witnesses in a church

In the former Abbey of Romainmôtier, an old monastery taken over by the Reformation in 1536 and which has become an important centre for the revival of Reformed liturgy, there

21 Edouard Diserens, *Le portail peint: Cathédrale de Lausanne. Guide du pèlerin*, Cabédita, Yens, 1996, underlined the ecumenical meaning of the presentation of Mary in this entrance.

is an ecumenical prayer fellowship bringing together Protestants and Catholics twice daily. In their prayer they have inserted the remembrance of biblical witnesses. They designed a project: to present a "book" in the Abbey for visitors in order to draw their attention to the fact that they are in a place where the church prays continuously every day. The idea is to give them the occasion to join in a meditation and a reflection on certain texts.

The project is made up as follows: there is a portrait of a person with a brief biography to situate it historically, a word, a characteristic phrase, and if possible a personal prayer. The fellowship has drawn up the first list of witnesses: St Roman, the father of the Jura and founder of the monastery, St Columban who restored it, St Wandrill, St Francis and St Clare of Assisi. Also Luther and Calvin. From the more recent times: Patriarch Athenagoras, Father Paul Couturier, Martin Luther King, Edith Stein, Dietrich Bonhoeffer, Mother Teresa, Oscar Romero, abbé Pierre, Brother Roger, Mother Geneviève, Théodore Monod, Albert Schweizer, Nelson Mandela…

The communities of Grandchamp and Taizé

The community of Grandchamp, which sprang from the liturgical and monastic revival in French-speaking Protestantism in Switzerland, has a rich experience in ecumenical commemorations of witnesses and martyrs. Every Thursday and Sunday they celebrate the last supper. Based on the example of the Rule of Taizé, Sister Minke writes: "It is thanks to the Eucharist that we came to realize, practically in a tangible manner, that 'our common prayer is to be found in the communion of saints',[22] in the communion of believers of today and of all times.".[23] The high point of the common praise is in the last supper, but it does not belong to the community, it is a gift entrusted in a special way to this community. Sister Minke adds: "the liturgy is an invitation to participate in the praise of the communion of saints in heaven and earth which passes through every period of time and space. It is our first service."[24]

In the community, the liturgical time of the church is mostly represented by biblical saints, but it has also integrated St Francis and St Clare, St Theresa of Avila and St Theresa of Lisieux, Dietrich Bonhoeffer, St Silouan, Edith Stein, Oscar Romero. They also keep in remembrance the Protestant martyrs of the St Bartholomew's Day Massacre and celebrate the feast of the Reformation on 31 October.

The community is also mindful of the days which made a mark on the conscience of humanity, such as 9 November, the Kristallnacht in 1938, plus the opening of the Berlin Wall. Coincidentally the community celebrates on that same day the first vows taken in 1952.

22 Rule of Taizé, 19
23 Soeur Minke, "La vie liturgique de la Communauté de Grandchamp" in Bruno Burki, Martin Klöckener, (eds), *Liturgie en mouvement*, Universitätsverlag, Freiburg, Labor et Fides, Genève, 2000, p.166.
24 *Ibid.*, p.174.

On the eve of the feast of the Transfiguration, 6 August, is the memorial day of the first atomic bomb on Hiroshima. There is a call to let oneself be transformed by the light of Christ and to repudiate the destructive light of evil. The community has rediscovered the various aspects of the life of Mary, a daughter of Israel and the mother of our Lord: her birth on 8 September, the Annunciation, the Visitation, and her *Dies Natalis* on 15 August. They pray for the Jewish people during their holidays. Finally they celebrate on every 7 December the remembrance of Mother Genevieve, the first Grandchamp prioress, and all the other sisters now in heaven.

These commemorations, which rhythm the church life, are a remarkable way of opening up to other churches and the world. Sister Minke also said that to remember those who fixed their gaze on Christ gives one strength to go forward with determination on the "new way" which he has opened up (cf. Heb. 10:20; 12:1).

On this point Taizé has taken a different path than Grandchamp. Although Taizé's previous prayer book included the remembrance of Mary, the apostles and the major witnesses,[25] it has discontinued them for pastoral reasons concerning the reception of the young generation, with the exception of a few hymns.

Taizé has nevertheless introduced a gesture of immense symbolical significance: a prayer around the cross lying horizontally on the ground. The young people place their foreheads on it as a sign of communion with the martyrdom of Jesus Christ and all the suffering endured by him. On 16 August 2008 the prior, Brother Aloïs reminded us of Brother Roger, this great ecumenical witness who inspired a prayer which still "expands the hearts" of thousands of young people:

> Oh God of love, on this day we remember our brother Roger. We give thanks for his life which he offered. He initiated a road to peace and reconciliation for us and for so many others throughout the world.
>
> Like him we wish to be the poors of Christ, with a burning fire of love inside us.
>
> Like him we wish to put into practice what little we have understood from the Gospel, so as to bring joy into the lives of those you have left in our care.[26]

25 *Office de Taizé,* 2nd edition, Presse de Taizé, 1963.
26 http://www.taize.fr/fr_article7051.html

Celebrating All Saints, the Known and the Unknown: An Orthodox Approach for an Ecumenical Commemoration of Witnesses

Job Getcha

Called to be Saints

At the divine liturgy, the eucharistic celebration of the Orthodox Church, the main celebrant invites the assembly to partake in the eucharist by saying: "The Holy Gifts for the holy". To this invitation, the assembly immediately responds: "One is Holy, One is the Lord, Jesus Christ, in the glory of God the Father. Amen"!

One is holy. Nevertheless every one is called to participate in this holiness. In the first epistle of Peter, we read: "As he who called you is holy, be holy yourselves in all your conduct; for it is written, 'You shall be holy, for I am holy.'"(1 Peter 1:15-16). The apostle Peter quotes here God's invitation: "Be holy, for I am Holy", which is found five times in the Old Testament (Lev. 11:44-45; 19:1; 20:7; 20:26). Saint Paul refers as well to this call in his epistle to the Corinthians, when he writes "the church of God that is in Corinth, to those who are sanctified in Christ Jesus, called to be saints."(1 Cor. 1:2).

The Orthodox do not "make up" saints, but strongly believe that holiness is the aim, the direction of Christian life. The Christian lives in the church, which is holy, and is being sanctified by the blood of Christ and the grace of the Holy Spirit. In the view of the Orthodox Church, the Christian life is a "life in Christ", a life enlightened by the Holy Spirit. Therefore the life of the Christian should reflect Christ: the Christian should be a witness of Christ.

As a matter of fact, in the early church, at times of persecution, the ideal of Christian life was linked with martyrdom. In Greek, the term "martys" means "witness". Therefore, the Christian martyr is not so much someone who has suffered and has died for Christ, as someone who has witnessed Christ in his life until the end. The early church commemorated the martyrs because it was convinced that they were models for others. With the end of the persecutions after the edict of Milan of 313, other kinds of witnesses appeared within the monastic movement, among the pastors of the church and among the laity as well. This is why the Orthodox Church commemorates them by celebrating their feast days and by reading their lives, considering that their example should be followed.

The Communion of Saints

But saints, in the Orthodox perspective, are not only models. They are also intercessors. The Orthodox believe that the church is not merely constituted by the Christians living here on earth, but that there is a mystical union between the earthly church and the heavenly church, which means that all believers of all times are united with and in Christ through prayer. As we pray for each other, the saints and the dead are also praying for us, since we all are alive in Christ. This is the meaning of what we call the "communion of saints", which is of course a christocentric notion.

This unity between the church on earth and in heaven is experienced through the celebration of the divine liturgy, of the eucharist, in which all are being united to Christ and in Christ. This is the main reason why, already in the early church, it has become a custom to celebrate the eucharist on the grave of martyrs on the day of their martyrdom. Later, the church continued to celebrate the eucharist on the feast day of the venerated saints as well as on the day of the death of each of its members, in order to show the unity which exists in Christ between the living, the dead and the saints. On this point, it is interesting to point out that the Byzantine anaphora of saint John Chrysostom prays *for* (*hyper*) the saints before praying for the departed and the living. On the other hand, the Byzantine anaphora of St Basil demands that "we may find grace with (*meta*) the saints".[1]

A Byzantine theologian and liturgist of the 15th century, Symeon of Thessalonika, develops in his writings an important point on the communion of saints. He underlines first of all that it is through the eucharistic sacrifice, which is, in his view identical to the sacrifice of Christ through a typological relation, that the saints participate in the divine glory, and that it is through this sacrifice in which they participate with us that they reconcile us with God when we celebrate their memory.[2] This vision would explain the antique tradition of the church to celebrate the eucharist not only on the days when we commemorate the dead but also on the days when we commemorate the saints. This is why, for instance, Cyprian of Carthage said, about the martyrs, that "we are continuously offering sacrifices for them".[3]

Difficulties for an ecumenical liturgical commemoration of saints in the Orthodox Church

Having in mind this profound unity among the living, the dead and the saints through the celebration of the eucharist, the Orthodox Church encounters a difficulty for an Ecumenical

1 Cf. G. Wagner, "La commémoration des saints dans la prière eucharistique", *La liturgie, expérience de l'Eglise. Etudes liturgiques*, J. Getcha & A. Lossky (eds), (AS 1). Paris, 2003, p.34.
2 The vision of Symeon of Thessalonica is the same as the one of Theodore of Andida: Theodore of Andida, *Protheoria* 28. PG 140, 456B. Cf.: Wagner, p.36.
3 Cyprian of Carthage, *Epist.* 39, 3. Cf.: Wagner, p. 36.

Liturgical Commemoration of Saints. We know well, especially within the WCC, that ecumenical liturgical celebrations are a touchy question and a problem in itself for the Orthodox Church. This problem is identical to the one of the so-called "intercommunion" or "eucharistic hospitality". As has been expressed on several occasions, the Orthodox Church does not believe that the eucharist is a means to achieve unity but an expression, a manifestation of a unity, which already exists. This is why it strongly believes that the partaking from one bread and the sharing of one cup could only be achieved among divided Christians once their divisions, whether they be doctrinal, disciplinary, historical or political, are overcome.

In the same perspective, the Orthodox Church does not commemorate *liturgically* saints that have not been in full eucharistic communion with it as it does not include them in its menologion or synaxarion, which is the list of saints for each day of the year. This problem is not merely a problem of discipline or of protocol, since we find sometimes figures that are being venerated by one Christian confession as saints and considered by another as heretics. Sometimes, those, whom one confession would venerate as martyrs, would be considered as persecutors by the others. This is not only a problem within the ecumenical (inter-confessional) dialogue, but also a problem for the dialogue of the Orthodox Church with the non-Chalcedonians.

Therefore, one cannot expect the Orthodox Church to commemorate saints of other confessions in its liturgy. Nevertheless, although it is impossible for the Orthodox Church to commemorate liturgically saints from another confession until the day full unity would be restored between this confession and Orthodoxy, this does not mean that the Orthodox Church excludes the possibility of holiness in other confessions. As a matter of fact, affirming such a position would deny the principle according to which holiness is a gift of the Holy Spirit, who blows where it wishes (John 3:8).

Furthermore, this does not exclude that it could see in exemplary figures of other confessions imitations of Christ and models for Christian life. For example, among the saints of the Roman Catholic Church, many Orthodox venerate Saint Francis of Assisi, whom they would compare very often to Saint Seraphim of Sarov. Nevertheless, a liturgical commemoration of Saint Francis as well as the inclusion of his name into the synaxarion of the Orthodox Church are not possible for the reasons mentioned above. One day, in the old days of Saint Sergius Orthodox Theological Institute in Paris, somebody offered a statue of Saint Francis to Father Kiprian Kern who had a great devotion for Saint Francis. Father Kiprian was embarrassed about what to do with this statue, since on the one hand the Orthodox Church does not have statues in its liturgical tradition, and on the other hand, Saint Francis is not a saint of the Orthodox Church. Father Kiprian finally decided to place the statue in the middle of the garden, thinking that this was a proper way to honour a saint who was so close to earthly creation... This story could help us to think about creative ways of commemorating Christian witnesses beyond the boundaries of the difficulties our confessions may encounter.

Opportunities for ecumenical commemoration of witnesses

Among the different opportunities for ecumenical commemoration of witnesses would be the establishment of a common day in the year. In the West, All Saints' day already exists on November 1. In the East, in the Byzantine tradition, this day is linked with feast of the Descent of the Holy Spirit since it is celebrated on the Sunday after Pentecost, underlining the link which exists between the saints and the salvific mystery of Christ as well as the gift of the Holy Spirit.

It might be interesting for our reflection to look at the different reasons given by the Synaxarion[4] of that day, that is the homily, which explains the meaning of this feast. One reason given is that it shows that the coming of the All-holy Spirit sanctifies and makes wise human beings, restores them and through Christ sends them to God, some by the witness of martyrdom and blood, others by their virtuous conduct and way of life. Another one, is that "it was necessary for the Saints who are celebrated individually day by day to be gathered together on one day, in order to demonstrate that, as they struggled for the one Christ and all ran the race in the same stadium of virtue, so they were all fittingly crowned as servants of one God and sustained the Church, having filled the world on high."[5]

But the second reason given by our Byzantine writer is very interesting and might be quite inspiring for an ecumenical commemoration of witnesses. He says that: "though many people have been well-pleasing to God, they were through outstanding virtue unknown to humanity by name, or for some human reason or other, but nevertheless have great glory in God's sight. [...] the most godly Fathers ordained that we should celebrate the feast of All Saints, honouring the earlier and later ones, the unknown and the known – all those in whom the Holy Spirit has dwelt he has made holy."[6]

Of course, many local Christian churches make commemorations of the witnesses or saints that are known to them. But the mystery of holiness is much broader since we are not making up saints: God is revealing saints to us, since the source of holiness, which is rooted in the mystery of Christ, is the sanctification by the Holy Spirit. Therefore, although many saints may be known to us, much more might exist and be revealed to us. Thus, on the

4 Written by Nikiphoros Kallistos Xanthopoulos (†1335). It is found in the *Pentecostarion* in the service for the Sunday of All Saints.
5 See in Appendix for Liturgical material The *Synaxarion* of the First Sunday after Pentecost.
6 *Ibid.*

grounds of the tradition of the Orthodox Church, the establishment of an ecumenical day of commemoration of Christian witnesses, known and unknown, around the feast of Pentecost, might be an opportunity to commemorate, in various ways, witnesses coming from different Christian confessions.

We know that the Ecumenical Patriarchate has established the day of prayer for the protection of creation on the new ecclesiastical year, September 1, and that a special liturgical service has been prepared. This idea was later picked up within the ecumenical movement: for instance the Conference of European Churches is now inviting its members to pray for the environment during the month of September. In the same spirit, a special day could be established around the feast of Pentecost for an ecumenical commemoration of Christian witnesses, known and unknown. For an ecumenical prayer service one could make use of the hymns and scriptural readings found for the Sunday of All Saints (First Sunday after Pentecost) in the Orthodox tradition.

Another opportunity could be "Ecumenical pilgrimages", during which Christians of different confessions could walk together to a place where a Christian witness may have lived, died or have been buried. Many Orthodox Christians have done the Roman Catholic pilgrimage to Saint James of Compostella. Last year, an Orthodox pilgrimage was organized to the concentration camp of Ravensbrück where the New Martyr, Mother Maria Skobtsova died, in which Christians from various confessions have taken part. As a matter of fact, Mother Maria is being considered as a saint not only by the Orthodox but by Christians from other confessions and is highly respected by Jews and even atheists. The former Roman Catholic Archbishop of Paris, Jean-Marie Lustiger, attended in person the ceremony of her canonization in the Russian Orthodox Cathedral in Paris. More recently an ecumenical pilgrimage was made to Iasi where the relics of St Paraskeva are found. Pilgrimages are not only a genuine Orthodox way of honouring Christian witnesses, but could also become a great ecumenical opportunity where Christians of different confessions walk and live together.

Some other already existing opportunities could also be used. For instance, each year, during the week of prayer for Christian unity, a commemoration of great figures of Christianity could be made by taking into consideration anniversaries that are fulfilled in the year and reflect on what could be taken from their life as example to enhance Christian unity today.

The existing Daily Prayer Cycle could be used by adding to it the commemoration, for each day of the year, of major Christian witnesses coming from the region and confession that is responsible for the material of that specific day. A short biography of the figure could be added to the produced material, reflecting how this example could be relevant for Christians living today.

To know better the life and the teachings of a Christian witness by commemorating him or her could be of a great benefit to the ecumenical movement. For instance, the St Silouan's Association, which was founded to promote the spiritual teachings of Silouan of Mount Athos, a Russian monk who died on the Holy Mountain in 1934 and who was popularized by Father Sophrony (Sakharov), gathers among its members not only Orthodox but Roman Catholics and Protestants as well, which shows the impact of the saint on the whole of contemporary Christianity. In fact, he could be, as many others, considered today as an "ecumenical saint". The book about his life and sayings is indeed extremely popular among all Christian confessions and the saint is not only known but also venerated by Christians of various denominations throughout the world.

These are at least four opportunities that could be seen, from an Orthodox perspective, as ways of having an ecumenical commemoration of witnesses, being aware that we are surrounded by a cloud of witnesses, known and unknown, united with Christ and filled by the Holy Spirit.

Ecumenical Opportunities for Commemoration: A Roman Catholic Perspective

Keith F. Pecklers

Introduction

Our ecumenical progress over the past 40 years has borne fruit in numerous ways: in shared study and pastoral outreach, in worship and mission, and in the recognition of common witnesses to the gospel of Jesus Christ and our desire to commemorate them. A mere glance at the Church of England's text *Common Worship* published in 2000 bears witness to this. On that liturgical calendar we find the names of Francis De Sales, Dom Bosco, Oscar Romero, Dietrich Bonhoeffer, Thomas More, Ignatius Loyola, Maximilian Kolbe, Martin Luther, Charles De Foucauld, Teresa of Avila and John of the Cross. Similarly, the Evangelical Lutheran Church of America's *Worship* published just two years ago in 2006 finds the names of Martin Luther King Jr., the Japanese and Ugandan martyrs, John and Charles Wesley, Oscar Romero, Martin De Porres, Francis Xavier, Teresa of Avila and John of the Cross. Such ecumenical commemoration in the different churches would have been unthinkable 30 or 40 years ago and is indicative of just how far we have come along the path towards Christian unity. It is extraordinary, for example, that there is now a statue of the slain Roman Catholic Archbishop of San Salvador, Oscar Romero, at Westminster Abbey in London along with other ecumenical witnesses. And it is equally significant that the Archbishop of Canterbury commemorated the Anglican Martyrs from the Melanesian Brotherhood in a chapel of the Roman Basilica of San Bartolomeo during Archbishop Rowan Williams' visit to Pope Benedict in November 2006. Yet despite such progress, there is much that remains to be done.

Challenges to Roman Catholic participation in an ecumenical commemoration

While recognizing the important ecumenical step forward that this symposium and ecumenical project might engender, the Roman Catholic Church has been reluctant to offer its full support. There is a concern, for example, about what is meant by the term "Christian witness" since the Catholic tradition of Blesseds and Saints is restricted to those who, following Christ more closely in a heroic manner have attained the glory of heaven, are worthy of imitation and have intercessory power. In a "Note" by the Congregation of the Cause of Saints issued on 28 December 1999[1], a distinction was made between "martyrs"and "witnesses of the faith", requiring the need for a distinction between martyrologies which include those who

1 "Nella Lettera apostolica", Notitae 36 (2000), pp. 51-54.

have officially been declared Blesseds or Saints and "witnesses of the faith" who have not been subject to the same canonical process. Thus, there are clear ecclesiological questions here about how the *communio sanctorum* is understood and who are the witnesses.

Having said that, however, that same "Note" of the Holy See encouraged initiatives to preserve and celebrate the memory of the "witnesses of the faith" so that commemoration of such Christian witness might become "an inspiration to the baptized". In encouraging such celebrations, however, the "Note" stated that it is expedient to avoid using concrete names of persons, indicating instead only categories of witnesses (witnesses during the persecution in Mexico, in Spain... under Nazism, under Communism...) Indeed, this was done at the ecumenical commemoration of witnesses at the Coliseum in which those commemorated were grouped into various categories so as to include different continents, various churches and ecclesial communities, and the victims of all the regimes and ideologies of the 20th century.

The Roman Catholic Church believes that such remembrance of Christian witnesses bears within it an inherent catechesis on the "universal call to holiness" borne in baptism, which reminds Christians of their radical fidelity to Christ – even to the point of shedding their own blood. Thus, such commemorations might "inspire in Christians of today an activism of faith in harmony with the radical newness from Baptism, which is itself an incorporation into Christ crucified and risen from the dead."

Ecumenical opportunities for commemoration

That Ecumenical Commemoration of Witnesses to the Faith in the 20th Century at the Coliseum on 7 May 2000 took place at the insistence of Pope John Paul II himself, even despite the reservations expressed by the Congregation for Saints only five months earlier. That event was linked to the holy father's statement in his Apostolic Letter *Tertio Millennio Adveniente*:

> In our own century, martyrs have returned, many of them nameless, "unknown soldiers", as it were, of God's great cause. As far as possible, their witness should not be lost to the Church... Their gesture cannot fail to have an ecumenical character and expression. Perhaps the most convincing form of ecumenism is the *ecumenism of the saints* and of the martyrs. The *communio sanctorum* speaks louder than the things that divide us. [no.37]

The Pope was keen to affirm an ecumenism lived in the giving of one's life in sacrifice for Christ regardless of one's ecclesial affiliation. Secondly, the ecumenical commemoration at the Coliseum was intended to be an invitation to all Christian communities to discern "the effective presence of Christ and of the Holy Spirit even in the midst of persecution and violence".

Thirdly, the commemoration was intended to serve as a strong reminder to present and future generations to learn from the example of their forebears who bore witness to the gospel of Christ and suffered persecution even as they forgave their persecutors. That ecumenical commemoration initiated by the Roman Catholic Church in the Jubilee Year of 2000 has set us on a path from which we cannot and will not turn back. Indeed, it offers a model for what is possible as we look towards the future – even despite our canonical and doctrinal differences.

The Agreed Statement of the International Anglican-Roman Catholic Commission for Unity and Mission (IARCCUM): *Growing Together in Unity and Mission* encourages "Visible expressions of our shared faith" in which Anglicans and Roman Catholics develop strategies to foster such visible expression. Specifically recommended is "more frequent non-Eucharistic worship, including celebrations of faith, …processions of witness (e.g. on Good Friday), and shared public liturgies on significant occasions." All of this is intended to reinforce their understanding of common mission borne in a common baptism. [no.102] Now, if we broaden the interpretation of that text beyond the Anglican-Roman Catholic dialogue to the wider mission of Christ's church, then such ecumenical commemorations offer the very "visible expression of our shared faith" that the Anglican Communion and Roman Catholic Church is actually encouraging. In other words, despite our sad divisions around the eucharistic table, we need to be doing as much in common as we possibly can where we are united, and the ecumenical commemoration of witnesses certainly offers one viable option for giving a visible expression of our common faith.

As always, much depends on the imagination, creativity and ecumenical commitment of pastoral leaders in our various churches and communities, but it would behoove us to seize opportunities for such ecumenical commemoration when they present themselves – whether at the local level or parish or diocese or in the context of larger international meetings or assemblies. In August 2007, during the Congress of the International *Societas Liturgica* held in Palermo, that ecumenical gathering of over 400 liturgical scholars gathered together at the Cathedral of Cefalù to remember our forebears in the faith and to re-affirm our own baptismal commitment of fidelity to Christ as instruments of God's mission within the world. Led by a Roman Catholic Archbishop – the Papal Master of Ceremonies at the time, Piero Marini and the Anglican Bishop of Salisbury, David Stancliffe, and in the presence of the Roman Catholic Bishop of Cefalù, the two bishops processed to the baptismal font in matching mitres and copes as the "Litany of the Resurrection" from the Church of England's *Common Worship* was chanted. At the font, the bishops led us all in a "Corporate Renewal of Baptismal Vows" and "Affirmation of Commitment" after which they moved throughout the cathedral sprinkling the assembly with baptismal water. Afterwards back in the sacristy, Archbishop Marini remarked to me: "Talk about visible unity! We had it here this morning."

In Rome we have a very active ecumenical clergy group which meets together monthly for prayer and study and collaborates regularly on various projects of common interest. The church where I serve collaborates closely with our neighbouring Anglican Centre and nearby Church of England parish. We meet together monthly for joint Evensong in one another's churches, celebrate an ecumenical blessing of palms on Ash Wednesday, and initiate Holy Week together each year with a joint procession and ecumenical blessing of palms. Interestingly, the Anglican parish is named "All Saints" and members of our Catholic community are regular participants at the Solemn Evensong there each year on All Saints Day – to celebrate their patronal feast. To date, however, we have never considered organizing an ecumenical commemoration of Christian witnesses. Certainly, one very good starting point would be a joint commemoration of the Ugandan Martyrs – Anglicans and Roman Catholics who died together in bearing witness to the Christian faith.

Unlike the Orthodox tradition, the Roman Catholic Church has no texts for Grand Vespers of All Saints, aside from what is found in the Roman Liturgy of the Hours for 1 November. The Roman Catholic *Book of Blessings* contains an "Order for the Blessing of Missionaries Sent to Proclaim the Gospel". Such a rite might provide a context for an ecumenical commemoration as those individuals are blessed and sent forth to preach the gospel, reminding them that they go forth within a long tradition of witnesses who have spent their lives in service of the gospel of Christ.

The restoration of the catechumenate after the Second Vatican Council offers numerous texts within the *Rite of Christian Initiation of Adults* that logically focus on mission, baptismal commitment and witness, willingness to die and rise with Christ etc. Here, as well, particular rites within the catechumenal process could appropriately take place within a wider ecumenical commemoration of witnesses whose own baptismal commitment can serve as an inspiration to those preparing to take up the same commitment. This would be especially fitting as the already cited Anglican-Roman Catholic document *Growing Together in Unity and Mission* actually encourages joint baptismal and catechumenal formation [no.100]. Moreover, as Lent is an especially intense period of final preparation for catechumens and candidates, it offers numerous possibilities for ecumenical commemoration in meditating upon the suffering of Christ in celebrations of the Way of the Cross, for example, or in the popular Taizé "Prayers around the Cross".

Certainly, the Easter season offers the occasion *par excellence* for such ecumenical commemorations. Christ, the risen one, opens the hearts of the faithful to the hope of everlasting life and gives meaning to suffering, tribulations and death itself. It is especially poignant that such a celebration happens in the context of Evening Prayer when Christians of diverse communities acclaim Christ whose joyful light pierces the darkness of the night.

Indeed, the ancient tradition of Easter Vespers with its procession to the baptismal font, renewal of baptismal promises, and sprinkling with baptismal water, would certainly offer a very real possibility for such an ecumenical commemoration. Within such a framework, the reading from 1 Peter [1:3-9, 13-21] is particularly apt as it speaks of the joyful faith of the baptized tried by fire, along with Matthew's gospel of the Beatitudes [5:1-12] reflected in the living icons of so many Christian witnesses over the centuries. As the conclusion of the great 50 days of Easter, the feast of Pentecost logically offers yet another opportunity with its inherent symbolism of mission and Christian witness which runs throughout the texts of the feast with a possible commemoration within the celebration of Evening Prayer either on the vigil of Pentecost or the feast itself.

Conclusion

Last April, during Pope Benedict's visit to the Church of San Bartolomeo in Rome, he spoke of the side altars in the small basilica. Each little chapel contains reminders of modern individuals who died for their faith or their love of others: a Bible belonging to a Catholic murdered while hiding in a church in Rwanda; a letter from Blessed Franz Jagerstatter, an Austrian beheaded for refusing to fight in Hitler's army; a missal used by murdered Archbishop Oscar Romero of San Salvador; a chalice, paten and stole used by Father Andrea Santoro, an Italian priest killed in Turkey in 2006. A large icon above the main altar pictures German Lutheran theologian Dietrich Bonhoeffer, executed by the Nazis; Russian Orthodox Patriarch Tikhon of Moscow, imprisoned by the communists in the 1920s; Father Gisueppe Puglisi, murdered by the mafia in Sicily; as well as scenes recalling the Armenian genocide and religious persecutions in Albania.

In commenting on such an ecumenical cloud of witnesses Pope Benedict asked: "Why did these martyred brothers and sisters of ours not try to save the indispensable gift of life at all cost? Why did they continue to serve the church despite serious threats and intimidation? Because these martyrs were following Jesus, who said there was no greater love than to give one's life for another."

LITURGICAL RESOURCES

LUTHERAN LITURGICAL RESOURCES

FROM *EVANGELICAL LUTHERAN WORSHIP* [1]

All Saints Day

A

Revelation 7:9-17

Psalm 34:1-10,22

1 John 1-3

Matthew 5:1-12

B

Isaiah 25:6-9

or Wisdom 3:1-9

Psalm 24

Revelation 21:1-6a

John 11:32-44

C

Daniel 7:1-3,15-18

Psalm 149

Ephesians 1:11-23

Luke 6:20-31

Almighty God,

you have knit your people together

in one communion in the mystical body

of your Son, Jesus Christ our Lord.

Grant us grace to follow your blessed saints

---

1 Evangelical Lutheran Church in America, 2006.

in lives of faith and commitment,
and to know the inexpressible joys
you have prepared for those who love you,
through Jesus Christ, our Savior and Lord,
who lives and reigns with you and the Holy Spirit,
one God, now and forever. Amen.

For the Commemoration of Saints

Micah 6:6-8
Psalm 9:1-10
1 Corinthians 1:26-31
Luke 6:20-23

Lord God,
you have surrounded us with so great a cloud of witnesses.
Grant that we, encouraged by the example of your servant/s [*name/s*]
may persevere in the course that is set before us and,
at the last,
share in your eternal joy with all the saints in light,
through Jesus Christ, our Savior and Lord,
who lives and reigns with you and the Holy Spirit,
one God, now and forever. Amen.

For the Commemoration of Martyrs

Ezekiel 20:40-42

Psalm 5

Revelation 6:9-11

Mark 8:34-38

Gracious God,

in every age you have sent men and women

who have given their lives in witness to your love and truth.

Inspire us with the memory of *[name]*,

whose faithfulness led to the way of the cross,

and give us courage to bear full witness with our lives

to your Son's victory over sin and death,

for he lives and reigns with you and the Holy Spirit,

one God, now and forever. Amen.

For the Commemoration of Missionaries

Isaiah 62:1-7

Psalm 48

Romans 10:11-17

Luke 24:44-53

God of grace and glory,

we praise you for your servant/s *[name/s]*,

who made the good news known in [*place of missionary work*].

Raise up, we pray, in every country,

heralds of the gospel,

so that the world may know the immeasurable riches of your love,

and to be drawn to worship you,

Father, Son, and Holy Spirit,

one God, now and forever. Amen.

For the Commemoration of Renewers of the Church

Jeremiah 1:4-10

Psalm 46

1 Corinthians 3:11-23

Mark 10:35-45

Almighty God,

we praise you for your servant/s *[name/s]* ,

through him you have called the church to its tasks and renewed its life.

Raise up in our own day teachers and prophets

inspired by your Spirit,

whose voices will give strength to your church

and proclaim the reality of your reign,

through Jesus Christ, our Savior and Lord,

who lives and reigns with you and the Holy Spirit,

one God, now and forever. Amen.

FROM *RENEWING WORSHIP: THE CHURCH'S YEAR*

– Propers and Seasonal Rites[2]

All Saints Day

The custom of commemorating all of the saints of the church on a single day goes back to at least the 3rd century. All Saints Day celebrates the baptized people of God, living and dead, who make up the body of Christ. On this day or the following Sunday, many congregations will remember the faithful who have died during the past year.[3]

It is indeed right,

our duty and our joy,

2 Evangelical Lutheran Church in America, 2006.

3 *Ibid.* p. 37.

that we should at all times and in all places
give thanks and praise to you,
almighty and merciful God,
through our Savior Jesus Christ.
By the witness of the saints
you show us the hope of our calling,
and strengthen us to run the race set before us,
that we may delight in your mercy,
and rejoice in your glory.
And so, with all the choirs of angels,
With all the faithful of every time and place,
we praise your name and join their unending hymn.[4]

FROM THE *LUTHERAN BOOK OF WORSHIP* [5]

Collect Prayer "The Saints"

We give thanks to you, O Lord our God,
for all your servants and witnesses of time past:
for Abraham, the father of believers
and for Sarah, his wife;
for Moses, the lawgiver,
and Aaron, the priest;
for Miriam and Joshua,
Deborah and Gideon,
Samuel and Hannah, his mother;
for Isaiah and all the prophets;
for Mary, the mother of our Lord;
for Peter and Paul and all the apostles;

4 *Ibid.* p. 48.
5 The American Lutheran Church; The Evangelical Lutheran Church; The Lutheran Church – Missouri Synod, 1978.

for Mary, Martha, and Mary Magdalene;
for Stephen, the first martyr,
and all your saints and martyrs in every time and in every land.
In your mercy, give us as you gave them,
the hope of salvation and the promise of eternal life;
through the first-born from the dead,
Jesus Christ our Lord.

LUTHERAN CHURCH IN AMERICA[6]

From the Vespers Litany

In peace let us pray to the Lord.

For the peace from above, and for our salvation, let us pray to the Lord.

For the peace of the whole world, for the well-being of the church of God, and for the unity of all, let us pray to the Lord.

……

For the faithful who have gone before us and are at rest, let us give thanks to the Lord.

Help, save, comfort, and defend us, gracious Lord.

(Silence for meditation)

Rejoicing in the fellowship of all saints, let us commend ourselves, one another, and our whole life to Christ, our Lord…….

6 *Lutheran Book of Worship*, 1978.

Prayer of the Day

For November 30, St Andrew, Apostle

Almighty God, as the apostle Andrew readily obeyed the call of Christ and followed him without delay, grant that we, called by your holy Word, may in glad obedience offer ourselves to your service: through your Son, Jesus Christ our Lord, who lives and reigns with you and the Holy Spirit, one God, now and forever.

For December 21, St Thomas, Apostle

Almighty and ever-living God, you have given great and precious promises to those who believe. Grant us that perfect faith which overcomes all doubts; through your Son….

For 26 December, St Stephen, Deacon and Martyr

Grant us grace, O Lord, that like Stephen we may learn to love even our enemies and seek forgiveness for those who desire our hurt; through your Son…..

For 27 December, St John, Apostle and Evangelist

Merciful Lord, let the brightness of your light shine on your church, so that all of us, instructed by the teachings of John, your apostle and evangelist, may walk in the light of your truth and attain eternal life; through your Son….

Similar prayers exist for

28 December, the Holy Innocents, Martyrs

18 January, The Confession of St Peter

25 January, the Conversion of St Paul

24 February, St Matthias, Apostle

25 April, St Mark, Evangelist

1 May, St Philip and St James, Apostles

11 June, St Barnabas, Apostle

24 June, the Nativity of St John the Baptist

29 June, St Peter and St Paul, Apostles

22 July, St Mary Magdalene

25 July, St James the Elder, Apostle

15 August, Mary, Mother of our Lord

24 August, St Bartholomew, Apostle

21 September, St Matthew, Apostle and Evangelist

29 September, St Michael and all Angels

18 October, St Luke, Evangelist

28 October, St Simon and St Jude, Apostles

1 November, All Saints' Day

Almighty God, whose people are knit together in one holy church, the body of Christ our Lord: Grant us grace to follow your blessed saints in lives of faith and commitment, and to know the inexpressible joys you have prepared for those who love you; through your Son, Jesus Christ our Lord, who lives and reigns with you and the Holy Spirit, one God, now and forever.

Prayer of the Day for the Commemoration of Saints

Lord, God, you have surrounded us with so great a cloud of witnesses. Grant that we (encouraged by the example of your servant/servants: *name/s*) may persevere in the course that is set before us, to be living signs of the Gospel and at last, with all the saints, to share in your eternal joy; through your Son, Jesus Christ our Lord.

Prayer of the Day for the Commemoration of Martyrs

Gracious Lord, in every age you have sent men and women who have given their lives for the message of your love. Inspire us with the memory of those martyrs for the Gospel (like your servant: *name*) whose faithfulness led them in the way of the cross, and give us courage to bear full witness with our lives to your Son's victory over sin and death; through Jesus Christ our Lord.

Such prayers exist also for the

- Commemoration of Missionaries
- Commemoration of Renewers of the Church
- Commemoration of Renewers of Society
- Commemoration of Pastors and Bishops
- Commemoration of Theologians
- Commemoration of Artists and Scientists

Preface in the great thanksgiving during the eucharistic liturgy for an Apostle's day:

It is indeed right and salutary that we should at all times and in all places offer thanks and praise to you, O Lord, holy Father, through the great shepherd of your flock, Christ our Lord who after his resurrection sent forth his apostles to preach the Gospel and teach all nations, and promised to be with them always, even to the end of the age.

And so, with patriarchs and prophets, with the apostle/apostles: *name/s* and with all the company of heaven, we praise your name and join their unending hymn: Holy, holy, holy.....

Preface for All Saints Day:

It is indeed right and salutary that we should at all times and in all places offer thanks and praise to you, O Lord holy Father, through Christ our Lord. In the blessedness of your saints you have given us a glorious pledge of the hope of our calling; that, moved by their witness and supported by their fellowship, we may run with perseverance the race that is set before us and with them receive the unfading crown of glory. And so, with the church on earth and the hosts of heaven, we praise your name and join their unending hymn: Holy....

Similar prefaces exist for All Souls Day.

REFORMED AND PRESBYTERIAN LITURGICAL RESOURCES

The Eucharistic Liturgy I[1]

Son of God, who is gone to heaven to prepare us a place, in your kingdom remember all those who have fallen asleep in your peace and in hope of resurrection to eternal life. Lord, grant them eternal rest and may perpetual light shine for them.

United through you in the communion of saints we remember all those who have glorified you on earth, by their faith or by their work; great is their reward in heaven: patriarchs, prophets, apostles, saints and martyrs.

We give you thanks for the gifts of your grace shown in them and also ask that you may grant us grace to follow their holy example, so that we too may one day with them partake in the glory of your heavenly kingdom.

Just as this bread which will be broken, was made from grain once scattered in the fields, and as this fruit of the vine, once dispersed on the hillsides, are here gathered and reunited on your table, so Lord may your church militant on earth and triumphant in heaven, soon be gathered to your kingdom from the farthest reaches of the universe, that you may be all in all.

The Ecumenical Liturgies[2]

Let us remember before the Lord all those who have left this world in faith, young or old, our fathers, brothers, sisters or children, those whose names are known to the Lord … May God give them the crown of life on the day of resurrection and may they be judged worthy of entering into the joy of their master, alongside the just whom he has deemed worthy. Let us commemorate before the Lord all his servants and witness of times gone by, particularly Abraham the father of believers, Moses, Samuel and David, Elijah, Isaiah, Jeremiah and all the prophets, John the Baptist the precursor, Peter and Paul, John and James and the other apostles, Stephen the first martyr, Mary our Lord's mother and all the saints, martyrs and doctors of the church in every century and every land.

Sunday Liturgy[3]

Lord God, as we approach your holy table where Christ receives us in your communion, we praise you for uniting us with you and with our fellow human beings; in your grace root us ever deeper in faith in the living Christ, with all those whom we remember.

1 *Liturgie de Communion I*. Église et Liturgie, Lausanne, 1931, p. 33.
2 *Liturgies de Communion*, Église et Liturgie, Lausanne, 1952, p.79.
3 *Liturgie du dimanche pour le temps ordinaire à l'usage des Églises réformées de la Suisse romande*, Lausanne, 1986, p. 219.

We remember those who have preceded us, and who have died in the expectation of resurrection: keep us united with them in the same hope.

We give you thanks for the cloud of witnesses that your Spirit, from the very beginning, has continued to call: the prophets and apostles, saints and martyrs of the past and of today; in the communion of a common faith, grant that we too may be able to serve and praise you all the days of our life.

As the grain once scattered in the fields is reunited in the bread, which we shall break, so too may your whole church soon be gathered into your kingdom from the farthest reaches of the earth. Amen.

For Those Who Partake the Communion[4]

At the holy table I commune with friends: with the disciples and those redeemed by the Lord – with St Paul, St John, St Augustin, St Elizabeth of Hungary, St Francis of Assisi, with Luther, Calvin, Pascal, Wesley, Oberlin, Livingstone, Coillard, Vinet, with the great cloud of witnesses, with those who live in invisibility on the other side of the veil, but also with all who have breath on earth, from the south pole to the north, those who struggle, love, pray, hope against hope, anonymous like leaves in a forest, but working night and day just as the leaves do, to purify the atmosphere of our globe.

Ceremony for the Protestant tertiary order "Les Veilleurs"[5]

In communion with the whole of your church past, with the church both visible and invisible of the present, with the church militant and triumphant, with the church at prayer which worships and with the missionary church which struggles, with the "assembly of the firstborn who are enrolled in heaven", and with the church of the future, one, pure, free, faithful, heroic, advocate of individuals and peoples, Father we are part of and wish to be ever more part of the mystical body of which Jesus Christ is the head.[6]

Oh Eternal God, you before whom stand the spirits of the living and the dead, Light of light, source of wisdom and goodness, you who live in all pure, humble and loving souls, we praise you for all who have worked for the salvation of humanity by bearing witness to your glory and proclaiming your truth; for the wise of every country and every race, and for the guides you have given to the human race over many thousands of years on its long pilgrimage!
For all of them we praise you!

---

4 Wilfred Monod, *Pour communier*, Paris, 1929, p. 64.
5 *Cérémonial du Tiers-Ordre protestant*, "Les Veilleurs", Delachaux et Niestlé, Paris-Neuchâtel, 1947.
6 *Ibid.* p. 46.

For the martyrs to our holy faith; for those who have borne faithful witness to Christ and not worthy of this world; for the Huguenot confessors and galley slaves, for the prisoners of the Tower of Constance; for those who resisted error and lies even unto suffering or death.
We praise you Lord![7]

Office de Taizé[8]

Remembering the saints is a reminder of the unity in Christ of all the faithful: through their life, witness and prayer they come to one another's aid in the communion of saints. We have mentioned the remembrance of saints of the New Testament: the Virgin Mary, John the Baptist, the apostles and writers of the gospels, Mary Magdalene, Stephen the first martyr. Remembering them should not exclude remembrance of other witnesses of the church, this remembrance is a sign of the presence of the cloud of witnesses who together with the church await the glorious manifestation of Christ at the end of time. This multitude is remembered at All Saints on 1 November. Remembering the saints is a liturgical reminder to the earthly church of its universal dimensions and of its unity with the heavenly church; it underlines that the liturgy of the church is part of the heavenly liturgy and that it is completely directed to the return of Christ: "The Lord your God will come together with all the saints."

Office of Crêt Bérard: Feast of saints and witnesses[9]

In communion with all the saints, let us pray to the Lord.

Lord have mercy

Christ have mercy

Lord have mercy

Christ hear us

God the Father, creator of the world

Have mercy on us

God the Son, saviour of humankind

Have mercy on us

God the Holy Spirit, source of communion

Have mercy on us

One God thrice holy

Have mercy on us

---

7 *Ibid.* p. 52
8 *Office de Taizé,* 2nd edition, Presse de Taizé, 1963, p. X.
9 *Office de Crêt-Bérard*, Genève, Labor et Fides, 1987, p. 296.

With the angels and archangels we praise you
Glory to you Lord

With the patriarchs and prophets, we bless you
Glory to you Lord

With the virgin Mary our soul exalts the Lord
Glory to you Lord

With the apostles and gospel writers, Lord we give your thanks
Glory to you Lord

With the martyrs to the faith, we give our life to you
Glory to you Lord

With all the people of the church, Lord, we proclaim you
Glory to you Lord

Final Prayer
Father of infinite goodness, kindle within us, as within all your saintly witnesses, the fire of the Spirit that Christ brought to the earth and which he so wished to set alight, he who reigns with you and the Holy Spirit, now and for ever and ever.

or
O God at all times you have given rise to a great cloud of witnesses from all peoples and languages; grant that we my be strengthened by their witness, be part of their prayer and be able one day to contemplate you in your glory, in communion with all the saints, by Christ our Lord.

Mary, the Lord's mother (August 15)
Holy God, you filled the blessed virgin Mary with a full measure of your grace and blessed her with spiritual gifts so that she prayed to you and magnified your name. May your Holy Spirit kindle our hearts and increase our desire to bless your name, through Jesus Christ, your Son our Lord and God, who reigns with you and the Holy Spirit, now and evermore.

All the angels, saints and witnesses (29 September and 1 November)
Almighty God, you come with the angels and all the saints to establish your kingdom and fulfil you victory; break the power of darkness, show forth your glory in our midst and make us part of your eternity, by Christ our Lord.

All saints and witnesses (1 November)
God of love, you gather us together in a single fellowship of communion with all of your friends throughout time. As have all your saints, grant that we may walk in the footsteps of Christ, surrounded by such a cloud of witnesses that we will enter into the joy of your presence, you who are blessed for ever and ever.

***Liturgy of the Reformed Church of France: Confession of Faith 5*[10]**

I believe, with all of the women and men of yesterday who deciphered his steps in history. A people freed from servitude and scolded by the prophets. A people who sang psalms and had the wisdom of proverbs. With the Palestinian crowd and the apostles who were witnesses to his human voice, I enter into the long line of those following the Nazarene: Paul of Tarsus, Francis of Assisi, Luther, Jean XXIII, Martin Luther King and all the others … they did not believe in vain.

"Our Forebears in the Faith" – a Litany

Almighty God: you built your church on the rock of human faith and trust;
we praise you for Jesus Christ, the foundation and cornerstone of all we believe.

R. *We praise you, God.*

For Abraham, Isaac, and Jacob; for Sarah, Rebekah, and Rachel; and for Moses, who led your people out of slavery and established the law in their hearts;

R. *We praise you, God.*

For the prophets who listened to your word and called your people back from disobedience and from the worship of man-made gods;

R. *We praise you, God.*

For those who foretold the coming of your Son Jesus Christ, and prepared the way for his birth:

R. *We praise you, God.*

For Mary and Joseph, who taught him to love you and trained him in synagogue and temple to serve you;

R. *We praise you, God.*

For Christ, our Savior, who loved us and gave himself for us on the cross;

R. *We praise you, God.*

10 *Liturgie* de l'Église réformée de France, 1996.

For the apostles and martyrs of the church, who gave their lives that we, in our day, might receive the good news of grace and forgiveness;

R. *We praise you, God.*

For the great men and women of every age, whose love for your church made it a willing instrument of your care and mercy; who placed you first in their lives and held to their faith in good times and in bad;

R. *We praise you, God, through Jesus Christ our Lord. Amen.*

Resources for All Saints Day[11]

Opening responses

Seeking your wisdom
R. *We seek your face*

Seeking your integrity
R. *We seek your face*

Seeking your forgiveness
R. *We seek your face*

Seeking your strength
R. *We seek your face*

Seeking your beauty
R. *We seek your face*

Closing responses

Summoned to holiness
Roused to justice
R. *We are called to live in love*

Granted forgiveness
Blessed with mercy
R. *We are called to live in hope*

11 Ruth Burgess, *Wild Goose, Candles and Conifers*, Iona, 2005, pp. 19-21.

Beckoned by saints
Encouraged by angels
R. *We are called to live in joy*

A prayer for All Saints Day

Holy and merciful God,
write the values of the beatitudes
into our hearts and lives;
and help us,
with all your saints and angels,
to seek your face
and happily walk in your ways. Amen

Bidding prayers for All Saints Day

God of warmth and welcome,
we come into your presence with wonder and praise;
caught up with the saints and angels,
we bring you ourselves and our prayers.
We pray for all who hunger and thirst for what is right, for those who are prepared to stand up for justice and defend unpopular causes.

God in your mercy
R. *Hear our prayer*

We give you thanks for the saints of Northumbria: for the vision of Cuthbert and the wisdom of Hilda, for the patience and trust of Aidan, for the poetry of Caedmon and the faithfulness of Bede. We thank you for their humanity, for their mistakes and successes, for their love for you. *(Include saints from your own country or area.)*

We pray for peacemakers; for peacemakers who live and work in places of conflict, for peacemakers who live in our communities and homes.

God in your mercy
R. *Hear our prayer*

We pray for those known to us who are ill, or in trouble, or in any kind of need

God in your mercy
R. *Hear our prayer*

We pray for those who have died, for those who, with the saints, are safe and joyful in God's keeping. Tell them we love them. Tell them we miss them.

God in your mercy
R. *Hear our prayer*

We pray for ourselves … called to be just and gentle … for our hopes, our needs, our dreams.

God in your mercy
R. *Hear our prayer*

Pilgrim God, lead us homewards.
May your saints encourage us,
your angels guard us,
and your little ones dance with us along the way.

ORTHODOX LITURGICAL RESOURCES[1]

Sunday of All Saints

The *Synaxarion* of the First Sunday after Pentecost[2]

On Saturday Evening at Great Vespers

At Lord, I have cried.

Stichera of All Saints.

The Spirit-inspired preachers, the Disciples of the Saviour, having become by faith instruments of the Spirit, distributed the holy proclamation, sowing it with right belief, to the ends of the earth, from which, by God's husbandry and grace, have sprung up the armies of Martyrs, who form an image of the holy Passion through many kinds of tortures, scourgings and fire; and with boldness they intercede on behalf of our souls.

Burning with the fire of the love of the Lord, they despised fire, and as lighted godlike coals the holy Martyrs by Christ burned up the brushwood insolence of error; while they stopped the mouths of wild beasts by wise entreaties, and when their heads were cut off they cut down all the regiments of the foe; and valiantly pouring out the streams of their blood they watered the Church, which then blossomed with faith.

The valiant Martyrs wrestled with wild beasts, were struck with swords, raked with claws, their hands were cut off and they were racked; without yielding they were burned with material fire, they were pierced and their joints were severed. They bore all most valiantly, as they looked forward to their coming rest, the pure crowns and the glory of Christ; to whom with boldness they intercede on behalf of our souls.

Let us, as is fitting, praise with sacred songs those who have competed by faith in all the ends of the earth, Apostles, Martyrs, godly-minded Priests, holy Women, a sacred gathering; for earthly beings were united with the heavenly and by suffering received through Christ's grace dispassion; and now like fixed stars they shed their light on us, as with boldness they intercede on behalf of our souls.

. . .

Godly choir of Martyrs, foundation of the Church, perfection of the Gospel, you have by deeds fulfilled the Saviour's words; for in you the gates of Hell, opened against the Church, have been shut; the flow of your blood has dried up the libations poured out to idols; your

1 Throughout the Orthodox Liturgical Resources some specific titles of the given prayers are removed in order to make these texts more widely accessible (Editors).

2 English translation from *Pentecostarion* by Archimandrite Ephrem Lash. http://www.anastasis.org.uk/allsaints.htm

slaughter has given birth the plenitude of the faithful; you have amazed the bodiless powers; bearing crowns you stand before God, whom you ceaselessly implore on behalf of our souls.

After the Prokeimenon of the day, the Readings.

The 1st Reading is from the Prophecy of Isaias [43:9-14[a]]

The 2nd Reading is from the Wisdom of Solomon [3:1-9]

The 3rd Reading is from the Wisdom of Solomon [5:16-6:3[b]]

...At the Liti we sing the Sticheron of the Saint of the Monastery; then the following Idiomels of All Saints.

...

In a harmony of faith let us all spiritually celebrate the festival of the whole world of those who from all time have been well-pleasing to God, the honour of the Patriarchs, the assembly of the Prophets, the adornment of Apostles, the company of Martyrs, the boast of Ascetics, the memory of all the Saints; for they intercede without ceasing that peace may be given to the world and to our souls God's great mercy.

Come, all you faithful, let us praise in psalms and hymns and spiritual songs the all-glorious memory of all the Saints: the Baptist of the Saviour, Apostles, Prophets and Martyrs, Hierarchs, Teachers, Holy Ones, Ascetics and Righteous, and the God-loving company of holy Women, as with reverence we call them blessed in harmony let us cry out: Christ our God, supremely good, at their prayers grant peace to your Churches, victories over enemies to our Christ-loving Sovereign, and to our souls your great mercy.

Come, let us rejoice in spirit at the memorial of the Saints; for see, it has come bringing us gifts of grace in rich abundance; and so with a voice of gladness and a pure conscience let us cry out and say: Hail, company of Prophets, who proclaimed the coming of Christ to the world and foresaw near at hand things far off. Hail, choir of Apostles, who caught the nations in a net, and who are the fishers of mankind. Hail, race of Martyrs, who were gathered from the ends of the earth into one faith, endured for it fierce torments and finally received the crown of your contest. Hail, swarm of Fathers, who trampled down your own bodies by ascetic struggle, and when you had slain the passions of the flesh you gave wings to your mind with divine love and took flight to heaven, and as you rejoice with the Angels, you enjoy eternal blessings. But, O Prophets, Apostles and Martyrs with Ascetics, insistently implore the one who crowned you that those who celebrate with faith and love your ever-revered memorial may be rescued from enemies visible and invisible.

. . .

Let us the faithful hasten together to the present festival; for a spiritual table and a mystical wine-bowl are set before us, filled with sweet foods of joy: the virtues of the Martyrs; for these brave-hearted ones from the ends of the earth offered to God as a rational sacrifice the many tortures of their bodily extremities and the prime of their years; some had their heads cut off, others were dismembered of hands and of every joint together; all the Saints became partakers of Christ's sufferings. But Lord, who gave them crowns as rewards of their torments, count us worthy to live according to their example, as you love mankind.

Theotokion

Come you faithful, let us today strike up a dance and devoutly keep festival and gloriously honour the glorious and revered memory of all the Saints, as we say: Hail, glorious Apostles, Prophets and Martyrs and Hierarchs. Hail, company of Ascetics and of the just. Hail, choir of honoured Women; and intercede with Christ for the world, to grant victories to our sovereign and to our souls his great mercy.

Theotokion

Clothed as in purple and fine linen with the blood of your Martyrs throughout the world, your Church cries out to you through them, Christ God: Send down your pity on your people; give peace to your commonwealth, and to our souls your great mercy.

Theotokion

The mystery hidden from all eternity and unknown to Angels has been revealed to those on earth through you, O Mother of God: God being made flesh in a union without confusion, and willingly accepting the Cross for us, through which he raised the first-formed man, and saved our souls from death.

At Matins

. . .

As I sing the praise of the ranks of your Saints, I beg you by your light to shed your rays on my soul at their prayers. For you are the unapproachable light, dispelling the gloom of ignorance by your torches, O Word of God, Christ giver of light.

As you were lifted up on the Tree, Master, you drew to knowledge of you the whole inheritance of the nations, and made it radiant with the light of the holy Trinity through your holy Apostles, through whom you drove out deception.

Obedient to your commandment, O Christ, your glorious Apostles devoutly renounced everything on earth; and by the light of grace they made bright the whole inhabited world as they preached you through the Gospel.

Rejoicing, the noble Martyrs took up the Cross and unflinchingly imitating your sacred passion, they did not tremble at the threats of tyrants, at fire, sword, scourges, not even starvation or death.

Theotokion

The virgins, having taken up a manly intent, unflinchingly endured the contests of martyrdom, and as in the Psalms, all-pure Virgin, following after you rejoicing together, inspired by God, they were offered to your Son, the king of all.

. . .

The Priests and Shepherds, clothed with sacred priesthood, wisely guided it, O Christ, and worthily adorned it, truly enriched with the word of teaching from on high.

Made fair by the beauties of that first created beauty, and revealed as unerring beacons, you made Christ's Church a heaven, O Saints, each in his place adorning it in varied ways.

Obedient to your law, the companies of the blessed, radiant with virtues of many kinds, have inherited with joy the heavenly mansions; for they all filled them worthily, each one their own.

Theotokion

Mother of God, from a virgin womb for us you gave birth to God the Word from God; whom pure maidens desired in a godlike manner, and in your train they all followed him.

. . .

As we celebrate the holy memory, Christ God, Forebears, Parents, Patriarchs, Apostles, Martyrs, Hierarchs, Prophets and your Holy Ones, Ascetics and Just, and each one whose name is inscribed in the book of life, we urge them all to intercession, as we beg: Give peace to your world through them, as you love mankind, that we may all cry out to you: O God, glorified in the Council of your Saints, you are truly the one who fittingly glorifies their memory.

Theotokion

Let us praise the heavenly gate and ark, the all-holy mountain, the radiant cloud, the heavenly ladder, the spiritual Paradise, the ransom of Eve, the great treasure of the whole inhabited world; because salvation was accomplished in her for the world and forgiveness of ancient offences. Therefore we cry to her: Intercede with your Son and God, to grant forgiveness of faults to those who devoutly worship your all-holy Offspring.

. . .

The company of your Saints, joined together through love and sincerely and purely delighting in you, dances in joy with the perpetual dance of the Angels around you, who see all, the God and Lord of all.

Glorious and all-blessed Martyr Priests, once gleaming with the divine anointing of the priesthood, you bound on like youths the Martyrs' wreath of victory; and so fittingly receiving double crowns, you rejoice with Christ eternally.

Godbearing Fathers, you subjected every fleshly thought to the spirit, withering their unruly assaults by fasting and ascetic discipline; and now aflame with the light of dispassion, you have received the rewards of your labours.

As Martyrs of Christ, the Protomartyr, you endured great torments, bravely and outstandingly, struggling, glorious Saints, as in bodies not your own; and now, revealed as heirs of the kingdom, you are source of healings for the faithful.

Theotokion

Bride of God, you became Mother of God; for you gave birth for us in bodily form to the Word before time, by whom women also have led holy lives and adorned through you by contests of many kinds, they have restored the fall of our Foremother.

. . .

As godly Prophets you were found worthy to foresee the things to come, longing for which with nobility of soul you purified yourselves by holy living, O Godbearers, enlightened by the strength of the Spirit.

The choir of the Saints is now made bright by divine gifts of grace, all those before the law, Patriarchs, Prophets, Apostles, companies of Martyrs, Ascetics, Teachers and Righteous with Priest Martyrs.

As we see the throng of your Saints shining today, O Saviour, with your brightness, and with unquenchable lamps of grace, we unceasingly sing the praise of your divine riches and unstinted blessings.

Theotokion

All-holy women, filled with love of most wondrous Offspring, reckoned the delights of life as nothing, O all-pure, and desiring passionately his brightness alone and his divine radiance.

. . .

The Saints, having found you, Master, in Sion placed as a precious, chosen cornerstone, an unshakeable foundation, built themselves on you as chosen stones.

When your side was pierced streams of blood dropped from it along with deifying water and refashioned the world and summoned a godly throng of all the Saints, O Benefactor.

With hymn most devoutly the inspired cloud of Martyrs, made radiant by grace and shining brilliantly with the purple of their blood and with the crimson of their valiant contest.

Theotokion

We all know you as most truly Mother of God, through whom women's nature was given strength, O all-blameless, and so competed on behalf of Christ and became filled devoutly with every virtue.

. . .

As first fruits of nature, Lord, creation's Planter, the world offers you, the god-bearing Martyrs; at their intercessions preserve your Church in profound peace, through the Mother of God, O most merciful.

. . .

Those who bore witness in all the earth and made their home in heaven, those who imitated the sufferings of Christ and who take away our passions, are gathered here today, revealing the Church of the firstborn, who bears the type of the one above, and which cries out to Christ: You are my God; keep me through the Mother of God, O most merciful.

The *Synaxarion* from the Menaion.

On this day, the Sunday after Pentecost, we celebrate the feast of all the Saints from throughout the inhabited world, in Asia, Libya and Europe, in North and South.

Verses

I sing the praise of each friend of my Lord,

If any would, let them now list them all.

Our most godlike Fathers decreed that we should celebrate the present feast after the descent of the All-holy Spirit, as showing in a certain way that the coming of the All-holy Spirit acted through the Apostles like this: sanctifying and making wise human beings taken from our mortal clay and, for the completion of that fallen angelic order, restoring them and through Christ sending them to God, some by the witness of martyrdom and blood, others by their virtuous conduct and way of life; and things beyond nature are achieved. For the Spirit descends in the form of fire, whose natural momentum is upwards; while dust, whose natural momentum is downwards, ascends on high, that dust which forms our mortal clay, the flesh added to and made divine by God the Word, which a short time before, had been exalted and taken its seat at the right hand of the Father's glory. But he now also draws all those who wish, according to the promise, just as God the Word had manifested the works of reconciliation and what was the end, most suitable to its purpose, of his coming to us through flesh and of his dispensation, namely that he brings those who were rejected before to union and friendship with God – human nature offering to God the ungrateful people from the nations like first fruits – those who were outstandingly well-pleasing to him. This is one reason that we celebrate the feast of All Saints.

A second reason is because, though many people have been well-pleasing to God, they were through outstanding virtue unknown to humanity by name, or for some human reason or other, but nevertheless have great glory in God's sight. Or again, because there are many who have lived following Christ in India, Egypt, Arabia, Mesopotamia and Phrygia and in the lands beyond the Black Sea, even as far as the British Isles themselves; in short, in both East and West, but it was not easy to honour them all properly because of their vast numbers, in the way that ecclesiastical custom has been received. And therefore, so that we may attract the help of them all, wherever on earth they were well-pleasing to God, and generally for those who would later become Saints, the most godly Fathers ordained that we should celebrate the feast of All Saints, honouring the earlier and later ones, the unknown and the known – all those in whom the Holy Spirit has dwelt he has made holy.

A third reason is this. It was necessary for the Saints who are celebrated individually day by day to be gathered together on one day, in order to demonstrate that, as they struggled for the one Christ and all ran the race in the same stadium of virtue, so they were all fittingly crowned as servants of one God and sustained the Church, having filled the world on high. They stir us also to accomplish the same struggle in its different and many forms, to the degree of power that each of us has to press onwards with all eagerness. (...)

Note that we are celebrating everything that the Holy Spirit, in giving good things, has made holy. I mean the highest and sanctifying Minds, that is to say the Nine Orders; the Ancestors and Patriarchs; the Prophets and sacred Apostles; the Martyrs and Hierarchs; the Priest Martyrs and Ascetic Martyrs; the Ascetics and the Just and all the choirs of holy women and all the other anonymous Saints, with them let there be all who will come afterwards.

But before all, in all and with all, the Saint of Saints, the most holy and quite incomparably mightier than the angelic Orders, our Lady and Sovereign, Mary, Ever-Virgin.

At the prayers of your all-pure Mother, Christ God, and of all your Saints from every age, have mercy and save us, for you alone are good and love mankind. Amen.

. . .

The ranks of Saints, as they praise in never silent hymns the One who rests among the Saints, now enjoy divine delight, and joyfully they dance and sing: Blessed is the God of our Fathers.

The companies of the Saints, suffused with divine rays of triple-sunned outpouring of light, devoutly proclaim a Unity in number three, the Father without beginning and the Son and the Holy Spirit.

When you appear, O God, in your ineffable glory in the midst of the gods, granting to each their desserts and apportioning crowns, then count all worthy to sing to you: Blessed is the God of our Fathers.

With gladness let us make melody to the throng of all the Saints, welded together from every race and rank and way of life, and let us sing with them: Blessed is the God of our Fathers.

Theotokion

All you maidens, having together formed a godly choir, cry out to Mary, the immaculate and all-holy Mother of God: Be glad, who made the source of our joy gush forth.

. . .

Rejoice, Martyrs, Prophets, Apostles, honoured company of Martyr Priests, godly choir of the Just, of Ascetics and Teachers, who all make melody with the Myrrh-bearing women: youths, bless; priests, praise; people, highly exalt him to all the ages.

Saints, who bear in yourselves the radiance beyond understanding and are filled with divine joy and gladness, you are called gods by your nearness to God; familiar with the rays which sanctify and enlightened by the beams of the ineffable glory, you highly Christ to all the ages.

Appearing as beacons with many lights, O Saints, you make the heaven of the Church radiant with gifts of grace of many kinds, and divers beauties; with justice, sobriety, courage and wisdom, as you cry: Priests, praise, people, highly exalt Christ to the ages.

Theotokion

With joy all women wise in God and made perfect in Christ by the Spirit, as you now stand round the all-pure Virgin and true Mother of God, who ransomed us from the curse of our foremother Eve, hymn her fruit to the ages.

...

The company of the elect, armed with the breastplate of hope and love and fenced about by faith, rejoiced as they nobly endured all the threats of tyrants, the tortures and scourges, for as outstanding witnesses of truth their wealth was Christ who gives victory in contests.

Let us now fittingly praise a haven of salvation, the Baptist, Apostles, Prophets and Martyrs, with Ascetics, godly Teachers and Priests, the company of Patriarchs and far-famed Martyr Priests, God-loving women, the holy and just.

Tested by the fire of temptations and not allured by pleasures, you rejoice sincerely, glorious company of the Saints, as you stand around the light-formed throne of the Master in heaven, now that mirrors have been abolished and shadow has passed away with the manifestation of the truth.

Theotokion

You appeared as the one who unites things that were parted; for through you humans have truly become companions of the Angels in heaven, and now the ranks of all the Saints bear witness as they hymn your Offspring, Virgin Mother of God, in everlasting songs.

...

Let us as is fitting crown with hymns the Baptist and Forerunner, the Apostles, Prophets, Martyrs, Hierarchs, Ascetics and Holy Ones, with Martyr Priests, God-loving Women and all the Just, and the ranks of Angels, imploring that we may attain the glory which they have from Christ the Saviour.

Theotokion

He who on high is divinely glorified by Angels, who ineffably was never parted from his Father's bosom, O All-pure, lived among those below; while you, pure Maiden, became the cause of this salvation, who beyond reason lent flesh to him from your pure blood; beseech him to give your servants ransom of offences.

At Lauds

...

The Lord has made his Saints wondrous on earth; for they received his marks and sufferings in the flesh, adorned by them and manifestly arrayed in godlike beauties; whom let us hymn as unfading flowers, as unwandering stars of the Church, as willingly offered sacrifices.
Verse: The righteous cried, and the Lord heard them; and rescued them from all their troubles.

Apostles with Prophets, Teachers with Ascetics, all the Just with Martyr Priests and those among women who struggled as Martyrs and lived the ascetic life with love, the multitude of the Saints and the ranks of the Just, let them be praised with sacred songs, as heirs of the kingdom on high and inhabitants of Paradise.

Verse: God is wonderful in his Saints, the God of Israel.

The Martyrs made the earth heaven by the radiance of their virtues, they imitated the death of Christ, they trod the way which brings immortality, they purified the passions of mortals by the surgery of grace, they competed nobly with their whole soul in all the world: let them be praised.

ROMAN CATHOLIC LITURGICAL RESOURCES

FROM THE ROMAN CATHOLIC *SACRAMENTARY*[1]

Collect Prayers for All Saints Day

Let us pray that the prayers of all the saints will bring us forgiveness for our sins
[pause for silent prayer]
Father, all-powerful and ever-living God,
today we rejoice in the holy men and women
of every time and place.
May their prayers bring us your forgiveness and love.
We ask this through our Lord Jesus Christ, your Son,
who lives and reigns with you and the Holy Spirit,
one God, for ever and ever.

Let us pray as we rejoice and keep festival in honor of all the saints.
[pause for silent prayer]
God our Father,
source of all holiness,
the work of your hands is manifest in your saints,
and the beauty of your truth is reflected in their faith.
May we who aspire to have part in their joy
be filled with the Spirit that blessed their lives,
so that having shared their faith on earth
we may also know their peace in your kingdom.
Grant this through Christ our Lord.

---

1 Edition 1974.

Litany of the Saints[2]

The cantors begin the litany; they may add, at the proper place, names of other saints (for example, the patron saint, the titular of the church, the founder of the church, the patron saints of those to be baptized) or petitions suitable to the occasion.

V. Lord, have mercy	R. *Lord, have mercy*
V. Christ, have mercy	R. *Christ, have mercy*
V. Lord, have mercy	R. *Lord, have mercy*

Holy Mary, Mother of God	R. *pray for us*
Saint Michael	R. *pray for us*
Holy angels of God	
Saint John the Baptist	
Saint Joseph	
Saint Peter and Saint Paul	
Saint Andrew	
Saint John	
Saint Mary Magdalene	
Saint Stephen	
Saint Ignatius	
Saint Lawrence	
Saint Perpetua and Saint Felicity	
Saint Agnes	
Saint Gregory	
Saint Augustine	
Saint Athanasius	
Saint Basil	
Saint Martin	
Saint Benedict	

2 From the Celebration of the Sacraments of Initiation.

Saint Dominic

Saint Francis Xavier

Saint John Vianney

Saint Catherine

Saint Teresa

All holy men and women

V. Lord, be merciful — R. *Lord, save your people*
From all evil
From every sin
From everlasting death
By your coming as man
By your death and rising to new life
By your gift of the Holy Spirit
V. Be merciful to us sinners — R. *Lord, hear our prayer*
Give new life to those chosen ones
by the grace of baptism
Jesus, Son of the living God
V. Christ, hear us — R. *Christ, hear us*
V. Lord Jesus, hear our prayer — R. *Lord Jesus, hear our prayer*

Preface: Holy Men and Women: The Glory of the Saints

Father, all-powerful and ever-living God,

we do well always and everywhere to give you thanks.

You are glorified in all your saints,

for their glory is the crowning of your gifts.

In their lives on earth

you give us an example.

In our communion with them,

you give us their friendship.

In their prayer for the Church

you give us strength and protection.

The great company of witnesses spur us on to victory,
to share their prize of everlasting glory,
through Jesus Christ our Lord.
With angels and archangels
and the whole company of saints
we sing our unending hymn of praise.

Preface: Holy Men and Women: The Activity of the Saints

Father, all-powerful and ever-living God,
we do well always and everywhere to give you thanks.
You renew the Church in every age
by raising up men and women outstanding in holiness,
living witnesses of your unchanging love.
They inspire us by their heroic lives,
and help us by their constant prayers
to be the living sign of your saving power.
We praise you Lord, with all the angels and saints
in their song of joy.

Preface: All Saints, November 1

Father, all-powerful and ever-living God,
we do well always and everywhere to give you thanks.
Today we keep the festival of your holy city,
the heavenly Jerusalem, our mother.
Around your throne
the saints, our brothers and sisters,
sing your praise for ever.
Their glory fills us with joy,
and their communion with us in your Church
gives us inspiration and strength

as we hasten on our pilgrimage of faith,
eager to meet them.
With their great company and all the angels
we praise your glory
as we cry out with one voice.

Solemn Blessing for All Saints Day

Bow your heads and pray for God's blessing.
God is the Glory and joy of all his saints,
whose memory we celebrate today.
May his blessing be with you always.
R. *Amen.*
May the prayers of the saints deliver you from present evil;
may their example of holy living
turn your thoughts to the service of God and neighbor.
R. *Amen.*
God's holy Church rejoices that her children
are one with the saints in lasting peace.
May you come to share with them
in all the joys of our Father's house.
R. *Amen.*
May Almighty God bless you,
the Father, and the Son, + and the Holy Spirit.
R. *Amen.*

Collect Prayers: Common of Martyrs

Father,
we celebrate the memory of your saints
who died for their faithful witnessing to Christ.
Give us the strength to follow their example,

loyal and faithful to the end.
We ask this through our Lord Jesus Christ, your Son,
who lives and reigns with you and the Holy Spirit,
one God, for ever and ever.

All-powerful, ever-living God,
turn our weakness into strength.
As you gave your martyrs
the courage to suffer death for Christ,
give us the courage to live in faithful witness to you.
Grant this through our Lord Jesus Christ, your Son,
who lives and reigns with you and the Holy Spirit,
one God, for ever and ever.

Lord,
may the victory of your martyrs give us joy.
May their example strengthen our faith,
and their prayers give us renewed courage.
We ask this through our Lord Jesus Christ, your Son,
who lives and reigns with you and the Holy Spirit,
one God, for ever and ever.

Lord,
hear the prayers of the martyrs
and give us courage to bear witness
to your truth.
Grant this through our Lord Jesus Christ,
your Son,
who lives and reigns with you and the Holy Spirit,
one God, for ever and ever.

God our Father,
every year you give us the joy
of celebrating the saints.
May we who recall their birth to eternal life
imitate their courage in suffering for you.
Grant this through our Lord Jesus Christ, your Son,
who lives and reigns with you and the Holy Spirit,
one God, for ever and ever.

God our Father,
your generous gift of love
brought your saints to unending glory.
Through the prayers of your martyrs
forgive our sins and free us from every danger.
We ask this through our Lord Jesus Christ, your Son,
who lives and reigns with you and the Holy Spirit,
one God, for ever and ever.

Lord,
we honor your martyrs
who were faithful to Christ
even to the point of shedding their blood for him.
Increase our own faith and free us from our sins,
and help us to follow their example of love.
We ask this through our Lord Jesus Christ, your Son,
who lives and reigns with you and the Holy Spirit,
one God, for ever and ever.

Father,
you gave your martyrs
the courage to die in witness to Christ and his gospel.
By the power of your Holy Spirit,
give us the humility to believe
and the courage to profess
the faith for which they gave their lives.
We ask this through our Lord Jesus Christ, your Son,
who lives and reigns with you and the Holy Spirit,
one God, for ever and ever.

God our all-powerful Father,
you strengthen our faith
and take away our weakness.
Let the prayers and example of your martyrs
help us to share in the passion and resurrection of Christ
and bring us to eternal joy with all your saints.
We ask this through our Lord Jesus Christ, your Son,
who lives and reigns with you and the Holy Spirit,
one God, for ever and ever.

Lord,
you gave your martyrs
the privilege of shedding their blood
for boldly proclaiming the death and resurrection of your Son.
May this celebration of their victory
give them honor among your people.
We ask this through our Lord Jesus Christ, your Son,
who lives and reigns with you and the Holy Spirit,
one God, for ever and ever.

God of mercy and love,
through the preaching of your martyrs
you brought the good news of Christ
to people who had not yet known him.
May the prayers of the saints
make our own faith stronger.
We ask this through our Lord Jesus Christ, your Son,
who lives and reigns with you and the Holy Spirit,
one God, for ever and ever.

THE ROMAN LITURGY OF THE HOURS FOR THE FEAST OF ALL SAINTS

Evening Prayer on the eve of the Feast Day

Psalm 113
Psalm 147
Canticle: Revelation 19:1-7
Hebrews 12:22-24

Office of Readings [Vigils]

Psalm 8
Psalm 15
Psalm 16
Revelation 5:1-4

Morning Prayer

Psalm 63
Canticle: Daniel 3:57-88, 56
Psalm 149
Ephesians 1:17-18

Daytime Prayer

Psalm 118
Isaiah 65:18-19
1 Peter 1:15-16
Revelation 21:10-11a; 22:3b-4

Evening Prayer on the Feast Day

Psalm 110
Psalm 116
Canticle: Revelation 4:11; 5:9,10,12
2 Corinthians 6:16b; 7:1

FROM *CATHOLIC HOUSEHOLD BLESSINGS AND PRAYERS* "ALL SAINTS AND ALL SOULS: VISITING A GRAVE"

Praise be to God our Father, who raised Jesus Christ from the dead.
Blessed be God for ever.
R. Blessed be God for ever.

The following Scripture texts may be read:

2 Corinthians 5:1 *"We know that if our earthly dwelling, a tent, should be destroyed, we have a building from God..."*

Romans 8:38-39 *"I am convinced that neither death, nor life, nor angels...will be able to separate us from the love of God..."*

After a time of silence, all join in prayers of intercession, or in one of the litanies or other prayers followed by the Lord's Prayer.

V. Lord God,
whose days are without end
and whose mercies beyond counting,

keep us mindful
that life is short and the hour of death unknown.
Let your Spirit guide our days on earth
in the ways of holiness and justice
that we may serve you
in union with the whole Church,
sure in faith, strong in hope, perfected in love.
And when our earthly journey is ended,
lead us rejoicing into your kingdom,
where you live for ever and ever.

V. Eternal rest grant unto them, O Lord,
R. *And let perpetual light shine upon them.*

V. May they rest in peace.
R. *Amen.*

V. May their souls and the souls of all the faithful departed,
through the mercy of God, rest in peace.
R. *Amen.*

V. May the peace of God,
which is beyond all understanding,
keep our hearts and minds
in the knowledge and love of God
and of his Son, our Lord Jesus Christ.

A Prayer for November 2 :

Into your hands, O Lord,
we humbly entrust our brothers and sisters.
In this life you embraced them with your tender love;
deliver them now from every evil
and bid them enter eternal rest.

The old order has passed away:
welcome them then into paradise,

where there will be no sorrow, no weeping nor pain,
but the fullness of peace and joy
with your Son and the Holy Spirit
for ever and ever.

ECUMENICAL COMMEMORATION OF WITNESSES TO THE FAITH IN THE 20th CENTURY[3]

The unfolding of the rite

The Ecumenical Commemoration takes place at Evening Prayer of the Third Week of Easter; it thus falls in the Easter Season and in particular on the Lord's Day, when the church celebrates the victory of the Risen Christ over sin and death. The Risen Lord opens the hearts of the faithful to the hope of everlasting life and gives meaning to suffering, tribulations and death itself. Evening Prayer is a time when the faithful of different churches and Ecclesial Communities celebrate Christ as the "Joyful Light of the Holy Glory of the Heavenly and Immortal Father" (Hymn Phos hilaron).

The site chosen for the Commemoration is the Colosseum which, together with other places nearby, like the Circus Maximus, calls to mind the witness of faith given by the early martyrs of the Church of Rome.

The Commemoration takes place outside the amphitheatre, near the Arch of Titus. It is made up of various ritual moments and is preceded by a preparation which respects the ecumenical and international character of the assembly.

Inside the Colosseum, prior to the start of the Commemoration, the Holy Father will offer a fraternal greeting to the representatives of the other churches and ecclesial communities.

1) Initial Rites

The initial rites include: a "station" inside the Colosseum, the procession to the area of the celebration outside the amphitheatre, the Holy Father's introduction and the opening prayer.

Inside the Colosseum. After the opening hymn, the Holy Father greets the assembly. An

3 Held in Rome, Colosseum, 7 May 2000.

invocation of praise to the Holy Trinity follows, recited by the representatives of the churches and ecclesial communities; it consists of a proclamation in different languages of texts drawn from the Book of Revelation (Rev. 4:11; 5:12; 5:9-10; 5:13). The assembly responds to each acclamation by singing: Amen . Alleluia.

At the end of the invocations, the procession with the Cross and the Gospel Book sets out from the inside of the Colosseum, while the choir sings the Hymn to Christ, the Lord of the Millennia.

A large icon of the Crucified Christ dominates the platform where the celebration will take place. When the procession arrives at the platform, the Gospel Book is enthroned and incensed. The Holy Father then begins the celebration with an introduction and the opening prayer.

2) The Readings

The Liturgy of the Word is made up of the following readings:

First Reading: 1 Pet. 1:3-9, 13-21: The faith of the baptized tried by fire

Song between the Readings: The wedding feast of the Lamb: Rev. 19:1-7

Second Reading: Heb. 12:1-6, 18-19a, 22-24: Surrounded by this great cloud of witnesses

Gospel Acclamation: Alleluia John 12:24-25: Unless a grain of wheat falls into the earth and dies, it remains alone; but if it dies, it bears much fruit...

Gospel: Matt. 5:1-12: Blessed are those who are persecuted for righteousness' sake, for theirs is the kingdom of heaven

The Gospel is proclaimed in both a Western and an Eastern language.

After the Gospel, the choir acclaims Christ, the Joyful Light, by singing the ancient Christian hymn Phos Hilaron.

The Holy Father then gives the homily.

3) The Profession of Faith, Testimonies and Prayers

The sign of peace follows the Holy Father's homily and precedes the profession of faith.

The two deacons, in Greek and in Italian, invite all present to exchange a sign of fraternal fellowship. Meanwhile the choir and the assembly sing the hymn Ubi Caritas.

The Holy Father then introduces the profession of faith. The Apostles' Creed is recited, using three different languages, by three representatives of the other churches and ecclesial communities. The assembly joins in each time by singing: Credimus, Domine, Amen.

After the profession of faith comes the specific commemoration of the witnesses to the faith in the 20th century. The witnesses are grouped in eight categories honoring the memory of Christians from all Continents and from the different churches and ecclesial communities: Catholics, Orthodox, Anglicans and Protestants.

Each commemoration or grouping is made up of the following elements: the reading of one or two significant testimonies (each testimony is introduced by a brief biographical note about its author); a prayer in the style of the Commemoration: Remember Lord...; and an acclamation by the assembly: *Kyrie eleison.*

At the end of the commemoration of each group of witnesses, a lamp is lit at the foot of the Crucifix which dominates the assembly and incense is burnt as a sign of the prayer of the just.

The testimonies and the prayers are meant to be a collective remembrance of specific groups of witnesses, evoking the different continents and the various situations in which Christians of various denominations have borne heroic witness to their faith.

The following groups of witnesses to the faith in the 20th century are commemorated:

1. Christians who bore witness to their faith under Soviet totalitarianism

   Two significant testimonies are read: the first is from the Russian Orthodox Patriarch Tikhon, while the second is from an anonymous witness from the gulag in the Solovki Islands. Both relate the ecumenism of suffering uniting Catholics and Orthodox.

2. Witnesses to the faith who were victims of Communism in other nations of Europe

   Two texts are read, one by the Romanian Greek Catholic Bishop Joan Suciu, the other by Father Anton Luli, an Albanian Jesuit imprisoned for seventeen years and then condemned to another eleven years of forced labor.

3. Confessors of the faith who were victims of Nazism and Fascism

   Tribute is paid to the courageous witness of the German Lutheran Pastor Paul Schneider in the Buchenwald concentration camp. The second testimony is that of Bishop Ignacy Jego, Bishop Emeritus of Koszalin-Kolobrzeg, one of the thousands of Polish priests interned in concentration camps. Ordained a priest on 20 June 1937, he was sent after four years of priestly ministry to Dachau as No. 37196.

4. Followers of Christ who gave their lives for the proclamation of the Gospel in Asia and Oceania

   Testimonies are read from Margherita Chou, the niece of the late Cardinal Ignatius Kung Pin-mei, Bishop of Shanghai, and from a group of Anglicans killed in a concentration camp in Japan.

5. Christian faithful persecuted out of hatred for the Catholic faith

   Witnesses to the faith in Spain and Mexico are commemorated: the former in the text of a moving document by the then Minister of the Republic Manuel Irujo and the latter in a sermon of the Bishop of Huejutla, José de Jesús Manríquez y Zárate, delivered in exile in Laredo, Texas, on the Feast of Christ the King, 27 October 1927.

6. Witnesses of evangelization in Africa and Madagascar

   The first testimony is that of Jolique Rusimbamigera, a seminarian who escaped the massacre at the minor seminary of Buta, Burundi, on 30 April 1997, in which forty-four Hutu and Tutsi seminarians were killed. The second testimony is that of a young Canadian Baptist missionary, W.G.R. Jotcham, who worked in the leprosarium of Katsina, in a Muslim area in Nigeria, and died a victim of charity in 1938.

7. Christians who gave their lives for love of Christ and of their brothers and sisters in America

   The testimonies remembered are those of the Capuchin missionary Bishop Alejandro Labaka, who worked tirelessly on behalf of the Amazonian people and died in Ecuador on 21 July 1987, and of Jesús Emilio Jaramillo Monsalve, Bishop of Arauca, Colombia, a Xavierian Missionary of Yarumal, kidnapped and killed at the age of 73 by a group of guerillas during a pastoral visit to rural parishes of his Diocese on 2 October 1989.

8. Witnesses to the faith in different parts of the world

   The first testimony is that of a monk of Tibirin, Algeria, Trappist Father Dom Christian de

Chergé, killed in 1996. The second text is by the Armenian Apostolic Patriarch Karekin I, who died in 1999; it evokes the sufferings and martyrdom of the Armenian people.

The series of commemorations ends with a collective remembrance of all those victims whose faith was known to God alone.

Between the various testimonies religious hymns are will be sung by choirs from different ecclesial traditions: a Lutheran choir, an Eastern Christian choir, an African choir, a Filipino choir and an Armenian choir.

The singing of the Our Father in Latin, preceded by a brief introduction and followed by the doxology Quia Tuum est Regnum, concludes the various testimonies and prayers.

4) Blessing and Dismissal

The entire Commemoration ends with an exhortation by the Holy Father to keep alive the memory of the witnesses to the faith in the 20th century in all the churches and to bear courageous witness to the Gospel of Christ in every nation and in every sector of society.

The Holy Father then imparts the Apostolic Blessing. The deacon dismisses the assembly and the choir sings the recessional hymn.

ECUMENICAL OFFICE OF THE MONASTIC COMMUNITY OF BOSE

THE COMMUNION OF SAINTS OF HEAVEN AND EARTH

Evening prayer – November 1[1]

Introduction

Lord, open my lips
and my mouth will sing your praise
God, make my ear attentive
so that I may listen to your word.

O favorite among peoples, o Lord Deut. 33:3
all his holy ones were in your charge
they marched at your heels
accepted direction from you.

Glory to the Father, to the Son
and to the Holy Spirit
as it was in the beginning, is now
and ever shall be. Amen.

Hymn

Those whom the burning bush has captivated
around you are gathered in your eternal kingdom
thirsting they have sought the light of your face
you only they have followed, and now they live in you.

To your eternal banquet with song they come
transfigured they surround your throne of glory
all expectations they have fixed on your true love
you shower them with light and make them like you.
The immense cloud of your holy witnesses
raises to you the new song that has no end
"Salvation is of God and of the immolated Lamb
we are but light in his innocent blood."

1 The English biblical texts are taken fron the New Revised Standard Version.

To you, o Father, creator of all things
through the Lord and redeemer of every life
we here on earth together with the saints of heaven
render praise forever in the Holy Spirit.

Psalms

Ant. *Let your light shine before others*
so that they may *give glory to your Father in heaven.* Cf. Matt. 5:16

Psalm 112

1 Praise the Lord!
Happy are those who fear the Lord,
who greatly delight in his commandments.

2 Their descendants will be mighty in the land;
the generation of the upright will be blessed.

3 Wealth and riches are in their houses,
and their righteousness endures forever.

4 They rise in the darkness as a light for the upright;
they are gracious, merciful, and righteous.

5 It is well with those who deal generously and lend,
who conduct their affairs with justice.

6 For the righteous will never be moved;
they will be remembered forever.

7 They are not afraid of evil tidings;
their hearts are firm, secure in the Lord.

8 Their hearts are steady, they will not be afraid;
in the end they will look in triumph on their foes.

9 They have distributed freely, they have given to the poor;
their righteousness endures forever;
their horn is exalted in honor.

10 The wicked see it and are angry;
they gnash their teeth and melt away;

the desire of the wicked comes to nothing.
Ant. *God brought down the powerful from their thrones*
and lifted up the lowly. Cf. Luke 1:52

Psalm 113

1 Praise the Lord!
Praise, O servants of the Lord;
praise the name of the Lord.

2 Blessed be the name of the Lord
from this time on and forevermore.

3 From the rising of the sun to its setting
the name of the Lord is to be praised.

4 The Lord is high above all nations,
and his glory above the heavens.

5 Who is like the Lord our God,
who is seated on high,

6 who looks far down
on the heavens and the earth?

7 He raises the poor from the dust,
and lifts the needy from the ash heap,

8 to make them sit with princes,
with the princes of his people.

9 He gives the barren woman a home,
making her the joyous mother of children.
Praise the Lord!

Ant. *There will be no more night*
for the Lord God will be the light of his servants. Cf. Rev. 22:5

Psalm 139

To the leader. Of David. A Psalm.

1 O Lord, you have searched me and known me.

2 You know when I sit down and when I rise up;
you discern my thoughts from far away.

3 You search out my path and my lying down,
and are acquainted with all my ways.

4 Even before a word is on my tongue,
O Lord, you know it completely.

5 You hem me in, behind and before,
and lay your hand upon me.

6 Such knowledge is too wonderful for me;
it is so high that I cannot attain it.

7 Where can I go from your spirit?
Or where can I flee from your presence?

8 If I ascend to heaven, you are there;
if I make my bed in Sheol, you are there.

9 If I take the wings of the morning
and settle at the farthest limits of the sea,

10 even there your hand shall lead me,
and your right hand shall hold me fast.

11 If I say, "Surely the darkness shall cover me,
and the light around me become night,"

12 even the darkness is not dark to you;
the night is as bright as the day,
for darkness is as light to you.

13 For it was you who formed my inward parts;
you knit me together in my mother's womb.

14 I praise you, for I am fearfully and wonderfully made.
Wonderful are your works;
that I know very well.

15 My frame was not hidden from you,
when I was being made in secret,
intricately woven in the depths of the earth.

16 Your eyes beheld my unformed substance.
In your book were written
all the days that were formed for me,
when none of them as yet existed.

17 How weighty to me are your thoughts, O God!
How vast is the sum of them!

18 I try to count them - they are more than the sand;
I come to the end - I am still with you.

19 O that you would kill the wicked, O God,
and that the bloodthirsty would depart from me -

20 those who speak of you maliciously,
and lift themselves up against you for evil!

21 Do I not hate those who hate you, O Lord?
And do I not loathe those who rise up against you?

22 I hate them with perfect hatred;
I count them my enemies.

23 Search me, O God, and know my heart;
test me and know my thoughts.

24 See if there is any wicked way in me,
and lead me in the way everlasting.

Ant. *Rejoice, O heaven, you saints and apostles and prophets!*
because God has given judgement for you.
Cf. Rev. 18:20

Canticle of the New Testament
Rev. 11:15.17-17; 12:10-12

We give you thanks, Lord God Almighty,
who are and who were,
for you have taken your great power and begun to reign.

The nations raged,
but your wrath has come,
and the time for judging the dead.

For rewarding your servants,
the prophets and saints
and all who fear your name, both small and great,
Now have come the salvation
and the power and the kingdom of our God
and the authority of his Messiah.

For the accuser of our comrades has been thrown down,
who accuses them day and night before our God.

But they have conquered him by the blood of the Lamb
and by the word of their testimony,
for they did not cling to life even in the face of death.

The kingdom of the world has become the kingdom
of our Lord and of his Messiah!
Rejoice then, you heavens and those who dwell in them!

Epistle

1 John 3:1-3

My little children, see what love the Father has given us, that we should be called children of God; and that is what we are. The reason the world does not know us is that it did not know him. Beloved, we are God's children now; what we will be has not yet been revealed. What we do know is this: when he is revealed, we will be like him, for we will see him as he is. And all who have this hope in him purify themselves, just as he is pure.
- Glory to you, o Lord!

Response

Rejoice in the Lord and exult, o saints.
- *Rejoice in the Lord...*
Servants of the Lord, shout with joy.
- *And exult, o saints.*
Glory be to the Father, to the Son and to the Holy Spirit.
- *Rejoice in the Lord...*

Silence

Ant. *The one who sanctifies and those who are sanctified all have one Father. Heb 2:11*

Canticle of Mary

Luke 1:46-55

46 My soul magnifies the Lord

47 and my spirit rejoices in God my Savior.

48 For he has looked with favor on the lowliness of his servant
surely, from now on all generations will call me blessed.

49 For the Mighty One has done great things for me
and holy is his name.

50 His mercy is for those who fear him
from generation to generation.
51 He has shown strength with his arm
he has scattered the proud in the thoughts of their hearts.

52 He has brought down the powerful from their thrones
and lifted up the lowly.

53 He has filled the hungry with good things
and sent the rich away empty.

54 He has helped his servant Israel
in remembrance of his mercy.

55 According to the promise he made to our ancestors,
to Abraham and to his descendants forever.

Litany of the Saints

Lord, have mercy!	*Lord, have mercy!*
Christ, have mercy!	*Christ, have mercy!*
Lord, have mercy!	*Lord, have mercy!*
Christ, hear us!	*Christ, hear us!*
Christ, grant our prayer!	*Christ, grant our prayer!*
Father, fount of life	*have mercy on us!*

Son, word made flesh
Holy Spirit, power of love
One only God thrice holy

Abraham, our father in the faith *pray for us!*
Sarah, fertile in your smile
Fathers and mothers of Israel, bearers of the promise

John the Baptist, the friend of the Spouse
Mary, Virgin and Mother of the Lord
Joseph, father of Jesus according to the law

Peter, rock of Christ's church
John, beloved disciple of the Lord
Paul, free prisoner of the love of Christ

Holy apostles who have heard, seen, and touched the Word
Holy evangelists, who have kept and spread the gospel
Holy disciples who have followed the Christ in his life

Stephen, first Christian martyr
Ignatius, Christ's wheat, milled and made bread
All you martyrs who have overcome the world

Basil, father of the cenobitic life
Augustine, who sang of the love of God

Gregory, man of holy desire

Antony, God's nomad in the heart of the desert
Pachomius, father of every holy community
Benedict, father of human and of divine service

Francis, poor man of Christ in perfect joy
Clare, great witness of radical evangelical life
All you holy monks and nuns

Little Therese, called to be love in the church
Charles de Foucauld, little brother of Jesus in the desert
Dietrich Bonhoeffer, holocaust for the life of his brethren

Dag Hammarskjöld, man of solitude and of communion
Athenagoras, man of passion for the unity of the churches
John, pope and prophet for the church and for the world

Holy mothers, who have borne children for the Lord
Holy fathers, who have kept the faith to the end
All you little and poor who have hoped only in the Lord

All you the pure of Israel
All you saints of the churches
All you just of the earth

Prayer

God of love
you gather us together with the saints, your friends,
in joyful brotherly communion;
grant that we like them may walk in the footsteps of Christ
and we, enveloped by such a great cloud of witnesses
may enter into your kingdom
blessed for all ages of ages.
- *Amen.*

Blessing

Let us bless the Lord.
- *Thanks be to God.*

May the God of peace himself sanctify you entirely;
and may your spirit and soul and body
be kept sound and blameless at the coming of our Lord Jesus Christ. 1 Thess 5:23
Amen.

THE FINAL MESSAGE TO THE CHURCHES

A Cloud of Witnesses: A Message to the Churches from a Symposium at the Monastery of Bose

1. Introduction

1.1 We, Christians from different churches and countries, gathered from the 29th October to the 2nd November 2008 at the Monastery of Bose (Italy) – as the Community celebrated the Feast of All Saints – in order to reflect on "A Cloud of Witnesses: Opportunities for Ecumenical Commemoration". This was a joint initiative of the Monastery of Bose and the Faith and Order Commission of the World Council of Churches, a continuation of a process which began with a meeting of representatives from six different confessional families who met at Bose in March, 2004.

1.2 The aims behind this project were: to recognize each other's witnesses of faith, when this is not mutually exclusive; to find ways of commemorating witnesses from various traditions at ecumenical meetings; to develop or recover the commemoration of witnesses in churches that do not have such a practice; to work towards a common ecumenical martyrology.

2. Who are the Witnesses?

2.1 Once again we began our conversation with our chosen biblical image of the great cloud of witnesses (Hebrews 12:2) going more deeply into our understanding of the meaning of witness (*martys*) and the composition of the cloud. Over the centuries the word "martyr" has been understood in different ways. The most common understanding of the term came to be that a martyr was a person who suffered violent death for their faith – a death freely accepted for Christ's sake but not sought out as an end in itself. In the course of the 20th century, the term came to include those who died confronting injustice for the sake of the gospel. We re-affirmed that the original and wider meaning of "martyr" was simply one who, Christ-like, witnesses to the truth of the gospel to the end. Those who may be termed "heroes of the faith", who witnessed to Christ throughout their lives but did not meet violent death, are certainly numbered among "the great cloud", the communion of saints – whether named or unnamed. In our reflections we take these definitions into account.

2.2 We listened to and claimed again the stories of the prophets, holy men and women of the Hebrew Scriptures and the saints and martyrs of the New Testament.

2.3 Together we revisited the past as a healing of memories. We began to see that what and who we remember can keep us apart, but our common remembering draws us together. This act of remembering can serve as an act of confession that opens before us a way of reclaiming together past witnesses. Repentance and forgiveness for past acts of inter-confessional violence are more likely to occur when we reflect together on those who in dying forgave their persecutors.

2.4 We listened to stories of witnesses unto death from the 20th century. These included the stories of those whose voices were silenced under totalitarian regimes (e.g., men and women in Argentina, Brazil, Chile, Germany, Romania and Russia); those who died resisting imperialism, colonialism and racial injustice (e.g., in Korea and South Africa); and the Armenians who were victims of the genocide at the beginning of the 20th century. Martyrdom continues in our own century. We heard the story of the Melanesian Brothers whose witness to the faith ended in death in 2003. These local stories transcend all boundaries by the truth and power of their witness in fidelity to Christ. We both wept and celebrated together. Within the context of grave persecution, the power of witness transcends all earthly divisions. It places us once again within the communion of saints.

2.5 There was a growing conviction among us that these witnesses to the faith do not belong only to individual confessional groups but, as in the first centuries of the Christian era, can be the joy and delight of all the churches. Similarly, significant heroes of the faith from the past no longer belong exclusively to the confessional groups in which they were formed but can be claimed the common heritage of the one, holy, catholic and apostolic church.

3. Discerning the Witnesses

3.1 Discerning witnesses together entails:

- Recognition in the witness of fidelity to baptismal faith expressed in a life conformed to the death and resurrection of Christ and a willingness to continue to the end, even to death itself. The Christ we recognize in the witnesses is the Christ who has suffered rejection, humiliation, even death on a cross. Their lives both feed the Body of Christ, the church, and draw it back to its calling.
- All baptized Christians are called to live in the Spirit and so participate in the new life in Christ. But within this communion, we recognize those witnesses who in a distinct sense become "Orators of the Spirit" who, open to the Spirit and in the power of the Spirit, proclaim the gospel.
- These witnesses are sources of inspiration. Their lives are authentic interpretations of the Beatitudes.
- Holiness is never solely an individual matter. Witnesses are shaped in discipleship by living in a particular community of faith. By affirming together their faithfulness, we celebrate the church that will be but is not yet.

- Witnesses offer us a foretaste of the kingdom and its justice. They possess an eschatological hope and joy, and a beauty that reflects their love of God. They point us to the fullness of the kingdom. Thus in their lives they unite us in Christ with the past, the present, and the future. The witnesses speak as members of the Body of Christ and draw us near to the mystery of this Body.
- The central act of the Eucharist is the remembering (*anamnesis*) of the death and resurrection of Christ in and through the power of the Holy Spirit. In the act of remembering, we are surrounded by the Cloud of Witnesses and with angels and archangels we sing, "Holy, Holy, Holy." That is why we long to celebrate the Eucharist together.

3.2 One difficult issue of discernment involves how we assess the witness of those who have felt compelled to engage in acts of violence in the pursuit of justice and peace, and in consequence have suffered torture and death.

3.3 In discerning the witnesses to Christ, we recognize that some have suffered without the support of their Christian community or its leaders. Furthermore, there are those who have suffered torment and death at the hands of other Christian communities, including our own. Our pilgrimage of faith requires a willingness to recognize ourselves as victimisers as well as victims – as sinners as well as holy people united with the Son of God. Commemorating such witnesses together brings about a reconciliation of painful memories of the past and is a step on our pilgrimage to visible unity.

3.4 Thus, witnesses help us on our pilgrimage of faith. They invite us to cross over to where Christ is, to the place where violence is endured and overcome. In this way they draw us deeper together into the life of the crucified and risen Christ. As we contemplate those whose lives were committed to peace we understand better our call to be peace makers and peace builders. Every time we commemorate the lives of holy men and women who have witnessed to the faith, we are confronted with our own failures and therefore called to repentance and to a deeper conversion to Christ and to one another in Christ.

4. Different Ways of Commemoration

4.1 In the communion of saints, all the faithful of every age and of all places are united by the Spirit in one fellowship. While we agree about this together, differences remain as to how we give expression to that reality. These differences include questions concerning the intercession of the saints, canonization, veneration of saintly relics, and the practice of indulgences. Disputes around these issues arose sharply in the 16th century and led to hardened confessional positions, to persecution, and to martyrdom. Nonetheless, there is today a growing consensus that emphasis needs to be placed on the commemoration of witnesses as a source of inspiration, for all ecclesial communities.

4.2 Secondly, churches differ in the ways they commemorate the great witnesses. Many churches do so through story telling, religious instruction, publications, and artistic expression. Some also commemorate witnesses as part of their daily liturgical life. Some churches formally identify saints through a process of canonization. Some have formal processes for including witnesses of the past in their calendars. Others regard the witnesses as a legacy for building up the life of the church, but have no formal process of recognition.

4.3 The lack of formal recognition and even more of a clear place in the liturgical life of some churches, has perhaps led them to undervalue the witnesses of the past. We have learned that some of these churches are beginning to value the commemoration of the witnesses. Other churches have had difficulty honoring those witnesses outside their own tradition. We have learned that these churches are beginning to recognize the witness of those from other traditions. This is variously expressed in ecclesiastical calendars, liturgies, books, catechetical materials, memorials, pilgrimages, and celebrations.

5. Commemorating Ecumenically Today

5.1 As well as commemorating together, churches have also broadened their commemorations of witnesses to include those of other traditions. Examples of this include the memorials in the Protestant Cathedral of Utrecht, the martyrology of the Romanian Orthodox Church, and the statues of 20th-century martyrs on the west front of Westminster Abbey.

5.2 We have heard encouraging stories of ecumenical commemoration of witnesses to Christ. There have been examples such as joint pilgrimages to sites where saints are commemorated (e.g., Nidaros Cathedral where St Olav of Norway is commemorated) and the ecumenical commemoration of witnesses at the Colosseum (7 May 2000). These examples encourage us to continue to search for more ways of commemorating together. The reconciliation and healing of memories that this involves is a way of making visible the degree of communion that already exists.

6. Possibilities for Future Commemorating Together

6.1 Arising out of our reflection came suggestions for the future. These are:

- build upon what is being done already;
- commemorate witnesses from different traditions annually on an appropriate occasion such as the Feast of All Saints, Reformation Day, a day in Lent or Holy Week, or in the Week of Prayer for Christian Unity;
- publish and exchange ecclesiastical calendars, biographies, and martyrologies;
- identify witnesses that both are and could be shared by different traditions;

- encourage Christians at local levels to exchange stories of their witnesses;
- convene more meetings such as the one held at Bose on the Cloud of Witnesses;
- encourage the World Council of Churches to include witnesses and their biographies into the ecumenical prayer cycle;
- develop an internet website which should include links to existing sites;
- encourage production of an annotated bibliography of key resources;
- help those churches that because of their cultural and missionary context are concerned to avoid anything which might suggest ancestor worship to distinguish between that and an appropriate honouring of the witnesses of earlier generations.

6.2 We reflected on the emerging convergence in the doctrinal bilateral and multilateral conversations, particularly in understanding the church as communion and the significance of baptism and eucharist for life in the Body of Christ. This convergence provides a firm foundation for celebrating together the witnesses to the faith of the church. It may be the right time now to ask the multilateral conversation in the Faith and Order Commission of the World Council of Churches to produce a short convergence text on the communion of saints that would gather together some of the rich insights of the bilateral dialogues, deepen the reflection, and in that context consider some of the remaining areas of contention. Such a text would provide a theological and ecclesiological basis for the project begun at Bose in 2004.

7. A Step Toward the Visible Unity of the Church

7.1 The boundaries of the cloud are always expanding as God adds to our number those whom he is calling. Furthermore, new faces emerge from the cloud as different historical and cultural circumstances lead us to perceive the significance of witnesses previously unacknowledged. We invite the churches to explore together the criteria for identifying individual witnesses and groups of martyrs from specific regions, eras, or events.

This work, undertaken together, can help heal the wounds of the past as we discover in the lives of the witnesses to the faith a determination to reflect the image of Christ. To re-discover the significance and power of the cloud of witnesses and to express this in common commemoration is an important step toward the visible unity of the church.

APPENDIX

Memorandum I

"Surrounded by a great cloud of witnesses"

Preface

At the invitation of the ecumenical Community of Bose, representatives of six different confessional families met together from 12th to 15th March 2004 at Bose to discuss the possibility of ecumenical commemoration of outstanding witnesses to the Christian faith.

The Community of Bose has recently edited an anthology of the lives of Christian witnesses, *Il libro dei testimoni* (*The Book of Witnesses*, Milan 2002), and is currently preparing a new edition in English. This compilation was inspired by a Report from the Bangalore Meeting of the Faith and Order Commission of the World Council of Churches in 1978, *Witness Unto Death* (Sharing in One Hope, Faith and Order Paper No. 92), which states: "*It is desirable that an ecumenical anthology of both early and modern accounts of martyrdom should be published for the use of the churches, since the recognition of martyrs already transcends confessional boundaries and brings us back to the centre of the faith, the source of hope, and the example of love for God and fellow human beings. The use of such a book would also strengthen the solidarity of all Christians in prayer and action with those who are in difficult or dangerous situations.*"

There is a growing awareness that contemporary witnesses to the faith do not belong only to individual confessional groups but, as in the first centuries of the Christian era, are the joy and delight of all the churches. Similarly, significant heroes of the faith from the past no longer belong exclusively to the confessional group in which they were formed but are the common heritage of the one catholic church.

Continuing ecumenical worship has created a demand for new content and this provides a context in which the commemoration of such witnesses might play an important role. This would meet at least in part the need many already feel to receive the gifts embedded in the history of others and encourage others to explore this rich and vital field of mutual understanding, and experience for themselves our membership of one Body (*cf* 1 Cor. 12:20-21).

Gathered here at Bose, we are united in wishing to help give shape to this exchange of gifts and in wanting to promote a wider and more comprehensively shared recognition of this "cloud of witnesses" (Hebrews 12:1).

Since the time of Bangalore, many churches have begun to contribute in their own way to this process and many historical misunderstandings are being addressed in a more eirenical way. Therefore the time is now ripe to recall Faith and Order to their 1978 challenge and to promote an exchange of views among its member churches.

The image of the cloud of witnesses

The Bible contains the stories of a great succession of witnesses, sometimes by offering us specific lists of individuals we are asked to remember (*eg.* Sirach 44 to 50 and Hebrews 11) and at other times revealing that the whole company is without number and impossible to name (Revelation 7).

These witnesses are mainly those who witnessed to the faith and the author of the Letter to the Hebrews suggests that we can find consolation and support for our own faith by becoming conscious that we are surrounded by so great a cloud of them.

The cloud of witnesses testifies to the corporate nature of salvation. It helps Christians to feel that they are part of a wider movement through history and that they are led and supported in their discipleship of Christ, "the pioneer and perfecter of our faith" (Heb. 12:2).

The cloud is not just an abstract concept, nor are its shape and visible boundaries established once and for all, unchangeable. Within the cloud individual names and faces are recognizable in every generation and we can hear their stories. This has given the churches courage over the centuries to name individuals whose example can offer us strength and comfort in all circumstances of life. In different eras, different names have emerged as relevant, partly because what is urgent and necessary may vary in different epochs and contexts, and partly because in all times and places God keeps giving new gifts to his children.

The importance of remembrance

Why is it important for the churches to remember together such a cloud of witnesses?

First of all, both at an individual and at a corporate level, the witnesses of the past help us bear witness to Christ. They show us how to conform our personal and community lives to the life of the one "faithful witness" (Revelation 1:5), who asked his disciple to learn from him, the "meek and humble of heart". By teaching this fundamental attitude and behaviour, Jesus sets an example for us, showing the way our mutual relations as Christians should be oriented.

What is at stake, however, is not just our own enrichment as individual believers or as Christian communities, but the future of Christian witness itself to the world. Such witness depends on our corporate conformation to Christ. In fact, how can we be credible proclaimers of the good news without being able to envisage paths of peace and reconciliation first of all among ourselves?

Recognizing together the cloud of witnesses which already encircles us is one of the most important steps most churches desire to take in order to provide new and fresh energy for the ecumenical endeavour. This is because it helps us all to feel more strongly the invisible communion between heaven and earth, a fellowship which is a gift God bestowed on us, a gift we should therefore acknowledge and receive with deep thankfulness and thanksgiving.

The witnesses of the past bring us closer to one another. We have not yet arrived at the goal of full *koinonia*, but the common memory of witnesses may help us to reduce our distance from one another, learning in particular from those among them who have been outstanding witnesses of reconciliation.

Finally, it has to be faced that the commemoration of those witnesses who gave up their lives has often been used powerfully for ill in times past as a weapon against those with whom a confessional group has disagreed. A measure of the success of the ecumenical movement is the way in which the memory of such martyrs has been recovered corporately in a way that is charged with penitence, hope and reconciliation. The celebration of a Christian witness is a celebration of resurrection faith, so to use a witness as a cause of offence to others is to offend against our corporate faith. Similarly, to make a weapon of one's own past suffering is no less an offence.

Who are the witnesses?

The basic meaning of *martys* in the New Testament is "witness". Christ himself is called the "faithful witness" (Revelation 1:4), and at the end of Luke's gospel Jesus tells his disciples: "The Messiah had to suffer and on the third day rise from the dead. Then repentance and forgiveness in his name would be proclaimed to all the nations, beginning from Jerusalem. Now *you shall be witness to this*" (Luke 24:46-48).

Beginning with the earliest account of Christian witness in Acts – Stephen's martyrdom – the life of the *martys* is described as Christ-like. Such life shows how God's strength is manifested in human weakness, and is ultimately the universal power of attraction and of reconciliation of the Cross.

The word *martys* came early to designate in a stricter sense a person suffering violent death *in odium fidei*, a death freely accepted for Christ's sake. Nonetheless, we prefer to refer to *martyres*/witnesses in a more literal sense.

Witnesses are for us signposts and models, sources of inspiration for the Christian life. They are people in whom the Spirit makes Christ visible, showing to all men and women the way to the full recovery of the divine image in them through a path of conversion and of assimilation to the Son of Man.

Witnesses are men and women who give their entire lives so that their brothers and sisters may also live. It is in this sense that true Christian witness is always "unto death", whether this may lead to martyrdom or just, more simply, mean that witnesses are called to serve God and their brothers and sisters every day of their lives, faithfully and tirelessly.

Such men and women of God constitute a tradition which is not confined to the past or concentrated in some local area. There still are and there will always be situations in the world which provide occasions for the Holy Spirit to inspire new Christ-like witnesses.

For this reason in each confessional family outstanding witnesses of all times are remembered, although in forms which may vary according to the confessional, cultural and historical sensitivities of each community. Some of these outstanding figures in our traditions have been in one way or another formally recognized as saints. Many other witnesses are known and honoured within their confessional group but have never been the subject of a formal canonization process.

Towards a sharing of witnesses

As we have observed above, the commemoration of ecumenical witnesses is already on the agenda of some churches. Such commemoration is already taking place in a variety of formal and informal ways. Some churches, for example, have revised their liturgical calendars to include outstanding witnesses to the faith from other traditions, thus enabling these persons to be remembered liturgically at the Eucharist and daily prayers. Local compilations of lives are already being used in some traditions in private devotion for instruction and edification, and to inspire penitence and prayer.

We would like to promote a greater sharing of memory between the different traditions. Some groups are already active in this field but all the churches might contribute to this task. This might be through publications, worship and symbolic acts on significant anniversaries, and through drama and works of art. The season of All Saints and the Week of Prayer for Christian Unity could provide contexts for the commemoration of the whole cloud of witnesses as it is known to God. We believe the churches could do this more effectively together, especially if better resourced.

The ecumenical anthology of lives of witnesses proposed at Bangalore in 1978 would provide the churches with a significant resource for the sharing of witnesses and a compelling symbol around which to focus their efforts.

An Invitation

We have noted earlier that the Ecumenical Monastic Community of Bose has already done a great deal of excellent work in this field and is in a position to continue to compile the core anthology and edit it for publication in a variety of forms. At present the resource is organized calendrically but it could also be made available in other ways according to need and denominational sensitivity.

The visible boundaries of the cloud of witnesses are always moving as God adds to its number. Consequently the core resource needs constantly to be updated with the addition of the lives of those whom the churches consider worthy of commemoration. To keep the resource within manageable bounds a measure of discernment, guided by a sense of the purposes of the anthology, is required by the churches.

Therefore we would like the churches to consider the following two questions:

- Can you identify outstanding Christian witnesses from *outside* your tradition whom you would wish to see included in the anthology?

- Who would you like to include from within your church?

Proposals might include those who bore witness in a non-violent way; witnesses who worked for social justice, in the midst of the poor and underprivileged; evangelists, prophetic voices, those who brought renewal to the church; witnesses who fell victim to persecution for their faith as the boundaries of Christendom were extended or under uncomprehending or totalitarian regimes; witnesses who were promoters of reconciliation, both among the churches and among different peoples and cultures. Above all the core resource should contain a universal distribution of witnesses, drawn from every nation, race, people and tongue (Rev. 7:9).

Two difficult issues

As we widen the range of witnesses commemorated by the whole church we encounter a number of difficulties. We have to acknowledge the problem that some witnesses of one church are viewed as heretics by another church. Considerable theological energy has been invested in this area in recent years in bilateral dialogues, but much still remains to be done. Experience shows that the modern ecumenical movement provides a framework where these issues may become theological and spiritual opportunities. This requires much love, respect and study, but it will undoubtedly allow us to see many protagonists of disputes with new eyes.

Perhaps even more crucially, we have to tackle the reality of acts of violence perpetrated by Christians against their brothers and sisters of other denominations. We cannot compile a list of noteworthy witnesses who died at the hands of fellow Christians without sincere acts of repentance for the evils which have been committed in inter-confessional conflicts. These may have been committed in the name of faith, doctrine and church order but they are wholly incompatible with the example set for us by Jesus Christ. Too often Christians have made use of force to impose the faith, and this is a contradiction of the essential message of the Gospel. Confession of sin alone is not enough. It must be accompanied by a thorough process of conversion in the attitude of persecutor to persecuted and of oppressed group to oppressor. We must always be open to the possibility that the death of a witness can become a "gift" to his or her persecutors; that the group he or she represents can become a "gift" to its enemies. This becomes a reality only if one church celebrates the other in such a way that the witness becomes a source of common grace and hope and an occasion of both penitence and thanksgiving.

Summary

The proposal outlined above draws its title from the 12th chapter of the Letter to the Hebrews. There the people of God, "surrounded by a great cloud of witnesses" (12:1) are urged to persevere on their pilgrim way, "looking to Jesus the pioneer and perfecter of our faith" (12:2). Today, after 2000 years, the cloud of witnesses has grown considerably in numbers yet the witnesses have become separated one from another only to surround this or that part of the church. Is this not the moment in history when the church should again allow itself to be surrounded by one great ecumenical cloud of witnesses? The agenda to which the church is called is stated with compelling clarity: "Pursue peace with everyone, and the holiness without which no one will see the Lord" (Hebrews 12:14).

Having drawn considerable guidance from the Letter to the Hebrews as we have met together at Bose in Italy, it seems appropriate to greet the churches with the final words of the Letter: "Greet all your leaders and all the saints. Those from Italy send you greetings. Grace be with all of you" (Hebrews 13:24-25).

Monastery of Bose, March 15th 2004

Br Enzo Bianchi (Roman Catholic),
Prior of Bose, Magnano, Italy

Br Guido Dotti (Roman Catholic),
Monastery of Bose, Magnano, Italy

Mgr Brian Farrell (Roman Catholic),
Secretary of the Pontifical Council for Promoting Christian Unity, Vatican City

Dr Tamara Grdzelidze (Orthodox),
World Council of Churches, Faith and Order Secretariat, Geneva, Switzerland

Dr Helmut Harder (Mennonite),
Mennonite World Conference, Winnipeg, Canada

Can Jeremy Haselock (Anglican),
Church of England Liturgical Commission, Norwich, England

Dr Dagmar Heller (Lutheran),
Evangelische Kirche Deutschlands, Hannover, Germany

Dr Päivi Jussila (Lutheran),
Lutheran World Federation, Geneva, Switzerland

Br Riccardo Larini (Roman Catholic),
Monastery of Bose, Magnano, Italy

Dr Lukas Vischer (Reformed),
Geneva, Switzerland

MEMORANDUM II

"Surrounded by a great cloud of witnesses"

In March 2004 representatives of six different confessional families met at Bose to discuss the possibility of ecumenical commemoration of outstanding witnesses to the Christian faith. After much fraternal discussion a memorandum was prepared for all the member churches of the WCC Faith and Order Commission asking them to respond to the substance of the memorandum and, in particular to four specific questions.

a) Can your church identify outstanding Christian witnesses from outside your own tradition whom you would wish to see included in a common commemoration?

b) Who would you like to include from within your own tradition – bearing in mind the particular ecumenical focus of the project?

c) What ways of commemorating such witnesses can you suggest, in both confessional and ecumenical settings?

d) How, in your view can common commemoration of such witnesses contribute to healing the wounds of the past?

A number of valuable written responses were received indicating an interest in the subject and providing a number of names in answer to the first two questions. In addition, several confessional groups were excited by the issues raised in the memorandum and organized conferences, dialogues and symposia on the subject. Some of these have resulted in valuable published essays and reflections which we list in the bibliography appended to this memorandum.

These varied responses encouraged the Bose steering group to believe that their initiative was valuable and to continue their work. Accordingly a further meeting was convened at Bose from 19th to 21st February 2007 to review the written responses in detail, to reflect on the new published material and to decide in which direction to continue the project. Some new members joined us for this second meeting, bringing valuable insights and offering practical expertise as well as an expression of warm interest from CEC. This second memorandum represents the fruits of this meeting and is by way of being a progress report with some further questions and recommendations.

Who are the witnesses?

Once again we began our conversation with our chosen biblical image of the great cloud of witnesses (Hebrews 12:2) going more deeply into our understanding of the meaning of witness (*martys*) and the nature of the cloud. We re-affirmed that the original and wider meaning of *martys* was simply one who, Christ-like, witnesses to the truth of the gospel. The narrower understanding of the term came to be the one most commonly understood today: a person suffering violent death *in odium fidei* – a death freely accepted for Christ's sake but not sought out as an end in itself. We take both these definitions into account in our reflections as those who may be termed "heroes of the faith" but who did not meet violent death are certainly numbered among "the great cloud".

Since the matter was first raised in Bangalore in 1978 many confessional groups have compiled martyrologies, or revised their calendars, or provided a biographical companion to their liturgical *ordo*. Added momentum was given when the late Pope John Paul II decided to commemorate the martyrs of the 20th century at the beginning of the new millennium. His initiative has led to the compilation of a large number of local martyrologies based on criteria derived from the second understanding of the term martyr: one who met a violent death at another's hands; for the Christian faith; submitting totally to the will of God and showing forgiveness for his or her persecutors. We welcome the huge amount of information generated by this diligent research which has shown the churches how the blood of the martyrs continues in our day to be the seed of the church.

To help us with our understanding of the wider definition of the term witness, we reflected together on the biblical criteria for holiness. They are witnesses in the great cloud if in a distinctive way their life reflects the image of Christ, living according to the Beatitudes, carrying their cross, or speaking in a prophetic manner to their generation or exhibiting the varying gifts of the unique Holy Spirit. Such persons have always been deemed worthy of commemoration in one way or another by the faithful and their memory continues to inspire today those who wish to lead the Christian life. We learn more and more how Christians from different confessional groups have witnessed together in the last century, indeed, within living memory. Their common witness is a call to the ecumenical movement to draw the churches together into unity with greater determination and to face together the challenges of today's world. In this respect we wish particularly to honour those who have given their lives for Christ in "the century of martyrdom" – we who are called to witness in the circumstances of our own lives wish to draw inspiration from the deep wells of those who have gone before.

Some suggestions for the ecumenical movement and the local churches

As we noted in our first memorandum, the commemoration of ecumenical witnesses is already taking place in a variety of ways in some churches. We would like to suggest a greater use of such commemoration in ecumenical acts of worship and other inter-church encounters. The Week of Prayer for Christian Unity is one such regular opportunity and we suggest that local planners research those witnesses whose stories resonate with the local community and make materials available for study, prayer and worship. At an international level we warmly invite the Joint Preparatory Commission to plan to provide material on this theme for all to use in a future year. The WCC Ecumenical Prayer Cycle "In God's Hands", with its weekly change of focus on groups of the countries of the world, might be extended in the future to include within the intercessory material the commemoration of appropriate witnesses from each country. We also suggest that the Commemoration of All Saints (November 1st in the Western tradition, a moveable date in June in the East) is an appropriate time to celebrate together the witnesses from all our traditions who have enriched our understanding of what it is to live the Christian life. More immediately the third European Ecumenical Assembly in Sibiu (4-9 September), might wish to introduce the commemoration of faithful witnesses into some of its acts of worship. Because the healing of memories among Christians must be seen as a vital component of the integrity with which Christians become involved in peace and reconciliation work, preparations for the final Convocation (IEPC 3-11 May 2011) at the end of the Decade to Overcome Violence (DOV) might profitably include reference to the ecumenical cloud of witnesses.

A fresh invitation to the churches

The boundaries of the cloud are always moving as God adds to our number those whom he is calling. New faces emerge from the cloud as different historical and cultural circumstances lead us to find new significance in witnesses previously unacknowledged. As the cloud grows, we invite the churches to explore together the criteria for identifying witnesses and martyrs for our time. This work undertaken in dialogue together can also help in healing the wounds of the past as we discover in the lives of our own heroes of the faith a common determination to reflect the image of Christ. Repentance and forgiveness for past acts of inter-confessional violence emerge more readily when we reflect together on those who in dying forgave their persecutors.

We invite the churches to share their criteria and to furnish us with carefully chosen examples of those who meet them so that all the Christian communities can make good use of this more widely drawn material. We will try to collect and collate this material and to offer some suggested formats or templates for publication. Please also feel free to send us examples of ways in which the commemoration of witnesses to the faith has featured in ecumenical acts of worship so that we can share good practice with others.

Appended to this memorandum is a preliminary select bibliography of work already accomplished to which we can add as new material is published. We invite the churches to contribute their suggestions to this also.

What happens next?

The Community of Bose has generously agreed to host a symposium in late October 2008 – "*Cloud of Witnesses*: Opportunities for Ecumenical Commemoration". This international ecumenical conference will explore more deeply the issues we have raised and the ways in which the churches can grasp the opportunity offered by the common celebration of their witnesses to the faith in revealing the unity of Christ's church.

Monastery of Bose, March 2007

Br Guido Dotti (Roman Catholic),
Monastery of Bose, Magnano, Italy

Dr Tamara Grdzelidze (Orthodox),
World Council of Churches, Faith and Order Secretariat, Geneva, Switzerland

Dr Helmut Harder (Mennonite),
Mennonite World Conference, Winnipeg, Canada

Can Jeremy Haselock (Anglican),
Church of England Liturgical Commission, Norwich, England

Dr Lukas Vischer (Reformed),
Geneva, Switzerland

Note on Bibliography

A selected bibliography on the topic can be found on the website of the Monastery of Bose: http://tinyurl.com/Bose-Cloud
The list was prepared on the basis of bibliographies suggested by the contributors to the Bose Symposium.